Reading and the Reference Librarian

W9-AVE-674

READING AND THE REFERENCE LIBRARIAN

The Importance to Library Service of Staff Reading Habits

by Juris Dilevko *and* Lisa Gottlieb

McFarland & Company, Inc., Publishers
Jefferson, North Carolina, and London

LIBRARY OF CONGRESS ONLINE CATALOG
Dilevko, Juris.
Reading and the reference librarian : the importance to library
service of staff reading habits / by Juris Dilevko and Lisa Gottlieb.
p. cm.
Includes bibliographical references and index.

ISBN 0-7864-1652-1 (softcover : 50# alkaline paper)

[1.] Reference librarians—Books and reading. [2.] Academic
librarians—Books and reading. [3.] Academic libraries—Reference
services. [4.] Public libraries—Reference services. [5.] Library
surveys—United States. [6.] Library surveys—Canada. [I. Title.]
Z682.4.R44D+ 2003021596

British Library cataloguing data are available

Cover image photograph ©2003 Corbis Images

Manufactured in the United States of America

*McFarland & Company, Inc., Publishers
Box 611, Jefferson, North Carolina 28640
www.mcfarlandpub.com*

Contents

Preface   1

I.   **General Concepts**   5

   1   Ideology and the Deprofessionalization of the Reference Function   7

   2   Reading and Reference Work   21

II.   **Academic Librarians**   27

   3   The Importance of Being Current   31
       How reading newspapers and magazines affects the
       work of academic reference librarians

   4   Developing a "Reader's Mind"   73
       How reading nonfiction and fiction affects the work
       of academic reference librarians

   5   You Can Lead Librarians to Knowledge, But You
       Can't Make Them Think   115
       Factors affecting how, and how much, academic librarians read

III.   **Public Library Reference Staff**   133

   6   Being a Jack-of-All-Trades   137
       How staying current affects the work of public
       library reference staff members

IV.   **Professors and Academic Librarians**   171

   7   Meeting the Expectations of Professors   173
       The need for academic librarians to read and
       think as if they were researchers

   8   Reading as a Species of Intellectual Capital   209

Appendix A.   Methodological Notes and Text of Survey Questions
Sent to Academic Reference Librarians   223

Appendix B.   Methodological Notes and Text of Survey Questions
    Sent to Public Library Reference Staff Members   229

Appendix C.   Methodological Notes and Text of Survey Questions
    Sent to Professors in the Humanities and Social Sciences   235

Appendix D.   Statistical Analyses of Selected Variables from the
    Survey Sent to Academic Reference Librarians   239

Notes   247

Bibliography   255

Index   261

Preface

As technological innovations have transformed all areas of library work, reference service has, in many respects, become a matter of typing search terms into a library's online catalog or into a web search engine, and then telling the patron the results of that search. Mechanical competency seems to be the order of the day. Reference librarians are no longer expected to know much about what they find; they are merely expected to find it.

This book suggests that there is another approach to providing quality reference service — an approach that relies on the acquisition of a wide range of general knowledge and subject area expertise through concerted and extensive reading of newspapers, magazines, and works of nonfiction and fiction.

After discussing, in Chapter 1, the philosophical implications of ever-increasing reliance on technological skills for the delivery of reference service, we turn to the results of original research conducted in 2000 and 2001. As discussed in Chapter 2 — a methodological overview of our work — we surveyed both academic reference librarians and public library reference personnel in the United States and Canada about various aspects of their reading habits as well as the ways in which their reading helps them to provide better reference service. We received more than 950 responses: 419 from public library reference staff members and 539 from academic librarians.

Chapters 3–5 focus on the academic library world. We present findings about the extent to which academic reference librarians read newspapers, magazines, nonfiction, and fiction books. We discuss some of their favorite general-interest periodicals and books. Most importantly, we recount and analyze their many stories about how reading has allowed them to be better librarians, not only at the reference desk, but also in terms of their collection development responsibilities, bibliographic instruction, faculty liaison tasks, and other activities. Chapter 6 examines the world of public library reference personnel from a similar perspective. What do they read, and how has it helped them in their work?

In Chapter 7, we switch gears to concentrate on what one user group — professors in the humanities and social sciences in North America — thinks academic reference librarians should do to improve reference service. Based on 236 survey responses, our results show that professors believe that the best reference librarians are those who have wide-ranging subject-based knowledge — a characteristic that is especially important in light of the growth of scholarly interdisciplinarity. In our concluding chapter, we position the act of reading — and the broad general and subject-specific knowledge gained from reading—as a piece of intellectual capital that librarians should proudly appropriate for themselves and employ as a distinct asset that defines them as professionals. In so doing, they might realize the abiding value of the type of subject-specific knowledge that comes from reading newspapers, magazines, and books, as opposed to the type of process-based and functional knowledge that is increasingly dominating the curricula of many programs of Library and Information Science or Information Studies.

In sum, this book has two intertwining themes. First, librarians are fervent and committed readers. Second, the vast range of reading that they undertake is crucially important for them in all aspects of their work, from reference service to collection development to bibliographic instruction. Reading leads to the accumulation of both generalized and subject-specific knowledge, which in turn allows library reference personnel to provide a high level of service to patrons. In the past few decades, however, this aspect of librarianship has been downplayed. We hope that this book, by bringing together a wealth of evidence based on the testimony of librarians and users of libraries, will allow librarians to appreciate just how vital reading can be to the provision of excellent reference help and other patron services. We suggest, too, how reading can lead to a re-intellectualization of the profession.

In some ways, this book complements Stephen Karetzky's *Reading Research and Librarianship: A History and Analysis*, published in the early 1980s. Karetzky's work is an eloquent historical overview of the research conducted by librarians "to ascertain the types of adults who read books and/or magazines, their motivation, their readings interests and habits, the sources and contents of their reading material, and the effects of reading upon individuals and society."[1] By examining closely what librarians read and how this reading affects their work lives, the present book presents the opposite side of the coin from Karetzky's work: the reading habits of librarians themselves are put under the microscope. The present book also complements the research of such scholars as Janice Radway and Catherine Sheldrick Ross, who, in the 1990s, studied at length how pleasure reading helps adults negotiate their daily lives by giving them facts about the world, models for identity, strategies for resisting and protesting unpleasant situations, confirmation of self-worth, connection with others, courage to make changes, and a sense of expanded possibilities, among other benefits.[2] By focusing on the extent of reading—and the effect of that reading—on the professional lives of librarians, our book contributes to the rich tradition of scholarship dealing with how reading benefits numerous groups and individuals. As examples of this tradition, we mention here only two books—Stephen Krashen's *The Power of Reading: Insights from the Research* and Jim Burke's compendium *I Hear America Reading: Why We Read, What We Read*.[3]

One final note: In parts II and III, we give names to many of the academic and public librarians who responded to our surveys. These are fictitious names created by us, and in no way are these names meant to identify, or to assign characteristics and opinions to, real librarians and reference staff members. Any relationship between a created name and a real person is entirely coincidental. Complete anonymity of responding librarians is therefore preserved.

We acknowledge the help of the following individuals: 53 students enrolled in FIS 1310, Information Resources and Services, and 13 students in FIS 2131 The Literature of the Humanities and Social Sciences, at the Faculty of Information Studies, University of

Toronto, during fall 2000 and fall 2001, respectively; 1,194 respondents to three questionnaires; Moya K. Mason, founder of MKM Rese@rch, who provided superb research assistance; Esther Atkinson, Gerstein Science Information Centre, University of Toronto, who informed us about journal clubs in the medical community; and Daniel J. Denis, Department of Psychology, York University, who assisted with statistical analysis. We also thank Marlo Welshons, Director of Publications, Graduate School of Library and Information Science, University of Illinois, for permission to use the following article: Juris Dilevko, "An Ideological Analysis of Digital Reference Services Models," *Library Trends* 50 (Fall 2001): 218–244. This article appears, in revised form, as parts of chapters 1, 2, and 8 of the present book.

I. General Concepts

Around 2000, oil discoveries in remote Equatorial Guinea began to stir interest in this long-neglected western African country, not the least because the United States was seeking new supplies of oil. American companies were already participating in, or making plans to participate in, oil ventures in nearby countries such as São Tomé and Príncipe, Angola, and Chad.[1] For an executive of an American-based oil firm or a company that supplies oil industry equipment, it would be natural to find out basic information about Equatorial Guinea. Where is the capital? Where does the government sit? Who are key contacts in the government, and where can I find them? One place that an oil executive might begin to look for answers to these questions is an academic or public library.

Once the question was received at the library, a reference staff member might look at a number of online and print sources and quickly conclude that the capital of Equatorial Guinea is Malabo. After all, recent editions of *The World Factbook*, published by the Central Intelligence Agency, identify Malabo as the capital. Other sources do so as well. However, an astute staff member might recall that some countries have two capitals. Bolivia has its seat of government at La Paz, but its legal capital and seat of judiciary is Sucre. *The World Factbook* provides this information about Bolivia, but for Equatorial Guinea the two-capital situation is not mentioned. The reference staff member would likely be confident that he or she was giving the oil executive complete information about Malabo being the capital and seat of government of Equatorial Guinea.

Unfortunately, this staff member would be only partially correct. As reported by Norimitsu Onishi in an article in the *New York Times*, Equatorial Guinea has adopted a "novel strategy" to "develop every town in the country." The strategy? Rotating seats of governments. In June 2000, for instance, the seat of government was moved to the city of Bata for a period of "perhaps … six months…. After that, the government will keep moving to other towns, returning to Malabo after an indefinite journey," reports Onishi, relying on the testimony of Gabriel Nguema Lima, secretary of state at the Ministry of Mines and Energy and son of the president of Equatorial Guinea.[2] Anyone searching for government officials in Malabo would probably not find them there.

How could a reference staff member have known this seemingly obscure piece of information? By reading newspapers and magazines for content-based factual information on a regular basis in order to stay current.

Reading newspapers is a simple act, but one that is often dismissed as unnecessary in an electronic age where large amounts of information can be found almost instantaneously, and where library administrators contemplate sophisticated, streamlined, and automated digital reference service paradigms. Librarians are told that they don't really need to know content, that all they "have to know is *how* to find things," the quicker the better. But, as this example makes clear, only the reference staff member who has taken the time and energy to sift through content-based information in a newspaper or magazine — and who has tucked away at the back of his or her mind intriguing bits of information that might later come in handy—could have offered a complete and accurate answer to the oil executive's question about Equatorial Guinea.

We start with this theoretical example as a way of drawing attention to the fact that, in the headlong rush to redefine reference service for the 21st century, increasing reliance on technological efficacy — e.g., the ability to type in a few keywords on a search engine — invariably decenters the human intellectual contribution to the reference transaction and erodes the value of the reference librarian. This concern was summarized in a 2002 *Newsweek* article detailing the profound sociocultural changes wrought by the emergence of the Google search engine because of "its seemingly uncanny ability to provide curious minds with the exact information they seek."[3] In that article, Joseph Janes, well-known as a strong champion of the development of digital reference models relying on technological innovation,[4] is quoted as saying, "But I worry about how over reliance on it [Google] might affect the skill-set of librarians."[5]

How, then, can the human intellectual contribution to reference work be placed front and center? We think that the answer revolves around the idea of reading — reading everything and anything, from biographies about historical figures to local and national newspapers to general-interest magazines to best-selling novels. After all, a librarian who had read Onishi's article about Equatorial Guinea would have been able to provide "added value" to the oil executive, perhaps creating untold good will for the library in the process. At the same time, there are broad philosophical issues connected with the emergence of reference service models relying almost exclusively on technological innovations. We address some of these issues in the first chapter. Chapter 2, after presenting a brief overview of what other library educators have said about the benefits of reading for reference work, describes the parameters of three studies that we conducted to determine the extent to which library reference personnel read, their opinion about whether reading helps them in their work, and the thoughts of one group of library users about whether reading should be an important aspect of reference work.

1

Ideology and the Deprofessionalization of the Reference Function

Some of the scenarios envisioned for reference services of the future are in danger of deprofessionalizing the reference librarian so that she or he becomes an assembly-line information worker not typically conversant with or cognizant of the information dispensed. At one time, however, the reference librarian was a person who was broadly familiar with contemporary social, cultural, political, and scientific occurrences. Such familiarity was important to delivering high-quality reference service because it added a fresh intellectual perspective and a new knowledge base to the question or problem at hand. Now, to judge from some recent proposals and models of digital reference service, the role of the reference worker is to be a mere technological gatekeeper, a guide who makes little intellectual contribution to the reference transaction beyond the perfunctory act of steering the user to web sites or databases without knowing a great deal about the issues underlying the request. In this opening chapter, we look at some of the new paradigms for reference service and demonstrate how they lead to a deprofessionalization of reference work.

Deprofessionalization and technology

Calls for a reformulation and rethinking of the concept of reference work make the human contribution either completely redundant or severely devalued and routinized. For example, John Richardson, Jr., reports on the Question Master "decision support system automating some of the more routine, fact-type reference questions encountered in libraries."[1] The system, comprising a series of web pages, is intended to guide librarians (and eventually end-users) "through a set of clarifying questions before making recommendations of an appropriate electronic or relevant print resource from WorldCat, the OCLC Online Public Union Catalog."[2] Noting that the accuracy rate of this system is about 64 percent, Richardson observes that, even in the beta stage of development, it performed better than the typical accuracy response rate of 55 percent provided by reference librarians. Ronald Heckart, extrapolating from the current functionality of advanced "intelligent agent" and "knowbot" systems, predicts a future for the emerging digital library in which machine help will replace human help.[3] A student will complete a paper and post it to the class web site "without ever visiting the physical library or talking to a real life library staff member." In an attempt to legitimize this vision, Heckart notes that corporations are "implementing virtual help desks, in which an employee finds answers by keying in a few key words on the corporate intranet" and in which, "if negotiation is needed to refine the request, the employee is automatically prompted with questions."[4] While Richardson and Heckart no doubt view their proposals as positive developments for reference librarianship, another way to interpret their visions is to understand them as rejections of the centrality of human presence — a human presence that is caring, experienced, educated, and profoundly well-read — in reference work.

Richardson and Heckart are closely related to another cluster of articles that suggest the call center model as something to which the digital reference library of the future should aspire. Writing specifically about academic reference service, Chris Ferguson postulates "electronic research environments that combine information resources, asynchronous tools and instructional aids, and real-time assistance [from] knowledgeable staff [skilled in] formulating research strategies and solving navigation problems."[5] One "critical component" of such a service is the "Internet call center, which integrates telephone, e-mail, chat, video, and other inputs into a single incoming queue" such that "an information specialist can employ FAQs, voice-recognition database queries, a ready reference collection at hand, electronic reference and other information resources, accumulated service histories within a C[ustomer] R[elationship] M[anagement] system, and a variety of service protocols ... in directly resolving queries, referring to experts on call, or making appointments with experts."[6] Viewing the call center as the anchor of the model digital reference library because it creates "economies of scale that allow increased flexibility in the allocation of resources for the greater and long-term good," Ferguson notes that the model depends upon "rich access to, and routine participation of, staff proficient in automatic call distribution (ACD), computer-telephone integration (CTI), CRM software, and Internet call center technologies."[7]

Steve Coffman and Matthew Saxton see the incoming call center as a model for networked reference service in public libraries. They envision reference workers as "agents ... tak[ing] calls at computer workstations where they ... have ready access to databases, lists of frequently-asked questions and answers, pre-written scripts for particular situations, and other tools needed to deliver ... information."[8] Susan McGlamery and Steve Coffman recommend the use of "web contact center software" (WCC) in public libraries, specifically pointing to the web site of a mail-order retailer such as Lands' End as a good model for WCC library reference service because the software available on that site "takes full advantage of collaborative tools, such as pushing, form filling, and taking control of the requestor's browser."[9] WCC provides the same functionality as traditional call center technology, but also takes advantage of the fact that many customers now have access to web browsers.

How would this work in practice? As described by McGlamery and Coffman, an individual in search of information about how to start a small business visits a library web site. From the library's business page, the user clicks on an icon marked "Talk to a librarian" and chooses to open a chat session. After providing some identification and perhaps a registration number, the user is put on hold while the library pushes web pages to the user's browser, much the same way as music is pushed to a person waiting in a telephone queue. Because the user has initiated contact from the library's business page, the user's request has automatically been directed to business reference staff. When the user does talk to an employee in the business department of the library, the employee makes use of a variety of software tools that have created "a hierarchical script based on the most commonly asked business questions."[10] The library employee listens to the user's request about information for starting a small business, finds the correct script based on a generic answer, and pushes it to the user's browser "in the form of a web page, a PowerPoint presentation, a page of frequently asked questions (FAQ), or any other electronic resource available to the library."[11] If the question is more detailed, the library employee could instruct the user how to use a business database with "follow me browsing," a process that allows the employee to take control of the user's browser and lead the user "through each step of the process."[12] In general terms, the "click here to talk to a librarian" icon can be placed anywhere on a public library's web site. If located on the catalog page, it would help the user find books with the aid of paraprofessionals; if located on a page containing reference databases, it would connect the user to someone skilled in searching databases. If located on a subject-specific page, it might refer the user to a reference librarian who, if she or he could not answer the query, would refer the user to other networked subject specialists at other libraries — whether academic, legal, or medical — in the local area.

The danger of deskilling in call centers

At first glance, library call center scenarios seem exciting and groundbreaking, allowing libraries and librarians to present themselves as forward-looking, cutting edge, and technologically adept. At second glance, however, the library call center model is part of a disturbing trend toward deskilling of the library profession. Roma Harris has identified deskilling as an important issue in librarianship, and presents evidence that certain library specializations, such as cataloging and collection development, are at various stages of risk. Citing the work of Nina Toren, Harris understands deskilling to involve "the delegation of routine activities to less qualified personnel [and] leaving the complex and difficult problems to the trained professional. Sometimes, however, not much is left to warrant a distinct professional status and its correlates."[13] Roma Harris and Victoria Marshall show that both budget constraints and rapid developments in computer technology have had the effect of "pushing tasks down the organizational hierarchy."[14] Tasks previously performed by professional staff are "now assigned to less expensive nonprofessional staff," and tasks that were "at one time performed by library staff at the bottom of the organizational pyramid may be pushed entirely out of the waged work structure in libraries."[15]

How can the call center model be understood as contributing to deskilling? Quite obviously, the call center is associated with the business world. Numerous companies have instituted call centers in order to become more efficient and to cut costs. Call centers try to set up interactive voice response (IVR) systems such that IVRs handle about 80 percent of incoming calls. A great deal of work goes into trying to make IVRs as flexible and information-rich as possible so as to handle an increasing percentage of calls. Simply put, IVRs do not require human intervention and are thus extremely cost-efficient. Those calls that cannot be handled by an IVR are put into an automated call distribution (ACD) queue, where they are routed to the next available agent. To manage the ACD queue in the most efficient way possible, the Erlang C algorithm is used to determine optimum staffing requirements. Developed in 1917 by A.K. Erlang, an engineer with the Copenhagen Telephone Company, Erlang C is a complex formula that takes into account the total traffic volume of arriving calls in a set period, the average amount of time spent per transaction, the average length of after-call processing time, and a carefully calculated acceptable service level, usually defined as 80 percent of calls answered within 20 seconds. Theoretically, companies can cut staffing requirements by lowering service levels — for instance, defining an acceptable service level as 75 percent of calls answered within 30 seconds — and by encouraging workers to spend less time on each client call and in after-call processing.

In the library realm, the quest for efficiency and cost-cutting is, on the surface, the primary force behind the fascination with call centers. Lurking beneath these ringing endorsements of streamlined, efficient service, however, is a barely contained disdain for the complexities of library reference work and a devaluation of those aspects not specifically connected to answering user queries. Consider Coffman and Saxton, who begin by suggesting that "the amount of down-time spent waiting around for somebody to ask a question" by reference librarians is a serious concern.[16] From the managerial perspective, such down-time is lost time because professional staff are not spending their entire time answering reference questions. Coffman and Saxton are more than a little disconcerted by the fact that librarians "try to fill up these slack periods by 'reviewing the professional literature' and other odd tasks" or by "keeping kids quiet, scheduling staff, ordering supplies, presiding over children's story times, checking books out, and other details of managing the building."[17] In their minds, circumstances such as these "only raise even more fundamental questions about what the true professional functions are in a library, and how and where they should best be performed."[18]

The scorn with which Coffman and Saxton view traditional reference work is palpable and visceral. Their use of quotes around the phrase "reviewing the professional literature" indicates that they do not think very much of this activity. They use the phrase "odd tasks" to relegate all other job duties of the reference librarian — such as readers' advisory services, keeping abreast of current events and current reference sources in order to anticipate future reference questions, collection development responsibilities, and so on — to a very low level of importance. Finally, they mock tasks associated with children and the smooth functioning of the library as a whole. In short, Coffman and Saxton do not put much stock in the view of librarianship as a female-intensive profession imbued with an ethic of caring and community service.[19] Instead, their watchwords are efficiency and cost-effectiveness. Their overall strategy is clear. First, raise questions about the value of reference work by showing that the job includes many tasks that ought not to be worthy of a professional. Second, because reference work does seem to encompass such tasks, remove reference work from the ranks of professional positions.

Having identified down-time as a serious managerial problem, Coffman and Saxton quantify exactly how much time staff at the County of Los Angeles Public Library system spend answering reference questions. The 88 branches of the system answer 3,016,619 million reference questions per year, with the average length of each reference question being 2.87 minutes (172 seconds). These 88 branches employ 116 reference librarians; total staff time spent answering reference questions is 144,338 hours. However, using the Erlang C algorithm and assuming an industry standard service level of 80 percent of calls answered on average in 20 seconds, they calculate that "a centralized reference center could handle all of the 3,016,619 million questions with a reference staff of only 67, a 42 percent reduction of the 116 staff required to handle reference services as we now provide it."[20] Moreover, these 67 staff would "be occupied and answering questions 89 percent of the time."[21] However, if the Erlang C algorithm was told that 116 staff would be working to answer all the questions, the staff occupancy rate would be only 51 percent, "which means they are spending half their time doing something other than reference."[22] Because Coffman and Saxton believe that anywhere from 50 to 80 percent of all reference questions "might not require" professional librarians, "a large percentage of the 67 staff needed to operate the networked reference service would not require professional degrees nor would they require professional salaries."[23] Because most of the 116 staff currently providing reference service do have professional degrees, the "potential cost savings of a centralized service staffed with a high percentage of paraprofessionals could be substantial."[24] The call center model allows not only for a drastic reduction in the number of reference staff positions, but also for a large-scale deprofessionalization of those positions that remain. Because the questions asked by patrons at reference desks are not really very difficult, they can best be answered by low-paid paraprofessionals who will do nothing else all day.

Yet Coffman and Saxton are not satisfied with this increase in efficiency and decrease in costs. For example, they are enthusiastic at the following prospect: "Reducing the average question length by just 22 seconds, from 172 seconds to 150, would reduce staff requirements by over 10 percent from 67 to 60 positions."[25] Here, queries are turned into mere commodities. The goal is to answer them as quickly as possible in order to process more each hour, raising the productivity levels of the call center by employing fewer people. Similarly, McGlamery and Coffman wax eloquent about developing library web pages so that more than 80 percent of user questions would be answered without recourse to human assistance. "We are calling these sites 'reference front ends'," they write, "and it is our hope that they will help answer a great many of the patrons' questions before they can be tempted to click on the "Talk to a Librarian" button."[26] Even if patrons do click on the "Talk to a Librarian" button, library staff "can be trained to use the resources on these key sites to answer the bulk of the questions."[27]

The drive toward efficiency and low costs is never ending. No matter the scenario, very little room is left for professional librarians in the call center model: very little room for them to display the specialized and generalist knowledge they have accumulated over the years and very little room for understanding the reference transaction as an important socio-cultural moment that requires sensitivity, care, and empathy. From a metaphorical perspective, the situation is very much as described by Harris and Marshall, who quote one library director who believes that paraprofessionals could be taught to handle reference questions "without running to mommy."[28] In effect, proponents of call centers view "mommy"—the disparaging term with which this library director referred to professional reference librarians—as superfluous. As libraries try to cut costs by employing fewer librarians and more paraprofessionals, the roles of librarians will tend to become very broad — a circumstance that "will eliminate their ability to specialize in the areas of expertise that have defined the core of the profession."[29] The result is a growing deprofessionalization of their jobs as librarians try to conform to the prevailing view that, as expressed by another library director quoted by Harris and Marshall, "It's a larger thing that makes a librarian [and] it's got something to do with management, and commitment, and analysis, and adapting to change."[30] Left unspoken is the danger that, as librarians evolve into managers, they risk losing the skills that made them librarians in the first place. As their jobs are continually simplified, as paraprofessionals take over these newly simplified tasks at a substantially reduced wage scale, as directors tell librarians that librarianship doesn't have anything to do with such "little things,"[31] as cataloging, collection development, and, now, reference service, are gradually outsourced, librarians may be forgiven for wondering about the intellectual content of librarianship and, indeed, whether there is such a thing as librarianship.

The politics of call centers

If librarianship is losing its intellectual component through such proposals, what is the face of the call center itself? First, the lists of skills that the new type of reference worker should possess mentions nothing about subject-area knowledge. Instead, necessary skills are confined to proficiency in various types of hardware and software packages, navigating already constructed web pages offering scripted answers, and keyboarding. Second, library call center proposals completely overlook the negative aspects of private-sector customer service call centers, often identified as electronic sweatshops. The neglect of these negative aspects is perhaps the most surprising feature of the embrace of the call center model by Coffman and Saxton, Ferguson, and McGlamery and Coffman.

There is a substantial body of evidence documenting how call centers, whether inbound or outbound, exploit and degrade workers. Building upon Michel Foucault's insight that Jeremy Bentham's design for the ideal prison, the Panopticon, is a metaphor for the workplace of the future, Sue Fernie and David Metcalf argue that the call center is the ultimate manifestation of employer control and worker powerlessness.[32] A philosophy of electronic surveillance discipline encourages an ever-faster pace of performance. Because the tasks performed in call centers are highly routine, highly intensive, and limited in range, Lester Thurow sees call centers as a significant step toward the industrialization of the service sector.[33] Ranald Richardson, Vicki Belt, and Neill Marshall point out not only that the "Taylorist fragmentation of work and flat organizational structures" in call centers restricts opportunities for career progression, but also that, because call centers have few links with local areas, they can "seek out even cheaper locations in order to achieve further reductions in the costs of production."[34] Finally, call center workers are at constant risk of being technologically displaced as newer and more sophisticated technologies take the place of their already routinized and automated tasks.

With regard to the working conditions in call centers, there is a long list of well-documented complaints. Ginger Conlon, reviewing the results of a survey by the Radclyffe Group, a management consulting firm, outlines three major factors that contribute to worker dissatisfaction: inflexible rules that restrict employee movement away from their desk or cubicle area; high call quotas; and strict monitoring of quantitative and qualitative performance levels through electronic surveillance and tracking of calls.[35] Mark Higgins describes the sense of isolation that call center workers experience: "It's supposed to be part of the new economy, but the setup is really very old fashioned — 'we're the boss, do what we say' sort of thing. At one place, they seemed to think they were the commanders on *Star Trek* — we all worked down on the floor, while the supervisors were on 'the bridge,' looking down on us."[36] David Menzies outlines the rigid adherence to a pre-determined script and the constant lurking of supervisors who reprimand any deviation from this script.[37] As Richardson, Belt, and Marshall, as well as Ruth Buchanan and Sarah Koch-Schulte,[38] observe, such conditions, taken as a whole, have resulted in serious health concerns: workers complain about tension, stress, sleeplessness, headaches, eye strain, voice loss, hearing problems, and burnout. Joan McFarland, describing strenuous governmental efforts (including tax incentives and resettlement bonuses) that resulted in a massive influx of call centers into New Brunswick, Canada, observes that local workers have no illusions about why call center companies choose to move there: "The company feels that New Brunswick is a cheaper place in wages and benefits. They see New Brunswick as desperate ... [where] workers will settle for anything as long as it is a job [but] the strategy of bringing in low-paying jobs is creating a poor society."[39] Reporting on the explosion in call center jobs in Jacksonville, Florida, Bruce Bryant-Friedland and John Finotti note that the annual average wage of $21,000 paid to call center employees does not compare well to the citywide average of $26,365 in all other industries.[40] As in New Brunswick, there was a concerted strategy by Jacksonville city officials to attract call centers in an effort to create jobs in a depressed area. Together with promises of cheap land and low building costs, business development officers touted "a plentiful supply of low-wage workers, especially Navy wives and college students,"[41] thus institutionalizing a permanent low-income ghetto. Studying the concentration of call centers in the depressed mining area of Newcastle in northeast England, Richardson, Belt, and Marshall observe that "the availability of a sufficient pool of quality labor at a lower cost than other regions" is the reason most cited by managers for the decision to set up shop.[42] It is therefore not surprising, as Angela Karr reports, that call center turnover rates average about 31 percent in the United States, significantly above the rate of 18 percent for companies in other industries.[43] Richardson, Belt, and Marshall cite one female call center agent who links infantilizing treatment with high turnover rates: "When I first came here.... I was like a small child, they were watching me ... I think most call centres are like that and that's why there's such a high turnover of staff ... because people just get fed up with it, the pressure."[44] Workers are beginning to unionize and embark on strike tactics to win better working conditions, increased autonomy, clearly demarcated career progression ladders, and overtime pay for working evenings, nights, and weekends.

Given the almost overwhelming derision with which call center work is characterized, many management consultants have proposed ways to improve call center working conditions. James Curtis recognizes that ways must be found "to make the job fulfilling as call centers get larger," and recommends that companies give serious consideration to "localization," that is, mini call centers "manned by between ten and 15 people, with the feel of a local community center."[45] Ruth Thaler-Carter suggests a series of incentive compensation plans to motivate call center employees, and especially lauds team-based and department-based objectives leading to low-cost or no-cost incentives such as "fun" gifts or prizes (plastic eggs in Easter baskets with a little prize or toy in each egg and a matchbox-size company car are two of the ideas mentioned) that go a long way to "encourage productivity and create energy."[46] Conlon outlines a proposal to encourage the creation of "an environment of personal and team accountability."[47] Although these ideas appear plausible on the surface, they do nothing to address the problematic structural nature of the call center industry as a disciplinary Panopticon. Indeed, they make employees themselves participants in surveillance activities. Instead of focusing on systemic inequities in the call center milieu that make for disgruntled workers, employees are urged to develop team spirit such that "if one rep is taking too many breaks, instead of reporting him to a manager, a teammate can confront that person herself about the behavior."[48]

Thaler-Carter's insight about team-based incentives that stress "fun"[49] (albeit infantilizing) rewards is thus a logical addendum to the Panopticon metaphor: employees motivated by team-based incentives will be more prone to participate in surveillance of their fellow employees, all in the name of winning prizes for the department as a whole. Instituting a policy of rewards does nothing to reduce the amount of electronic surveillance. It even encourages workers to process calls more quickly because those who do not win incentives understand that, insofar as the automated call distribution (ACD) system tracks the amount of time spent on each call, rewards are based on pre-determined quantitative measures that can be increased at the discretion of management. Even Curtis's notion that mini call centers are the wave of the future does not alter the fundamental nature of call center work because technology exists to monitor productivity across a virtual and decentralized network. Even though people may be working in small groups of 10 or 15 people, or even at home by themselves, each computer is still being centrally monitored. In addition, the mini call center model allows companies to avoid a rising wage structure such as might develop at large central facilities because of possible low employment rates in the surrounding area or unionization pressures. As Curtis notes, the small telecenter approach allows the company "to set up cost effectively wherever there are people willing to work,"[50] a wily euphemism for a constant search for low-wage geographic pockets.

Critics of call centers have, of course, themselves been criticized for adopting a doom and gloom perspective. Stephen Frenkel, Marek Korczynski, Karen Shire, and Mary Tam, in a book entitled *On the Front Line: Organization of Work in the Information Society*, argue that call centers fall "within the general parameters of knowledge work" insofar as they allow for significant levels of employee input, discretion, and creativity.[51] Scholars have begun to take note of such variables as "size, industrial sector, market conditions, complexity and call cycle times, the nature of operations (inbound, outbound), the precise manner of technological integration, the effectiveness of representative organisations, and management styles, priorities, and human resource practices."[52] When call centers prioritize quality as opposed to quantity in their workflows, that is, when such characteristics as "targets soft, flexible or no scripts, relaxed call handling times, customer satisfaction a priority, possibility of off-phone task completion, statistics modified by quality criteria, task cycle time long, low call volumes, high value of calls, high level of operator discretion"[53] are present in the working environment, some researchers suggest that the type of regimentation and routinization that marks quantity-oriented call centers decreases substantially or disappears completely. However, Phil Taylor, Gareth Mulvey, Jeff Hyman, and Peter Bain show that this is not the case. Examining two call centers—one generally characterized by quality-oriented workflows and the other by quantity-oriented workflows—Taylor and his colleagues find that there is very little difference in how workers perceive the level of control they exert: "Even in the workflows where the emphasis is on quality, significant numbers are reporting an absence of control over key aspects of their jobs."[54] Moreover, workers in so-called quality-workflow situations perceive their task performance as "highly routinised," limited as to the possibility of "customization" and "highly constrained by managerial imperatives."[55] In both call centers, the emphasis is continually on cost reductions, the consequences of which are "further growth of routinisation and intensification" even though a "minority of operators might enjoy higher levels of discretion and creative responsibility."[56]

Despite the numerous drawbacks of call centers, it is somehow appropriate — although no less disconcerting—that Steve Coffman embraces the retailer Amazon.com as a model for the library of the future.[57] He could not be more fervent in stating his belief that Amazon.com is the epitome of a successful and technologically innovative organization with a firm commitment to superior customer service. Using the Amazon.com paradigm, he pictures the ideal local library as providing access to 43 million items (the approximate total of all items listed in the OCLC database), all accessible through a catalog designed "for the selection decision, with records that carry reviews, cover art, tables of contents, excerpts, and any other kind of content that could help a person."[58] Accessible seven days per week and 24 hours each day, the new library will even provide home delivery of requested books so that patrons' time is not wasted. Customer service representatives will always be friendly, knowledgeable, and willing to help patrons with their questions and book selections.

The reality of Amazon.com is starkly different from Coffman's vision. Customer service representatives—the backbone of Amazon's operation — make only between $10 and $13 per hour. As Mark Leibovich reports, they are expected to respond to 12 e-mails per hour; "lagging productivity—fewer than 7.5 e-mails an hour for an extended period — can result in probation or termination."[59] Employees complain that their self-worth is measured in "how many e-mails I could answer": "we're supposed to care deeply about customers, provided we can care deeply about them at an incredible rate of speed."[60] Another employee recounts how, after a telephone conversation lasting three or four minutes with a customer to whom he recommended a Civil War–era fiction book, he was chastised by a supervisor who warned him to "watch the schmoozing."[61] In other words, everyone is expected to work constantly at an "uptime" pace. The infamous Amazon memo entitled "You can sleep when you're dead" is a brutal reminder of how unforgiving work expectations have become for customer-service representatives. As Mike Daisey writes of his experience at Amazon, "We were all moving at this sickening, accelerated, and unreasonable rate together, aging at the same incredible speed like that bad

Star Trek episode where the content makes everyone old.... Conventional wisdom held that Amazon Time was equivalent to Dog Time, which meant that one human year equaled seven Amazonian ones. You lived through a year [of working there] and you might look twenty-four, but you were really thirty-one."[62]

Amazon regularly orders mandatory overtime to deal with backlogs of unopened e-mail and telephone calls. Managers outline goals to be met — goals couched in the rhetoric of team-building and sacrifice: "You own this goal. I own this goal. We all will share in the consequences of failing to meet this goal." "Fun-productivity" races held at midnight — where the prizes are "sundaes, smoothies, trail mix, pretzels, award-winning coffee and other yummy things" — are presented as "great news" even though they count as required overtime. But for many customer-service representatives, management methods such as these are "like Communist China under Mao.... You're constantly being pushed to help the collective. If you fail to do this, you're going against your family. But if this is a family it belongs on Jerry Springer."[63]

In addition, the physical and spiritual landscape of Amazon is, literally, frightening. One Amazon call center had very little light, making it like "something from the accounting halls of Dickens' *Bleak House*."[64] There were only "four small frosted windows that served four hundred of us" — a situation that resulted in confrontations in bathrooms between employees about who would have a "a seat that received a few feeble rays [of sunlight] for a few hours a day."[65] Even more disturbing was the constant flashing lights and shrill noise when quotas were not being met. "Hanging everywhere were readerboards showing the number of calls on hold and the average response time. When the numbers got too high they would turn red and a fearful, piercing whistle would go off, hooting over and over."[66] Employees understood that the whistle was a form of "conditioning" meant to inspire them to work faster because they knew that when the "horrible" noise stopped, they would feel "intense relief" and a substantial reduction in tension.[67]

When losses mounted and stock prices collapsed in 2000, the concept of family and "goal ownership" evaporated very quickly. Amazon instituted a round of layoffs and began to outsource customer service representative jobs to Daksh.com, with the expressed goal of having about 80 percent of its customer service work done in India.[68] Whereas Amazon custom service representatives in the United States earn on average $1,900 per month, Indian workers can expect to earn no more than $109 to $175 per month.[69] In an effort to reach acceptable levels of profitability, Amazon is thus participating in the global outsourcing movement, taking advantage of countries with relatively weak labor standards and low wage structures. It was perhaps inevitable that dissatisfaction with Amazon work practices reached such heights that persistent efforts were undertaken to form a union. As one worker bluntly explains, "Amazon may be the symbol of the new economy, but it has the worst of the working conditions of the old economy."[70] Preaching the mantra of ownership and family, Amazon responded with anti-union activities, distributing instructions to managers about how to dissuade workers from signing union membership cards.[71]

In short, Amazon.com stands as a case study of the negative features associated with call centers and customer service centers. The fact that Coffman has unlimited praise for the Amazon.com business model and management ethos is troubling to say the least, considering his desire to make call centers the heart of the 21st-century library. Even if his vision of call centers processing reference questions includes quality-oriented workflows, the research conducted by Taylor, Mulvey, Hyman, and Bain suggests that high levels of regimentation, work intensification, and cost containment will still be a characteristic feature of such work environments. Whether a call center is quality-oriented or quantity-oriented, the reference transaction will become automated, regimented, and depersonalized, further eroding another facet of the intellectual and cultural base of librarianship.

Women and call centers

Perhaps the most salient and intriguing feature of call centers is the preponderance of female employees. Most scholars agree that about 70 percent of call center employees are women and that many employees find themselves on "the periphery of the labor market for some reason," usually poverty, transience, or lack of education.[72] While the part-time student component of call center work tends to be evenly distributed between men and women, full-time work is dominated by women who, as one worker put it, "probably have not progressed beyond high school or who have families or for some other reason would not be able to find a job."[73] This division of labor has gendered consequences, namely the ghettoization of women in routinized, low-paying jobs without much chance for advancement. Buchanan and Koch-Schulte also document how sexism plays a role in such gender imbalance. Women may modulate the pitch of their voices in order to deal effectively with male callers. "Guys will respond to you better if you speak in lower tones like a husky voice…. It's almost a sexual preference. In that sense, I think women get the short end of the stick because it almost brings them down to sexual objects…. I think we should give women more credit than just pretty faces and nice-sounding voices."[74]

Although inbound call centers tend to provide more stability and chances for advancement, Buchanan and Koch-Schulte suggest "the dynamics of the industry are such that the 'good jobs' are disproportionately distributed to the few young men in the labour force."[75] Indeed, relatively high-paying inbound call centers that require special expertise (like mutual fund sales) and that consequently require phone representatives to pass exams are almost exclusively dominated by men. In broad terms, men working in call centers have specialized skills that give them numerous opportunities for advancement, while women tend to be concentrated in positions that demand sympathy, listening, interpersonal, conflict resolution, and communication skills—care-giving functions that may be summarized as "emotional labour."[76] Moreover, women do not have much opportunity to learn new and challenging skills that would lead to better-paying jobs simply because they are valued for their care-giving role and for their ability to keyboard quickly.[77] Thus, despite the gleaming appearance of many call centers, with rows of high-powered computers and sophisticated web-based digital interfaces, many female workers view their workplaces as nothing but factories. "You think this is an advanced office and this is on the cutting edge of technology; or whatever. It is not that at all. It is a factory."[78]

As libraries move toward the visions of Coffman, Saxton, Ferguson, and McGlamery outlined above, where paraprofessionals in call centers perform functions previously the preserve of reference professionals, there is a danger that they will become even more complicit in what Steven Ellis identifies as "the economy of offshore information production."[79] For instance, many cataloguing and document conversion tasks are performed in less-developed countries for low wages and in unsafe working conditions. These are low-skill data entry jobs held by women at a rate approaching 98 percent. Reviewing other studies on the subject, Ellis summarizes that these "data-entry women are locked into physically damaging work with little or no opportunity for making transitions to traditionally male (and increasingly scarce) technical or supervisory roles." He quotes one supervisor of data-entry clerks who notes, "Women are better at this kind of job [because] they are more dexterous, more disciplined, more caring about the quality of work and more agile."[80] This echoes the comments of a call center supervisor worker interviewed by Buchanan and Koch-Schulte, who attributed the preponderance of women in the industry to the fact that "there were more typing skills among women, and also, I suppose, you aren't trained to [do] anything else.... It's a great job for somebody who types real fast and sits there."[81] Studying the phenomena of data processors in various Caribbean countries, Ewart Skinner also offers evidence for the mostly female composition of data clerks. One government official is of the opinion that "women have a natural proclivity for work that is tedious and monotonous" and that "a man just won't stay in this tedious kind of work, he would walk out in a couple of hours."[82]

Indeed, McFarland compares call centers in New Brunswick to free-trade zones (so-called "maquiladoras") in Third World countries insofar as both are "the outcome of strategies based on outside investment by footloose industries attracted by government incentives, have similarly structured workforces subject to the same worker 'burnout,' and involve the relaxation of laws and regulations affecting workers' health."[83] Transnational companies that operate call centers and maquiladoras search for locations where there is "the prospect of a docile labour force, unorganized and unorganizable," and some scholars have suggested that it is not a coincidence that the vast majority of employees in call centers are female. Swasti Mitter, for example, writes that "it is not the genetic characteristics of women workers that make them the preferred labour force in [worldwide factories of transnational corporations], but rather their marginal role in the mainstream labour movement."[84] There are, of course, large differences between call centers and maquiladoras, but it is nevertheless true that, in the same way that maquiladoras do not pay a great deal of attention to health and environmental issues, jurisdictions such as New Brunswick, in an effort to attract call centers, emphasize that workers will not receive compensation for "health problems caused by workplace stress."[85] As we have seen, stress is perhaps the defining feature of life at call centers, and it is therefore revealing that workplace compensation programs do not cover health costs associated with such stress.

Lenny Siegel observes that the Silicon Valley high-tech workforce also has characteristics of gendered labor segmentation. Even though women make up only 38.1 percent of these workers, women constitute 79.1 percent of clerks, versus 22.6 percent of managers.[86] These statistics indicate the larger forces currently affecting library restructuring and reorganization. Harris and Marshall remind us that a prevailing attitude among some library directors is that the work traditionally performed by higher-paid women in the library system is overrated, silly, or comprised of what Coffman and Saxton call "odd tasks."[87] Thus, in the view of library directors, "it makes good sense to pass it on to other women who are a little lower-paid, and who can, with training, take on increased responsibility."[88] This deprofessionalization of reference responsibilities is, from one perspective, tantamount to a ready acceptance of a large number of female call center clerks. They would perform tasks that are tedious and monotonous, partaking in what Noah Kennedy calls "the industrialization of intelligence."[89] At the same time, this approach implies the valorization of managerial and systems-administrator tasks which, according to the statistics gathered by Siegel, are held mostly by men.

Even though proponents of digital reference call centers in academic and public libraries would strenuously argue that their vision of the future is very far removed from the electronic sweatshop model, the call center analogy used to describe digital reference work is, on both practical and symbolic levels, very telling. Since librarianship is a female intensive profession that has traditionally paid relatively high wages, any attempt to offload reference functions to paraprofessionals working in a setting characterized by constant electronic surveillance, low wages, labor segmentation, work routinization, stress, and high levels of employee churn is a worrisome setback. Library directors currently do not seem overly concerned about "the economy of offshore information production" described by Ellis, so it is not inconceivable that they would come to accept as normal, and perhaps even desirable, a situation in which clerical workers process reference questions under less than stellar working conditions.

When all is said and done, library directors who are enthusiastic about call centers appear to be willing victims of technological determinism. It is almost as if they are saying to themselves: If the technology exists and if everyone else is using it, why shouldn't I use it too? The opportunity to cut costs and show oneself to be an adept and forward-thinking manager is irresistible. Scant heed is given to Antonio Gramsci's warning against the danger inherent in blindly accepting that which seems to be the commonsensical approach and "the spontaneous philosophy which is proper to everybody."[90] In short, unexamined acceptance of late 20th-century information technology (IT) has created a hegemonic dynamic insofar as non–IT-based solutions are held to be without much value.

Revaluing reading as the basis of reference work

To be sure, there are numerous suggestions about how to improve the call center experience. Buchanan and Koch-Schulte propose a series of significant ameliorative actions, including monitoring the "gender and racial segmentation of workers" in call centers, ensuring that call centers create intellectually challenging "good jobs" that provide advancement and career opportunities, regulating the working conditions with regard to pace and stress, and emphasizing the value-added and skilled nature of call center work.[91] These changes, if instituted, would certainly improve library reference call centers. Yet dangers remain. Not only would the "bad jobs" prevalent in call centers assume an increasing share of the totality of jobs in a library universe heretofore characterized by "good jobs," but the fundamental human-centered and caring aspect of traditional reference work would also be eviscerated in the rush for efficiency and cost effectiveness.

Ferguson would disagree with this assessment. Instead, he believes that a three-tiered integrated "on-site/remote service matrix"[92] would ensure that the "enduring service values [of librarianship] can be reinterpreted and sustained in meaningful ways by promoting user satisfaction that derives from personal contact and by increasing the ability to verify customer satisfaction in arenas not currently monitored well."[93] He envisions first-tier gateway services ("basic use and finding questions related to core information resources") staffed by students and paraprofessionals who make use of asynchronous user aids through Customer Support Centers; second-tier intermediate services ("general research support and initial triage of complex software or hardware issues; referral to experts") staffed by paraprofessionals, computer consultants, and librarians making use of e-mail reference; and third-tier expert and specialized services ("subject or resource experts by appointment or during office hours") staffed by librarians and computer consultants.[94] Yet, at the same time, he foresees that an "Internet call-center" would be the cornerstone of all these services, dealing around the clock with most questions and problems, and making only a small number of referrals to librarian experts.[95] Keeping in mind that, according to Coffman and Saxton, the primary purpose of library call centers is to increase efficiency and reduce costs by decreasing time spent per call and hence the number of staff required to take calls, the nature of the "personal contact" that Ferguson still believes to be possible is problematic.

From another perspective, Ferguson's plan also devalues the majority of reference questions and information requests by assigning them to less qualified personnel. In effect, he forgets that each reference question comes with a complex history and, often, a psychosocial context. As Brenda Dervin has shown, individuals seeking reference assistance may be thought of as experiencing a gap in their understanding of a given situation, whether intellectual, psychological, emotional, practical, or recreational.[96] They have a discontinuity in their knowledge about something, and they are unable to continue on their journey of achieving knowledge without obtaining "gap-bridging" information.[97] Reference staff may therefore be instrumental in offering a series of "helps" that can assume such diverse forms as initiating a new idea or a new way of looking at things; offering a sense of direction; assisting in the development of a new skill; regaining control; moving out of a bad situation; or obtaining support, comfort, or reassurance.[98] Carol Kuhlthau, moreover, sees the librarian as a counselor who establishes, with the patron, an ongoing dialogue "that leads to an exploration of strategy and to a sequence for learning."[99] Typically, the dialogue may be reformulated, redefined, and nuanced throughout the many stages of the information-seeking process, as librarians "facilitate understanding, problem solving, and decision making."[100] In the call center model, with its emphasis on speed and rote answers through electronic FAQs, the opportunities for caring, personalized reference service delivered by library professionals who understand the psychological insights of Dervin and Kuhlthau would seem to be few and far between.

Is it possible to re-intellectualize reference work in the 21st century? In the next chapter, we suggest that renewed emphasis on voluminous reading is a prerequisite for the revalorization and reintellectualization of the reference function because reading has the potential to provide the basis for the reference librarian to make the kinds of intellectual, cultural, and, if necessary, interdisciplinary connections that add real value to the reference transaction.

2

Reading and Reference Work

Early practitioners of library reference work were convinced that general-interest reading, especially reading of newspapers and magazines, was an integral aspect of success on the job. In 1925, Frank Keller Walter urged librarians not only to promote reading among the public, but also to realize that "[i]n self defense the librarian [too] must read if she wishes to succeed."[1] More specifically, to keep up with the pace of world events, "One often must get out of the current to see the progress of the stream and to notice that it is the stream and not the banks which moves."[2] Continuing his analogy, he suggested that, because "[i]nformation is the real water of life to the mind," it is "most often in books, in magazines and newspapers that one can get the best perspective of social progress in the limited periods of leisure [available to the librarian]."[3] In 1930, James Ingersoll Wyer recommended that librarians "[f]aithfully read at least one local newspaper" and "[k]eep somewhat in touch with affairs of state and nation as well as city … through a metropolitan daily or an able review."[4] In 1944, Margaret Hutchins was adamant about the central role that newspapers play in the provision of superior reference service. She noted, first, that "a very large proportion of the reference work in practically all types and sizes of libraries is accomplished by means of periodicals and newspapers.[5] Newspapers and periodicals are "indispensable" because they "supply the most up-to-date information on all subjects."[6] In 1961, Shiyali Ramamrita Ranganathan also insisted on the value of reading newspapers and periodicals on a regular basis because "sometimes research studies and investigations are reported in the newspapers at their inception. Sometimes newspapers have feature articles on important conclusions brought to light."[7] Accordingly, a "close scanning of both newspapers and periodicals is really necessary for useful, intelligent long-range reference service" because the reference worker must constantly anticipate the types of questions that could possibly be asked, and because periodicals "provide opportunities for the reference librarian to keep himself [or herself] abreast of the world's progress in knowledge," in effect "keep[ing] ahead of the game [and at] the very wave-front in the advance of knowledge."[8] When reading newspapers and periodicals, "the variety of questions actually brought up by enquirers and of the questions anticipated on the basis of local knowledge and contemporary happenings should get interlaced in the mind of the reference librarian."[9]

The emphasis on reading current publications seems to be undergoing a renaissance. Companies are beginning to recognize that general-interest reading (referred to as "environmental scanning") by their in-house corporate librarians contributes to profitability.

For example, the librarian for Highsmith Inc. spends "20 percent of her time scanning newspapers, magazines, on-line databases, and Web sites ... and her antennae are always up for interesting tidbits from television, radio, advertising, or casual conversation."[10] The point here is that she never knows what she is looking for, or what she will find. Instead, she must be alert to a wide variety of issues, themes, social trends, and occurrences, and her perusal of media sources must be sufficiently detailed so that she can reject material as well as flag it as potentially valuable. As a result, she becomes a walking, well-informed resource for everyone in the company, not just those who have assigned her specific tasks and searches. In addition, Elizabeth Thomsen suggests that one important way for librarians to survive constant change and to provide the type of service users expect in a fast-paced world is to read newspapers, magazines, and generally make themselves into "active and informed citizens" through a diversified and continuous current awareness program.[11] Indeed, in order to anticipate the myriad questions and concerns that affect "the lives of our patrons and sends them off in search of information" and to avoid embarrassing gaps in their own cultural knowledge, Thomsen argues that reference librarians "should spend several hours a day reading a variety of newspapers and magazines—cover to cover—listening to National Public Radio (NPR) and watching CNN."[12]

In sum, intensive reading of a wide array of current publications gives librarians intellectual tools with which to confront an equally wide array of information requests. They can then use this knowledge to understand the comprehensive context of the question and to make innovative connections to other fields and subject areas, giving the library customer a richer and more robust answer than if they had very little background knowledge about the particular question. Or, quite simply, they can provide the answer in a shorter time, thus fulfilling one of the desiderata of reference work in the digital era.

How does this work in practice? To give some idea about the range of situations where knowledge of information contained in newspapers and magazines has had or could have a demonstrated positive effect in reference work, we present four documented examples from often overlooked reference texts. In one of his reference case studies, S.R. Ranganathan tells the story of the "Kra Canal Enquiry." Here, "a young graduate stepped into the library. Mentioning an alleged agreement between Siam and Japan, he asked for information on Kra Canal." Unfortunately, the librarians "were absolutely ignorant" of [the problem]."[13] A long and frustrating hunt for the desired information commenced. Librarians and the patron worked hand in hand, searching unsuccessfully through the following sources: encyclopedias; books on Siam; book on Japanese foreign policy; books on naval bases in Singapore; and books on Far Eastern problems. Subsequently, periodicals were searched, with a little more success. The magazine *Pacific Affairs* contained an article called "The Kra Canal: A Suez for Japan?" which included a number of footnotes leading to the *Parliamentary Debates*, which in turn gave a number of references to key articles in *The London Times*.

Denis Joseph Grogan describes how "a young girl obviously on her way home from school" approached the reference librarian wishing to know as much as possible about the astronaut Sally Ride.[14] Vaguely aware of the recent publicity surrounding Sally Ride, the librarian searched first (unsuccessfully) in the American, British, and international versions of *Who's Who*. He then searched *Biography Index* and found references to only very brief articles that he knew would not be very useful to the patron. He then remembered the existence of a magazine entitled *Current Biography*, looked at the cumulative index of the most recent issue, and located a reference to a cover story on Sally Ride in an issue about three or four months old. The article was about three pages long and contained a wealth of personal information about the astronaut.

Grogan also recounts how a public librarian was asked about spontaneous human combustion. Convinced that such a thing could not exist, she looked in five encyclopedias, but only found that this phenomenon occurs in hay, coal, and other such substances.[15] After consulting the *Oxford English Dictionary*, which stated that human combustion is possible in people who consume much alcohol, she then searched the library catalog. Finding nothing there, she was "at something of a loss where to turn next" when she asked a senior colleague, who immediately told her that "there was a letter in *The Times* about that a year or so ago."[16] Once located, this letter turned out to be the key to finding a vast array of information about spontaneous human combustion.

Finally, Grogan describes a request for information about the present whereabouts of Noah's ark. The unsuccessful search encompassed, again, numerous encyclopedias, numerous periodical indexes, and the *British National Bibliography*. Two books that sounded promising were found, but did not contain the desired information. Grogan then relates how "[t]his was the point at which the librarian indicated that he had taken the search far enough."[17] But, some months later, "by one of those chances that happen so frequently in reference work," the librarian noticed "in his routine scanning of *The Times*" a story, datelined Ankara, that reported on a recent discovery of "a boat-shaped formation found 5,000 ft. up Mount Ararat in Eastern Turkey" which the archaeologist was confident would turn out to be Noah's Ark.[18]

In the first two examples, intensive reading of newspapers or magazines could have made finding an answer much easier. Librarians would have been aware that they had read about the Kra Canal in a newspaper and would have immediately gone to *The Times* index to find the appropriate issue. Or, if the article in question was too recent to have been indexed, they could have leafed through back issues to locate the correct article. Either way, much time could have been saved. Similarly, in the case of the young girl and Sally Ride, even the most cursory scanning of recent magazines and newspapers—the idea of environmental scanning as practiced by the librarian at Highsmith Inc.—would have allowed the librarian to locate the cover story article about this famous American astronaut. The last two examples provide ready evidence that newspapers do serve a valuable function. Even a seemingly innocuous letter to the editor can become the starting point for finding an answer to a difficult reference query such as the one about spontaneous human combustion. And, as the Noah's Ark example demonstrates, even the most intractable queries can frequently be resolved through careful attention to information contained in newspapers. As Grogan suggests, newspapers are irreplaceable repositories "of much information completely unavailable elsewhere," all the more so because "a substantial minority of the enquiries in all types of libraries stem from the news of the moment" and because they present "the best source there is for assessing the *Zeitgeist*, the life of the time as seen through the eyes of contemporaries."[19]

These examples, of course, come from an era when online information sources were nonexistent or in their infancy. Are newspapers and general-interest magazines still valuable sources of information for librarians and reference personnel in both academic and public libraries? In broader terms, does reading, keeping up with current events, and being aware of trends in social and intellectual culture make a positive difference in the ability of reference personnel to satisfy the information needs of contemporary patrons? How many newspapers and magazines do librarians read in their spare time? How many fiction and nonfiction books do they read in their spare time? Does reading newspapers, magazines, and books help in reference work? What do 21st-century patrons feel that librarians should do in order to better serve them? For instance, should academic librarians actually know content and be subject-specialists in one or two areas, or is content-based knowledge an outmoded concept for academic librarians in an era of digital services?

To answer questions such as the above, we conducted a series of three survey-based studies during fall 2000 and fall 2001. All three studies involved graduate students in a Library and Information Science program at a Canadian university. These students were asked, as part of their class assignments, to send questionnaires to a wide variety of academic and public library reference staff, as well as to professors in the humanities and social sciences. Detailed information about procedures is contained in Appendices A, B, and C.

In the first survey, we asked academic librarians to tell us how often they read local newspapers, national newspapers, and magazines in their spare time. What sorts of general-interest publications do they read? How often do they read works of fiction and nonfiction on their own time? Which ones? Do they think that reading any of these materials helps in their reference work? Does it help in other aspects of their jobs? Can they think of any concrete examples where reading newspapers, magazines, or books has helped them? Would they like to read more? Would they like to have paid time at work to read?

We received 539 completed surveys from academic librarians, and their cumulative answers are not only a rich portrait of their intellectual life outside of work, but also an eloquent record of the numerous ways that reading has helped them to do a better job at their daily tasks. Complete texts of the 23 questions, as well as a brief discussion of some salient demographic characteristics of respondents, are in Appendix A. We also conducted statistical analyses with a view to determining whether the amount of reading that academic librarians engage in has a significant relationship with instances where such reading helped them in their reference work or in other aspects of their jobs. The results, presented in Appendix D, show that, in general terms, the more one reads, the more it helps on the job.

In the second study, we sent a slightly different questionnaire than the one described above to public library reference personnel — professional librarians as well as paraprofessionals. From an overall perspective, we wanted to know about the ways they keep up with information sources. How do they stay current? Do they read newspapers and magazines on their own time? What do they read? Do they watch television and listen to the radio? Has reading newspapers and magazines helped them in reference work or in other job functions? Has watching television and listening to the radio helped them in reference work or in other job functions? We also asked whether their respective institutions provide them with current awareness services, and whether they engaged in shelf-study and browsing online sites to discover information that might potentially be useful. (Because the focus of the present book is on reading, we do not discuss these last two issues here, but we will return to the idea of shelf-study and current awareness services in subsequent journal-article length work.) We received 419 completed surveys from public library reference personnel; their responses, taken as a whole, paint a multi-hued portrait of the vital role that reading newspapers and magazines plays in their work lives. Complete texts of the 19 questions that were sent to public library reference personnel, as well as a brief discussion of some salient demographic characteristics of respondents, are in Appendix B.

In the third study, we turned to library users and asked them what they thought about the service they had received and how it might be improved. Specifically focusing on professors in the humanities and social sciences, we wanted to know what they thought about the issue of whether academic reference librarians should have subject-based knowledge in one or more fields. We focused on professors because, traditionally, professors have been one important group of users of academic reference services. They may not ask as many questions at the reference desk as undergraduate and graduate students, but they often set the tone for how their students perceive librarians and library services through their comments in class, the degree of emphasis they place on acquiring library research skills so that students may successfully complete assignments and essays, and their willingness to involve librarians in their classes as experts in bibliographic instruction. The views of professors are therefore a good baseline by which to gauge whether academic reference librarians should have subject-based specialties and knowledge in order to provide high-quality reference service in university and college settings.

We asked professors to assess the quality of reference service that they had received in the past and to compare that level of service with an ideal level that they themselves would offer, if they were suddenly transformed into academic reference librarians. How many times had they asked a question related to their field of study at the reference desk in the past two years? Were they satisfied with the answers? How would they describe the service they received? Have they ever been impressed (or disappointed) with the subject-specific knowledge of an academic reference librarian at their institution? Do professors make a point of going to one or two reference librarians, and if so, why? What advice would they give to reference librarians about how to improve service to patrons such as themselves and to stay current in various subject fields? Responses from 236 professors in 13 different subject areas were received. The complete texts of these 15 questions, as well as a brief discussion of some salient demographic characteristics of respondents, are in Appendix C.

Taken together, the results of these three surveys give a well-rounded picture of the way in which intensive and continuous reading helps reference work in both academic and public library settings. We have the testimony of academic librarians, who speak mainly about their dealings with students. We have the testimony of public library reference personnel, who speak about their interactions with diverse members of the general community. Finally, we have the testimony of a demanding user group, professors in the humanities and social sciences. Judging from the stories recounted in the following chapters, all of these groups agree that reading—whether it be newspapers, magazines, scholarly journals, fiction, or nonfiction—is an element of reference service that cannot be overlooked and that, in many ways, separates the truly wonderful reference librarian or staff member from someone who provides only average service.

One of our aims in writing this book is to suggest that the implementation of digital reference models of the kind described in Chapter 1 is not the only way that reference service can be improved in the 21st century. Encouraging reference personnel to read broadly and deeply in various subject areas and across a broad range of materials is, based on the evidence presented in the following chapters, an equally valid way to raise the level of reference service in both academic and public settings.

II. Academic Librarians

Valerie has been an academic reference librarian for more than 20 years. She does little reading outside of work, describing most of what is published these days as "right-wing propaganda." She occasionally picks up magazines with an alternative or feminist bent — *Sojourner, The Nation, In These Times, Ms.* — and the odd newspaper. None of these materials has helped her provide better reference service, nor does she feel the need to spend any more of her free time reading.

The idea of spending more time reading strikes Francine as somewhat odd, seeing as she reads all the time, indulging in two poetry books a week and spending the past few months on four works of nonfiction about Keats, two about Shelley. She reads literary magazines at least once a week, cover-to-cover, along with the *New York Times*, though she does not give the newspaper quite the same attention as the literary magazines. But she will skim the headlines and glance at the first few paragraphs of articles before settling down to read those that really interest her. Once a month she reads *The Earlville Leader*, the local paper from a small town in Illinois. What it lacks in national or international news, it makes up for in the caliber of its obituaries, which she very much enjoys. Unlike Valerie, Francine does see a connection between the reading she does outside of work and the quality of reference service she provides. In fact, she believes that literature and poetry make her not only a better librarian, but also, as she phrases it, "a better everything."

Like Francine, Myles is a voracious reader, though his weakness is literary fiction — novels such as Saul Bellow's *Ravelstein* and Philip Roth's *The Human Stain*, both of which he just recently finished. He is, to apply a word that many librarians seem anxious to avoid, bookish — a person who characterizes himself as "someone totally in love with books" and whose devotion to them is seemingly boundless. Even though he already reads over 50 novels a year, Myles still wants to read more. Yet family responsibilities in the form of "a wife, grandchild, and a few family friends that interrupt my reading and writing life" preclude him from finding the time. "They seem to be more important," he muses. "I'm not always sure they are."

Finding few books to his liking, Howard insists that he is "not the typical librarian." His favorite reading materials are the newspaper (a regional paper, read daily) and *Reader's Digest*, though he does peruse works of nonfiction published in the field of American Indian Studies, a subject on which he himself has written five books. Rather, he prefers to spend his free time watching television, playing music, or enjoying outdoor activities. Nonetheless, Howard believes that whatever one reads will somehow help in answering reference questions, an idea that he summarizes as "the more knowledge, the better the service."

These four profiles— representing a fraction of the 539 librarians who responded to our survey— provide a glimpse of the diverse perspectives academic librarians have on reading and its applicability to their work. These perspectives begin to take shape with librarians' responses to the question of what they most enjoy reading during their free time. Some academic librarians are voracious readers, but even the concept of voracious reading has differing connotations. There are individuals with catholic tastes who "read everything" or "read broadly"—fiction and nonfiction, newspapers and magazines— and who describe themselves as being "eclectic" or "peripatetic" readers. Other voracious readers, like Francine and Myles, concentrate their attention on a particular genre or will immerse themselves in a topic "and then read extensively about it," like Kayla, who spent the past year "focused on fiction by southern Africa women writers." Indeed, while some librarians identify their favorite reading material as simply "fiction" or "nonfiction" without going into further detail, others define genres and topics with astounding specificity: "British Naval fiction"; "murder and mayhem"; "romance (but not the cheapo writers, the better written ones)"; "military weapons development"; "readable history (not anything published by an academic press)"; "compelling nonfiction about families"; and "cosmology and the development of massive bodies such as galaxies."

Other librarians, like Valerie and Howard, simply are not that interested in reading, sticking to a few newspapers and magazines, avoiding, for the most part, books. Even librarians with less stringent opinions of book publishing than those two individuals list newspapers and magazines as their favorite reading materials. Of the 537 librarians who indicated their reading preferences, 56 (or 10.4 percent) mention newspapers and 99 (or 18.4 percent) mention magazines— everything from news publications to *Vanity Fair*, from "ladies' magazines" to *The Hockey News*.

Despite the variation in academic librarians' reading proclivities, the majority of respondents believe that, in general, the types of materials they read outside of work— novels and works of nonfiction, newspapers and magazines of various types— somehow help them to provide better quality reference service. As Table 1 shows, 473 librarians (88.2 percent) feel that is the case, while only 40 (7.5 percent) think this is unlikely, and 23 (4.3 percent) see no possible connection between outside reading and reference work. Those who do see a positive relationship between reading and reference work construe this relationship in a number of different ways. First, they explain that any reading contributes to a person's background knowledge, making them better informed in general. "All my reading provides me with a wonderful background on the world," writes one librarian, while another comments that reading "helps fight parochialism." This background knowledge, in turn, means that the librarian will be "better able to process difficult questions," will be able "to ask more pointed questions in a reference interview," and can better assess the applicability of resources and "point out the authors whose work is most respected" within a field. Warren touches on all these points in his assessment of the impact of outside reading on reference work. Reading, he explains,

> opens your mind to whole different worlds and cultures. By its nature, reading makes you think and evaluate what you've read. These critical thinking skills you develop help tremendously at the reference desk where finding information is not difficult, but finding

the RIGHT information is quite challenging. Reading broadens your perspective, and that is critical in the reference interview when you are trying to correctly determine a person's actual needs, which [are] often different from what they are asking for. Simply stated, it enables you to communicate more effectively and that is the most difficult part of working the reference desk.

In fact, librarians equate communication skills not only with the verbal exchange of the reference interview, but also with knowing the vocabulary to conduct a targeted and thorough search. This means understanding and selecting appropriate search terms, whether they be "specialized discipline jargon" or "new catch phrases" from current newspapers and magazines.

Table 1. Could reading newspapers, magazines, nonfiction, and fiction somehow help provide better quality reference service? (Question 18 in Appendix A)

Response	No. of academic reference librarians (n = 536)
Yes	473 (88.2%)
Possibly	40 (7.5%)
No	23 (4.3%)

Academic librarians are particularly adamant about the importance of keeping abreast of current events, with one person commenting, "I've watched a lot of reference librarians over the years. Those who are up on current events, follow the issues and are more well rounded individuals are better reference librarians." Another puts it more bluntly: "If you don't know about an event or a book that has been a best seller, and a student requests information concerning it, you look like an idiot. How can we expect to be considered professional if we don't maintain this very basic level of knowledge?" At the same time, being informed of current events sets a good example for students by providing librarians with "a chance to reinforce the idea that reading even a current newsmagazine is important." But beyond this didactic role, familiarity with current events — and not just hard-news issues, but popular-cultural topics as well — enables the librarian to share in patrons' interests and to be more "in tune" with their needs. "I think that current newspapers and newsmagazines ... are essential to providing the best of reference service," Joo-Mee writes. "It keeps me up on latest news, fads, etc., which undergrads are likely to express an interest in. It's important to indicate an interest by showing some familiarity with the topic at hand."

Where do the librarians who see little or no connection between what they read outside of work and improved reference service stand on these issues? In fact, many of the 23 individuals who answered "no" and the 40 individuals who responded "possibly" (see Table 1) raise similar concerns, differing only in the tenacity with which they hold these viewpoints. Some of these librarians say that library experience trumps the information they could accrue from outside reading, as do mastery of online search skills and "knowledge of [the] reference collection." One person insists, "I have always felt as a librarian that the search strategies and research skills I have are paramount. Specific knowledge of a given topic isn't necessary to provide really good reference service." Estimating that the reading he does outside of work makes the reference service he provides "about 10 percent more" effective, another librarian concludes that "[b]eing a 'techy' has become as important as having a bank of knowledge."

For some of the librarians skeptical about how their outside reading could improve reference work, the primary argument is that, with the probable exception of newspapers and newsmagazines, what they read during their free time would not coincide with the queries they field at the reference desk. In contrast to those who believe that "the best reference librarians are people who are widely read," they feel that outside reading would have an impact on their work only if this reading were discipline-specific. In other words, a business librarian might see the advantages of reading *Business Week*, but the latest John Grisham is a different story. While some librarians see the benefit of reading widely manifested in the serendipity of having just read something on a topic and then being asked a question on that very topic by a patron, others do not see the likelihood of this ever happening. By the same token, they feel that trying to mesh one's reading interests with probable reference queries is an exercise in futility, given that "it is impossible to know everything." Bryn suggests that "each reference question is unique and no one of us can be expected to be an expert in every discipline. I believe that good research skills and knowledge of where information can be found is as good as trying to be a mini expert in many different disciplines." Leslie agrees, observing that "the questions we get are largely confined to topics related to [students'] research papers.... But the world of information is so incredibly broad now that the chance I might have read something which would apply to their research topic is very slim."

Over the course of the next three chapters, we explore these issues in depth, examining not only what academic librarians read, but also how they have applied these materials to their work. We begin with the outside reading that respondents cite as particularly beneficial: newspapers and magazines. In Chapter 3, we look at the newspaper and magazine reading habits of academic librarians before turning to the stories respondents provide about the impact that reading such publications has made at the reference desk and in other areas of their work. Chapter 4 follows the same format, but with a focus on works of nonfiction and fiction. Finally, in Chapter 5, we look at whether academic reference librarians would like to spend more time reading and the various environmental and psychological factors that inform their decisions. We conclude this section with their views on whether reference service would improve if they were given paid time for reading newspapers, magazines, fiction, and nonfiction at work.

3

The Importance of Being Current

How reading newspapers and magazines affects the work
of academic reference librarians

We asked academic librarians whether, in their experience, the reference service they provide has ever been improved by reading newspapers and magazines during their free time and whether reading these materials has helped them in other aspects of their job. The answer in both cases was an emphatic yes. As Table 2 shows, 443 respondents (88.8 percent) have experienced first-hand the benefits of reading newspapers and magazines when fielding reference queries. These benefits derive from the sheer volume of current-events related questions they receive, as well as the high level of coincidence between articles they have read and the relevance of those articles to patrons' information needs. As one individual describes it, "Almost every day someone asks a question related to something they have read in a newspaper." Another observes, "Often a patron will begin a reference interview with the statement, 'Did you read the story about...?' It helps when I have read that or a related story."

While librarians stress the importance of keeping abreast of current events when providing reference service—the idea expressed by one respondent that "you need to know what Bosnia is to function at our desk"—they note that keeping current is crucial away from the reference desk as well. A total of 435 librarians (86.1 percent) indicate that reading newspapers and magazines during their free time has had a positive impact on non–reference related work, and they provide examples that touch upon many different aspects of their professional life. Some of these are readily identifiable facets of librarianship: collection development, bibliographic instruction, dealing with personnel issues, implementing new technology, even bibliographic control. Others are so not easily labeled: conversing with colleagues and faculty, maintaining their professional credibility, and contributing to their personal, as well as professional, growth. These are not skills that would necessarily appear on a list of job responsibilities, but they nonetheless form an integral part of the daily working life of an academic reference librarian. Like reference work, these facets of librarianship are significantly affected by what an individual reads in newspapers and magazines outside of working hours.

Table 2. Academic librarians assess the impact at work
of reading newspapers and magazines
(Questions 20 and 21 in Appendix A)

	Has reading newspapers and magazines helped in reference work? (n = 499)	Has reading newspapers and magazines helped in areas outside of reference work? (n = 505)
Yes	443 (88.8%)	435 (86.1%)
No	56 (11.2%)	70 (13.9%)

That the majority of academic librarians who participated in our survey view reading newspapers and magazines on their own time as beneficial to their work leads to the following question: *Which* newspapers and magazines are these librarians reading? Do they consider some publications to be more helpful than others? Do they prefer local newspapers to national ones? How often do they pick up a magazine? Do they read these materials from cover to cover no matter what happens to be the content that week, or do they focus on selected articles that truly interest them?

We begin this chapter by examining the newspaper and magazine reading habits of academic librarians. We then turn our attention to what librarians see as the many advantages reading these materials can bring to the reference service they provide. Finally, we look at how they use newspapers and magazines to meet the myriad other issues and challenges they face at work.

Reading newspapers

To find out which newspapers academic librarians read and how they read them, we asked them a series of questions that focused exclusively on their newspaper reading habits, beginning with how often they read local or regional newspapers (publications such as the *Fresno Bee* or the *Wichita Eagle*), and how often they read national newspapers (publications such as the *New York Times* or the *Wall Street Journal*). The results are shown in Table 3.

Table 3. Frequency with which academic librarians
read newspapers on their own time
(Questions 5 and 6 in Appendix A)

Rate of reading	National newspaper (n = 532)	Local or regional newspaper (n = 535)
Daily	103 (19.4%)	281 (52.5%)
Two to five times per week	110 (20.7%)	100 (18.7%)
Once a week	80 (15%)	80 (15%)
Once a month	76 (14.3%)	22 (4.1%)
Less than once a month	107 (20.1%)	24 (4.5%)
Never	56 (10.5%)	28 (5.2%)

The figure that commands the most attention concerns the readership of local and regional papers: more than twice as many librarians read these newspapers on a daily basis (281, or 52.5 percent) than read a national newspaper (103, or 19.4 percent). In fact, national newspaper readership changes surprisingly little from category to category, as compared with local and regional newspaper readership. For example, while 10.5 percent of librarians never read a national paper, only 19.4 percent read them on a daily basis. Similarly, while 80 respondents (15 percent) read a national newspaper once a week, almost the same number (76, or 14.3 percent) read these publications just once a month. In contrast, the range between academic librarians who never read a local or regional paper and those who read one on a daily basis is 5.2 percent–52.5 percent — an astounding difference compared to the numbers for national newspaper readership. These differences become especially pronounced when librarians' newspaper reading habits are plotted in Figure 1. While the progression of the line representing national newspapers varies little across the six reading categories, the line representing local and regional papers drops sharply over the course of the first four categories before finally leveling off.

The frequency with which academic librarians read national, regional, and local newspapers reflects national averages of how often the general adult population reads these publications in both the United States and Canada. According to National Opinion Research Center (NORC) data about the newspaper reading habits of Americans between 1972 and 1998, 53.2 percent of the 25,214 individuals surveyed (and giving an answer) read a newspaper every day.[1] While the NORC data does not differentiate among national, regional, and local newspapers, we can nevertheless see a strong affinity between the NORC figure of 53.2 percent and our figure of 52.5 percent of academic librarians who read a local or regional newspaper on a daily basis. Likewise, NORC data suggests that 21.2 percent of Americans read a newspaper "a few times a week," while in the corresponding "two to five times per week" category in our survey, 20.7 percent of academic librarians read a national newspaper and 18.7 percent read local or regional newspapers.

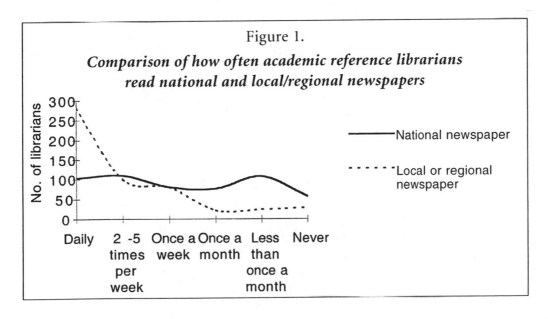

Figure 1.

Comparison of how often academic reference librarians read national and local/regional newspapers

Data from Statistics Canada about the reading habits of Canadians follow a similar pattern: in 1998, 48.9 percent read a newspaper on a daily basis, while 27.2 percent read a newspaper "at least three times a week."[2]

The academic librarians in our survey, then, read newspapers at roughly the same rate as the general population. But do they read the same newspapers as the general population? We therefore asked survey respondents to name any and all newspapers— local, regional, and national — that they read at least once a week outside of their work hours. Of the 524 librarians who responded to this question, 484 (92.4 percent) read at least one newspaper a week, as opposed to only 40 (7.6 percent) who do not read a newspaper on a regular basis. In fact, academic librarians read an average of 2.2 newspapers on a regular basis, ranging from individuals who follow the news in only one publication to a few industrious people who read seven different newspapers per week.

We then categorized the titles provided by librarians according to five different newspaper types, which are listed and defined in Table 4: national; major regional; regional; local; and outside North America. The first three categories are based, in part, on a newspaper's relative ranking in terms of circulation numbers, using a 1999 report by the Audit Bureau of Circulations (ABC).[3] For example, newspapers that we classify as "major regional" have rankings between 6 and 50 on the ABC list of "Top 100 Newspapers by Circulation," regional papers are those ranked 51–100 according to this list, and so on. Since the ABC report covers only newspapers published in the United States, we added to each category the relevant Canadian newspapers cited by respondents. Finally, we defined as a local newspaper any publication that is not included on the list of "Top 100 Newspapers by Circulation" and is published in North America. For many librarians, local papers include publications that emanate not only from the town or city in which they live, but also the college or university where they work.

While the data presented in Table 3 reveal that academic librarians read a local or regional newspaper on a daily basis more often than they do national newspapers, Table 4 shows the popularity of local papers in particular. A total of 287 librarians (59.3 percent) read at least one local paper every week — slightly more than is the case with national newspapers and significantly more than either major regional or regional newspapers. At the same time, some of the most intriguing examples of newspapers, and newspaper reading habits, come from the local newspaper category. For example, outside of work Keshia eschews the widely circulated national papers and reads only "[n]ewspapers dealing with the African American population" such as the New York *Amsterdam* and the Chicago *Defender*. As she points out, "Most libraries do not subscribe to online or print newspapers related to this population."

While local papers may be the most popular newspapers for many librarians, they are closely followed by national newspapers, which are read on a regular basis by just over half (55.4 percent) of the respondents in our survey. Table 5 lists the eight publications mentioned by librarians that qualify as national newspapers. The *Wall Street Journal*, *USA Today*, the *New York Times*, the *Los Angeles Times*, and the *Washington Post* together form the first five listings in the ABC list "Top US Newspapers by Circulation." To this list we added two national newspapers published in Canada — *The Globe and Mail* and the *National Post*— as well as the *Christian Science Monitor*, which was cited by six respondents. The majority of academic librarians who read a national newspaper on a

Table 4. Types of newspapers academic reference librarians read on a regular basis (Question 7 in Appendix A)

Newspaper category	Definition	Examples	No. of librarians who read at least one newspaper in this category (n = 484)*
National	Top 5 US newspapers by circulation, plus *The Christian Science Monitor*, plus relevant Canadian papers	(See Table 5)	268 (55.4%)
Major Regional	Nos. 6–50 of top 100 US newspapers by circulation, plus relevant Canadian papers	*Boston Globe* *Charlotte Observer* *Chicago Sun Times*	203 (41.9%)
Regional	Nos. 51–100 of top 100 US newspapers by circulation, plus relevant Canadian papers	*The Grand Rapids Press* *Honolulu Advertiser* *Lexington Herald Leader*	84 (17.4%)
Local	Newspapers not included among top 100 US papers by circulation, including campus newspapers	*Erie Times News* *Independent Florida Alligator* *Tahoe Daily Tribune*	287 (59.3%)
Outside North America	International papers that are not published in the US or Canada	*London Times* *Le Monde* *Sud-Deutsche Zeitung*	8 (1.7%)

*Numbers do not add to *n* and percentages do not add to 100% because respondents cited multiple categories.

regular basis choose the *New York Times*. The 64.6 percent of *New York Times* readers is distantly followed by the 17.5 percent of respondents who choose *USA Today* and the 13.1 percent who choose the *Wall Street Journal*. In other words, while the general population prefers the *Wall Street Journal*, academic reference librarians opt for the *New York Times*, with both groups choosing *USA Today* at about the same relative rate.

Table 5. National newspapers that are read most frequently by academic reference librarians

Newspaper	No. of librarians (n = 268)*	Ranking according to ABC (1999)
1. *New York Times*	173 (64.6%)	Third (3rd)
2. *USA Today*	47 (17.5%)	Second (2nd)
3. *Wall Street Journal*	35 (13.1%)	First (1st)
4. *Washington Post*	24 (9%)	Fifth (5th)
5. *The Globe and Mail* (Canada)	22 (8.2%)	NA
6. *Los Angeles Times*	17 (6.3%)	Fourth (4th)
7. *National Post* (Canada)	11 (4.1%)	NA
8. *Christian Science Monitor*	6 (2.2%)	NA

*Numbers do not add to *n* and percentages do not add to 100% because respondents cited multiple newspapers.

Of course, not all of the newspapers read by academic librarians are published in North America. Eight respondents (1.7 percent) read seven different European newspapers at least once a week. The majority of these papers are from Great Britain, including the *London Times*, which is cited by four librarians, the *Financial Times*, and the *Scotsman*. Other examples are non–English language publications such as *Le Monde*, mentioned by two librarians, and the *Göteborgs-Posten*, which hails from Gothenburg, Sweden. Librarians note that access plays a large part in determining which international publications they can read on a regular basis. One individual comments, "I used to read both *The Guardian* and *Le Figaro*, but I no longer have access to either." Others mention reading international publications online rather than in print.

We assigned each of the newspaper titles supplied by librarians to one of the five categories shown in Table 4 for two reasons. First, we wanted to see which type of newspaper academic librarians most often read on a regular basis. But we also wanted to examine what *combinations* of newspaper types these individuals read. In other words, we were interested in finding out, for instance, whether academic librarians read local newspapers exclusively, or whether they tend to pair a local or regional paper with a national publication. Since the content of newspapers differs according to type, the implication is that someone who reads only one type of newspaper would have access to a limited range of information. For example, someone who reads only *USA Today* would be familiar with international and national events, but not necessarily with issues of importance to his or her local community or regional area. The reverse could be true as well: individuals who read only local or even regional papers would lack the depth of international news coverage provided by a national newspaper.

Table 6. Types of newspapers read by academic reference librarians

Category or category combination	No. of librarians (n = 484)
National only	49 (10.1%)
Major Regional only	35 (7.2%)
Regional only	20 (4.1%)
Local only	77 (15.9%)
National, plus any other category	222 (45.9%)
Major Regional plus Regional and/or Local	69 (14.3%)
Regional plus Local	12 (2.5%)

We can see from Table 6 that most academic librarians do in fact simultaneously read multiple types of newspapers. The most frequently occurring combination, which applied to 45.9 percent of respondents, is to read a national newspaper with at least one major regional, regional, or local paper. In contrast, no more than 16 percent of respondents read newspapers from any one of these categories exclusively. This suggests that academic librarians' newspaper reading spans international, national, and some local coverage, depending on whether the national paper is read in conjunction with a major regional, a regional, or local publication. Librarians are also more likely to pair, say, the *Orange County Register* — a major regional paper — with either a regional paper such as the *Los Angeles Daily News* or a local paper such as the *Claremont Courier* than they are to read the *Orange County Register* or the *Daily News* alone. An exception — though perhaps not a surprising one given what we have already seen of librarians' newspaper-reading tendencies— is the number of respondents who read only local papers on a regular basis. In fact, the 77 librarians (15.9 percent) who listed only local papers make this the second most popular category in Table 6.

We also asked academic librarians to characterize how they read newspapers (regardless of how often they read them). Do they read every page, cover-to-cover, or do they just skim the headlines? As Table 7 shows, most librarians prefer to zero in on the articles of most interest to them and, at the same time, to familiarize themselves with other news items. By far the largest percentage of respondents (77.3 percent) accomplish this by first skimming the paper's headlines or glancing at the first paragraphs of most stories and then reading fully the articles of particular interest to them. The second most popular reading style, although employed by significantly fewer librarians, is based on the same principle of trying to get the whole picture of a day's events while concentrating one's full attention on selected articles. In this case, the articles happen to comprise a specific section of the newspaper: 52 individuals (9.9 percent) said that they read certain sections of the newspaper in their entirety and then glance at or skim articles in other sections.

Some of the librarians who choose not to read a newspaper on a regular basis describe other sources from which they get their news, namely, television, radio, and online news sites such as CNN.com, ABCNews.com, and Yahoo! Online news. As one individual notes, these sites can be tailored "to give only articles in my area of interest," the implication being that people can read exactly what they want, when they want it. This issue of efficiency informs a number of librarians' viewpoints on the subject of print newspapers (and, indeed, print sources in general). Take, for example, the comments made by Jason, a self-described "Gen-Xer," who suggests that "there are other venues available to get the same kind of information" that newspapers supply. "Reading," he continues, "is a slow/tedious process. Audio/visual means of communication are more effective/efficient ways of distributing information." The fact that Jason is a "Gen-Xer" is not insignificant, as Robert Putnam explains in *Bowling Alone*, a book that examines civic engagement at the end of the 20th century. Putnam points out that reading a newspaper "is a lasting habit established early in adult life"— a habit that is experiencing a "precipitous decline

Table 7. How academic reference librarians read newspapers (Question 8 in Appendix A)

Newspaper reading style	No. of librarians (n = 525)*
Skim headlines only	30 (5.7%)
Glance at first paragraphs of all or almost all stories	18 (3.4%)
Skim headlines, glance at first paragraphs of all or almost all stories, then read fully articles of interest	406 (77.3%)
Read everything in certain sections, then skim and glance at stories in other sections	52 (9.9%)
Read everything from cover to cover	19 (3.6%)

*Percentages do not add to 100% because of rounding.

... due to the by now familiar pattern of generational succession."[4] He notes that, while 75 percent of Americans born before 1929 read newspapers on daily basis, "[f]ewer than half their boomer children are carrying on the tradition," a percentage that drops to 25 percent "among their X'er grandchildren."[5]

Putnam also points out that, although it is easy to jump to the conclusion that successive generations have "simply shifted their news consumption from the printed page to the glowing screen," the issue is more complicated. Newspapers and television news "are complements, not substitutes"—a concept supported by the fact that Americans who watch the evening news "are *more* likely to read the daily newspaper than are other Americans, not *less* likely" (original emphasis).[6] In fact, this idea of complementary news sources is evident in a number of librarians' descriptions of how they keep up with current events. Lori, for example, reads the *Loveland Daily Reporter-Herald* for its local news, but gets her national news from ABCNews.com. In addition to perusing CNN online, Haeyong regularly reads the *Chicago Tribune* and the *New York Times*. Academic librarians note that the various news sources they read, watch, and listen to all come into play when helping patrons at the reference desk. In terms of fielding reference questions, one librarian remarks, "Sure, it happens all the time that I read something of national or international significance that I use to guide the reference interview, but I am much more likely to be knowledgeable on these matters by listening to *All Things Considered, Morning Edition, Weekend Edition, The Connection,* and *Fresh Air* on NPR [National Public Radio]." Another respondent has noticed that the answers to reference questions "may be readily known from watching TV as well," leading her to conclude that "being part of society helps you answer reference questions, not just reading." This may often be the case. But, as we will see, the experiences of academic librarians point to a clear role for reading newspapers and magazines in their reference work.

Reading magazines

As with newspapers, we asked academic librarians to discuss their magazine reading habits, beginning with how frequently they read news, business, science, history, or cultural feature publications (i.e., *Time, Business Week, Scientific American, Smithsonian, Harper's*) outside of their work hours. As Table 8 shows, most librarians read these types of magazines between two and five times a week (31.4 percent) or once a week (24.1 percent). Although less than 15 percent of respondents make these news-based publications a daily habit, less than 15 percent of librarians read them only once a month or less than once a month, respectively.

We also asked librarians to tell us how they read these news-oriented (or science- or history-oriented) magazines. From their responses, presented in Table 9, we found that four times as many librarians read magazines cover-to-cover (77 individuals, or 15.3 percent) than was the case with newspapers (19 individuals, or 3.6 percent). In addition, librarians are less likely to read only the first few paragraphs of each magazine article and then stop (5 individuals, or 1 percent)—a practice that proved to be more popular with newspapers (18 individuals, or 3.4 percent). These distinctions notwithstanding, the approach to reading magazines shared by the overwhelming majority of respondents

(346, or 68.8 percent) corresponds with librarians' preferences for reading newspapers as well. As with newspapers, librarians are select readers: most shop around a bit within a particular magazine, kicking the tires, so to speak, and taking articles for a test spin by reading a little bit from each story before deciding whether to invest the time to read the article fully.

Table 8. Frequency with which academic reference librarians read magazines on their own time (Question 9 in Appendix A)

Rate of reading	No. of librarians (n = 528)
Daily	68 (12.9%)
Two to five times per week	166 (31.4%)
Once a week	127 (24.1%)
Once a month	78 (14.8%)
Less than once a month	65 (12.3%)
Never	24 (4.5%)

Table 9. How academic reference librarians read magazines (Question 10 in Appendix A)

Magazine reading style	No. of librarians (n = 503)
Check the Table of Contents and then decide what to read	75 (14.9%)
Read only three or four paragraphs of each article	5 (1%)
Read a little bit from each article, then read fully those articles that are of interest	346 (68.8%)
Read everything from cover to cover	77 (15.3%)

While the previous two questions focused on how, and how frequently, academic librarians read news-oriented and cultural feature publications, we also wanted to get an overall sense of their magazine preferences. We therefore asked librarians to list all the magazines that they read on a regular basis, which we defined as being at least six times per year. Here respondents were free to name any and all publications: their weekly *TV Guide*, the specialty magazines that feed a particular interest or hobby, the gardening magazine with the beautiful glossy photographs that seems to find its way into the grocery cart each month. We then assigned each of the titles provided by the 509 librarians who responded to this question to one of the broadly defined categories of magazines displayed in Table 10.

As Table 10 indicates, weekly news publications such as *Time, Newsweek,* and *The Economist* are read on a regular basis by the greatest percentage of academic librarians (53.6 percent). While this is not surprising in the case of individuals whose work is predicated on collecting and distributing information, it does mark a departure from magazine industry estimates of what Americans over the age of 18 prefer to read. In fact, there are a number of discrepancies between the magazines favored by academic librarians and those that are most popular among the general adult reading population. Table 11 compares the top 15 magazines read by academic librarians with the rankings of those publications in Mediamark's Fall 2000 Magazine Audience Estimates.[7] While *Newsweek* and *Time* are the two publications most often cited by academic librarians, in contrast these publications rank 22nd and 18th, respectively, on the Mediamark list. Similarly, while *U.S. News & World Report* is the sixth most frequently mentioned publication by librarians, it is ranked 40th by Mediamark. There are only four instances where the top 15 magazines as identified by librarians correspond with the national audience estimates: *National Geographic, People, Better Homes & Gardens*, and *Reader's Digest*.

Table 10. Categories of magazines read by academic reference librarians (Question 11 in Appendix A)

Category	Examples	No. of librarians (n = 509)*
News	*The New Republic, Newsweek*	273 (53.6%)
Home/Gardening/Cooking	*Gourmet, Real Simple*	205 (40.3%)
Health/Science/Technology	*Scientific American, Wired*	151 (29.7%)
Cultural feature/Social issues	*Harper's, The New Yorker*	148 (29.1%)
Professional	*American Libraries, Library Journal*	124 (24.4%)
History	*Archaeology, National Geographic*	117 (23%)
Travel/Regional	*Condé Nast Traveler, Pittsburgh Magazine*	102 (20%)
Gender or culture specific	*Ebony, Woman's Day*	75 (14.7%)
Sports/Automotive	*Car and Driver, Runner's World*	74 (14.5%)
Celebrity/Movie/Television	*Entertainment Weekly, Soap Opera Digest*	73 (14.3%)
Business/Investing	*Forbes, Kiplinger's Personal Finance*	65 (12.8%)
Fine Arts/Music	*Art in America, Rolling Stone*	59 (11.6%)
Animals/Nature/Outdoors	*Birdwatcher's Digest, Sierra*	57 (11.2%)
Collecting/Hobbies/Crafts	*Classic Toy Trains, Stamping Arts and Crafts*	50 (9.8%)
Progressive/Alternative	*Mother Jones, Utne Reader*	47 (9.2%)
Literary	*Granta, Prairie Schooner*	37 (7.3%)
Religion/Philosophy	*Ensign, Guideposts*	36 (7.1%)

*Numbers do not add to n and percentages do not add to 100% because respondents cited multiple categories.

The first and second place ranking of *Newsweek* and *Time* on the librarians' list of top 15 magazines stands out for another reason as well, namely, that the difference in the relative popularity of these two publications—with *Newsweek* mentioned by 31.6 percent of respondents and *Time* cited by 31.4 percent of respondents—is minimal. One explanation for these virtually identical figures is that reading *Time* and *Newsweek* is not an either/or proposition for academic librarians. Instead, they read both, a phenomenon not unlike what we saw with newspapers, where academic librarians read national and regional or local papers concurrently. While the *Newsweek-Time* pairing is most frequent, this pattern emerges with other news magazines too. Indeed, librarians who list at least one news magazine more likely than not read multiple news-oriented publications, whether the magazines themselves are categorized as "News" or as "Progressive/Alternative" (see Table 10). Thus we have librarians who regularly read *Newsweek, Time*, and *U.S. News & World Report*, as well as those who read such intriguing combinations as *The New Republic, The Nation*, and the *National Review*. It is this last example especially that suggests that academic librarians read multiple news magazines not simply to learn the facts of major events, but also to gain different perspectives on current issues.

Table 11. Top 15 magazines read by academic reference librarians

	Title	No. of librarians (n = 509)*	Ranking in Mediamark Research's Fall 2000 Magazine Audience (Adults) Estimates (000)
1.	Newsweek	161 (31.6%)	22 (19,594)
2.	Time	160 (31.4%)	18 (20,809)
3.	The New Yorker	92 (18.1%)	157 (2,982)
4.	National Geographic	55 (10.8%)	12 (29,892)
5.	Smithsonian	52 (10.2%)	62 (7,665)
6.	U.S. News & World Report	43 (8.4%)	40 (10,582)
7.	People	40 (7.9%)	10 (34,430)
8.	Good Housekeeping	33 (6.5%)	16 (24,128)
9.	Southern Living	28 (5.5%)	31 (13,080)
10.	Better Homes & Gardens	27 (5.3%)	9 (35,177)
11.	Atlantic Monthly	25 (4.9%)	229 (1,057)
	Reader's Digest	25 (4.9%)	8 (42,987)
13.	Cooking Light	24 (4.7%)	70 (6,863)
	Sports Illustrated	24 (4.7%)	19 (20,252)
15.	Consumer Reports	23 (4.5%)	24 (16,130)
	Maclean's	23 (4.5%)	NA (Canadian publication)

*Numbers do not add to n and percentages do not add to 100% because respondents cited multiple magazines.

Following "News" as the type of magazine most often read by academic librarians is the category of Home/Gardening/Cooking (see Table 10), which encompasses not only topic-specific publications such as *Cook's Illustrated* and *The Herb Companion*, but also "shelter" magazines like *Real Simple* and *Martha Stewart Living*, geared toward a reading public that prefers "sticking around the house and 'nesting.'"[8] An interesting pattern emerges when the popularity of this category in general is juxtaposed with the top 15 magazine titles read by academic librarians, as listed in Table 11. While the top two magazines correspond with the most popular category of magazine (in other words, *Newsweek* and *Time* fall within the most-often cited category of news magazines), *Good Housekeeping*, read by 6.5 percent of respondents, is ranked only eighth among the 15 titles, despite being in the second most popular magazine category. In another example, *The New Yorker* is the third most frequently mentioned magazine, read by 18.1 percent of academic librarians. Yet the category that this publication falls within—Cultural feature/Social issues—is ranked fourth, just below the category of Health/Science/Technology. Despite being the third most popular magazine category, however, no health, science, or technology publication is among the top 15 titles read by academic librarians.

The discrepancies between the most popular *categories* of magazines and the most popular *titles* are instructive for understanding academic librarians' magazine reading preferences. To be sure, the relatively weak standing of any particular Home/Gardening/Cooking magazine in the list of top 15 titles could be attributed to the sheer quantity of these publications available. Even a cursory glance at the magazine racks of a major bookstore chain suggests that there are more shelter magazines with the word "living" or "home" in the title (e.g., *Southern Living, Country Living, Midwest Living, Traditional Home, Metropolitan Home, Country Home*) than weekly news magazines. With so many options to choose from, the chances of any one publication standing out are diminished. The ubiquity of these publications also suggests that they are somewhat interchangeable. There is the distinct sense from respondents' comments that they do not feel especially wedded to any one of these magazines even though they enjoy them as a categorical type.

Indeed, just as librarians proved to be select readers when it comes to choosing which articles to read within a given publication, many are equally selective when it comes to shopping for magazines, purchasing whichever happens that week or month to have "the best" articles. For example, one librarian explains that she will read "any gardening magazine that I find has interesting articles," while another summarizes the "various gardening magazines" that she picks up with the comment, "I do not read any one title with loyalty." Librarians make similar observations about magazines from other categories as well. Some respondents note that, with the exception of a few titles that they read on a regular basis, their choice of which magazines to read is often based on circumstance. While newsstand browsing is certainly a factor in which magazines are purchased, magazine selection is also contingent upon "what the dentist, the hairdresser or airline offer" or "whatever is available in the doctor's or other waiting area." The combination of choosing whichever publication happens to have the most relevant articles and a reliance on circumstance means that popular types of magazines do not always translate into most popular titles read.

While academic librarians may or may not feel any loyalty toward specific publications, there is ample evidence that many of these individuals are constant readers of specific types of magazines. Librarians often list multiple publications within the categories shown in Table 10, as is the case with David, who reads "three wine publications" plus *Gourmet* on a regular basis, as well as Mindy, who feeds her interest in financial planning with *Business Week*, *Money*, *Smart Money*, *Bloomberg*, *Better Investing*, and *Individual Investor*. As one might expect, such a concentration of magazines on one topic results in little opportunity (or perhaps inclination) to read magazines in other areas. There is the example provided by Eric, whose selection of magazines read on a regular basis consists of *Trains*, *Classic Trains*, and *Railplace*. And there is Dolores, who reads *Country Living*, *Country Home*, *Traditional Homes*, *Classic Homes*, *Home Companion*, *Romantic Homes*, *Country Living Gardener*, *Country Home Gardener*, *Chicagoland Gardening*, *Herb Companion*, and *Herb Quarterly*—11 different magazines, all of which are about home or garden.

In fact, cases like that of Eric and Dolores are the exception, not the rule. In other words, while academic librarians voraciously read within a favorite genre of magazine, they also read broadly across a number of different magazine categories. In fact, we calculated the average number of categories of magazines read per librarian to be 3.5. A perfect example can be found in the magazine list provided by Kay. While her reading of *Soap Opera Digest*, *Soap Opera Update*, and *Soaps in Depth* indicates a keen interest in daytime dramas, Kay's regular magazine consumption also includes *Time*, *Newsweek*, *Business Week*, *Fortune*, *The New Yorker*, *Ladies' Home Journal*, *Redbook*, *Reader's Digest*, and the *Michigan State Bar Journal*. Similarly, science-fiction and astronomy fan Steven complements his reading in this area (including two Star Trek–related publications) with *The Nation*, *The Economist*, *Atlantic Monthly*, *Utne Reader*, and two Canadian news magazines: *Maclean's* and *L'actualité*.

"The difference between an adequate librarian and a great reference librarian": How reading newspapers and magazines improves reference service

As we noted at the beginning of this chapter, when we asked academic librarians to consider whether the various newspapers and magazines they read during their free time have in any way helped them in providing reference service, 443 individuals (88.8 percent) responded that they have experienced a connection between, on the one hand, reading newspapers and magazines and, on the other, dealing successfully with patron queries (see Table 2). Many of these librarians illustrated their statements with concrete examples recalled from their own experiences at the reference desk. Often anecdotal, sometimes even admonishing in tone, their stories provide valuable insight into how reading newspapers and magazines outside of working hours, in the words of one respondent, "means the difference between an adequate librarian and a great reference librarian." More specifically, this difference comes from the librarian's ability to apply to various reference situations what he or she has read in newspapers and magazines.

Take, for example, Kurt's summary of the impact of reading newspaper and magazines on the quality of his reference work. Noting that he uses newspapers to find out about "new laws, new rulings, Congressional hearings, new products, lawsuits, marketing campaigns, you name it!" he comments, "One student asked who Gandhi was—pronounced it Gandy—when he died. Another question: 'Have you ever heard of a nun called Mother Teresa? I think she did something in third world countries?' Another one: 'There was a guy assassinated who was involved in the peace talks at Camp David....' You get the idea. If I didn't read newspapers, I wouldn't have a clue. I usually answer their questions, telling them what I know and point them toward local papers, national papers or books on the subject."

Kurt's experiences highlight how reading newspapers directly contributes to good reference service by strengthening important related abilities: the ability to recognize the names of international figures, to directly answer specific questions, and to recommend sources for further research. All these abilities come from keeping abreast of recent events and current trends.

Kurt's is by no means an isolated example. From the stories that librarians provide about the positive effects that reading newspapers and magazines have on the quality of their reference service, five themes emerge: increasing one's background knowledge; directing patrons to specific newspaper or magazine articles; selecting search terms; assisting students in selecting topics for their assignments; and using newspapers and magazines to identify new or alternate resources. These themes are summarized in Table 12. We will now examine each of these themes in detail, relying on librarians' own accounts of how these factors affect reference service at academic libraries.

Increasing background knowledge

Cited most often (47.4 percent), this theme is also the broadest conceptually. At the most basic level, the idea is that reading newspapers and magazines improves reference

Table 12. Five ways in which reading newspapers
and magazines helps in reference service
(Question 20 in Appendix A)

Effect on reference service	No. of librarians (n = 443)*
Increasing background knowledge	210 (47.4%)
Directing patrons to specific articles	129 (29.1%)
Selecting search terms	24 (5.4%)
Helping students select topics for assignments	17 (3.8%)
Using newspapers and magazines to identify new or alternate resources	12 (2.7%)

*Numbers do not add to *n* and percentages do not add to 100% because not all librarians provided specific responses in their answers. The *n* is taken from the total of "yes" responses in the first column of figures in Table 2. While 443 respondents stated that reading newspapers and magazines helps in reference work, some of these respondents merely indicated "yes" with no subsequent description of "how" such reading helps. Conversely, some respondents gave more than one "how" reason. We did not choose *n* = 392 (the sum of the five ways) so as not to overstate percentages.

service by increasing the librarian's background knowledge. One individual describes how she is "constantly putting together bits and pieces of things" that she has read — a comment that brings to mind the process of completing a jigsaw puzzle. As the librarian fits together these pieces of information, a picture emerges— one that is composed of world and local events, prominent figures, socioeconomic trends, and bits of specialized knowledge. The fullness and clarity of this picture — this background knowledge — means better reference service.

At a more detailed level, one way in which background knowledge contributes to better reference service is by enabling the librarian to understand the reference question, to have what one person identifies as "some rudimentary knowledge" of whatever topic or event forms the focus of a patron's query. As one librarian explains, "I am much more capable of following reference questions when I have some idea of what the patron is asking. In the realm of current events, major authors, whatever the subject at hand may be, I find that I can relate to people better and provide higher quality reference service when I have had some exposure to the material or topic in question."

Respondents most often describe how their background knowledge contributes to understanding patron queries in the context of current events–related questions. Jessica, for instance, writes that "[s]tudents/faculty often phrase a reference question based on something that has been in the news lately—'Considering the current cost of gasoline, how would I find out the last time it was this high?' I will have a better starting point having read the papers and knowing how high gas is, what part price fixing may play, what part Middle Eastern politics and economics might play, etc." More than simply providing a starting point, a number of librarians note that the background knowledge of various subjects that they have gained by reading newspapers and magazines helps them to zero in on the specific information sought by a patron. Louise provides the following example: "A retired surgeon came last week looking for information about new treatments and survival rates for intranodal breast cancer. I had read in *Technology Review* about a new means of treatment using microwaves to pinpoint the cancerous tumor, and had also read about a fairly new means of detection, which used dye to show how far the cancer had spread. This knowledge helped me target what he wanted." Louise also credits her reading habits in general with her ability to help this patron, commenting, "I try hard to read about a wide variety of subjects to help me to understand the reference questions I receive."

When librarians discuss how reading newspapers and magazines helps them to understand reference questions, they do not always have in mind queries on especially sophisticated or esoteric topics. Frequently, understanding comes down to what one librarian identifies as being able "to untangle mangled reference questions." Respondents seem to relish the opportunity to describe their question-untangling feats. One individual recalls the student who wanted to find out about "as he put it, Boss something. He wanted info about Bosnia but all he could remember was Boss." And then there was the "student who asked for a biography on a famous lawyer — 'Dr. Rovey Wade,'" more commonly known as the Supreme Court case *Roe v. Wade*. Carlos provides an example where the "patron wanted information about the ee-bowl-eye organism," explaining that "[w]hen I asked that he write out the word, he wrote E. boli. Because I listen to and read the news, I suspected that he was referring to either E. coli or the Ebola virus. During the course of the interview we determined that it was the latter term he was after."

The core of many of these mangled reference questions consists of what academic librarians refer to as "hot topics" — current events that students research for their assignments. When respondents were completing our survey during fall 2000, these hot topics included the Ford Explorer–Firestone tire controversy, the Napster court case, prescription treatments for attention deficit disorder, school vouchers, the Rick Lazio vs. Hillary Rodham Clinton New York Senate race, and, of course, the 2000 presidential election. Daniel contributes the following anecdote about another "hot topic" — cloning:

> [A] biology student [was] told to come read about Dolly, to find out what was important about Dolly. Except the first librarian thought he meant "Dalí," as the student simply asked for books about the subject and didn't say what class it was for, and that librarian's interests include art. Well, so do mine, but this answer, of course, did not help, as the student didn't know how this pertained to biology and also did not know what he was supposed to be finding or the spelling of Dolly, since the assignment had been given orally. So he came back to ask me. "Dolly who?" was indeed a reasonable question for both of us. If not Dalí, who could possibly be known by that name alone? Ah, it came to me. "Dolly" the cloned sheep. Now that makes sense. I'm a specialist in federal publications but I had read about cloning and knew about Dolly and where to help the student find information.

Daniel's story not only points to the way in which current-events awareness can be used in deciphering reference questions, but also highlights the benefit of reading widely and of being familiar with a number of different subject areas and topics. As Daniel observes, both he and the first librarian consulted by the student are interested in art. Professionally, his subject specialty is federal publications. Nonetheless, by reading about current events, he was able to make connections that extend beyond his own areas of interest and expertise in order to assist the student — something the first librarian failed to accomplish.

In fact, a large part of understanding the reference question is filling in gaps. Returning to the idea that background knowledge is composed of pieces of information that complete a mental jigsaw puzzle, respondents stress how the background knowledge they have gained from newspapers and magazines has enabled them to supply key pieces of information during the reference interview. "Lots of users remember only parts of an event — maybe a passing of a law or certain legislation — but they can't remember the exact name or date it took place," one librarian explains. "I am often familiar with it due to my reading in newspapers and newsmagazines, even if it took place years ago." Another writes, "There have been several times when students have come looking for newspaper articles on company takeovers, for instance, or review articles on books or movies without the specifics as to date, time, geographic location, etc. Because of my own reading habits, I've been able to help them add the missing details needed to locate the information they've been seeking."

The specific examples that academic reference librarians provide reveal a diverse range of topics to which they have added "the missing details." Dina describes how "[a] student had heard about controversial treatments for leprosy, but did not know the name of the drug or why it was controversial. I knew he was referring to thalidomide, because I had been reading about it. I probably could have found this eventually but searching medical databases is so overwhelming, and I am not confident I could have located this promptly." Kara recalls a case during the 2000 presidential election campaign where a student needed information concerning the candidates' ties to the oil industry and "was especially interested in Dick Cheney's relationship with oil companies." She explains how the student "was having a difficult time getting started, but because I knew that Cheney had worked for Halliburton, I was able to give him a little extra information on which to search. In addition, because I was aware that Al Gore has some ties with Occidental Oil, I was able to ask if that would be of further assistance, which it was." At the same time, another librarian notes that being able to fill gaps in students' reference questions and being able to quickly locate articles "helps prevent frustration and discouragement on the students' part."

Being familiar with a given event from newspapers or magazines can also spare a patron embarrassment or pain. Ginger, for example, was able to avoid painful questions in a reference interview by supplying the relevant facts herself. She writes, "A woman called and asked if we carry 'older newspapers.' [It] turns out that her son had been murdered about two years earlier and because of the emotional pain it had caused, everyone close to her had thrown out the papers with the news coverage to save her more grief. She now felt she could read the coverage. She found it so hard to even ask the question that I was pleased I remembered reading about the incident. I was able to tell her that she didn't need to fill me in on the details, that I remembered the event."

Just as Dina remarked that knowing the specific name of a drug enabled her to locate information promptly without having to search an unwieldy medical database, some academic librarians describe how the background knowledge they have acquired from reading newspapers and magazines significantly streamlines reference service. As one individual observes, "Having a grasp of current events and 'hot button' issues can speed up the reference process, so I don't have to ask a whole lot of questions about a current issue to help the patron." Some librarians cite the advantages of being able to supply a timeframe for topics, commenting, for instance, that "[i]t helps that I already ... know when a piece of legislation was passed, so that I can jump into the right year of *Con-*

gressional Quarterly Almanac without tracking down a date first." One librarian recalls helping a patron who "wanted to read the Mississippi Supreme Court's decision in the case about Robert Johnson's estate, whether it goes to the person who was the child of Mr. Johnson's alleged illegitimate child or the descendant of one of his siblings," explaining that "[b]ecause I had read about the case in the newspaper, I was able to pinpoint the timeframe of the Court's decision and locate the information for the patron." At the same time, librarians also state that by being able "to pinpoint the timeframe" of an event, they can avoid futile searches in non-contemporary sources. Lauren, for example, assisted a patron who had "asked for interviews or speeches given by Vashti McKenzie." She remarks, "Because I keep up with current events, I had read a few weeks previous that she had just been elected the first female bishop of an African church. This meant that I could avoid searching the religion databases, because they would not have been updated that recently."

A number of other librarians also comment on the connection between being familiar with a topic from reading a newspaper or magazine and knowing which sources are most likely to yield the information sought by a patron. Phil writes: "I feel that I bring my personal knowledge base into every reference transaction. My understanding of a topic or question dictates what reference source I would direct a student to." This is the case for Maggie as well, who notes that "when a patron asks, for example, for biographical information and has no idea about the nationality of the person or when he/she lived, I can often use information I have read to decide what sources to check. Or when a person asks about some concept I know about, I am better able to select the right database to begin a search." The result is not simply faster reference service, but also better quality reference service. In this regard, Julie's comments are revealing.

> Currently we have an issue on the California ballot next week to legalize voucher schools (private schools to be funded by tax money). Several students have been writing papers on this proposal in the last year or so, and if I did not read current newspapers I probably would not have known much about what they were talking about. Because I know who the proponents and opponents of voucher schools are, and what their arguments are, I have been able to direct our students more knowledgeably to the best sources, to suggest the databases and web sites that would be most helpful, etc. If I knew nothing about this issue, I would have been making the recommendations in the dark, and they would not have been as good. If I knew nothing about the issue, it would also have taken me longer to answer these questions, because I would have been learning about it during the course of answering the questions. It always takes longer to answer a question when you're floundering around blindly trying to figure out what it's about.

As Julie explains, the contextual framework of names, places, and dates that she constructed by following the California school vouchers debate in newspapers enabled her to assist patrons expeditiously. Yet, the utility of this framework extends beyond providing prompt service. Julie notes that her familiarity with the issues made her confident not only in selecting materials that would have information on the topic, but also in judging which of these would be "the best sources" and "the databases and web sites that would be most helpful."

The stories thus far have focused on the ways in which reading newspapers and magazines leads to solid background knowledge, which in turn enables academic reference librarians to identify where a patron can find the answer to a question or to recommend sources for further research. Librarians explain that the articles they read contextualize various issues and topics, giving them a better understanding of relevant reference questions and allowing them to fill in gaps or otherwise untangle these queries. Necessary information can therefore be found more efficiently and with more confidence. But librarians also point to another positive effect of this contextual framework, namely, the ability to answer reference questions directly themselves, using their background knowledge, as opposed to identifying where the answer might be found. As one individual observes, "With my background information, I can jump right in and answer the question."

Academic librarians cite a variety of examples. One self-described "avid reader of newspapers and news magazines since junior high school" was able to answer a "recent question regarding [the] Tidal Basin Incident, 1974 ... from information read 26 years ago."[9] Corinne recalls a patron who was looking for a children's book that is also "a parable on the free-coinage-of-silver question in the 1890s." She explains, "I had recently read something about *The Wizard of Oz* being such a parable (the yellow brick road being the gold standard, etc.) and was able to help her." George answered the question of "whether a parent of a kidnapped child could claim the child as [a] deduction on income tax," having "just read a financial column in the local newspaper about this." (The answer, he explains, is yes, but "only in the year of the kidnapping, not in subsequent years.")

Not surprisingly, many of the questions to which librarians supply the answer concern current events "hot topics" or "hot button issues." Xiu Ping assisted a student who needed to know "if the wife of the Ford CEO was related to the Firestone family." "I remembered reading that William Ford, CEO of Ford, was the great-grandson (or grandson) of Harvey Firestone," she explains, and this information prompted the appreciative student to exclaim, "Aha! That's what the teacher meant!" Another individual observes that "[c]urrently the senate race between Rick Lazio and Hillary Clinton is a very popular topic on campus. Reading newspapers and magazines has helped me answer basic questions such as where did Hillary buy her house and what issues are being discussed more than others." In another example tied to elections, Bob describes deciphering political cartoons for a patron, observing that he "[c]ouldn't have done it without understanding jokes thanks to political points recounted in the [*New York*] *Times*."

The connection between reading newspapers and providing answers to current events-related questions has motivated many librarians to take a proactive approach to reference work. Specifically, these individuals read the newspaper with an eye to anticipating future questions and having the necessary information readily available. One individual explains that students come to the reference desk "every Tuesday afternoon trying to find out what happened in world news that would affect them at home. By reading the newspaper that weekend I can give them a quick answer." Lewis similarly comments, "Our students always want to know about the hottest companies, both public and private, but especially those that will be going public soon or have just gone public. I have found that if I read the Sunday *Globe* or *NY Times* business sections I can learn about the coming IPOs." Michelle explains how "[s]omething I've read in the *New York Times* will often allow me to anticipate reference questions. Usually an article will discuss some legislation or some statistics, and I will sometimes think that I might get a question on that, so I do some research on the topic before I work the desk."

Respondents repeatedly cite the usefulness of following Supreme Court decisions, observing that, on days when the decision is reported in the newspaper, "our first preoccupation [at work] would be to find the decision, ready to answer a question." Noting that Supreme Court decisions are discussed in great depth in "the major newspapers," Kurt writes, "I love to see what is being argued because I will get questions. *Roe v. Wade* will never go away as a topic." By the same token, there will always be students who ask for information on "Dr. Rovey Wade." But as librarians' stories demonstrate, keeping abreast of what is reported in newspapers and magazines enables them not only to anticipate queries about current events, but also to disabuse patrons who lack or otherwise confuse key pieces of information. In either case, librarians are indeed able to "jump right in and answer the question," a skill respondents attribute to the background knowledge that comes with reading newspapers and magazines during their free time. As Ellen concludes, "Being current gives you a starting point rather than relying solely on the 'reference interview' and the student's (sometimes limited) knowledge of a topic."

Directing patrons to specific articles

While a plurality of librarians provided examples of how the background knowledge acquired by reading newspapers and magazines helps in various facets of reference work, 129 individuals (29.1 percent) cite instances where they addressed patrons' queries by recommending an article they had read themselves. One respondent estimates that "[a]t least twice in the last year, I have been able to recommend reading an article on the topic recently, and knowing which magazines I read regularly, found the article for the student." Another individual comments that "every day I directly refer students to specific newspaper/magazine articles" which she herself had recently read. In fact, these librarians often express amazement at the serendipity of having just read an article on a topic and then being asked for information on that same topic or on a related issue. Maxine once "helped a student who was looking at the way in which computers are influencing education" by pointing out an article she had read in *USA Today* "about a school in Florida that is totally online." In some cases, serendipity is tied to the X factor of what the librarian happened to read during his or her lunch break. "I was putting a *Forbes* back on the rack after lunch, when [a student] asked me a question about [baseball] caps," Tina recalls. "He was writing an ENG 100 paper on his hobby. I pulled the *Forbes* off the rack and turned right to the article on a tycoon who got rich making caps. The student was amazed and very pleased. He didn't think we could find anything on his topic." In another example, the librarian had a student ask "how many young people vote Republican or Democrat." Explaining that the student "needed specific numbers, not anecdotal information," this individual remembers how "[t]hat day at lunch I picked up the *Christian Science Monitor* and they had a story and chart on voting by age groups and party."

Academic librarians also recall instances where they were able to lead patrons not only to articles they themselves had read, but also to visuals within the articles that matched patrons' information needs. In one example, the respondent writes that an

"Italian language teacher needed to show her class current pictures of life and culture in Sicily today. I had [a] magazine I read at home, *Italy Italy*, that I remembered in several issues covered this nicely." Another librarian used an image printed in a regional newspaper to fill a patron's request when other resources could not be located: "I had a student that was looking for a visual to use with her report on students' rights. She requested a video on student rights. After thoroughly searching in the catalog on that topic I remembered reading in the *Minneapolis Star Tribune* an article on schools that were not allowing female students to attend school in tank tops. A photo accompanied the article. We found this, and the student made a copy, pleased with the outcome." Had the librarian not read this newspaper story herself, she could not have made the innovative and subtle connection between a photograph that illustrates an article on a students' rights issue and the patron's original request for a "video on students' rights." In all likelihood, the student would have left the library empty-handed.

The ability to recall a visual image from having read a newspaper or magazine is a distinct advantage, considering that images are often not indexed. Filling patrons' requests for these materials therefore becomes what one librarian calls "a needle-in-a-haystack search." Indeed, even when indexed, searching for an image that meets a patron's requirements can be a daunting task, since search terms for images tend to be object-based (e.g., "woman," "tree," etc.) rather than subject-based. In other words, chances are one would *not* find an image indexed under the phrase "students' rights" in most databases.

Librarians discuss the issue of indexing in the context of print materials as well, describing their ability to "refer a patron to an in-depth article in the *New York Times*, for example, without even consulting an index." Respondents cite the fact that patrons are often pressed for time or simply would rather not have to wade through a multitude of database "hits" in order to locate a single article. In these situations, the librarian can instead directly refer the patron to an article he or she has read, effectively bypassing the entire search process. Irene "[o]ften refers patrons to [articles in] *The New Yorker* or *Working Woman* which were relevant to their topics, especially when they don't want to sort through indexes but just want a quick article." Librarians note that these articles generally turn out to be "just what the patron needed." Christopher tells how a "recent issue of *American Scholar* carried an excellent article on electronic books." He continues, "Yesterday, a student came to the reference desk needing to find an article on that very subject. I referred her to *American Scholar*. Later she came back and told me it was just what she needed." Librarians also use articles that they themselves have read as a starting point before consulting relevant databases and indexes. "Had a student once looking for information on symbiotic relationships between plants and insects," one librarian writes. "I had just read an article on the subject (in *National Geographic* I think) and was able to point her to the magazine. It was a current issue so it isn't likely that the article would have shown up in the indexing yet. Of course we did look for other articles in various databases that we have access to."

The experiences of many librarians indicate a fundamental problem with relying on indexes or databases, one which respondents often mention when describing how reading newspapers and magazines improves reference service: there are no records for the most recently published articles in indexes and databases. Academic librarians note that students in search of articles on current events immediately gravitate toward the periodical indexes, not realizing that there is a time delay between when the article appears in the newspaper or magazine and when it appears in these resources. One librarian writes, "Calgary, a few years ago, had a referendum on chlorine in the drinking water. Students in one of the environmental courses had been asked to look for how the story was reported in the media. They were trying to look in article indexes, but of course, because the stories had just come out, they hadn't been indexed yet." Another person notes that she "sometimes point[s] students to a particular article in *The Nation* that is too recent to be in indexes." Through their reading of newspapers and magazines, librarians are able to alert patrons to recent articles that otherwise could not be easily located. This is equally true of articles published in newspapers and magazines that are not included in the databases and indexes to which the library subscribes. Aaron recalls that a "patron needed information on the reintroduction of the wolves in Montana for a report. We used indexes, but I remembered reading a well-researched article in *Montana Outdoors* by the Fish, Wildlife, and Game Department." Likewise, another librarian was able to locate, based on her recent reading, "several articles and series in local newspapers (not indexed) that were pertinent" to a patron's request for information on "acid rain in the Great Smoky Mountains National Park."

In addition to bypassing indexes and databases, librarians describe another advantage of being able to lead patrons directly to a relevant article. As one person comments, "Part of any reference librarian's job is to evince an interest in the question," "to be inviting and engaging in reference encounters," and to stay "informed of local, national, and international news, and generally about topics of scholarly and general reading interest [which] help one to connect with the questions and discussion during a reference encounter." The instances where librarians have recommended an article that they themselves have read illustrate the role these recommendations play in expressing an interest in a patron's query. Rose explains that "a student was looking for articles about women's alteration of their body image, specifically using girdles (for an art class). I had recently seen an article on this in one of the magazines I read and was able to talk knowledgeably about the comeback of girdles and refer her to this article." Mike also recalls providing a patron with an article that he had just read, in this case from his own copy of the magazine: "There was a time recently when someone asked for a *Consumer Reports* that was missing from our collection. He wanted to buy running shoes. I was able to bring him my own copy of *CR* as well as a *Runner's World* chart comparing various types of running shoes. He was happy."

To be sure, librarians can "evince an interest" in the reference question, and therefore establish a rapport with the patron, simply by recognizing the topic at hand. This rapport can be strengthened, however, through the common bond created by shared reading interests. In the mind of the patron, the focus of the query evolves from a topic of which the librarian is simply aware into a topic that the librarian takes the time to read about, as demonstrated by the fact that he or she just happens to have read a terrific article on that very subject. As one librarian summarizes, "I can remember innumerable times saying to someone, oh yes I just read about this and here are some sources you can consult. I think this also helps me put the patron at ease. They know I care enough about their topic because I read about it."

Selecting search terms

While academic librarians remark on the fact that reading newspapers and magazines means that they often can identify articles without using databases, online searching is, of course, an ineluctable component of reference work. As Table 12 shows, 24 respondents (5.4 percent) mention that database searches are facilitated by reading newspapers and magazines, specifically by providing ideas for keywords and search terms. As one librarian explains, "I keep up with current issues (national and international) through the newspapers. I have had reference questions related to politics, international disasters, etc., for which subject headings or search terms would not have been obvious without some knowledge of the situation." Another remarks that reading newspapers and magazines outside of work helps "with the spelling of 'hot topics' or names, and gives me ideas of keywords to search under."

At the same time that they describe the search strategies they have developed from reading newspapers and magazines, librarians also identify the limitations of popular databases. Just as Dina noted earlier that "searching medical databases is so overwhelming" in her example of answering a patron's query about leprosy treatments, others explain that searching databases is faster and less frustrating when armed with concrete ideas for search terms. Beth remarks: "I deal with undergraduate students mostly, and many ... have been looking for recent information in newspapers on currently argued law cases in Los Angeles ... and the handling of the cases by the LA Prosecutor's Office. Lexis/Nexis searches (not always easy given the type and size of the database) are definitely easier because both the students and I have read about them so we know what keywords to use in the database." Another respondent recalls "having trouble finding material on effects of forest fires in the environment [when] looking in databases that didn't have controlled indexing.... [K]nowing to put in Yellowstone and other place names as part of the search at the time got some good material."

Not surprisingly, the specific search terms and keywords that librarians mention are often "new catch phrases" and other examples of terminology that enter the general lexicon through newspaper and magazine coverage of current events. One librarian remembers "getting questions about AIDS years ago when it was just being identified," noting that "[p]eople didn't know what it was called, but I had read about it and knew what the medical subject headings were at the time that you needed to find information about it." Being familiar with the terminology used to identify and discuss issues in current newspapers and magazines allows the librarian to construct what one respondent calls "a mental thesaurus" of synonyms that can be consulted during the search process. Haeyong remembers a student who was researching the topic of "educational vouchers." She advised the student to conduct his search using "the phrase 'school vouchers,' which seems to be the preferred terminology." At the same time, librarians explain that they not only recognize relevant search terms, but, by reading current newspapers and magazines, can also understand the underlying concepts these terms embody. This proved to be the case for Sadie: "Recently a patron asked me to help her find academic articles for a paper on depression. I knew that she would need to focus her topic but wanted to help her by showing her the thesaurus in PsychInfo. After typing in depression and going to the thesaurus entry we saw a number of related terms and narrower divisions.

My reading of *Discover* magazine gave me the knowledge to know what each of these terms meant."

Helping students select topics for assignments

The connection between reading newspapers and magazines outside of work and helping students at the reference desk is a recurring theme in many librarians' stories. But the notion of assisting students with their assignments extends beyond helping them locate information. As Table 12 indicates, 17 librarians (3.8 percent) recall situations where they have assisted students by either proposing or refining the topic to be researched for the assignment, responding to such questions as "How can diabetes education be focused into a doable 5-article literature review?" and "What serial killer will I find enough information on to speak for one hour?" Once again, academic librarians' ability to answer these questions—to "offer up topics for papers when students are on the fence"—stems from their reading of newspapers and magazines outside of work hours. One respondent explains, "Students often ask me (instead of their instructors) to help them define a research topic. Current awareness magazines help me with this process as I can suggest topics that are currently of interest and in the news." Another librarian explains that "[a] common assignment at the beginning of 2000 was to write a paper about some event in the last century or decade. Most students had no idea what to choose and would ask for suggestions. If I hadn't read newspapers, etc., I would have nothing to suggest."

Indeed, many of the topics that respondents helped devise or refine were used for open-ended assignments, which Amy, for one, feels often overwhelm students. She remarks, "Most of our students need assistance in picking topics, understanding the topics they pick, and narrowing the topic down so it can be written about in a five page paper." Joyce laments the demise of "reading lists and topic suggestion lists," commenting, "I think too much is left up to students who are simply not aware of the variety of topics/people they could research." This combination of a loosely defined assignment and a poorly informed student produces situations where the student needs help in selecting a topic and where reading newspapers and magazines makes the academic librarian's job a little easier. Mary Jo recalls helping a number of students: "Last month a class had an assignment in which they were required to find 25 articles on a news event in a third world country (poorly designed assignment). Many students were at a loss to come up with topics, and although I don't read a lot of foreign news, I read enough that I was able to help them come up with topics of interest."

Using newspapers and magazines to identify new or alternate resources

Twelve librarians (2.7 percent) mention that they learn about new or alternate resources from newspaper and magazine articles. In other words, the newspaper or magazine article forms a bridge that connects the librarian to another source or reference tool. At the same time, respondents note that, had they not read about them in a newspaper or magazine, these sources would have escaped their notice. As Rhea explains:

[A] student was working on a paper — she believed that the shape of the human throat while meditating [you know, ohm...] had a resemblance to the shape of arches in a Gothic cathedral and the acoustics thereof. Let me say, it was very hard to find anything on this. Then, while reading the paper, I saw an article about a recent study done by a doctor at a university in Florida which relates in some aspect to her idea. The study was as yet unpublished, but through the article we were able to track down the doctor's name, then we used other means to locate him, and she was going to contact him to discuss her idea.

Some respondents have also discovered Internet resources by reading newspapers and magazines, describing how "newspaper and magazine readings ... alert me to web sites that may provide me with the 'perfect answer.'" In one case the librarian notes that "[h]aving read about the wildland fires this year in the west, I was able to access an agency on the Web that I would not have heard of otherwise. It had fabulous stat[istic]s and maps, when a simple search on the Web brought up not much." Likewise, another person remarks, "I was able to find some specific U.S. Government information faster by reading in the newspaper about a new web site called Firstgov.gov." In fact, the recognition that newspapers and magazines can be a fruitful source for learning about Internet sites is reflected in a number of librarians' reading habits. Eleanor comments: "I always read the *New York Times*' 'Circuits' section and the *New York Post*'s 'Access' section.... I have learned about great Internet sites and especially the latest news about search engines and how to search them. We have many academic databases here. However, sometimes we just want to see what is out there on the Internet. I recently read that my favorite search engine, Altavista, has a 'clean' sister site, www.raging.com." It is interesting to note that, in all these examples, librarians became aware of "great Internet sites" not through professional journals, but instead through daily and weekly publications geared toward the general reading public.

Which newspapers and magazines have helped librarians in their reference work?

Considering the priority that most academic librarians place on keeping up with current events, it is not surprising that national newspapers such as the *New York Times*, the *Wall Street Journal*, and the *Christian Science Monitor* feature prominently in their stories. As one respondent remarks, "Reading a quality national newspaper is absolutely essential if the reference librarian is to be effective in that capacity." Librarians' stories are also rife with references to newsmagazines such as *Newsweek* and *Time*. These two publications have been used to answer queries on genetic engineering, diabetes, RU-486, the effect of music on brain development, the 2000 presidential election, and euthanasia, to name but a few topics. Librarians also refer to various topics they have read about in history and cultural feature publications—for instance, water rights and Chinese statuary in *National Geographic*, or a musical based on *Huckleberry Finn* in *The New Yorker*. One person explains that she often makes use of the "breadth of information on sciences, arts and history" found in *Smithsonian*, while another describes *The New Yorker* as "really crucial" to her work.

Not all the magazines mentioned by librarians, however, fall into the category of newsmagazines, nor are they "high culture" publications such as *The New Yorker* and *National Geographic*. A number of respondents recall situations in which popular, non–news oriented publications—for example, entertainment, lifestyle, hobby and craft magazines—have assisted them at the reference desk much in the same way as news-oriented materials. Ralph comments: "I recently had to help a patron identify a type of wood that he had a sample of. It turned out to be Zebrawood, a rare, expensive, tropical wood. I knew it on sight and helped him locate a picture of it here in the library and also what the tree looks like. If I did not have [the] hobby of woodworking and read craft magazines, I would not have known the answer. The other two people who tried it first did not have a clue." Similarly, Phyllis explains that "[b]ecause of my interest in antiques, I read several antiques magazines. Recently, a student doing research for a play being staged on campus was looking for appropriate props. I was able to find materials that fit the era she needed—both in pictures and actual materials." In other words, hobby publications should not be discounted as valuable sources of information that are potentially useful for answering a broad range of queries at academic library reference desks.

When it comes to entertainment and lifestyle magazines, academic librarians have found that these publications can provide them with a timeframe for events much in the same way as newspapers and newsmagazines. Consider the following story told by Rita:

> I read entertainment magazines. I have never been a *Seinfeld* fan, and seldom, if ever, watched the show. A student was researching *Seinfeld* and looking for reviews of the television program. He wasn't finding much and came to ask if I knew how he could get more information. I knew magazines that our databases didn't cover at the time that the show began, and that the show was slow to catch on. I needed to find materials that would cover an earlier time period. I would have figured that out if I hadn't known the dates, but it did speed the question along.

While Rita cites entertainment magazines in general, many of the examples of how librarians have applied information read in entertainment publications come from dedicated readers of *People* magazine, ranked seventh on the list of top 15 magazines read by academic librarians (see Table 11) and which Jeanne dubs "a pop culture expert." She recalls the following patron query concerning a popular soft drink advertisement that featured a curly-haired child actress: "A student was writing a paper on advertising and wanted some information on the little girl that does the Pepsi ads, where she changes her voice (so it seems). I had read about her and remembered enough about her name to find the article in *People* magazine. My Head of Department was amazed." Librarians also mention *People* in the context of reference queries that fall outside of the entertainment industry. Discussing newspaper and magazine coverage of the 2000 presidential election, one individual observes that "[e]ven *People* magazine has been helpful and informative in providing some of the lighter information on the candidates and their spouses." Another librarian remarks that she has found information in *People* on the "hard news" topics of "charter schools and prayer in schools."

These stories do more than illustrate the usefulness of *People* magazine. They also demonstrate how the answer to a question or the solution to a problem can come from what, at first glance, might be considered an unlikely source. At the same time, they challenge preconceived notions of both the content of popular magazines and the contribution they can make to educative and scholarly pursuits. In fact, there are clear advantages to being able to direct patrons to articles geared toward a general audience. Linda notes that such materials often serve as a good starting point for research, as she explains in the following example. "A student needed information on tofu for a food and nutritional science class. The student had no clue what tofu was. A magazine (*Martha Stewart Living*) had done an entire focus on soy and in addition to recipes talked about nutritional yield and benefits and origins. This was a useful article to refer the student to for accessible background reading before tackling the more scientific literature."

The idea that the perfect article, the ideal resource, or the missing piece of the puzzle could be in the next magazine you leaf through at the supermarket check-out counter, rather than in a scholarly journal, has informed a number of academic librarians' views on what it means to be information-literate. Mike stresses that librarians need to know not only what is happening in the world, but also which newspapers and magazines convey this information. Describing reading these periodicals as "all-important," he writes, "We need to know various types of periodicals available and the kinds of content each specializes in — and that's everything from the *Journal of Neurobiology* to *Soldier of Fortune*. If we are teaching information literacy, we need to be information literate ourselves." Furthermore, some respondents explain that knowing the content of various publications also means being aware of the potential biases of various newspapers and magazines—for example, what issues are covered and the extent of this coverage. Hugh observes that "the magazine *FAIR* has done a number of articles on biased reporting in the media that encourages me to be careful when selecting or advising users on information resources." Another librarian adds that "it helps to be able to compare how magazines approach the same event and to talk [to patrons] about the range of content in various disciplines' magazines and scholarly journals."

At the same time, the experiences of many academic librarians point to a role for newspapers and magazines that is often assigned solely to the professional literature of librarianship. There are respondents who have directed patrons to health-related web sites that they had first learned about in *Redbook* and who have helped students decide on a paper topic based on a book review published in *Elle*. As with the *Martha Stewart Living* example, these magazines might be considered unlikely sources. In other words, academic librarians would not necessarily turn to *Redbook* to find out about health information web sites, considering this subject instead to be the domain of either journals on health sciences librarianship or technology review publications. Similarly, book reviews are typically associated with professional reviewing tools such *Choice* or *Library Journal*. Although some survey respondents feel that only "[l]ibrary related literature keeps us up-to-date with our profession," they are unaware of both the potential contribution of newspapers and magazines and of the limitations of not looking beyond the professional literature. As the examples in this section demonstrate, librarians who read publications such as *Elle* and *Redbook* know that these magazines can have as great an impact on providing quality reference service as professional journals such as *College & Research Libraries*. Furthermore, as we turn our attention away from the reference desk, we will see that newspapers and magazines also play a significant role in other facets of academic librarianship.

From collection development to cocktail conversation: The impact of reading newspapers and magazines on other areas of academic librarianship

As we note at the beginning of this chapter, when asked whether reading newspapers and magazines has helped in aspects of their job *other* than providing reference service, 435 out of the 505 academic librarians who answered this question (86.1 percent) replied that it has, in fact, had a positive impact on a number of different areas of their work (see Table 2). Some indication of the breadth of this impact can be found in the categories listed in Table 13. Each of these 11 categories, identified from respondents' own experiences, represents a different aspect of their job that has benefited from reading newspapers and magazines outside of work. To understand the depth of the impact that reading newspapers and magazines has on these various facets of academic librarianship, we again turn to the thought-provoking stories librarians shared with us.

Many librarians revisit some of the prominent themes that characterize their experiences at the reference desk. For example, just over one-fourth of the respondents (26.4 percent) emphasize the contribution of reading newspapers and magazines to being a well-rounded individual who is aware of current events. Brenda comments: "Again, knowledge of current events gives me a better understanding of the world — other countries, conflicts around the world, etc." Another person pointedly observes, "I would feel like a 'bad' reference librarian if I weren't up to date on certain topics." While the theme of well-roundedness is familiar, a number of respondents recast this issue, focusing less on the specifics of answering reference queries and more on the importance of being a "culturally literate human" in general. Lewis explains that he keeps up with current events not simply to answer research-oriented reference questions, but also to be able to respond knowledgably to queries that reflect the concerns of everyday life:

> In general I have found that patrons often expect reference librarians to know bits of information that don't really fit into the category [of] a traditional reference question.... A patron may ask, "Where is next week's presidential debate being held?" If you cannot give a satisfactory answer off the top of your head to this question, because you didn't read about the debates in the newspaper, the patron may walk away as disappointed as if she had asked a wonderful multi-part question related to the OECD's reporting of the main economic indicators for the United Arab Emirates and you replied "What's that?"

Other librarians also discuss the importance of keeping abreast of not only hard news, but popular culture as well. As Beverly observes, "Newspapers and magazines help to keep my finger on the pulse of culture. By reviewing what editors print and people read, I can begin to 'feel' the cultural shifts as they happen." At the same time, Anita identifies an additional benefit that derives from being able to understand "what my clients (college students) may care about in terms of pop culture": that "it may help me to relate to them," which, in turn, leads to better library service overall. Of course, librarians have their own individual sense of what it means to be "in tune" with popular culture, whether it be by "remaining knowledgeable about popular performing arts such as TV, movies, [and] pop music," or simply "know[ing] what movies are playing" at the local cinemas.

Another familiar theme is that of discovering databases and web sites in newspapers and magazines read outside of work. The 21 librarians (4.8 percent) who discuss this issue, however, point to an application for these sites other than answering reference queries: they add these newly discovered tools to their library's home page or to other electronic resources that they have developed or maintain for the library. As Chris explains, reading newspapers and magazines "can help in identifying web sites that I can add to the pages for which I am responsible. A recent editorial in the *Denver Post* mentioned a site at HUD that describes and maps environmental hazards by geographical locale; it is especially good for superfund sites. I added it to one of my pages." In addition to home pages, librarians also have linked web sites they read about to their library's "virtual reference desk" or to "web subject resource guides" they have created. June remarks that "reading ... articles on consumer health and health care in America can help in the selection of web-based resources for a library web page devoted to consumer health." Likewise, Sharon recalls that when "constructing an 'election resources' web page," she included links to a number of different sites she had first "seen mentioned in the papers/magazines."

Table 13. Aspects of academic librarianship, excluding reference work, that have benefited from reading newspapers and magazines (Question 21 in Appendix A)

Aspect of academic librarianship	No. of librarians (n = 435)*
Being well-rounded/keeping up with current events	115 (26.4%)
Collection development	93 (21.4%)
Bibliographic instruction	62 (14.3%)
Making conversation	51 (11.7%)
Workplace/professional issues	46 (10.6%)
Implementing new technology	26 (6%)
Discovering databases/web sites	21 (4.8%)
Personal enrichment/independent research	20 (4.6%)
Maintaining/increasing credibility	18 (4.1%)
Outreach and programming	13 (3%)
Bibliographic control	4 (0.9%)

*Numbers do not add to *n* and percentages do not add to 100% because respondents cited multiple aspects.

The other nine aspects of academic librarianship that we identify in Table 13, and the stories from which these categories emerged, concern different ways in which reading newspapers and magazines outside of work facilitates the myriad responsibilities and activities of academic librarians. It is on these other responsibilities and activities that we now focus attention. As one librarian observes, "It is difficult to describe how my wide-ranging interests coupled with intense reading have helped me in a specific way that I can apply to a specific reference question. Rather, it informs and influences the way I approach my job." The experiences and examples that academic librarians relate shed light on the breadth of their job. Yet, these stories do more than provide insight into how librarians apply what they read in newspapers and magazines to specific tasks. They also illustrate how outside reading "informs and influences" respondents' perceptions of what it means to be an academic librarian at the beginning of the 21st century and their sensitivity to how other members of the academic community view this role. We have therefore organized respondents' stories into two sections. The first section examines the relationship between reading newspapers and magazines and librarians' specific job responsibilities: collection development; bibliographic instruction; dealing with workplace issues; implementing new technology; outreach and programming; and, finally, bibliographic control. The second section explores the relationship between reading newspapers and magazines and librarians' personal growth and sense of professional identity. It covers the following categories: making conversation; personal enrichment and independent research; and maintaining or increasing professional credibility.

Specific job responsibilities

COLLECTION DEVELOPMENT

Just as librarians have used newspapers and magazines to construct a frame of reference for current issues when providing reference service, 93 individuals (21.4 percent) note that reading newspapers and magazines enables them to develop "a frame of reference for purchasing items for the library." Again, this frame of reference consists of the general knowledge they have developed from their outside reading, including their familiarity with current events. Although a frame of reference usually is a conceptual construct, as when librarians place a reference query within a temporal or geographical context, this frame takes on physical form through the act of collection development. Because it influences the collection decisions he or she makes, a librarian's frame of reference is mirrored in the range of materials that ultimately appear on the library shelves. A narrow frame of reference — one which is uninformed by reading newspapers and magazines— results in an equally narrow collection that fails to address current issues, concerns, and trends that are relevant to the library's user community. Conversely, collection decisions that are made within a broad frame of reference — one which is based on the recognition and understanding of different perspectives on a range of pertinent issues— result in a collection of similar breadth and depth.

For many academic librarians, having a broad frame of reference means looking beyond the courses taught at their university or college when adding items to the library's collection. Pointing to the fact that "understand[ing] the basics of the world around you" not only helps provide better reference service, but "can also aid in your collection development activities," Daniel observes that "[w]e live in a global economy where our actions impact and are impacted by other countries in the world. Ignoring the world and local media only isolates you in [an environment] where awareness should be required for its intrinsic value.... Responsible citizens should keep abreast of current events and at least be familiar with the top books being currently sold. As information professionals we should take that a step further since we are the gateway to the resources that help responsible citizens find and use this essential information." Gail similarly emphasizes the need to extend one's professional gaze beyond the academic environment. She writes, "I think general knowledge about what is happening in the world is very helpful in collection development. It is important to know national and international trends when building up a collection. Students are interested in things that are happening in the world, not just things that are taught at this institution." Carlos also considers students' interest in world affairs when purchasing materials for the library, commenting, "I select reference materials for purchase based on timely topics like AIDS or home schooling or social conditions because I am aware of current and ongoing interests."

Others see the information contained in newspapers and magazines as a way to bridge "the real world" and "the academic world" for library users. When describing how reading newspapers and magazines affects collection development these librarians speak of how national or local trends affect either academia in general or, more specifically, the academic disciplines that coincide with their collection development, responsibilities. Julie recounts how reading periodicals outside of work has provided insight into the ongoing canon formation debate and the effects of this debate on collection development policies.

> My reading, as it touches on hot issues in academe, is often helpful in understanding some of the larger issues that affect the educational world in general, and my campus in particular. Arguments of late regarding the traditional canon of great authors and challenges to it (sometimes known as the "dead-white-male" debate) have been much bandied about. My reading of various views on many aspects of this issue has helped me in dealing with our faculty and in determining how to build the library's collections to support our curriculum as it changes in response to this debate. If I were ignorant of this issue, I would be building a collection that would be out of touch with the authors our students are reading these days in their assignments.

This desire to build collections that reflect what "students are reading these days" is also expressed by subject specialists who wish to develop collections that reflect current trends or developments in various fields. In this regard one individual remarks, "I select books in the computer science/electronics area and the faculty here are very up-to-date/cutting edge. Science/high tech info in the news helps me to see what the current hot topics are." In fact, examples of respondents developing collections in light of current trends and issues span a number of academic disciplines. Myra, a bibliographer "in the visual arts area," notes that she could not imagine fulfilling her collection development responsibilities had she "not always read widely in this area." Specifically, when reading current newspapers and magazines, she takes note of "awards, exhibitions, and renewed attention [paid] to specific artists, photographers, and architects." Similarly, Xiu Ping's experiences as a business librarian demonstrate that "doing collection development for a business library requires knowledge of the hot topics in business." She provides the example of being "able to order books on supply chain management before [she] was actually asked for them."

While some librarians describe how reading about new trends in academic fields or disciplines has motivated them to purchase books on that topic for their library, others cite the crucial role that book reviews play in alerting them to new materials. And while some of these individuals read library publications outside of their working hours in order to "learn about collection issues," others stress the benefit of using reviews in newspapers and magazines that "fall outside of normal library publications"—namely, that "reviews in non-library magazines or newspapers" provide a wider frame of reference for collection development than professional literature alone. Perhaps not surprisingly, the *New York Times* is most frequently mentioned as a source for book reviews, though it is by no means the only newspaper consulted. One librarian has found that "[r]eading book reviews in the Sunday issue of the *Denver Post* has brought a number of new books and local interest books" to her notice. Another person explains that she sometimes purchases a book "based on an interview of the author in a magazine." At the same time that a book review in a non-library publication can influence what is selected for a collection, it can also influence what does *not* get selected. Kathleen asserts that she has, on occasion, chosen not to purchase a book "because of an article pointing out some characteristic of it that makes it inappropriate for the collection." Likewise, Yukiko recalls that a *Newsweek* review of *Dutch,* a controversial biography of former President Ronald Reagan, "made me alert for the appearance of the book in our approval shipments, and I rejected it because of what I had read."

BIBLIOGRAPHIC INSTRUCTION

The 62 librarians (14.3 percent) who cite bibliographic instruction as a facet of their work that is improved by reading newspapers and magazines explain how they use the events and issues they read about in these publications as search examples in their instruction sessions. There is, of course, the assurance of "demonstrating a news database to a class and knowing [that a given news] item will call up a good number of hits," as Regina observes. Librarians also point out that, by reading newspapers and magazines, they have a wide range of search examples to choose from and can therefore select those most likely to attract and hold the interest of their students: "Using the Love Bug Virus or Napster, or whatever is currently being discussed in the newspaper, usually gets more attention and response."

Indeed, librarians describe how they have incorporated "hot topics" in their instruction sessions. After seeing "Ralph Nader featured in several of the magazines" she was reading at the time of the 2000 presidential race, Rose "chose third party candidates as a demo topic." Kit used the topic of "elite athletes and drugs" to teach a WebQuest class, while Charlene "used the Microsoft antitrust case to show students how to search Lexis/Nexis." Others tailor their sessions to the course in which the students are enrolled, selecting events in the news that have a direct bearing on the subject matter being taught. Recalling that "[a] particular class in social work research methods was doing research on the homeless," Abby mentions that she selected as a search example a relevant article on that topic that she had read in *Time* magazine. And Meredith recounts, "I often pull references to research reported in newspapers or magazines for library instruction presentations in psychology. A year or so ago, there was an article about a national report surveying how girls were doing in math. I remembered seeing a cartoon portraying the controversy over (at the time) a new talking Barbie that said, 'Math is tough.' So I used this research and the cartoon tie-in to lead a search strategy for a PsychInfo database demonstration for Psych 101."

Current events "hot topics" are not the only issues that librarians transform into search examples for instruction sessions. Charlene has found that animal topics also tend to be a big hit with her students, citing her use of an article she had read on "chimpanzees and communication as an example for how to search ProQuest." And while librarians frequently introduce their stories by mentioning the need to use search examples that are "of interest to 17- and 18-year old" first-year university students, students are not the only group that have their instruction sessions tailored to highlight individual interests. Betty writes, "When I was teaching Lexis/Nexis to faculty, there was a faculty member who was a big baseball fan. I had read a story about studies of the design of baseballs and the increase in home runs. We used this topic as an example in the training session and the faculty member seemed to appreciate the interest."

Dealing with workplace issues

Copyright infringement, filtering, intellectual freedom, personnel concerns, fundraising, the implications of introducing e-books into the library — these are just a few of the issues that academic librarians grapple with on a daily basis. As Table 13 shows, 46 librarians (10.6 percent) comment on how reading newspapers and magazines outside of their working hours has enabled them to competently and confidently address these workplace and professional concerns. In many cases, newspaper and magazine articles have "offered concrete advice on how to handle work issues" that respondents, in turn, have applied to their own work situations. Rahma explains that she is able to see "how other libraries function elsewhere," which furnishes her with "ideas about changes that might be implemented in our library." Dawn remarks that "[r]eading about relationships, workplace environment issues, etc., has provided me with data and stimulation in library and college reorganization efforts and personnel concerns." Librarians mention everything from how to get along with co-workers to salary issues. As one individual quips, "By reading *The Chronicle of Higher Education*'s annual statistical issue, I learned that I was grossly underpaid." When personnel concerns extend to hiring practices, librarians use the issues and topics that they themselves have read about "to sound [job candidates] out on topics in their field of expertise or their region." In essence, reading newspapers and magazines plays a double role: the awareness of events and issues that comes with outside reading prepares the librarian for the role of interviewer and, at the same time, forms a criterion by which candidates are evaluated. As another respondent points out, "People want to hire people who are at least aware of their environment."

In fact, librarians describe innovative ways in which they have put into practice information and ideas they have read about in newspapers and magazines. Phyllis, whose reading of antiques magazines came to the aid of a drama student, also notes that art and architecture publications have provided direction for construction projects at her work place, commenting that "when we recently renovated our floor in the library I was able to help discuss spatial and aesthetic needs." Another respondent used an article on "planning office space" from *The Journal of Light Construction* "to help with [a] review of staff work areas at the library." News items in the local paper often have a direct bearing on library operations as well. Lydia explains that "reading the local newspaper is often the best way to find out information about state funding and actions of the State Board of Higher Education or the legislature that may affect our jobs or salaries." This is also true of non-governmental funding, with one librarian using the local newspaper to garner ideas "for fundraising possibilities by reading about local philanthropists."

Academic librarians apply what they read in newspapers and magazines not only to issues that affect the library as a whole, but also to their own personal work practices. "I have used various techniques that I've read about in meetings and in one-on-one situations at work," Emily observes. "I've used some 'stress reducing' exercises on particularly rough days. I've used some organizational methods that I've read about to help control the clutter that is my office!" While Emily uses these techniques to address specific problems or issues that impact the daily routine of her job, Priscilla uses what she has read to better understand the significance of her work in a wider context, noting that "*The Chronicle of Higher Education* has many news and feature articles that help me understand higher education in general and my role as an academic librarian in particular." Part of interpreting their role as academic librarians involves stepping back from any self-created image of their profession and seeing themselves instead through the collective lens of society. Non-library publications provide this viewpoint, giving librarians insight into what one individual refers to as the "public perception of libraries" and their role in society today. Explaining that "[r]eading the culture and technology sections of newspapers and magazines always gives an interesting outside perspective," Miranda tells how reading an article in *The New Yorker* "about the San Francisco Public Library weeding uproar certainly gave a richer perspective to the classic library stance on weeding." Jodi states that reading this type of publication "[b]roadens my knowledge of what society thinks of libraries (I read a *New Yorker* article about the card catalog a few years ago). I've read many articles in popular magazines about libraries." Another individual makes a point of noting that he subscribes to an online "current awareness service for newspaper articles about libraries."

While academic librarians realize that they can gain perspectives on their profession by reading popular publications—the idea, as one respondent put it, that "reading both newspapers and magazines help me stay in touch with the trends and attitudes toward librarianship"—they also note that they can use examples of libraries in the news to influence their patrons' perceptions. Rhea cites "an editorial in the local newspaper about the new university library down the street from our college [that] touts its community service function." She describes how she used the editorial as a way of "explaining to students that libraries have reasons for existing." At the same time, Rhea also transformed the editorial into public relations tool for her library by pointing out to students that libraries are not homogeneous institutions, but instead have unique strengths and weaknesses. She continues, "And though the [university] library is newer and bigger, the university does not have a physical therapy program. We do; therefore, we have a better collection in that area, though our overall library is smaller."

IMPLEMENTING NEW TECHNOLOGY

Just as librarians use newspaper and magazine articles to examine the "public perception of libraries" in general and to address specific workplace issues in their own libraries, a similar dichotomy between the general and the specific characterizes the stories provided by the 26 respondents (6 percent) on the topic of technology-related issues in various newspapers and magazines. Stuart describes how these publications give a better understanding of how technological advances affect the broad mission of the library.

> Staying abreast of broad technological developments has helped me bring a deeper under-
> standing of what is happening in the marketplace to what is happening in the "library
> world." As key players in the "information society" it is imperative that we evolve to
> maintain our mission of providing information for free or at minimal cost. In a society
> that increasingly recognizes information and the delivery of information as a commodity,
> libraries need to work at staying in the game, for no other reason than to insure that
> information is available to all members of the community — not just those who can pay
> for it.

Academic librarians also have applied the information about new technologies that they
have read when making specific decisions for their own libraries. "I've had various computer and database related responsibilities in several library positions," one individual
recalls. "Many of the decisions I've made have been based in a broader understanding of
the computer industry I've gained through newspapers, magazines, and other sources."
Dawn notes that, because of her outside reading on these issues, she is "informed of technology developments and trends and use[s] this information to make library automa-
tion suggestions and decisions."

Some librarians rely on a small group of publications to stay informed or when faced
with a decision about what hardware or software to purchase. One person explains, "I
always read the *New York Times'* Thursday section called "Circuits" and bring information about new technology back to work," while another cites *PC Magazine* in conjunction with the selection of HTML editing software. For others, there is the serendipity of
locating sought-after information when least expected in such places as a physician's
waiting room: "Usually, magazines and newspapers have helped me in library purchasing decisions. When DVDs first came out, I was assigned the task of reading up on the
latest *Consumer Reports* to advise the college librarian which DVD would be best suited
for our library's needs. I found the perfect article while waiting in the doctor's office."

OUTREACH, PROGRAMMING, AND BIBLIOGRAPHIC CONTROL

Although mentioned by fewer respondents than the previous aspects we have examined, outreach, programming, and bibliographic control are also areas where academic
librarians have experienced the positive impact of reading newspapers and magazines
outside of work. The examples provided by 13 individuals (3 percent) in the outreach-
programming category encompass a diverse range of activities. Deborah explains how
she reads "*The Chronicle of Higher Education* regularly (at home or at work) and update[s]
the education faculty about news found in the *Chronicle*, new reports available online,
etc." Citing a different form of outreach, Brian remarks that the information in local and
regional newspapers he reads has helped in the area of partnerships: "The L.A. papers are
the primary source of information about K-16 education institutions in the Greater L.A.
area, and we get information from the papers that assists in planning future coordina-
tion, cooperation, goal-sharing, etc." Other respondents allude to their use of newspapers and magazines to furnish ideas about whom to select as keynote speakers for
library-sponsored conferences. Angela is responsible for recruiting women in science "to
participate in an annual conference devoted to interesting junior high school girls in
math and science fields." She recalls, "I have come across names in the newspaper, and
we in turn ask those individuals to participate in our annual conference." Harry notes,

"I am on a committee that brings in a well-known scientist to speak every year. I read enough popular science magazines that it has helped me make suggestions about who we might want to bring in."

Four individuals assert that reading newspapers and magazines can facilitate work in the area of bibliographic control. Rebecca recounts the pleasant surprise of finding a newspaper article relevant to her current cataloging task.

> I have even had occurrences when my general reading has helped [with] cataloging issues. I am currently cataloging over 50 titles in the Loeb Classical Library series. I was amazed to see an article in the Minneapolis newspaper about the re-issuing of some titles in this series with new or revised translations that were done to more accurately reflect the coarse language that had been used in the originals. This information informed my interpretation of the dates used on the verso of the title pages on some of the editions I had.

In addition to the serendipity factor, there is also a trickle-down effect in which outside reading contributes to a librarians' background knowledge, which, in turn, expedites the cataloging process. "Current reading contributes to on-going education and updating one's knowledge of the world," Vicky observes. "That knowledge aids making decisions when, for example, assigning subject headings to works being added to the library collection or assigning classification numbers." For Steven, this process has become second nature: "Believe it or not, as a cataloguer, I sometimes, entirely unconsciously, start, in the back of my mind as I'm reading a newspaper story ... assigning LC subject terms to [the] article. This has certainly enhanced my ability to more quickly determine the exact LC subject term needed to analyze the contents of an item needing original cataloguing."

Personal growth and professional identity

In describing the impact of reading newspapers and magazines on the three remaining factors listed in Table 13 — making conversation, increasing and maintaining professional credibility, and personal enrichment and independent research — librarians' comments take a self-reflective turn. The focus of the stories in each of these categories is not on the specific professional responsibilities that define their jobs, but rather on how reading has formed a type of scaffolding on which their interactions with co-workers, faculty, and students are built. The strength of this scaffolding, in turn, determines not only librarians' credibility within the academic community, but also their own sense of belonging to this world and the contributions they make there.

Fifty-one librarians (11.7 percent) describe how reading newspapers and magazines outside of work makes them better, more interesting conversationalists at work — the idea, as expressed by one respondent, that "the reading of these materials makes for livelier conversations around the coffeepot." "My knowledge of certain subjects helps generally in establishing a sense of collegiality among myself and other reference librarians and the director," Edna elaborates. "There is a level of awareness of culture that comes from reading newspapers and magazines." This awareness serves as a common denominator in building and maintaining relationships among a diverse group of co-workers.

Through the shared experience of reading about and discussing current social, political, and cultural events, librarians establish a basis for communication that is not circumscribed by the library environment itself, with the result that "work is more fun when one can have lively discussions."

Librarians call attention to the need for maintaining "the friendly atmosphere of [a] small library" and for establishing a sense of shared experience in libraries that have a high staff turnover rate. "Reading magazines provided me with interesting tidbits to share with colleagues," Maria observes. "They provide conversation starters, which help us build community. Having a 'stash' of conversation starters helps because Library and Information Services ... has hired about 13 new professional staff members in the last 18 months." Conversely, without this common "level of awareness that comes from reading newspapers and magazines," the librarian is at a distinct disadvantage, unable to share in or contribute to the collegiality of the workplace. As one respondent rhetorically asks, "Who wants to talk to a co-worker who isn't aware of the presidential debates?" Similarly, William recalls an exchange with a colleague that would have lost its piquancy had it not been for his recognition of a phenomenon popularly known as "Bushisms": "I told a colleague the other day about a strange question I got. The question was 'What is the cause and effects of recess?' Her remark was 'That sounds like a question Bush would ask.' If I didn't read in the news about Bushisms, I would be unable to understand her witticism."

In addition to conversing with colleagues, librarians also describe how reading newspapers and magazines has helped them to interact with students and faculty. While respondents had earlier commented on the need to keep abreast of current events for reference interviews, here their focus is less on librarian-client interaction than on human interaction and understanding in a broader sense. Won-Young, remarking that reading newspapers and magazines "has allowed me to make personal contact with students and faculty who are concerned with some current news item or problem, and I am able to join in the conversations and contribute information," emphasizes how "[t]his helps to create an esprit de corps with the students." Another person explains that reading about world events yields "[i]ntelligent conversation with multicultural and multinational students." At the same time, an awareness of world events can create not only more intelligent conversationalists, but more sympathetic listeners as well. This was true for Holly, who explains that her reading of newspapers and magazines has helped in her interactions with "foreign researchers," especially when "sympathizing with a Turkish scholar right after [an] earthquake" devastated his native country. In other cases, librarians note that reading newspapers and magazines on their own time prepares them for situations such as unavoidable—and often dreaded—business-social events on campus. Two respondents mention their reading helps with "cocktail conversation," while another explains that it "has helped me in participating in a luncheon conversation at the Faculty lounge."

Being able to converse intelligently in "business-social situations" relates to another aspect of librarianship that respondents say is directly affected by reading newspapers and magazines—that of maintaining and even increasing their professional credibility. Eighteen individuals (4.1 percent) agree with Kerry's assessment that "[t]o seem knowledgeable and interested in a situation adds to my reputation." These respondents also note that, conversely, "[i]f you are unaware, it leads others to believe you are missing 'it.'"

While some librarians cite the need to maintain their credibility with colleagues, most examples in this category focus on establishing and sustaining credibility with students and faculty through an awareness of the various topics that are of importance to a diverse academic community. As Vincent explains, "A good reference librarian has to appear smart in order to be trusted and taken seriously (particularly in an academic environment)." Indeed, respondents feel the need not only to establish their own reputation as knowledgeable and helpful individuals, but also to foster a positive image of librarians in general. Evidence of this connection can be found in one person's comment that "by being a bit knowledgeable, I do my bit towards maintaining a favorable image of professional librarians." This seems to be especially crucial when it comes to faculty members, who, according to another respondent, "tend to regard ... librarians as overpaid clerical workers." As Arlene observes, "When faculty know librarians are current and aware of important events, it assists [in] our networking efforts and in projecting a knowledgeable image."

Arlene's comments hint at the fundamental goal of establishing credibility in an academic environment: to bring more people into the library. The more knowledgeable the librarians, the greater the chance that faculty will recommend to their students that they avail themselves of the services that these librarians provide; the greater the number of students who use these services, the more entrenched the library itself becomes in the university community. Respondents acknowledge this domino effect, which begins with the librarians' reading newspapers and magazines and ends with well-respected librarians and a well-used facility, observing that "if [faculty members] see us as knowledgeable, they're more likely to use our services and send their students to do so too." Similarly, they suggest that, if students "think we 'know everything,' they'll be more inclined to ask for help again." One individual feels that it is this process of establishing academic librarians' credibility in order to increase the use of library services that makes reading newspapers and magazines outside of work time well spent, commenting that "the value of 'outside' reading may be more political than it is substantive in terms of helping to answer specific questions."

Respondents also see a connection between reading newspapers and magazines and their own perceptions of themselves as individuals. In fact, a slightly higher number of respondents (20, or 4.6 percent) see reading as a form of personal enrichment or as a means of pursuing independent research interests outside of work, than as a means of establishing credibility with outside parties (18 respondents, or 4.1 percent). Some librarians remark that newspapers and magazines "enrich my life" or have influenced the direction their lives have taken. As one of these individuals notes, reading "keeps us grounded as private citizens. It empowers us." The examples of ways in which respondents feel personally empowered by what they read covers everything from assistance in making "sound financial decisions and plans for retirement" to becoming "a more informed citizen [and] a better voter." One respondent explains how an article in *Forbes* that she had read on an airplane provided "some ideas for ... career development." Another observes that information from a magazine "led me to ask for my migraine medication in the form of pills rather than shots." Outside reading has also served as the motivation for independent research projects, as with Ralph, who is examining how the Boy Scouts of America is "used as an identifying group in studies of youth, as done by outside, non-scouting groups." Still others see reading newspapers and magazines as a way to recharge their batteries. Ruby believes that "it keeps my curiosity alive on days where I've explained how to do an online journal search for the umpteenth time." Another person writes, "Reading is inspirational and refreshing. It is a way to 'put something back in' instead of your thoughts always, and only, 'going out.'"

The arguments against reading newspapers and magazines to benefit library work

To be sure, not all academic librarians feel that reading periodicals during their free time has any beneficial effect on their job, a viewpoint epitomized by the comment that "I found out that it was useless and that is why I stopped years ago. Only young people who don't know any better or library school teachers who haven't worked in libraries in years would even consider it useful." As we noted earlier and as shown in Table 2, 56 respondents (11.2 percent) have *not* found that reading newspapers and magazines outside of work helps in reference work, while 70 respondents (13.9 percent) have not noticed any impact on non-reference aspects of their job. A number of librarians in both of these groups believe that "just knowing how to search online databases is the key," or that "one could probably discover the necessary resources by understanding and applying good search techniques only." Similarly, one librarian contends that "[i]f the students need help with newspaper reference questions, I can help them access electronic or paper newspaper indices to which our library subscribes." In another example, an individual working at "a branch campus of a large state university system [where] the students ... are upper-level undergraduates or graduate students" explains that these students are "not doing the type of research that is helped by *outside* reading. What they need and most appreciate are recommendations for relevant databases and search skills."

The stories we have related in this chapter supply ready evidence for refuting the argument that database searching alone "is the key." Respondents repeatedly cite examples where "the perfect article" was not indexed, either because it was published too recently or because it originated from a source that simply is not indexed within the library's searchable databases. They also point out that patrons often want "a quick article" without having to spend the time wading through any number of database "hits." Furthermore, there is the question of what happens when the patron then asks which of the numerous print sources identified through this search would be best geared for his or her research needs. In order to successfully answer this question, the librarian would need to have some basic knowledge not only of the topic, but also of the differences among the print sources themselves—their relative strengths and weaknesses, as well as the scope of their content and any potential biases. As one librarian explains, "[W]hen someone starts talking about some current topic such as the Euromarket ... I at least have some reference point from which to do my searching and I appear to the patron to have some knowledge of the subject. I feel that the more current emphasis in Library School on sources, rather than content, lessens the librarian's desire to even want to know what is contained in a journal, magazine, etc."

The credibility factor discussed above by a number of librarians also provides a counter-argument to claims that, because upper-level undergraduate and graduate students do not undertake "the type of research that is helped by outside reading," the newspapers and magazines that constitute this outside reading are not beneficial to library work. Rather, we need to examine this issue in terms of respondents' comments that they are better able to handle the reference interview when they have some sense of the topic at hand — a frame of reference constructed from the knowledge accumulated by reading current newspapers and magazines. At the same time, librarians describe how this frame of reference enables them to impart better search skills to the user by recommending, for instance, very precise search terms that they have encountered in their outside reading. In addition, while third- or fourth-year students might not need the type of assistance in selecting or refining assignment topics that first- or second-year students do, they would still benefit from hearing about a terrific web site on their research topic that the librarian just happened to have read about in a mainstream magazine or newspaper — a scenario recalled by more than one survey respondent. While some librarians may believe that the key to good reference service is being able to conduct a search on a given topic regardless of their familiarity with the topic itself, there is nevertheless the assumption on the part of patrons that the librarian will at least be able to recognize the principal players, the timeframe, or the basic terminology of a given topic, no matter whether it concerns general interest current events or advanced scientific research. As a result, as one respondent points out, "if [patrons] come to you with a topic you know nothing about, it can sometimes make them doubt your ability to help."

The role of local newspapers

Among the academic librarians who describe the importance of reading newspapers in various work situations is an extremely vocal contingent emphasizing the special role that local newspapers, as opposed to regional or national publications, play in improving the service they provide. We have already heard local papers discussed in terms of publications that often are not indexed. But the role of local newspapers extends beyond the issue of database searching. Consider Nora's comments on *The Ithaca Journal*, one of the local publications that she reads.

> For a small city paper, [*The Ithaca Journal*] reports more scientific news than an average newspaper. Specific instances where this newspaper has helped have been... 1. Breaking news about a discovery. For example, a student was researching prions, and it hadn't been covered in many of the popular scientific or generic newsmagazines, but our local paper covered it. A recent Cornell student discovery of a protein found in butter [that] protected cells in the breast against cancer. 2. They frequently feature information about the latest developments in search engines, which we then try out at work. They wrote up a comparison/critique of Google.com long before I read about it elsewhere.... 3. The newspapers frequently cover local statistical data, which is seldom published in a national or even regional format.

Of course, not everyone's local paper has "a strong research institution [Cornell University] looming large in the background," as Nora observes of her "townie newspaper." Nevertheless, 26 librarians provide examples of how reading local newspapers has proved to be invaluable in answering reference queries, while 21 individuals describe non-reference situations in which keeping up with local news is essential to their work.

First, there are patron queries concerning local events and people. Heather comments that "[r]eading the local paper is a must for knowing what is going on in your community. Even though we are an academic library we are asked endless questions about agencies in our area, 'Who does xxx in town,' and miscellaneous other items." This is especially true of out-of-town students who "do not know the local area well, do not read the daily local news," and often need assistance with researching local current events topics. Meredith recalls a student who needed help on his "thesis about a local city mayor." "Having read local newspaper articles about a recent mayoral scandal," she explains, "I was able to pinpoint … the only public library in the area that archives that paper. He [the student] of course made use of the library's clipping file on the mayor for both of his administrations." In other cases, students who are new to the area simply want to find out more about their adopted environs. As one respondent from Nashville remarks, "Many students from out of town want to know about Nashville — where to go, what to do, where does Dolly Parton live, etc. Several locally published magazines and newspapers highlight local people and events." Librarians emphasize how their reading of local periodicals has helped them either in directly answering a patron's question or in recommending sources for further information.

Often, it is not the student who is the out-of-towner, but rather the librarian. Respondents who have found themselves in this situation explain the necessity of reading local publications in order to understand patrons' queries. Emily remembers the following incident: "I am not from Louisville originally, so I was not aware of the controversy surrounding a proposed new bridge over the Ohio River between Kentucky and Indiana. While the controversy had been ongoing for about 10 years now, it wasn't until I read an article about it in *Louisville Magazine* that I became aware of the details. A patron asked for material on the topic for a class debate, and this background helped me to supply at least one article off the top of my head, plus let me know what they were talking about to begin with!" For Hilda, recognizing the importance of following local news came with hindsight: "I had a phone call from a patron who needed to know the names of board members of a certain company. I had no idea what she meant when she used the company's name, because I was new to the area. (The company has been involved in highly controversial land use.) It took some digging to figure out just what the young lady was talking about. [Had I] been reading the local newspaper in town, I would have known all about it." The incidents to which Emily and Hilda refer have achieved a certain degree of prominence within their communities. In one case, there is a controversial building proposal that spans two states and 10 years; in the other, a controversy embroils a local company. Because of their prominence, patrons would assume the reference librarian to be at least familiar with the rudiments of these cases. While librarians may recognize the need, as one respondent put it, "to know what Bosnia is to function at [the reference] desk," this same principle applies to local news items as well.

Academic librarians also explain that reading the local paper makes them feel part of the community — both in terms of the geographical area in which they live and the university or college at which they work. One person notes that this is especially crucial when "fitting into a new community [and] feeling more comfortable in a new environment." Even those who are not new to a community describe the importance of "knowing what is happening and what issues are important to people in your community." Examples range from being aware of voting registration deadlines to knowing "when and where local events" will take place. Much like the individuals who read the local paper in order to stay informed of issues that affect their libraries, some librarians track issues in the local paper that "may impact campus life" more generally, including press coverage of the university itself. As one respondent observes, "It has been helpful to read anything concerning [the] university or its faculty that appears in local newspapers." Roger agrees, noting that "[r]eading the local paper helps me to know what is going on at the university where I work. There are frequent articles in the paper about state funding of public universities, etc. Sometimes these are issued before we hear the information through in-house channels. This has helped me be informed of what is going on here"— a telling observation about the often secretive nature of institutional politics and turf wars.

Academic librarians' enthusiasm for local newspapers is reflected in their reading habits. Returning to the data in Table 4, when asked to identify the newspapers that they read at least once a week, 59.3 percent of responding librarians mention one or more local newspapers—a higher percentage than that of any other newspaper category. Additionally, more than twice as many academic librarians read a local or regional newspaper on a daily basis than read national newspapers (see Table 3). While these figures point to the fact that academic librarians read more local and regional newspapers on a regular basis than national papers, the data for local newspaper readership can also tell a different story. In other words, the fact that just over half (52.5 percent) of responding librarians read a local or regional newspaper on a daily basis or that 59.3 percent of these individuals read a local newspaper at least once a week also means that approximately 40–50 percent of librarians are not regular readers of local or regional newspapers. Given the numerous, insightful examples that respondents have provided about the fundamental role that reading local newspapers plays in providing better reference service and in facilitating other areas of their library work, the fact that 40–50 percent of academic librarians do not bother to turn to local publications is troubling.

What accounts for this lack of interest in the local world? It may be, as Janine has found in her own work experiences, that "many professionals don't read the local paper" because they "consider it too mundane." The inevitable result, she continues, is that these librarians "have no idea of what is happening locally." But information about local events is often exactly what academic library patrons seek. Furthermore, being knowledgeable about local events can stimulate interest in national and world events. Indeed, newspaper and magazine coverage of local events enables librarians to comprehend, on the one hand, the national implications of these events, and, on the other hand, how national and international issues play out at a local level.

4

Developing a "Reader's Mind"

How reading nonfiction and fiction affects the work
of academic reference librarians

The stories related in the previous chapter are evidence of the positive impact that reading newspapers and magazines has on reference service and other aspects of academic librarianship. Are there similar benefits to reading nonfiction and fiction? Does reading nonfiction and fiction outside of work hours help in providing reference service? Does reading these materials help in other aspects of an academic librarian's job? Of the 501 librarians who responded to the question concerning the relationship between reading fiction and nonfiction and reference work, 382 individuals (76.2 percent) say that reading these materials outside of work has helped them in their reference work, while 119 (23.8 percent) see no benefits (see Table 14). The figure of 76.2 percent is slightly less than the 88.8 percent of academic librarians who state that reading newspapers and magazines has helped them in their reference work. The greater relevance that academic librarians attribute to newspapers and magazines is evident in the comments of some of the 119 respondents who could not recall any instance where the books they read outside of work positively affected their reference work. "I think my magazine and newspaper reading [is] more beneficial than my book reading in this regard," one respondent concludes. Another feels that, for the most part, newspapers and magazines are more applicable to the information needs of the majority of her patrons, namely, students. She suggests that "reading fiction or nonfiction would come more into play with public librarians. The students here are usually concerned with current events, which are covered more in papers and magazines."

Table 14. The impact at work of reading nonfiction and fiction for academic librarians
(Questions 22 and 23 in Appendix A)

	Has reading nonfiction or fiction helped in reference work? (n = 501)	*Has reading nonfiction or fiction helped in areas outside of reference work? (n = 492)*
Yes	382 (76.2%)	398 (80.9%)
No	119 (23.8%)	94 (19.1%)

Rather than focusing on the comparative advantages of reading newspapers and magazines, most of the academic librarians who see no connection between reading books during their free time and improved reference service introduce a new variable: the *type* of fiction or nonfiction that they read. Coverage of current events varies from newspaper to newspaper and among different news magazines—a fact that academic librarians recognize in their decision to read both national and regional papers each week, or to complement *Time* with *The Nation*. This variation, however, pales in comparison with the panoply of subjects contained in books, which mirrors the exploration and production of knowledge that takes place in colleges and universities. As one librarian points out, "We are dealing with the entire range of human knowledge in an academic environment." Given this range, what is the likelihood that the interests a librarian pursues through his or her leisure reading of books will coincide with the information needs of patrons?

Respondents who say that the books they read have not facilitated reference service feel that there is a disjunction between the topics of these books and the focus of either the library at which they work or the studies and research interests of their patrons. Jennifer, who works in a business library, writes, "I cannot recall a single instance when having read a nonfiction or fiction work helped me in my reference work (I do not read business books)." Nicole identifies her favorite reading materials as "books on history and classic novels," but notes that "[w]e don't have many history majors here, and not too many students read classical literature (which is unfortunate on both counts)."

Other librarians believe that the specificity of their reading interests is a problem. In the introduction to the section on academic librarians, we mention that Kayla spent a year "focused on fiction by southern Africa women writers." She subsequently notes that, unfortunately, "last year's focus on southern African women writers and their works has not been called upon yet. I hope it will be in the not too distant future." There is also the argument that "No, my outside reading is for my enjoyment," with the implication that pleasure reading can have no bearing on academic librarianship. Merle, a dedicated fan of British mystery novels, writes: "I cannot think of any examples of specific instances where my personal reading informed my reference work. I guess that there is some reason to believe that a widely-read person will be a better reference librarian, but reading British mysteries (my fave source of personal reading pleasure) doesn't seem too terribly pertinent to reference work."

Table 15. Frequency with which academic librarians read books (Questions 12 and 14 in Appendix A)

No. of books read in the past 12 months	Fiction (n = 535)	Nonfiction (n = 520)*
None	32 (6%)	53 (10.2%)
One to five	127 (23.7%)	190 (36.5%)
Six to ten	79 (14.8%)	113 (21.7%)
Eleven to twenty	105 (19.6%)	88 (16.9%)
Twenty-one to fifty	121 (22.6%)	62 (11.9%)
Fifty-one to one hundred	29 (5.4%)	11 (2.1%)
More than 100	42 (7.9%)	3 (0.6%)

*Percentages do not add to 100% because of rounding.

But the experiences of the 382 academic librarians who describe how the books they read during their free time enable them to provide better reference service emphasize the very point that Merle tentatively acknowledges— that "a widely-read person will be a better reference librarian." Noting that "the first two words out of the mouth of my reference instructor in graduate school [were] READ EVERYTHING," Kara affirms that "[s]ounder advice for the reference librarian was never given." And in keeping with this advice, the books that respondents say have had an impact on their work are not all of an academic or scholarly nature, but instead encompass a wide range of topics and genres. There are books for different types of "Dummies," books about religion and books of devotion, travel literature that spans the world, and, yes, even mysteries, to name but a few examples. Moreover, the various works of nonfiction and fiction they read have an even greater impact outside of reference work. While 76.2 percent of librarians discuss how reading books during their free time has helped them in their reference work, 80.9 percent provide examples of how their reading assists them in other areas of their work.

We began our investigation of the nonfiction and fiction reading habits of academic librarians by asking survey respondents to tell us roughly how many books they have read over the past year. Interestingly, the most often cited range — between one and five — is the same for both nonfiction and fiction. As Table 15 shows, 127 librarians (23.7 percent) have read up to five fictional works over the past twelve months; in the case of nonfiction, the number of respondents in this range is 190 (36.5 percent). The similarities between nonfiction and fiction reading, however, end there. For example, while 6 percent of librarians have not read a novel, play, or book of poetry over the past year, this percentage jumps to 10.2 percent in the case of nonfiction. Similarly, 42 librarians (7.9 percent) have read more than 100 works of fiction over the course of the last twelve months, compared to just three individuals (.6 percent) who have read more than 100 works of nonfiction. When librarians' reading habits are plotted in Figure 2, we can see that the lines representing fiction and nonfiction both form sharp peaks at the one-to-five book range and

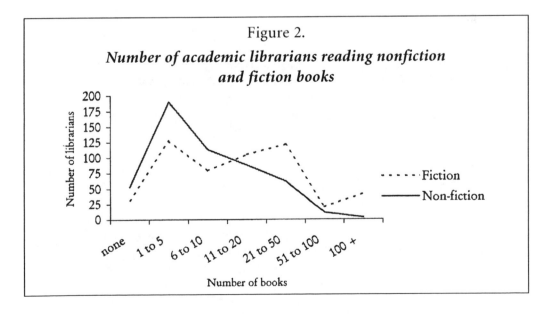

Figure 2.

Number of academic librarians reading nonfiction and fiction books

then subsequently diverge. While the line representing nonfiction steadily descends as the number of books increases, the line representing fiction re-ascends, taking into account the 19.6 percent of librarians who read between 11 and 20 fictional works a year and the 22.6 percent of respondents who read between 21 and 50 works of fiction annually. Of even greater significance than the quantity of books academic librarians read are the titles of these works.

We start this chapter much in the same way as the previous one: by examining what academic librarians read, looking first at fiction before turning our attention to nonfiction. We then examine how librarians have applied both of these materials in their reference work and in other aspects of their jobs, once again using their own stories from their work experiences.

Reading fiction

We asked survey respondents to name the author or title of two or three works of fiction they have recently read, with the intent that these titles and authors would form a backdrop for the stories academic librarians relate about the impact that reading fiction has on their work. J.M. Coetzee, William Dean Howells, Rumer Godden, Truman Capote, Anita Desai, Upton Sinclair, Chaim Potok, Ha Jin, Euripedes, Willa Cather, Elmore Leonard, Washington Irving, Tupac Shakur, Anita Brookner, Cormac McCarthy, and Flannery O'Connor are but a few of the authors mentioned by the 480 librarians who identified the author of the books they have recently finished. In some cases, librarians cite an author in conjunction with a specific work, either one that had been published around the time of the survey—*Plainsong* by Kent Haruf, for example—or a renowned novel, such as Michael Shaara's *The Killer Angels*, which won the Pulitzer Prize in 1975. In other instances, librarians have read or are in the process of reading multiple works by the same author, as witnessed by responses such as "I'm currently on a Neal Stephenson bender" or "I'm systematically plowing through all of Ann Perry's Charlotte and Thomas Pitt mysteries." Non–English language material is also well represented among examples of recently read fiction. French language works are mentioned by a number of librarians, with citations ranging from Victor Hugo's *Notre Dame de Paris* to *Rue Deschambault* by Gabrielle Roy. One individual who enjoys "contemporary Mexican literature in Spanish" recently completed *El Tunel* by Ernesto Sabato, *Benedíceme Ultima* by Rudolfo Anaya, *Macho* by Victor E. Villasenor, and *Pubis Angelica* by Manuel Puig. Another librarian comments that he has recently "read some Japanese novels."

While the various works of fiction mentioned by academic librarians collectively form an eclectic bibliography, suggesting a diversity of tastes and interests among survey respondents, this eclecticism is somewhat tempered by the frequency with which some authors are cited. We deliberately use the phrase "somewhat tempered," since the list of frequently cited authors in Table 16 reveals an interesting pattern in which individual tastes intersect with current literary and cultural trends. Take, for example, the first category listed: "Cited by 15 or more librarians." Only three authors are mentioned by at least 15 respondents, with the first two authors in this category garnering the reading attention of 27 librarians each. Considering that 480 librarians provided authors or titles for recently read works, 27 individuals translates into just 5.6 percent of respondents reading each of the top two authors. Collectively, the "Cited by 15 or more librarians" category accounts for works of fiction that 15.2 percent of academic librarians have recently read. Yet, the fact that the three authors in this category are Barbara Kingsolver, J.K. Rowling, and John Grisham is significant. In fact, Table 16 in many ways acts as a mirror that reflects not only the reading habits of academic librarians, but also the popular tastes and trends of the general reading public at a specific point in time — namely, fall 2000, when this survey was completed.

Using the 45th and 46th editions of *The Bowker Annual Library and Book Trade Almanac*, which record the *Publishers Weekly* bestsellers for the years 1999 and 2000, respectively, we can examine the authors and titles most often cited by academic librarians in terms of larger cultural and literary trends. We begin with Barbara Kingsolver. Academic librarians cite in their responses a number of novels written by Kingsolver, including *Pigs in Heaven* and *Animal Dreams*, but none as frequently as *The Poisonwood Bible*, which chronicles an American missionary family caught in the midst of the Democratic Republic of Congo's transition from Belgian colony to independent nation. First published in hardcover in 1998, 662,842 trade paperback copies of the novel were sold in 1999[1] and 1,759,929 copies in 2000.[2] The immense popularity of *The Poisonwood Bible* can be attributed, in part, to its being named an Oprah Book Club selection. Daisy Maryles, executive editor of *Publishers Weekly*, points out that the novels with sales of over 1,000,000 copies in trade paperback in the year 2000 were "either titles in the phenomenally bestselling Left Behind series or Oprah Book Club picks."[3] In addition to *The Poisonwood Bible*, three other novels listed in Table 16 fit Maryles' description. There is the Left Behind series itself (mentioned by nine respondents), *Daughter of Fortune* by Isabel Allende (mentioned by eight individuals), and *She's Come Undone* by Wally Lamb (mentioned by seven respondents). Both of these last two titles were Oprah Book Club selections.

The other two authors in the "Cited by more than 15 librarians" category have an even stronger grip on the attention of the general reading public than does Barbara Kingsolver. Maryles observes that "[i]n 2000 John Grisham led the pack again, this time with *The Brethren*, with sales of more than 2.8 million copies. In fact, Grisham has held the lead position on these annual charts each year since 1994."[4] As Table 16 shows, 19 librarians have recently read one or more of Grisham's legal thrillers, yet no single title stands out among survey responses. In other words, librarians are just as likely to have read *The Brethren* as *The Street Lawyer* or *The Runaway Jury*. A few individuals simply write "a John Grisham"—a response suggestive of both the ubiquity of Grisham's novels and a probable lapse of memory on the part of the respondent. In fact, Grisham's novels not only annually achieve bestseller status in hardcover, as Maryles points out, but they perennially maintain their popularity in paperback, as both the listings of mass market sales and academic librarians' reading habits make clear.

Table 16. Authors most frequently read by academic librarians: Fiction (Question 13 in Appendix A)

Frequency of citation	Author	Genre	Most frequently mentioned title
Cited by 15 or more librarians	Barbara Kingsolver (27)	General	*The Poisonwood Bible*
	J.K. Rowling (27)	Fantasy	The Harry Potter series
	John Grisham (19)	Legal thriller	NA
Cited by 10 — 14 librarians	Sue Grafton (14)	Mystery	NA
	Patricia Cornwell (13)	Mystery	NA
	Tony Hillerman (11)	Mystery	NA
	Margaret Atwood (10)	General	*The Blind Assassin*
	Janet Evanovich (10)	Mystery	*Hot Six*
	Arthur S. Golden (10)	General	*Memoirs of a Geisha*
Cited by 5 — 9 librarians	Maeve Binchy (9)	Domestic	NA
	Jan Karon (9)	Domestic	The Mitford series
	Stephen King (9)	Horror	NA
	Tim LaHaye/ Jerry B. Jenkins (9)	Christian/ inspirational	Left Behind series
	Anne Perry (9)	Mystery	NA
	Jane Smiley (9)	General	NA
	Isabel Allende (8)	General	*Daughter of Fortune*
	Tom Clancy (8)	Espionage thriller	*The Bear and the Dragon*
	Dick Francis (8)	Suspense	NA
	Charles Frazier (8)	General	*Cold Mountain*
	John Irving (8)	General	NA
	Melissa Bank (7)	General	*Girls' Guide to Hunting and Fishing*
	Wally Lamb (7)	General	*She's Come Undone*
	Toni Morrison (7)	General	NA
	Kathy Reichs (7)	Forensic thriller	NA
	Tom Robbins (7)	General	*Fierce Invalids Home from Hot Climates*
	Jane Austen (6)	"Classics"	NA
	Mary Higgins Clark (6)	Suspense	NA
	Michael Cunningham (6)	General	*The Hours*
	F. Scott Fitzgerald (6)	"Classics"	NA
	David Guterson (6)	General	*Snow Falling on Cedars*
	Sharyn McCrumb (6)	Mystery	*PMS Outlaws*
	Robert B. Parker (6)	Mystery	NA
	Rosamunde Pilcher (6)	Domestic	NA
	Carol Shields (6)	General	NA
	J.R.R. Tolkein (6)	Fantasy	NA
	Colin Dexter (5)	Mystery	NA
	Seamus Heaney (5)	General	*Beowulf* translation
	Carl Hiassen (5)	Crime thriller	NA
	Anne McCaffrey (5)	Science fiction	NA
	Philip Roth (5)	General	NA
	Mark Twain (5)	"Classics"	NA

While the 2,875,00 copies of *The Brethen* that were sold in 2000 is a staggering figure, it is diminished by another statistic. Describing J.K. Rowling's Harry Potter series as "[t]he biggest sales story of the year (and not just on the children's front either)," Diane Roberts, the senior editor for children's books at *Publishers Weekly*, points to the fact that "a grand total of 23.3 million Harry Potter books were sold in the United States in 2000."[5]

Certainly, the comments of the 27 librarians who have recently read one or more of these books serve as a testament to the phenomenal popularity of the Harry Potter series among adult readers. These respondents were quite adamant that the Harry Potter books are not "children's books." "I think Harry Potter is not just for children," one librarian states. "Here at my library we shelve it in the General Collection, and not the Juvenile Collection." Another individual comments on "the fact that [the Harry Potter books] are certainly being read by plenty of adults." Another notes that she "had great fun with that series."

Outside of the phenomena of the Oprah Book Club, the Left Behind series, Harry Potter, and John Grisham, there are other titles that have achieved popularity both with academic librarians and the general reading public. The same general popularity that characterizes the top three most frequently read titles and authors applies to many of the listings in the "Cited by 10–14 librarians" and the "Cited by 5–9 librarians" categories in Table 16. For example, Arthur Golden's *Memoirs of a Geisha*, which was recently read by 10 academic librarians, sold over 2,000,000 trade paperback copies in 1999.[6] Within this same category, Margaret Atwood's *The Blind Assassin*, winner of the 2000 Booker prize, made an eight-week appearance on the *Publishers Weekly* bestseller list, as did Janet Evanovich's *Hot Six*.[7] Likewise, Tom Clancy's latest espionage thriller *The Bear and The Dragon* was number three on the *Publishers Weekly* 2000 bestsellers list for fiction.[8]

Of course, the fact that some authors are read more frequently by academic librarians than others cannot always be understood in terms of societal tastes and trends. As we glance at Table 16, only the arbitrariness of individual preferences and interests can serve as an explanation for why F. Scott Fitzgerald is more popular than Mark Twain, and why both of these authors have been read by more librarians than Somerset Maugham, who is not listed in Table 16 but whose work nonetheless was cited by two respondents. Yet, while not all of the reading preferences expressed by academic librarians can be tied to bestseller lists and book clubs, the fact that *The Poisonwood Bible* and the Harry Potter series are the titles cited most frequently means that academic librarians, to borrow a phrase used by one respondent in the previous chapter, have their "finger on the pulse of culture." Furthermore, these librarians are attuned to popular literary trends not simply by reading *about* them, but by reading the materials around which these trends form. As one academic librarian points out, "It is not possible to relate to the craze over Harry Potter if you have not read any of it."

Before we turn our attention to the works of nonfiction that academic librarians are reading, it is interesting to note that a few individuals replied "Can't recall" or "Don't remember" in response to the question of what fiction they had read recently. These two seemingly nondescript phrases provide a number of insights into the reading habits of academic librarians. In some cases, what the librarian "can't recall" is the last time he or she even read a work of fiction. For some respondents, this is a conscious choice: one librarian whose favorite reading material is Jewish philosophy comments that she has "not read fiction in a very long time," while another respondent who enjoys reading the newspaper writes, "It has been years since I finished a fiction title." For other librarians, however, the inability to recall the last time they finished a novel is a reflection not of reading preferences, but rather of the reality of not having enough time. "Quite honestly, I can't remember the title of the last book I was able to read from start to finish," one fan of mysteries explains. "I read to my kids all the time, but I haven't had time to read for myself in recent memory." We examine the issue of time — or, more specifically, a lack thereof — and how it affects the reading habits of academic librarians in Chapter 5.

In other cases, the fact that academic librarians have trouble remembering the last novel they read is simply a case of failing memory. "I can't even remember the names of the two mysteries I am currently reading nor the name of the latest Dick Francis I read a couple of months ago," confesses one respondent. Another mentions that she recently read "a mystery novel that was lying around my parents' house over the holidays. I can't remember the name of it." Failing memory, however, seems to be a selective affliction, with librarians easily recalling the authors and titles of some works they have read while forgetting others. In other words, the inability to remember bibliographic information is tied to the impact the book made on the reader rather than the memory capacity of the respondent. For instance, one librarian dismisses the fiction he has recently read with the comment, "None memorable enough to list here." Another individual observes, "[I] don't pay a lot of attention to remembering titles. This is mostly just 'pleasure' reading which I consider somewhat inconsequential most of the time." Yet, while some librarians feel that the novels with which they occupy their free time are not worth remembering, we will see that the majority of academic librarians have found their pleasure reading to be anything but inconsequential — a fact that applies to everything from literary prize winners "to the latest Dick Francis."

Reading nonfiction

Fewer academic librarians provided the names of authors or titles of nonfiction they had recently read outside of work than was the case with fiction. While 480 respondents cited specific fictional works, 446 identified recently read nonfiction — a fact that reflects the overall popularity of fiction for leisure-time reading. Nonetheless, the same diversity that characterizes librarians' fiction reading is also evident in the range of nonfiction topics to which academic librarians devote their attention. Table 17 presents a categorical breakdown of the primary subject areas of the nonfiction books recently read by academic librarians, as well as two sample titles for each category.

As Table 17 shows, academic librarians' interests cover 21 different broadly defined subject areas — everything from travel literature to health and psychology books, from humorous musings to outdoor adventures. Most frequently cited were Autobiographies/Biographies and History/Geography, with 141 (31.6 percent) and 140 (31.4 percent) respondents, respectively. The category Religion/Spirituality/Philosophy follows, with half the number of respondents (70) as each of the previous two categories. At the same time, librarians are reading about an astounding range of topics within each of these categories. For example, titles in the Religion/Spirituality/Philosophy category examine such diverse subjects as Native American spirituality, Buddhism, Catholicism, Evangelicalism, Judaism, and the Shakers. There are canonical religious texts, such as the Bible and the Koran, as well as histories and guides to these texts, including *The English Bible and the 17th Century Revolution* and *The Bible for Dummies*. There are books that weigh in on the creationist debate and books that tell you to count your blessings.

Table 17. Subject areas of nonfiction recently read by academic reference librarians

Type of nonfiction	Sample titles	No. of librarians ($n = 446$)*
Autobiographies/Biographies	*It's Not About the Bike* (Lance Armstrong); *The Color of Water* (James McBride)	141 (31.6%)
History/Geography	*Isaac's Storm* (Erik Larson); *In the Heart of the Sea* (Nathaniel Philbrick)	140 (31.4%)
Religion/Spirituality/Philosophy	*Black Elk Speaks; Art of Happiness* (Dalai Lama)	70 (15.7%)
Travel	*Under the Tuscan Sun* (Frances Mayes); *Encore Provence* (Peter Mayle)	60 (13.5%)
Cultural, Social, or Political Issues	*Bobos in Paradise* (David Brooks); *Fools for Scandal: How the Media Invented Whitewater* (Gene Lyons)	56 (12.6%)
Science and Technology	*Does Jane Compute?* (Roberta Furger); *Genome: The Autobiography of a Species in 23 Characters* (Matt Ridley)	48 (10.8%)
Psychology/Health	*Reviving Ophelia* (Mary Pipher); *Eating Well for Optimum Health* (Andrew Weil)	45 (10.1%)
Anthropology/Sociology	*Confederates in the Attic* (Tony Horwitz); *An Anthropologist on Mars* (Oliver Sacks)	35 (7.8%)
Adventure/Outdoors	*Into Thin Air* (John Krakauer); *Touching the Void* (Joe Simpson)	33 (7.4%)
Literary Studies/Linguistics	*How to Read and Why* (Harold Bloom); *Into the Looking-Glass Wood* (Alberto Manguel)	32 (7.2%)
Art/Architecture/Design	*The Art of the Renaissance* (Bertrand Jestaz); *Shaker Built* (Paul Rocheleau)	29 (6.5%)
Nature/The Environment/Pets	*All Creatures Great and Small* (James Herriot); *The Man Who Listens to Horses* (Monty Roberts)	26 (5.8%)
Food/Gardening	*Kitchen Confidential* (Anthony Bourdain); *The Orchid Thief* (Susan Orleans)	21 (4.7%)
Work-related	*Literature in English: A Guide for Librarians in the Digital Age; Statistical Reasoning for the Behavioral Sciences*	17 (3.8%)
Film/Television/Media	*Hitchcock at Work* (Bill Krohn); *About Town: The New Yorker and the World it Made* (Ben Yagoda)	15 (3.4%)
Crafts/Home Renovation/Hobbies	*Shabby Chic* (Rachel Ashwell & Glynis Costin); *Landscapes and Illusion* (Joen Wolfrom)	9 (2%)
Music	*Dictionary of Electronic Music and Instruments; Swing Shift: All-Girl Bands of the 1940s* (Sherrie Tucker)	8 (1.8%)

Type of nonfiction	Sample titles	No. of librarians (n = 446)*
Humor	*Dave Barry Turns Fifty* ; *The Onion Presents Our Dumb Century* (Scott Dikkers)	7 (1.6%)
Business/Economics	*Business @ the Speed of Thought* (Bill Gates); *The Crisis of Global Capitalism* (George Soros)	5 (1.1%)
Feminism/Women's Issues	*Blues Legacies and Black Feminism* (Angela Y. Davis); *The Last Gift of Time: Life Beyond Sixty* (Carolyn Hellbrun)	5 (1.1%)
Sports/Automotive	*Wait Till Next Year* (Doris Kearns Goodwin); *Best of Car Talk with Click & Clack* (Ray Magliozzi)	3 (.7%)

*Numbers do not add to *n* and percentages do not add to 100% because respondents cited multiple types of nonfiction.

The diversity of academic librarians' nonfiction selections can also be viewed in the context of the most frequently read titles. As shown in Table 18, there are few titles in common: only 10 titles have garnered a place on the recent reading lists of more than five librarians.[9] The fact that there are so few overlaps suggests that, with the exception of a few especially popular titles, academic librarians tend to forge individualistic reading paths reflective of their unique areas of interest. At the same time, the titles that are listed in Table 18 present a snapshot of what was popular with the general reading public at the time respondents were completing our survey, much in the same way as the fiction titles listed in Table 16. While not exactly new publications, books such as the two Frank McCourt memoirs *Angela's Ashes* and '*Tis*, as well as *The Perfect Storm* by Sebastian Junger, have had runs on major bestseller lists that were sustained, in part, by movie tie-ins. Likewise, 5.2 million copies of Mitch Albom's *Tuesdays with Morrie* have been sold since its publication in 1997;[10] it was also the number one nonfiction bestseller on the *Publishers Weekly* list for 1999, before falling to number four the following year.[11] Somewhat more surprising — at least in terms of their first place ranking alongside the McCourt memoirs — is the unquestionable popularity of Bill Bryson's travel narratives. As was the case with John Grisham, academic librarians are just as apt to mention earlier Bryson titles as they are his more recent publications, with the dual result that no one title stands out and that respondents collectively have logged miles in Bryson's company from Australia (*In a Sunburnt Country*) to Appalachia (*A Walk in the Woods*). In fact, there are a good number of armchair travelers among survey respondents, with Travel being the fourth most frequently read nonfiction subject area.

"Connecting the dots": How reading books outside of work affects reference service

It should come as no surprise that the diversity of interests and tastes evident in academic librarians' book selections would produce a lively debate about how these materials help during reference work. We noted at the beginning of this chapter that 76.2 percent of academic librarians believe that reading books outside of work improves the

Table 18. Most frequently read titles: Nonfiction
(Question 15 in Appendix A)

Frequency of citation	Title	Author	Category
Cited by 15 or more librarians	*Angela's Ashes*; *'Tis* (20) Multiple titles, including *I'm a Stranger Here Myself*, *A Walk in the Woods*, and *In a Sunburnt Country* (20)	Frank McCourt Bill Bryson	Autobiography/Biography Travel
Cited by 10–14 librarians	*Tuesdays with Morrie* (12) *The Perfect Storm* (10)	Mitch Albom Sebastian Junger	Autobiography/Biography Adventure/Outdoors
Cited by 5–9 librarians	*The Greatest Generation* (9) *Into Thin Air* (9) *Galileo's Daughter* (9) *The Professor and the Madman* (7) *The Endurance: Shackleton's Legendary Antarctic Expedition* (5) *How the Irish Saved Civilization* (5)	Tom Brokaw John Krakauer Dava Sobel Simon Winchester Caroline Alexander Thomas Cahill	History Adventure/Outdoors Science History Adventure/Outdoors History

quality of the reference service they provide (see Table 14). As Table 19 shows, the experiences that these respondents talk about collectively point to six different areas of reference work that benefit from their reading, ranging from an increase in general background knowledge to readers' advisory services. What the data presented in Table 19 fail to convey, however, are respondents' diverse viewpoints regarding how, exactly, reading nonfiction and fiction helps librarians in each of these areas.

Table 19. Six ways in which reading nonfiction
and/or fiction helps in reference work
(Question 22 in Appendix A)

How reference service helps	No. of librarians (n = 382)*
Increase in general background knowledge; being well-rounded	88 (23%)
Awareness of specific titles and authors	65 (17%)
Directing patrons to specific books	60 (15.7%)
Increase in subject specific knowledge	40 (10.5%)
Readers' advisory services	19 (5%)
Selecting search terms and keywords; increasing vocabulary	15 (3.9%)

* Numbers do not add to *n* and percentages do not add to 100% because not all librarians provided specific responses in their answers. The *n* is taken from the total of "yes" responses in the first column of figures in Table 14. While 382 respondents stated that reading newspapers and magazines helps in reference work, some of these respondents merely indicated "yes" with no subsequent description of "how" such reading helps. Conversely, some respondents gave more than one "how" reason. We did not choose *n* = 287 (the sum of the six ways) so as not to overstate percentages.

Consider the comments of Joyce, who writes: "My ability to help people at the reference desk is based more on the totality of my educational background/life experiences/

good memory/current and past reading habits, etc. than simply my ability to recall one specific time I read one book that helped me answer a reference question." Other librarians also suggest that developing a foundation of general knowledge is a gradual, cumulative process, which makes it difficult to link specific pieces of information they know to specific books that they have read. Kara, for instance, reflects, "I am constantly building on the knowledge that I already have, and even though I may not be completely aware of the source when I am using it, I do know that my job performance would be on a much lower plane if I did not read as much as I do." Yet, some librarians do, in fact, attribute their ability to supply a patron with a particular piece of information to having read a particular book. Explaining that "[w]hen you get a reference question about something you read, you can get to the source quicker knowing where to look," Carla notes, "I just had a reference question about 7th century Ireland and how women had equal rights with men. Had I not read any of Peter Tremayne's books, I would not have known that Ireland, during the 7th century, had equal rights for women."

Echoing Joyce's contention that it is "the totality" of reading, learning, and living, rather than reading individual books, that makes her a better reference librarian, Daniel does not see much difference between reading newspapers and magazines and reading books when it comes to improving reference service. "It doesn't matter where the information comes from," he argues. "Books vs. email discussion groups vs. personal communications or the Internet. Content is what matters—a matter of currency and depth of coverage. Credibility and accuracy always matter too." Another librarian similarly concludes, "I do not see a difference between books and magazines/newspapers in helping with reference questions." While few would disagree about the importance of current and credible content, the librarians who have recommended specific books to patrons as sources for research, provided readers' advisory services, and bought books for their library's collection based on their own reading might reasonably disagree with the idea that there is no distinction in how reading newspapers and magazines versus books assists them in providing reference service.

We turn our attention now to each of the various aspects of reference work that academic librarians identify as having benefited from the books that they read during their free time. Beginning with how the background knowledge that is a product of reading works of nonfiction and fiction helps librarians to address patron queries, we pay careful attention to the myriad ways in which respondents utilize specific materials within each of the aspects of reference work listed in Table 19. The issues that respondents raise in these discussions provide valuable insight into how academic librarians process and apply different forms of information, whether it be a best-selling novel, a work of scholarly research, or a "how-to" guide. Taken together, their views suggest that academic librarians are very inclusive in their use of texts: all and sundry reading materials both inform and facilitate reference work.

Increase in general background knowledge and being a well-rounded individual

As was the case with newspapers and magazines, academic librarians most frequently find that reading nonfiction and fiction outside of work contributes to an increase in their general background knowledge and to their own sense of being a well-rounded individual. The experiences related by 88 respondents (23 percent) fall into this category. For many, this background knowledge manifests itself, first, as the ability to make connections between materials from disparate sources, genres, and time periods and, second, as the ability to elucidate this interconnectivity in the context of answering specific reference questions. In Chapter 3 we make the analogy between the pieces of information that academic librarians discover by reading newspapers and magazines and the pieces of a jigsaw puzzle. The more the librarian reads in current newspapers and magazines, the more complete a picture he or she has of local and world events, figures, and trends. In the case of books, however, there is no pre-determined picture of events to be filled in. Instead, the image that emerges is an entirely original creation whose pattern is determined not only by the books that a librarian reads, but also by the connections he or she makes among these diverse works. Respondents explain that the various pieces of knowledge accumulated over many years of reading nonfiction and fiction are raw materials that they weave together, with the resulting tapestry of information stretching across traditional boundaries of academic disciplines and genres. Mike observes, "I'm at an age where a lot of the fragments and bits I knew before are starting to come together into a coherent whole. Knowledge may by its very nature be contradictory and incomplete in a lot of ways, but things are beginning to come together for me in ways they didn't before. It is important to me as an information provider to know that this sort of coherence is possible."

Some academic librarians explain how the sense of coherence that Mike describes affects the quality of the reference service for the better. "When I get a less-than-perfect question, I immediately place it in light of all its possible contexts, line up the access points and start whittling away at it," Florence observes. "At the same time, one's own specific resources must be kept in mind, to actually answer the question. Because I read and have a reader's mind, I am used to hanging concepts out there in space and connecting them with other concepts." Frank stresses the need for reference librarians to be able to make connections among concepts, a process he refers to as "connecting the dots."

> Not ten minutes ago I was working with a student on a Whitman assignment. He was creating an annotated bibliography on *Leaves of Grass*. I was able to sit with him while he went through the MLA and tell him about the various critics, especially one who happens to be a fairly known poet (WD Snodgrass) but whose name means nothing to most people unless they read modern poetry. From there I was able to tell him about a book on American literature by Borges which offers some wonderful insights in period literature. I have no doubt that the search experience was enriched by my having read the poetry of Snodgrass, the fiction, poetry, and essays of Borges, and connecting those dots with the student.

While Frank's story demonstrates the process of making connections within a field, other respondents cite instances where they have "connected the dots" across various disciplines in order to assist patrons. Miranda recalls a situation in which she "had a patron come and launch into a convoluted explanation of a project he was embarking on, still in the incubation stage as far as thinking about it. Had to do with similarities in architecture and philosophy of Eastern religions and Egyptian mysticism. My background gave me at least a context in which to respond to his query, and to understand where he might be trying to go with the first steps of his research — understanding that there were religious, architectural, linguistic, and cultural aspects to his intellectual problem."

Librarians explain that their ability to identify the various intellectual contexts relevant to a patron's query also enables them to recognize the types of sources that will best meet the patron's information needs. Observing that "the more you read the better knowledge you have of subjects and how they relate to one another," Charlene suggests that "[r]eading indirectly helps you in categorizing and thinking generally and specifically. When I read about science topics, namely, the environment and animals, I get a better sense of where to go in the reference collection for what topics. Specific example: the topic 'animal habitat endangered by logging' sent me three places: the government section for laws, the psychology section for bioethics and the agriculture section for animals." At the same time, the ability to break down a reference query into its essential parts that Charlene describes also means that the librarian can recognize when the context of a query extends beyond the library's collection. Thus Erin describes the advantage of her reading books outside of work as "general knowledge — knowing when a question is not really a legal question but is, rather, a philosophy or sociology question. Materials will not be found in the law library."

As was the case with the background knowledge they acquired from reading newspapers and magazines, librarians note that reading nonfiction and fiction often means that they can immediately produce the answers to specific queries without having to first consult reference sources. And, as was also the case with newspapers and magazines, the examples respondents provide display an impressive array of knowledge collected from a disparate range of sources. One librarian recounts how "[r]eading a book on the human genome project helped ... answer biology students' questions for their lab reports on transcription." Another writes, "I had a student ask me if I knew of a black social worker that she could write a report on. I suggested Charles Spurgeon Johnson. The student came back at a later date to say that she had used my idea and was pleased to have earned an 'A' on her report." Historical topics are often featured in examples of reference questions that librarians answered directly, history being the second-most often cited subject area for recently read works of nonfiction (see Table 17). Faith notes that "[r]eadings in medieval history allowed me to explain feudalism and its breakdown to the rise of the modern nation state to a befuddled student." Exclaiming that reading books outside of work "helps every day," Nadine provides the example of "a student [who] asked for help finding a speech Benjamin Disraeli made at the Crystal Palace Exhibition. Since I have read a lot of British history, I was able to help [the student] without having to spend a lot of time figuring out what he was after."

While the previous examples focus on nonfiction, academic librarians also recall cases where reading fiction outside of work has helped them to directly answer patron queries. What distinguishes many of these examples is the fact that the queries being answered have nothing to do with literature. In fact, librarians explain that reading fiction has assisted them in tackling everything from history to science-based questions— subject areas that are more typically associated with knowledge of nonfiction sources. Nevertheless, Judy has noticed that "[h]istory and facts learned from fiction also give me background knowledge. The fiction I read tends to have some science and history background," while Mary Jo comments that "[b]ooks like *The Poisonwood Bible*, though fiction, reflect a historical era and therefore give me background on a time and place with which I am not familiar." Edna, who also enjoys reading novels with historical themes, observes that "students sometimes have a vague assignment like 'read a book on history before 1400 and find a review on it.' Reading historical fiction helps me to suggest a country or a character to them." Likewise, Barbara recollects that "[f]rom reading Colleen McCollough's Roman series I was more familiar with Roman history and was able to help a student narrow down a question."

While Edna and Barbara's experiences demonstrate how works of fiction can provide a historical backdrop that enhances an individual's understanding of a geographical place or time period, other stories illustrate how academic librarians have used the background knowledge gained from novels to answer very specific, non–literature related reference questions. Lucy explains that reading Barbara Kingsolver's *The Poisonwood Bible* enabled her to help "a student [who] wanted example of U.S. interference in African government and politics." Specifically, she remembered that "the Church hearings were mentioned" in Kingsolver's novel. While Lucy points out that "[t]here were lots of other ways to find the hearings," she also stresses that "it just saved time because I remembered the dates and the committee" from having read the novel. Sally also mined factual information embedded in a work of fiction — in this case in Robert McNeil's *Burden of Desire*, which she describes as "a novel set in Halifax around the time of the First World War." She explains that one of the novel's characters "is an Anglican priest and there is mention of the Anglican hymnal or prayer book being revised. Knowing the date that happened helped me with a reference question."

The stories recounted thus far illustrate how academic librarians use the background knowledge they have developed from reading nonfiction and fiction to help students devise and refine topics for assignments, to direct researchers to appropriate sources, and to answer queries directly. Respondents also point out that the books they read outside of work have assisted them in deciphering cryptic — or, as one librarian phrases it in the previous chapter, "untangling mangled" — reference questions. As with newspapers and magazines, librarians are able to supply key pieces of information based on their reading of nonfiction and fiction that facilitate the reference interview. "General historical and literary knowledge is often useful when library users mix up names, events, characters, book titles, etc.," one librarian observes. "We would probably get to the answer eventually, but it's quicker if my reading gives me a clue." Specific examples of getting to the answer quickly include "a question about 'the lines seen from the air in South America'," to which the librarian was able to apply material "read about three years ago about the Incas and their predecessors," and a question received by another respondent about a flying monkey, in which case the librarian knew that the patron wanted information about "a colugo, sometimes called a flying lemur, although it is not related to the primates."

Fiction once again plays an interesting role in helping academic librarians decipher patrons' reference questions. In many cases, what needs "untangling" are the fictional and factual components that have become intertwined in a patron's query. Librarians note that patrons come to the reference desk armed with a fictional character name or locale and ask for information — as was the case with one respondent who reports that "[t]he other day a [patron] asked me to identify Mrs. Dalloway"—fully believing that these characters or locales exist outside the context of the novel, that they are, in fact, part of "real life." Librarians also explain that their familiarity with the books from which these characters and locales originate enables them to disabuse the patron. Neil writes, "Because of my interest in science fiction, I was able to help one of my staff who was puzzled by a question from a community member who wanted background information on the country of Mu. The question was asked as if it were an actual country existing today, and not as if it were an imaginary, hypothetical place." Roy provides the following example from his experiences working in a law library: "A student was looking for the case of Jarndyce and Jarndyce. I started the search in the normal law library way. The case name was familiar. Then it hit me, that case is at the heart of Dickens' *Bleak House* and is entirely fictional (although based on the realities of the Court of Chancery). I could have spent a lot of time looking for that had I not read that book in university."

More than simply providing examples of how patrons can blur the boundary between fact and fiction, Roy's story also illustrates how the reference questions librarians receive offer resistance to the cognitive boundaries that define the collections and services of various academic libraries. While Victorian literature is not generally considered to be the domain of academic law libraries, this fact is of little consequence when the librarian is faced with a query about Jarndyce and Jarndyce. These stories suggest that the impact reading books, newspapers, and magazines can have on reference work should be construed not simply in terms of the narrowly defined context of a specific type of library, but rather in light of the more protean nature of the type of queries librarians receive. This applies not only to cases of "mangled" reference questions, but to the entire range of general queries librarians field because patrons often have broadly conceived notions of what services a library — any library — will provide. And, as we will see in the next section, patrons have similar preconceptions as to the knowledge a librarian who works in an academic library possesses.

Awareness of specific titles and authors

Roy's "Jarndyce and Jarndyce" episode points to another theme that characterizes respondents' stories. As Table 19 shows, 65 academic librarians (17 percent) note that having an awareness of specific authors and titles is crucial in providing quality reference service — an awareness that comes with reading nonfiction and fiction outside of work. One of these individuals remarks that "when dealing with undergraduates who are studying literature, the more I have read, the better off I am when trying to help them with their reference questions." Academic librarians have fielded queries from graduate students and faculty, as well as undergraduates, using their awareness of both nonfiction and fiction. What differentiates these examples from the Jarndyce and Jarndyce story and others categorized under the theme of general background knowledge is the fact that the patron's query itself purposively focuses on a specific title or author. The helpfulness of the librarian therefore depends upon his or her previous awareness of that author or title.

Academic librarians identify two separate components of author-title awareness in providing reference service, both of which are summarized in a comment made by Cybil.

She writes, "If the librarian has never heard of the author, it can take longer to locate information for the student. It can also help [when] the student is not sure who the author is of a particular work or what genre or time period the work is from." While both of these components underscore the need for academic reference librarians to exhibit some familiarity with authors and their works, in the case of the first component — the idea that "[i]f the librarian has never heard of the author, it can take longer to locate information" — the onus falls squarely on the librarian. These are not instances where the patron has failed to include, or has muddled, key pieces of information in his or her query. Rather, these are situations where the patron naturally assumes that the reference librarian is already familiar with the author or title cited in the query. For example, a student might need assistance in researching Gershom Scholem for an assignment, but would consider it unnecessary to have to identify Scholem as a 20th-century scholar of Jewish Mysticism when asking for help. "If you are in an academic setting and not erudite, then what good are you?" Priscilla pointedly asks. "Students have the reasonable expectation that faculty and librarians will be better educated than they are." In practical terms, the idea that the librarian "will be better educated" than the patron translates into an expectation that the librarian will be familiar with the titles and authors about which the patron is inquiring, meaning that the patron does not have to supply background information during the reference interview.

Interestingly, even librarians who indicate in their responses that they see no connection between reading nonfiction and fiction, on the one hand, and improved reference service, on the other hand, nonetheless cite the type of patron expectations described by Priscilla. At the same time, they see these expectations as a reflection of time-tested stereotypes of librarians — what one individual identifies as "a stereotype that all librarians read the classics or great literature." Tom acknowledges that "[w]hen a student comes to the desk with a question, he or she expects that a librarian has read lots and can answer literature questions. I am a science specialist and don't have a great interest in reading. It is strange to the students to encounter my reference interview questions about authors or types of works. I usually find what they need, but they find it hard to believe that librarians don't sit at their desks reading all day." While Tom emphasizes the fact that he is a "science specialist," what he fails to recognize is that patrons — and students in particular — tend to connect academic librarians to the environment in which they work. In other words, there is an underlying assumption on the part of students that librarians working in what Priscilla referred to as "an academic setting" will have been exposed to, at the very least, the same realm of information that the students themselves are now studying. As Nathan points out, "Reading is a fundamental element of an educated person, and when one works at a university, it makes sense to embrace the word, written or electronic!" If the university itself is a locus of wisdom and erudition, it is only natural that students would suppose that academic librarians would also be wise and erudite across a broad range of topics.

Librarians' stories stress the need to be aware not only of "the classics" but of new and current authors as well. On the one hand, there are comments such as those made by Keshia, who observes that it "helps if someone tells you they want to write a paper on *Madame Bovary* and you already know who the author is and that encyclopedias of French Literature might help." On the other hand, there are examples of how an awareness of recently published works also facilitates reference service. Martha remembers that "[a] student was looking for information on the author Sandra Cisneros. I knew that her work was only recently discovered and could explain why the Gale set 'Contemporary Literary Criticism' did not have an entry for her yet. We knew to look into other information sources." Similarly, Keith recalls that a patron "needed to find a review of the book *Welcome to My Planet* and because I had read it I knew it was published in 2000 and to look for it on the electronic databases instead of the print indexes as I would have if the article had been older."

Academic librarians emphasize the importance of being familiar with both "classics" and current literature in the second component of author and title awareness as well. While the first component focuses on the librarian's ability to efficiently and effectively deal with patron queries without having to ask basic background questions during the reference interview, the second component concerns the librarian's ability to fill in gaps in patrons' queries based on his or her awareness of authors or titles — the idea initially expressed by Cybil that reading "can also help [when] the student is not sure who the author is of a particular work or what genre or time period the work is from." Examples of this type of gap-filling include queries on everything from canonical literature to bestsellers. Jill recalls an instance where "a student asked for a book written by *Les Misérables*," and she was "immediately able to tactfully suggest that *Les Misérables* might be the title, not the author." Rita was able to identify an author even when the patron came armed with an incorrect name: "[A] woman was looking for a poet. She told me his name, ... that the poet was British and married to a famous American, who has died. I didn't find anything under the supplied name, but the more the patron talked, the more I began to suspect she was looking for Ted Hughes. Without my own knowledge, I would have said 'we don't own anything,' and the patron would have been out of luck." Charles remembers that "some years ago" a patron "wanted to read a book he had heard about that was about the North Carolina mountains and had a funny title with words like flowers or something unusual or colorful.... I had read Tom Wolfe's *Kandy-Kolored Tangerine-Flake Streamline Baby* and remembered that it had a chapter about bootlegging in the North Carolina mountains. This was the book the patron wanted." Charles concludes his story by observing that "I would never have found the answer if I had not read the book."

The missing pieces supplied by academic librarians often answer queries concerning books that have recently become popular through film or book-club tie-ins. Essentially, these materials are analogous to the current events "hot topics" that respondents mention in the previous chapter. Describing the recent outpouring of interest in one of these "hot topic" books, one respondent writes, "I believe the media coverage influenced the inquiries." Brooke recalls that she could supply the title *The Perfect Storm* when a student inquired about "the book about swordfishers who drowned that was made into a movie." Donna tells of the influx of requests for a specific work that a movie tie-in can produce.

> I remember when a new movie based on a story by Stephen King came out.... It was called *The Shawnshank Redemption*, and EVERYONE wanted the novel/movie tie-in to this film. Well, the "novel" was actually a short story contained in a collection written by King sev-

eral years earlier, and IMPOSSIBLE to find or even identify that well. The collection had a different title than just one story contained within it, and we all felt sure that a newer collection must have also had the story anthologized or republished. Only it didn't, and no one was prepared to accept our word that this was it for the movie tie-in.

At the same time, movie tie-ins often produce a heightened interest in other books focusing on the same theme, time period, characters, or locale as what is shown in a newly popular film. Reference librarians therefore need to be aware not only of the work on which the film is based, but also sources that relate to this broader context. Faith recalls assisting a "faculty member [who] wanted to know what other books on Horatio Hornblower had been written after seeing recent movies."

Of course, books that top various bestseller lists also garner much media attention, with the result that academic librarians "try to be aware of bestsellers and the like." Gail observes that patrons have come to her with the query, "I'm looking for a book by the woman who wrote *The Poisonwood Bible*, do you know who that is?" As we note at the beginning of this chapter, at the time respondents were completing our survey, *The Poisonwood Bible* had entered the literary consciousness of the general reading public. It follows, then, that patrons who had read this novel would be interested in finding out about Kingsolver's earlier or later works, including *Prodigal Summer*, which was published in hardcover in 2000 and which ran for 17 weeks on the *Publishers Weekly* bestseller list that year.[12] Pam provides another example, this one concerning Mitch Albom's memoir *Tuesdays with Morrie*. In fact, Albom's memoir can be associated with two forms of media coverage already mentioned—bestseller lists and movie tie-ins—and has an Oprah tie-in as well. Pam recalls, "Very recently a patron had been told about a book which chronicled the final period of a professor's life. He thought that one of the professor's students had written this book. The student wanted to know: the name of the professor, the name of the student, the name of the book, what disease the professor had that caused his death, and if the story had been made into a movie which he might watch, rather than having to read the book." She explains that since she had read the book herself, she was able to answer all of the above questions, including the fact that "the professor's name was Morrie Schwartz; the student's name was Mitch Albom; ... The disease from which the professor suffered was Lou Gehrig's disease and that Oprah Winfrey had bought the rights to the book from which a movie, starring Jack Lemmon (as Morrie), was made."

Academic librarians' stories demonstrate how reading books outside of work produces an awareness of authors, the titles of books they have written, and the years in which these works were published—all of which result in respondents' being able to effectively and efficiently guide patrons to information sources or to directly answer their queries. Many librarians link their ability to recognize a title, even from partial information provided by patrons, to their having read the book themselves, as Pam does in her story about *Tuesdays with Morrie*. Likewise, Gail writes, "I have been asked by people questions like, 'Oh, there's a book out now about an interracial marriage—it was written by the son, would you know that book?' It was *The Color of Water*, and I had just read it." The argument could be made, however, that knowing this type of information—for instance, that *The Color of Water* is a memoir written by an African American author about his Caucasian mother, or that Professor Morrie Schwartz suffered from Lou Gehrig's disease — does not necessarily depend upon having read these books. Rather, it could also be the product of what Joyce had termed the "totality" of knowledge which comes from being a generally well-read and culturally aware individual. In the two examples just cited, one could argue that this information could be gleaned from book reviews in the *New York Times*, for example, or from an interview with the author published in a magazine or conducted on a morning television program.

Indeed, a few respondents indicate that their familiarity with some books is not a result of reading them, but rather of skimming through them as they come into the collection. These individuals regularly shelf-study both reference and non-reference materials, a practice which Brian, for one, thinks has been seriously neglected in librarianship of late. Observing that "[f]amiliarization with reference books as they come into the collection has helped in the past," he notes that "[w]e've become so needful of keeping up on the electronic database interfaces that there's been a falling-off of this practice, which has had some unfortunate consequences. Students are not finding some of this information, [which is] not available online, because the reference librarians don't know about it." Kevin provides an example of shelf-study in action, recalling, "A professor wanted a list of all the Academy Award winning movies for a collection development project. A senior reference librarian could not put her hands on the list and I happened to be nearby and overheard the question. The previous weekend I had been skimming through the *World Almanac* to see what kind of information was included. I remembered that there was a list of Academy Award winning movies.... It was exactly what the professor was looking for."

Nonetheless, librarians cite instances where the quality of the reference service they provide has been enhanced by having read the book (or play, or poem) on which the patron's query is based. Molly remembers when "[a] student came in trying to find some material for a paper on Shakespeare's *Richard III*. I have read almost all of the plays, including *Richard III*, so I was able to assist this student in looking for resources. Plus, the student can tell that I've read the play, so we can jump right into the research process." Part of being able to "jump right into the research process" means understanding the work in question and therefore having a better sense of what sources the patron might need. "I have been able to discuss ... concepts with a philosophy student based on both of us having read the same book," Peggy asserts, "and that made it easier for me to anticipate where he would be taking his research." Likewise, Eric comments, "I recently re-read some works by James Joyce. When a patron came up to find criticism on Joyce, I could relate better." (He adds the editorial aside, "By the way, the more I read of Joyce the less I like him.")

In some cases, the search process is expedited because the librarian is familiar not only with a given book, but also with the relevant literary criticism, having looked up this material for his or her own interest. Edith notes that "[s]everal years ago I was reading some of Barbara Kingsolver's novels and became familiar with her writing style. Students at our college read her books and ask for literary criticism and biographical information, and I am able to suggest a number of different resources to them (beyond *Contemporary Biography* and *Contemporary Literary Criticism*) because I know her work." Similarly, Diane recalls that "a student was asking for criticism about Tim O'Brien's fiction book *The Things They Carried*. I love the book and had already looked up some criticism for myself."

In addition to facilitating the search process, librarians also note that having read a particular book in advance of receiving a query about it allows them to provide insights into the work that can be of further assistance to the patron. In some cases, this means helping the patron to understand the meaning of the work in question. One of these individuals writes: "Based on my reading, ... I have also been able to comment on works or authors when they come up as part of reference searches and give students a better idea of what the book is about or the author's style." Shannon provides the following example: "Because I had read Annie Dillard, when a student came in complaining of not understanding [Dillard's] use of language, much less [being able] to write a paper about her work, I was able to explain the idea of being able to accept ideas even when we disagree with them and that [the ideas] don't necessarily have to be linear and discrete. We looked at a passage and gleaned the beginnings of an idea for a paper." At the same time, librarians also can act as a sounding board for patrons' own interpretations of a book. Ben remembers, "I had a student that joined a book club and needed to sound out her reactions to [Caleb] Carr's *The Alienist*. I had just finished reading the book and listened to her comments." In addition, having read specific titles enables librarians to provide their own insights regarding public reactions to these works. As one respondent who is "frequently asked about censorship of particular books" observes: "It's an enormous help if I've read the book myself when I answer why a work has been challenged." Not surprisingly, librarians mention J.K. Rowling's Harry Potter series in this context, with one individual noting that "[h]aving read the Harry Potter series, I was able to discuss it with a patron in conjunction with a discussion about children's literature, banned/challenged books, and freedom to read."

The ability of librarians to address issues surrounding the publication and reception of recent books such as the Harry Potter series points to the issue of temporality. As we note at the beginning of this chapter, a number of librarians cite their educational background in general, and in particular the books they read during the time of their formal education, as playing a key role in developing a foundation on which they base their reference service. Mildred explains that "with a Masters in English & Comparative Literature and an MFA in Writing, I can much better help students with literary criticism reference questions." While this undoubtedly is the case, other respondents emphasize the need to continue building upon this foundation by keeping current — in other words, by reading materials that have subsequently entered the literary and popular cultural realms. Explaining that "[r]eading fiction helps familiarize the librarian with authors and nonfiction helps librarians learn more about different subjects," James stresses that "[b]eing well read on a variety of subjects is essential in providing reference services, and it is not possible to simply rely on what you've read in college."

Directing patrons to specific books

As with the issue of author and title awareness, this third most often cited theme of how reading nonfiction and fiction outside of work facilitates reference service also concerns a librarian's familiarity with specific books. Rather than providing examples of how their awareness of books has coincided with patrons' queries on those very same titles, here librarians recall instances where they have recommended books that they themselves had read as research sources for patrons. As Table 19 shows, the stories provided by 60 librarians (15.7 percent) fall within the category "Directing patrons to specific books." These stories resemble the situations described in the previous chapter in which academic librarians were able to direct patrons to newspaper or magazine articles they had read — materials that turned out to be exactly what the patron needed.

Academic librarians identify a number of advantages to guiding patrons directly to a work of fiction or nonfiction that are similar to those first mentioned in the context of recommending specific newspaper and magazine articles. One of these advantages is being able to locate materials that might not be unearthed through online searching, including images. Won-Young recounts how "[a] professor wanted the picture of the earth from space taken by Apollo 10 as well as the moon viewed by Apollo 13 for slides in a class demonstration. Because specific pictures are not included in the indexes of most books, this would normally present something of a problem. Since I read books on astronomy almost every day, I remembered seeing these pictures and was able to find them rather quickly." Respondents have faced this same challenge in cases where online searching would not yield bibliographic records for essays in an anthology or individual topics within a book. Because they have read the books themselves, however, librarians are cognizant of the specific issues addressed in these works and can therefore recommend a wider range of sources to their patrons. Carolyn recalls that "[a] student needed a book on the Black Death. We had a few books specifically on it. But, I had read Barbara Tuchman's *A Distant Mirror*, which has a wonderful section on how the plague altered life in the 14th century, and helped create our modern world. I would not have found this book with a traditional subject heading search." For this very reason, Irene "keeps logs" of the books she has read, recording bibliographic information and an abstract for each entry. Not only is the log "useful for reference questions" because a book "previously read might have a chapter on what the patron is seeking," but this system also "impresses the patron."

While such examples demonstrate an unmistakeable interest in the patron's query, they also suggest that academic librarians are well-versed in the strengths and weaknesses of the library's collection. In other words, by reading books outside of work, the reference librarian is knowledgeable about not only the information to be found in numerous books, but also the books that can be found in the library's collection. To a great extent, this knowledge comes from librarians using the collection to feed their own intellectual interests. Doris writes of a patron who "wanted books or tapes to teach themselves Italian. Because I had had the same need I could tell about the books and tapes in our collection from first hand experience." In some cases, knowing "first hand" about materials in the collection enables the librarian to guide the patron to less obvious choices. This was the case with Peggy, who, having "read quite a few plays and monologue books" was able "to steer [a student] to some material that was not as mainstream." In other cases, reading within a collection translates into the librarian knowledgeably assisting patrons with queries that technically fall outside of his or her own area of expertise. Mark describes a patron's "question about the significance of a set of petroglyphs in the region" where he works. "I could have directed the person to the social sciences librarian but I try to read most of the books about the southwest," he states, noting that he therefore was able to supply the patron with "an author's name."

Increase in subject-specific knowledge

As Table 19 shows, 40 librarians (10.5 percent) describe the impact of the books they read outside of work in terms of augmenting their knowledge of a specific subject area — knowledge that has subsequently helped them deal with patron queries at the reference desk. Their stories provide an interesting contrast to the comments made by librarians who discussed the contributions that reading books during their free time has made to their general background knowledge. While not discrediting the advantages that a general background knowledge can bring to reference work, librarians' responses in the "Increase in subject specific knowledge" category stress the importance of reading books in a given area of expertise. In some cases, these individuals are published authors, and their identity as a scholar within a field means that they are, either by job title or by reputation, the resident expert in that field at the library where they work. Because of their role as both researcher and subject specialist, these librarians need to keep current in their field of interest. Howard, who we noted earlier has written five books in the field of American Indian Studies, observes that "students and faculty expect me to know my field and be familiar with general histories and cultures of tribes." For this reason, a few librarians point to books as being more helpful in their reference work than newspapers and magazines. "I tend to get difficult Renaissance questions referred to me," explains one of these individuals. "It is only because I've been reading both fiction and nonfiction about this era for 20 years that I could pinpoint the answer to such questions. Speaking for myself, I have found reading books to have been more valuable to my service as a librarian than reading newspapers and magazines."

Some librarians explain that their knowledge of a subject area has grown over time and over the course of many years of advanced education. Tim writes: "Although I am a reference librarian, I am also a historian with several books and numerous articles under my belt. So anyone who comes in with a project in American history is pointed my way. After 8 years in graduate school in history, it would be very difficult for me to give you a case where a single book or even two that I read outside of working hours allowed me to answer a reference question." Yet, because of their knowledge of a field — a knowledge that is built upon their educational background and reinforced by independent research — these librarians have an innate familiarity with the resources in their area, placing them in an ideal position for fielding relevant reference questions. Bonnie, who has two master's degrees and a doctorate in Biblical Studies, describes how "I can always go directly to the shelf and pull off just the right resource (or resources) without even making a trip to the card catalogue. I know the subject and reference books so well." She provides the example of a student "working on a paper on Cathedrals. His classmates had checked out all of the books on cathedral architecture from the stack. In moments I had open before him Eliade's *Encyclopedia of Religion*."

Readers' advisory services

Academic librarians also identify readers' advisory services as an aspect of reference service that is improved by their reading of books. As Table 19 shows, 19 individuals (5 percent) describe instances where the nonfiction and fiction titles they read during their free time have enabled them to provide patrons with "recommendations of a 'good' book to read." Additionally, 10 librarians separated readers' advisory services from other aspects of their reference work. They therefore elected to describe this particular facet of their job in response to the last question of the survey, which addressed how reading nonfiction and fiction impacts non-reference-related work (see Table 20). The comments of these 10 individuals are included here.

Readers' advisory services are not usually associated with academic libraries— a fact mentioned by a number of respondents. And yet, academic librarians do recall times where they have been called upon to make recommendations of this type. In contrast to instances where librarians recommended books for patrons' research projects, here respondents are filling patron requests for books (and novels, in particular) that they can read for pure and simple enjoyment. For some academic librarians, these requests are a rare occurrence. Rita recalls having a student ask her for recommendations of "a suitable book to read to an elderly woman." She points out, however, that "[t]his kind of readers' advisory seldom comes up in the academic setting, although it is a staple of reference work in the public library." For others, readers' advisory service is a regular facet of their work — one that stems from the fact that "people always seem to ask a librarian, 'What have you read lately?'" In other words, the issue of whether the librarian works in an academic or public library is immaterial to the patron. At the same time, a number of respondents note that their libraries have facilities akin to what Pearl describes as "a Recreational Reading section in the browsing area of the library." The idea that patrons would want recommendations "for something good to read" is a natural result of the availability of such materials.

The patrons who most often ask for advice on what to read are students. "I sometimes have students ask me what I would recommend for 'fun' reading," Emily notes, "and I can often recommend something I've just read myself such as *Open House* [by Elizabeth Berg] or *Sis Boom Bah* by Jane Heller." Kurt reports that "last month a volleyball player needed a good read. I suggested P[atricia] Cornwell." And Rosalind has found that readers' advisory services are especially in demand "around the end of the semester when students are starting to look for books to read for pleasure." In contrast to the library where Pearl works, with its "Recreational Reading section," Rosalind's library does not "have a large fiction collection." She has, however, compensated for this lacuna by lending books from her own personal collection "to students over the break," observing that "[m]uch of what I read is not too 'reference' oriented."

In addition to general requests for "a good read," librarians have also been called upon to recommend books that meet certain criteria. In some cases, patrons want "more of the same" in terms of a certain style of writing, setting, or time period. Noting that reading on his own time "definitely helps in readers' advisory reference queries," Joe elaborates: "It's helpful to be able to tell a patron (with confidence arising from my own reading experience) that if he/she enjoyed reading Flannery O'Connor, they'd probably also enjoy Walter Percy, Eudora Welty, Carson McCullers, etc." In fact, Joe mentions that providing this service makes him feel "[s]ort of like Amazon!"— a reference to the online bookseller Amazon.com, where similarities among authors and titles are highlighted in a feature called "Customers who bought this [book] also bought...." In an example that focuses on setting, Erica recalls a case where she "had a patron wanting to get a book, a work of fiction, set here in Colorado." She writes: "I had just finished reading a book by James Doss set in southern Colorado just a couple of hours' drive from here. I recommended this author to the patron and it seemed just want he wanted." At the same time, Erica also notes the difficulty she would have had filling this request had she not read Doss' work herself. "Since I had read this author's books and knew they were in our collection, the question was very easy to handle. Trying to find this info on the online catalog would have been much more difficult."

Selecting search terms and keywords and increasing vocabulary

As was the case with readers' advisory services, respondents mention the role that reading nonfiction and fiction plays in helping them to select search terms and to increase their vocabulary in the context of reference service and other areas of academic librarianship. As Table 19 shows, 15 individuals (3.9 percent) describe how reading books during their free time assists them when devising search strategies. In addition, ten librarians (2.5 percent) discuss issues related to keyword searching and use of vocabulary in response to the final survey question, which focuses on non-reference related aspects of academic librarianship (see Table 20). The following discussion incorporates librarians' responses to both the reference-focused and non-reference focused questions.

The idea of being able "to offer alternate search terms and strategies for [the patron] to use in the catalog and the periodical indexes," as one librarian describes it, echoes earlier discussions of the usefulness of newspapers and magazines in identifying the most fruitful keywords or subject headings. Librarians again point to the fact that, in addition to suggesting search terms, the books that they read outside of work enable them to understand the underlying concepts those terms embody. Specific examples include a case where "[a] student was irate" because of an apparent lack of materials on the topic of "feminist Christology." Because the librarian "had read several books on the topic," she was able to use these volumes to point out "subject headings that would net [the student] more than 40 books." Similarly, it was Maria's reading on the topic of "Birth Order Effects" that enabled her to recommend that phrase as a search term to a psychology student using a periodical index.

April points out that the ability to recognize key terms helps not only with searching for books and articles through library-based catalogs and indexes, but also when trying to navigate the Web. "Students were asking for information on Homo sapiens, [and] the other term they used was human morphology," she recalls. "Because of my interest in and reading about anthropology [and] archaeology I knew that they wanted a cladistic tree of the human family and I helped them find a web source." She also remembers the time when "[a] faculty member was setting up a course on early tool use. My anthropology reading came in handy there also, and I was able to use a variety of terms to locate web resources."

At the same time, academic librarians credit reading nonfiction and fiction outside of work with their ability not only to wield subject-specific terminology when conducting online searches, but also to expand the vocabulary they use in all types of reference encounters. Theresa has found that "my reading has helped me develop a large vocabulary and

a stock of bits of handy information. I have been asked what a Swedish turnip is and somehow knew it was a rutabaga. I have been asked about myasthenia gravis (I went and
found the printed information for the patron but I could tell them at the start what kind
of a condition it is)." And Charles recalls the time when "[a] student came to the desk
and said he was trying to remember a word that he thought was classical in origin and
meant something like haughtiness or pride. I suggested hubris and he said he was
delighted because this was the word he was trying to remember."

The generalist/specialist debate

Before we examine the impact of reading nonfiction and fiction outside of work on
non-reference related aspects of academic librarianship, we would like to address an issue
that appeared repeatedly in respondents' comments concerning many of the areas of reference service listed in Table 19, but that is most relevant to the idea of reading books as
means of increasing a librarian's general background knowledge and of reading as a means
of bolstering a librarian's knowledge in specific subject areas. Academic librarians tend
to view the utility of the materials they read during their free time in terms of one of the
following two concepts: that reference work mainly benefits from reading broadly across
many fields, topics, and academic disciplines; or that reference work mainly benefits from
reading within a few targeted, specific subject areas. In many cases, a librarian's alle-
giance to either of these viewpoints was first evident in their responses to the survey
question of whether reading outside of work — regardless of the format of the materials
read — can help to provide better reference service (Question 18 in Appendix A). As we
note in the introduction to this section on academic librarians, and as is shown in Table
1, the majority of respondents (88.2 percent) feel that reading does, in fact, improve reference service, and they emphasize the importance of keeping up with local, national,
and international events and contemporary cultural issues by reading newspapers and
magazines. But beyond these current events and issues, the question of what information is most beneficial to reference librarians and what materials—fiction or nonfiction,
scholarly or popular works— would be of most assistance in providing reference service,
becomes more complex.

As librarians express their views on the impact that reading nonfiction and fiction
outside of work has on the quality of the reference service, two groups emerge. On the
one hand, there are the generalists, who endorse the idea that academic reference librarians should read broadly across a number of fields and disciplines. One respondent from
this group even suggests that reference librarians be called "professional generalists."
Another individual comments, "I can't imagine someone who has not read widely doing
well in this position." On the other hand, there are the specialists, who believe that academic reference librarians should concentrate their reading on a specific topic or subject
area. This viewpoint is best summarized by the following observation: "I feel that the
broader your base of knowledge, the better reference service you can provide. However,
I do feel that you need an area of expertise."

Academic librarians from both the generalist and specialist camps provide con-
vincing arguments and examples to support their views. Among the generalists, there is
the idea that the broader your knowledge base, "the better you are at understanding cus-

tomer needs." The librarian is able, at the very least, to construct a framework for understanding patron requests on many different topics. Hugh writes: "My reading in nonfiction allows me to be aware of current thinking in a variety of areas that come up during reference interactions. Having a broad background allows me to move from topic to topic. It gives me a feel for where to start" in areas that are not his specialty. Hugh's comments allude to an important fact, namely, that some respondents who espouse the generalist viewpoint nonetheless are specialists in given subject areas. Yet, these individuals do not feel that the benefits of reading outside of work are confined to their areas of expertise. In fact, they see their leisure-time reading as a way to gain a handle on areas outside of their own specialties. As Lori explains: "Even if I am not an expert in a particular subject, it helps to have some idea of the topic in order to provide a more in-depth reference interview. My students frequently comment on the variety of topics with which I am familiar and my ability to help them focus their research as a result." Colin notes, "I specialize in business, communications and law, so I need to have a general understanding and awareness of current events in those areas." Yet he also observes, "All of us answer questions in a wide variety of disciplines, so the wider your reading and exposure to all materials, the chances are that at least you will have read something on the topic(s)."

The generalists acknowledge that it is impossible to know something about everything, and that therefore "you are bound to get questions on subjects about which you have no clue." Paula clearly recognizes the inevitability of these questions when she writes, "I certainly don't read anything with the express intention of providing better reference service." Instead, she explains that "[y]ou never can tell what will be useful! Because of what I've read, I feel very confident in dealing with a lot of obscure humanities-types of questions." Noting that "[s]erendipity is the key here," another librarian observes: "I cannot predict how my reading will assist, nor will I change my personal reading habits to 'bone up' for work." In fact, librarians' comments point to the fact that there is no need to change their "personal reading habits." As Maxine notes, "All of what I read can be useful in a reference situation. The questions are always varied and they are not always academic and scholarly."

Conversely, other librarians emphasize the benefits of concentrating on a few subject areas in their outside reading. Lauren's comments are typical.

> I think that, by reading various types of materials outside of work, I provide better quality reference service to some people who use my library. Because I choose to read subject areas like literature, history, political science, as well as current events, I think I provide better quality reference to people asking questions in those areas. If I know more about the topic, I can ask them specific questions to determine what exactly they need. In a subject area such as chemistry or physics, I may take longer to get the answer, or I may not give them exactly what they need, because I do not feel as comfortable in those subject areas.

In contrast to Paula, who does not read "with the express intention of providing better reference service," respondents such as Lauren select reading materials with an eye to providing better reference service in designated areas. As another librarian writes, "I do specific 'work' reading in my spare time because I want to increase knowledge in my subject areas." Therefore, while these librarians believe that "[r]eading material helps very much

[to] provide better quality reference service," they also believe that this reading "should be focused on the specialty of the librarian."

Indeed, it is not difficult to see how the experiences of librarians such as Lauren would reinforce the benefits of reading in a few specific subjects areas. Consider a scenario in which an academic reference librarian whose personal interest in, say, the art and politics of Italian city-republics from the twelfth through seventh centuries has led her to read widely in this area. Over time, this individual might notice that, because of her reading, she is able to effectively answer questions concerning the cultural and political history of Venice, Rome, and Turin to help guide patrons in their research, and to recommend good titles that she has read. She also begins to develop a reputation among students, and by association, faculty, as being an expert in this field — a reputation that is cemented by co-workers who send patrons with questions on Italian medieval and Renaissance history her way. The high repute in which this librarian is held is part of a score of obvious benefits that arise from reading works of nonfiction and fiction about this specilized topic, thereby fueling the librarian's interest in reading more of the same.

Arguably, the inclination to read broadly across many subjects or deeply within a few also depends on the nature of the library where the respondent works. On the one hand, a member of the generalist contingent explains, "I work in a general academic library, i.e., we cover all subject areas. I just find the wider read you are, the easier it is to help people out. This type of environment rewards the generalist, and my reading certainly contributes." On the other hand, respondents who work in specialized, rather than general, academic libraries tend to tailor their reading to these specific areas, as in the case of Jan, who works in a design library and therefore is "studying and reading about design." Business librarians Todd and Francesca also try to focus their reading, with Francesca commenting that reading "nonfiction in my subject area, which is business, is very helpful." Similarly, Lee-Ann notes that "[m]ost of our programs are technical and vocational, such as Nursing, Telecommunications, Computer Science, Business, and Engineering Technology. Many of our reference questions tend to be technical in nature." She therefore gravitates toward business and health-related topics when selecting reading materials.

Some librarians who work in specialized academic libraries call into question the idea that only reading in their field can prove useful at the reference desk, as well as the idea of coordinating reading to these specialized subjects. Xiu Ping — a business librarian — makes comments that provide an interesting contrast to those of Todd and Francesca: "[T]hough we are a business library, I've had questions about Handel's 'Messiah' by students who didn't understand that it is a piece of music. My general knowledge was invaluable in answering this question. I increase my general knowledge through my reading." Roy's story of how a student came looking for a legal case that existed only within the pages of a novel by Charles Dickens is another example of how general reading can play a significant role in providing reference service even in as specialized an environment as a business or law library. In addition to getting a handle on patrons' queries, another benefit of reading widely, Louis suggests, is to garner ideas that can then be applied to one's own field: "Reading literature away from my immediate area of specialization (U.S. history) can also be beneficial in keeping one's mind open to new ideas and topics." The idea, then, is to find a balance between reading in one's specialty and reading broadly in order to be a well-rounded individual. As one respondent neatly summarizes, "Reference librarians are one of the last 'Renaissance' people left, and the more we know, the better our service."

The good, the bad, and the inevitable: The impact of reading nonfiction and fiction on other areas of academic librarianship

At the beginning of this chapter, we noted that a greater percentage of academic librarians said that the books they read during their free time are more beneficial to non-reference related aspects of their job (80.9 percent) than to reference work itself (76.2 percent). Their stories touch upon a wide range of job aspects—14 in total, as listed in Table 20. Some of these stories have familiar themes. When asked to describe how reading nonfiction and fiction has helped them in areas of librarianship other than reference service, some respondents reiterate factors discussed in the context of reference work: an increase in their general knowledge and a sense of being well-rounded individuals; familiarity with specific authors and titles; readers' advisory services; and the ability to select appropriate search terms and comprehend the topics to which they apply. Table 20 shows the number and percentage of librarians who mention these four factors outside of the context of reference work; the specific points these individuals raised have already been addressed.

Table 20. Aspects of academic librarianship, excluding reference work, that have benefited from reading nonfiction and fiction (Question 23 in Appendix A)

Aspect of academic librarianship	No. of librarians (n = 398)*
Collection development	78 (19.6%)
Increased knowledge; being well-rounded	51 (12.8%)
Personal outlook	46 (11.6%)
Making conversation	41 (10.3%)
Maintaining or increasing credibility	37 (9.3%)
Bibliographic instruction	35 (8.8%)
Relating to people	25 (6.3%)
Outreach and programming	21 (5.3%)
Workplace/professional issues	21 (5.3%)
Familiarity with specific authors and titles	15 (3.8%)
Implementing new technology	14 (3.5%)
Readers' advisory	10 (2.5%)
Selecting search terms and keywords; increasing vocabulary	10 (2.5%)
Bibliographic control	3 (0.8%)

*Numbers do not add to *n* and percentages do not add to 100% because respondents cited multiple aspects.

Other respondents revisit areas of librarianship that benefit from reading newspapers and magazines outside of work as well: collection development; making conversation; maintaining or increasing credibility; bibliographic instruction; outreach and programming; workplace and professional issues; implementing new technology; and bibliographic control. Respondents in the "Outreach and programming" category note that the books they read during their free time have helped them with everything from mounting exhibitions at the library to "proactive liaison work" with various departments. As an invited speaker at a book club — one where club members "do not actually read the book" but instead "hire a speaker to describe the book to them" — Maxine discussed a work she had recently read. She characterizes this experience as "good PR for my university." Similarly, librarians who relate their experiences of implementing new technology (14 respondents, or 3.5 percent) explain that they directly apply the knowledge they have gained from books on technological subjects, the general idea being that "[r]eading Internet, Web, and HTML books is invaluable in Web design and Web searching."

Librarians also apply the books they read outside of work to various situations they encounter at work. The 21 individuals (5.3 percent) in the "Workplace/professional issues" category cite reading material that ranges from standard management texts to Caroline Knapp's *Drinking: A Love Story*, with the respondent in this case noting that "my reading of highly autobiographical work re-sensitized me to struggles evident with some employees in my division." Julie has also used nonfiction to handle personnel issues, remarking, "One of the nonfiction books I read most recently, Barbara Pitcher's *Drama of Leadership*, has helped me tremendously by giving me valuable insight in understanding leadership styles and the types of people one works with and how to deal with them when they are in positions of power." Citing a different workplace issue, Elliot explains that his "reading of Neil Postman's *Technopoly* was very interesting given that we are living in the information age." He mentions "the current discussions on 24/7 reference [service] and the debate on how our work is driven by technology" as areas in which "Postman's book has given me some good insights."

The fact that the same aspects of academic librarianship benefit from reading books, newspapers, and magazines would seem to suggest that there is little difference among these materials. In other words, all information regardless of specific format is beneficial — the same viewpoint expressed by a few respondents in terms of how reading improves reference service. In fact, while librarians' stories cover many of the same aspects of librarianship, the specific themes of the stories are unique. We first look at academic librarians' experiences in four of these areas: collection development; making conversation; maintaining and increasing professional credibility; and bibliographic instruction. These are areas in which respondents identify a distinct role for reading nonfiction and fiction in facilitating the work of academic librarians. We then turn our attention to two new aspects of academic librarianship that benefit from reading nonfiction and fiction outside of work: "Relating to people" and "personal outlook." We conclude this chapter by examining the types of books academic librarians cite with unmitigated enthusiasm as having had a positive impact on their work, both at and away from the reference desk.

Collection development

Seventy-eight librarians (19.6 percent) describe how they have applied their reading of nonfiction and fiction to collection development issues. Collection development is not only the most often cited aspect of academic librarianship listed in Table 20, but is also a good example of how reading nonfiction and fiction helps academic librarians in ways that both correspond with and diverge from those associated with reading newspapers and magazines. In the previous chapter, respondents describe how newspapers and magazines enable them to establish "a frame of reference for purchasing items for the library," alerting them to topics or books that should be represented in their collection. The connection between having a broad frame of reference — one that is informed by knowledge of current events and topics of concern to the library's user community — and having a collection that covers all of that community's needs applies here as well. The primary distinction, however, is that librarians are able to recommend for the library's collection specific books that they themselves have read.

One benefit of making purchasing decisions based on first-hand knowledge of a book is that it avoids costly missteps. As one librarian explains, "We have a very limited book budget. Having read a book, I feel more able to determine its worth in adding to our collection." One aspect of determining a book's worth is being able to judge the validity of its content. Nicole has found that "simply reading books on history" enables her not only to increase her knowledge of "the area of history that the author is writing about," but also to "learn more about an author's 'authority' on a subject." William notes: "If I hadn't read Mark Williams' translations of Endo Shusaku's novels before, I wouldn't [have recognized] that his latest book on Endo is an authoritative one and confidently ordered it for the library." The ability to recognize or to question a particular author's authority that comes with having read this individual's work has led Joe to wonder about the pertinency of the various reviewing tools that generally inform collection development decisions. He writes: "There have been many instances in which, judging by book reviews, I would have decided for or against the selection of a particular item, BUT due to my knowledge of the author's talents or non-talents from my own reading experience, I have decided the other way."

In addition to authority, another aspect of determining a book's worth is being able to ascertain its suitability for certain types of collections. Vera knows that "[t]here are certain authors that I would not recommend for an academic fiction collection" based on her own reading of these authors' work. Other librarians explain that reading, and enjoying, the work of a specific author leads "to selecting or adding other titles by the same author." Librarians also describe the influence of reading nonfiction and fiction on their collection development responsibilities in terms of knowing the suitability of topics. One respondent explains that she intends to add to her library's collection the book she is currently reading "about gifted but mostly poor students at a Los Angeles high school since it is a good book on education with a local angle." Often, a librarian's own interest in a topic results in the addition of material on this subject to the library collection. As Dina points out, "I have ... been able to recognize gaps in collections, which prompts me to go on book hunts." For Edith, "personal concerns about cell phones" prompted her "to find some new books for the library in the technical and medical areas relevant to cell phone usage."

A librarian's interest in a subject area is expressed not only through the act of collection development, but collection maintenance as well. Brad, a self-described "armchair climber," explains, "We have a School of Recreation Administration with both graduate and undergraduate students. My interest in climbing books ... has helped in collection development in this area. For example, I made sure that a replacement copy of *Into Thin Air* [by John Krakaeur] was purchased when the library copy disappeared, realizing that it includes a valuable discussion of the roles and responsibilities of professional guides—a topic of interest to our Rec. students and faculty." An interest in given authors can also lead a librarian to pay greater attention to collection maintenance issues. As Shelley notes, "I read *Mrs. Dalloway* by Virginia Woolf and this motivated me to look more closely at our holdings on Woolf, which caused me to realize that a number of copies of her novels were considerably the worse for wear, so I ordered new copies."

The stories provided by these respondents demonstrate how a librarian's personal interest in a specific topic or author results in a renewed focus on the library collection itself. Prompted by intellectual curiosity, these librarians have assumed the role of patron, objectively examining the library's holdings in a subject area of interest, discovering that the books they seek are missing, or that works by certain authors are in disrepair. In fact, Shelley adds that her focus on the state of the Virginia Woolf novels at her library "also inspired me to pay more attention to the physical condition of other frequently read authors and to replace some copies."

Making conversation

As Table 20 shows, 41 academic librarians (10.3 percent) discuss the advantages that reading nonfiction and fiction bring to making conversation — a slight decrease from the 51 respondents (11.7 percent) who in the previous chapter cite newspapers and magazines as helping them with this same aspect of librarianship (see Table 13). While respondents use newspapers and magazines to develop a sense of collegiality with students, co-workers, and faculty by discussing current events at the reference desk, the water cooler, or the faculty party, here this sense of collegiality is established by sharing views about recently read books. Librarians explain that discussing popular books is a particularly useful way to "build working relationships" with faculty or other library staff members. Melanie and her library colleagues, for instance, regularly discuss authors that they enjoy, with Jonathan Kellerman and Patricia Cornwell being special favorites.

Some librarians emphasize the role that book discussions play in generating extradepartmental conversation. "Librarians at our institution are considered part of the faculty, so when we gather in department meetings and parties, it is helpful to have read various types of material," Phyllis explains, adding that "[r]ecently, a group of us discussed David Guterson's *Snow Falling on Cedars* and its movie adaptation." Adele even notes that the majority of her reading "other than mysteries has been done due to a suggestion from one of the faculty members. Any time a faculty member or administrator mentions an author or title, I try to look at the book. This gives me a talking point when I see them and makes for good relations for the library." Other librarians agree that, more than simply a way of sharing bibliographic interests, reading books outside of work can be a public relations tool for the library. This fact has prompted two librarians to join faculty book clubs at their respective universities. Dorothy reports, "I joined a faculty book discussion group. The interaction with this group has helped tremendously in other areas of faculty collaboration."

The experiences of other respondents in the "Making conversation" category focus on developing strong relations with students. As one respondent sees it, books provide "areas of common interests to talk about. In terms of patron relations, that means I'm not that mysterious 'library lady.' I'm a person who has the same reading habits they do." Meredith recounts, "Since I am allowed to read non-professional literature while I am at work, I often read fiction during slow times in the evenings at the reference desk. While I was reading *The Fight Club* [by Chuck Palahniuk], a student noticed and sat down to talk to me about the book/movie. We had a very provoking conversation and I have no doubt that this kind of rapport-building and good will spreads [to] that student's friends and makes them more likely to ask me for help." Helen, explaining that incoming freshman at her university are assigned a specific book for summer reading and that she has led discussion groups about those books, notes that these assigned readings often "are books I have read already, so it gives me an opportunity to share my feelings about the books with a group of students and compare our reactions."

Some librarians recollect having the type of stimulating conversations described by Meredith and Helen about the Harry Potter books. Based on their accounts, these conversations are less about the plot lines of the books than they are about librarians' reactions to the entire Harry Potter phenomenon. Peter notes that "[p]eople have seen my copies of Harry Potter books on my desk and ask about them — if I've enjoyed them, do I think they deserve all the negative publicity, etc. It's refreshing to share comments with others who have similar interests (in juvenile fiction, not witchcraft!)." The focus of these conversations suggests that academic librarians benefit not only by keeping abreast of popular cultural trends, but by actively participating in them as well — the idea expressed earlier by one librarian that "[i]t is not possible to relate to the craze over Harry Potter if you have not read any of it." At the same time that reading these books enables librarians to relate to what is happening outside of the academic realm, it also allows them to contribute to and benefit from a sense of workplace collegiality. As one respondent explains, "Well, when everyone in the library has read the *Harry Potter* books, you have a common thing to talk about."

Maintaining and increasing credibility

As Table 20 shows, 37 librarians (9.3 percent) describe how they have been able to maintain and even increase their professional credibility by reading nonfiction and fiction outside of work — an even greater percentage of respondents than those who discuss in the previous chapter the impact of reading newspapers and magazines on this aspect of their job (18 librarians, or 4.1 percent). As was the case with newspapers and magazines, academic librarians explain that reading books "gives the impression ... that, in general, I sometimes know what I am talking about." This impression, in turn, reflects well not only on the individual, but also on the library profession as a whole. "I'm just a more interesting person, and I can have a meaningful conversation about almost any topic," Eleanor remarks. "I think I am a positive representative of the library profession." Vincent agrees, commenting that "[p]atrons tend to take you more seriously if they sense that you are well read. They respond positively when you make reference to current titles or recently reviewed books."

Some academic librarians see the benefits of reading nonfiction and fiction in terms of defining their own professional reputation. Indeed, while reading newspapers and magazines is construed as means of establishing a basic professional credibility, the knowledge respondents have acquired from reading books outside of work has enabled them to stand out as individuals within the profession. Kyle explains:

> [G]eneral reading is particularly useful as I work with other college faculty. I am conversant with topics important to their research or writing and it gives us a basis for interaction. Clearly they respect me more when I know about their fields (incidentally, it rarely works in the reverse. They rarely appreciate the changes in the library field and we don't judge them for that lack of knowledge, but we are expected to know about theirs). Being a librarian often seems an uphill battle to gain faculty respect and reading in other subject areas (including literature) is invaluable.

Likewise, Sadie notes that her "ability to communicate with many of our subject specialists in the language of their field(s) is a direct result of reading nonfiction. This ability has helped me gain their respect. This in turn has afforded me greater freedom to engage in projects of my choosing, and to teach a variety of instructional classes."

Like Sadie, some academic librarians emphasize that they have gained the "respect" of faculty members—respect that is often manifested in various forms of professional accolades. Kyle has been "asked to serve on search committees and evaluation committees in other departments because [the faculty] feel I am a colleague aware of and knowledgeable in their field." In another example of committee appointments, Sonja reports that her "deep interest in environmental reading got me a position on the Environmental Studies Steering Committee," noting that "no other librarians have been asked to do this sort of thing." Chuck explains that "[b]ecause of knowledge gained in reading books on technology and multimedia use in education, I have been asked to assist many faculty members ... in developing courses" on this topic. Librarians attribute the professional honors they have earned to reading fiction as well as nonfiction, with one respondent observing that "I have often introduced lecturers at forums or participated in workshops or served on panels as a result of my background knowledge of literature, specifically current fiction."

Bibliographic instruction

The 35 librarians (8.8 percent) who discuss the impact that reading nonfiction and fiction has on their bibliographic instruction work make a point similar to that of their colleagues who discuss this aspect of librarianship in relation to reading newspapers and magazines. Reading widely enables them to develop search examples that will grab and sustain the attention of students. As Lois writes,

> My favorite example of this has to be from a Composition 2 class that has a film/movie theme. While explaining to a class how to locate film criticism and information about the writers/directors, the instructor began explaining how today's movies [have] their roots in the silent era. I could see several students tuning her out because they had no way of relating silent films to today's action dramas. I started talking about how Chuck Jones and the writers for the Looney Tunes cartoons used slapstick humor to create many of the Bugs Bunny and Daffy Duck gags and it was obvious they were able to translate those ideas in

the modern films. If I had not read several books about the creation of the Looney Tunes cartoon, I would not have been able to bridge that gap.

Like Lois, Grace also uses the books she reads to "bridge that gap" between past and present, as well as the generation gap between students and instructors. Remarking that she is more likely to accomplish this feat "than some younger and less well-read librarians," she recalls the presentation she gave to students in a literature survey class. By comparing the "Congo setting and anti-colonialism" theme of *The Poisonwood Bible* to Joseph Conrad's perspective from 100 years earlier in *Heart of Darkness*, she was able "to stir the interest of the class."

Librarians also note that the books they read during their free time assist them in highlighting issues within their instruction sessions. Because she is familiar with the literature that students are assigned, Ellen uses as search examples themes and issues that students might wish to investigate later in their assignments. She explains: "[I]f I am giving a lecture to an English class and I am familiar with the works the class is reading, I can usually give a more thorough and in depth lesson on using the library because I'll know what types of themes, meanings, etc. the students will probably want to look for in a particular book—i.e., a student reading *The Catcher in the Rye* will probably want to research adolescent identity or a similar variation of the 'coming of age' theme." Having read *Killer Algae* by Alexandre Meinesz, Sam used the topic of this book—the introduction and subsequent invasion of the alga *Caulerpa taxifolia* into the Mediterranean Sea—to compare "the development and reporting on alien species in the popular and scholarly journal" in a research methodology class.

Personal outlook

We now turn our attention to two new aspects of academic librarianship that are affected by reading books outside of work. As Table 20 shows, 46 librarians (11.6 percent) discuss how reading nonfiction and fiction titles informs their personal outlook, or as one respondent describes it, "contributes to my well being." In fact, there are three different components to how reading affects academic librarians' well being, both at and away from work. First, a number of respondents explain that the nonfiction and fiction they read during their free time helps them to flex their mental muscles. "I feel that reading books makes me think and keeps my mind nimble," Phil observes. Other librarians echo this sentiment with such piquant phrases as "keeping one's synapses well oiled" and "helps keep my mind from going to mush." The result of keeping one's mind in a suitably firm state is the ability to be critical, objective thinkers. "THAT," Nadine emphasizes, "permeates everything we do."

While some librarians stress that reading books outside of work helps them to keep their minds in good working order, an even greater number of respondents claim that it prevents them from losing their minds altogether. When the issue of stress relief came up in the previous chapter, respondents commented that they often utilize stress reduction techniques they had first read about in newspapers or magazines. Here, however, the librarians note that reading books outside of work is itself a means of reducing stress. As Jackie remarks, "Reading is my therapy." Likewise, Don finds that reading books "is very good for my mental health." In fact, a number of respondents describe the effect of reading as preserving their sanity, including Harriet, who explains that "the less I read, the less sane I am," and Daryl, who writes: "Saves my sanity, which I use on the job."

Daryl's comment raises another valid issue, namely, that it is not only the reference librarian who benefits by staying stress-free, but also the librarian's patrons and colleagues. Emily addresses this trickle-down effect, explaining that "[r]eading fiction outside of work relaxes me and gives me the chance to 'recharge' myself in order to be a nice, relaxed librarian the next day at work!" Marcus adds, "Reading is a big part of my life ... keeping me sane and happy, therefore it has got to help with all aspects of my job." Part of being able to "recharge" after work is removing oneself not only physically, but also mentally from the work environment. As Roy explains, "[A]nything that helps keep you relaxed and grounded in life outside of work is bound to help. If all I read were reports and professional journals, I'd be a basket case in a year or two." While Roy reads in order to stay "grounded in life outside of work," others see reading as an escape route from reality. Leah, for example, observes, "I get to live a bunch of different lives vicariously within this one that I have." Noting that "[r]ecreational reading is very good at relieving stress and taking me away from workplace worries or concerns," Lorna reports that she was able to escape both mentally and physically from a seemingly endless project at work by reading a mystery at home: "I recently was working on updating many web page links—hours of very tedious and time-consuming work. After work I got engrossed in a mystery set in the Yorkshire Dales. I soon forgot about the web updates and was able to relax and return to work the next day ready to finish up the project."

While academic librarians explain that reading books during their free time provides both mental stimulation and respite from job-related stress, some respondents also point to a third aspect of how reading affects their personal outlook: it provides inspiration and motivation both at and outside of work. They suggest that reading is more than simply a means of escaping quotidian stresses; rather, it engenders "a rich inner life" that they can draw upon. Frank describes reading as a means to "keep the mind alive. The body willing. And the spirit engaged." He notes that it "[g]ives me something to look forward to, a reason to go home" at the end of the work day. For some, this "rich inner life" is not simply a source of comfort, but of confidence as well. Peggy asserts that being well-read contributes to "my personal sense of worth." For others, reading serves as reminder to continue to strive, both personally and professionally. "It has helped me to be a better human," writes Shirley. Marion simply states that "sometimes it inspires me to try harder."

Relating to people

Perhaps the most intriguing area of academic librarianship that benefits from the fact that librarians read both nonfiction and fiction outside of work is the area of relating to people. The experiences categorized in Table 20 as "Making conversation" involved specific types of social interactions, whether discussing the Harry Potter series with students or using the latest Tom Clancy novel to make small talk at a cocktail party. The stories that we have characterized as "Relating to people," however, focus more intently on the theme of understanding human behavior in general—an understanding that 25 academic librarians (6.3 percent) say is greatly enhanced by the books they read during their free time. Sylvia comments are typical: "The most consistent type of help that my reading has [provided] in my job is helping me to understand different types of people and how variable the human species is in interests, attitudes, beliefs, etc., which makes my job easier since I deal with so many patrons and other personnel." Penny has also come to understand "how variable the human species is" through the books she reads outside of work, prompting her always to "to see something from another's point of view."

How exactly does reading nonfiction and fiction allow librarians "to see something from another's point of view?" One answer is that books have introduced them to diverse people, conditions, and cultures, resulting in their being "more open ... to diverse people and their needs for information" at work. Hugh explains that "[b]eing alert to conditions in other regions of the world has given me an increased sensitivity to working with students from those and other regions." Another librarian observes that by reading widely "[y]ou become a citizen of the world, even if you don't travel." Likewise, Gloria notes that her interest "in many authors who grew up and/or [are] living outside the U.S." means that she can begin to understand people in "very different circumstances" than her own. For other librarians, the concept of diversity refers to people's various individual abilities, rather than cultural background. Paige remarks that the information she has picked up "about learning disabilities via reading ... has helped me recognize problems with student workers and with patrons.... [W]ithout this knowledge I might have assumed these workers or patrons were dumb or weird." Agnes agrees, commenting that "[t]he book I'm reading by a person with autism will help me better understand those with autism. Hopefully this will make me better able to respond to their requests if they come into the library."

Fiction plays a very prominent role in helping academic librarians relate to the diverse people they encounter each working day. As with nonfiction, reading fiction — especially novels — provides what one respondent describes as "additional insight into human behavior and relations that supplement our own life experience." While reading nonfiction enables a person to travel the world, fiction helps the reader to explore the world of emotions and to apply the understanding one takes away from these fictional encounters to actual situations. Describing "the reading of fiction as an indispensable tool," Stuart explains that it provides him with "insight into life experiences other than my own, which helps me develop a sense of empathy and understanding that ... make me a more patient professional. I am more willing to listen and understand constraints under which the students find themselves as they try to meet educational and personal demands."

Other respondents take the idea that fiction provides insight into human behavior a step further, casting fictional characters as prototypes for people they expect to encounter in their working life. Just as patrons sometimes confuse fictional and factual situations in their reference queries, librarians explain that they sometimes intentionally blur the distinction between reality and fiction in preparation for their work. In other words, while the patron may come to the reference desk asking the librarian to identify Mrs. Dalloway, the librarian is mentally prepared for the possibility that the patron approaching the desk just might be like someone out of a Virginia Woolf novel. "Well-drawn characters in fiction, especially the unusual ones, give me a dry run so to speak on meeting new and unusual people," Agnes reports, adding that "[t]his can be a bit more challenging in 'real' life." Two other respondents also use fiction as a type of test run for future "real life" encounters, including Gloria, who comments, "My reading of fiction … has helped me in the sense that many of the characters in a novel are similar to people I meet." Noting that "[r]eading fiction helps me to understand human beings generally," Edward elaborates, "Fictional characters represent people we meet daily…. I often find it amusing when I meet these people in daily life."

Which books have helped academic librarians in their various job responsibilities?

Considering the variety of sources that respondents cite in their stories, the question of what types of books academic librarians have found to be most helpful in their work is largely rhetorical. We have seen that some accounts feature bestsellers that librarians themselves have just recently read — titles such as *The Poisonwood Bible* and *Tuesdays with Morrie*, for example. Tasha's interest in the writings of Isabelle Allende (whose novel *Daughter of Fortune* is listed in Table 16 among the works of recently read fiction) enabled her to enlighten a patron who "had a vague idea that there was some relation between George III and the Chilean author." The connection? "Isabel Allende's daughter Paula died from porphyria," Tasha explains — the same disease that plagued the British monarch and that the patron had seen portrayed in the film *The Madness of King George*. Likewise, we have seen examples of how librarians have applied their readings of canonical works, including Shakespeare, Virginia Woolf, and Charles Dickens, to name but a few.

In fact, librarians cite everything from "a lengthy report on German dyes" to *Clear Your Clutter with Feng Shui* as having helped them answer patrons' reference queries and in other aspects of their work. "I'm into Icelandic sagas," one respondent confides. "When our English instructor was considering using Eyrbyggja saga as a text for an introductory literature class, I was able to recommend it." Dwayne mentions that "[m]ost recently there was a book on presidential communication and one on Star Trek … which helped me answer questions at the desk." This same diversity characterizes the stories librarians provide about how reading non–English language materials enhances the quality of the service they provide, both at the reference desk and in other capacities. Rose recalls that "a professor wanted a copy of a Garcia Marquez book in Spanish; we didn't have that work in Spanish in our library, but I was able to supply him with a copy from home because of my own reading habits and interests." And Annette writes, "The outside reading [of] books in Italian helps me to skillfully interpret foreign language sources of information," referring to how the "knowledge I absorb on Italian language and culture and history" assisted her in the processing of a recent "donation of a large collection of Italian history books."

Often, respondents refer to the advantages of reading genres rather than individual titles. Yolanda credits travel literature — the fourth most popular category of nonfiction materials recently read by academic librarians (see Table 17) — with helping her to "know where places are in the world." "I'm often surprised that a lot of people do not know geography," she reflects. "It has come up before that I was able to identify places for people who have heard that something happened somewhere and they have no idea where the place is. Example: East Timor." A number of librarians are quite vocal in pointing out the benefits of reading "self-help" or "how-to" books on all sorts of topics. Bryn explains that one can

> [n]ever know what will be useful to a reference librarian. One of the first questions I got where my library flat out did not have the answer in its large collection came in the second month I was a librarian, i.e. in August 1972. The local public library had not been able to answer it, so the user came to the university library instead. The question? "What are the hand signals used to tell a sheepdog what to do when it is herding?" I now know the answer, both from experience watching sheepdog trials, training dogs and talking to trainers, and [from] reading … how-to books and magazines.

And, as Kurt observes, self-help books also help in resolving workplace issues: "[they] have helped me cope with difficult personalities (including my own) here at the workplace. I have worked with alcoholics, with tyrants, with nutcases, and nuisances. I trudge right along."

Just as academic librarians have found that a variety of books can assist them in their work, their stories point to a similarly diverse range of instances where a specific genre of materials has helped them. These instances cover a number of different factors that we have examined over the course of this chapter. An example of this phenomenon is the genre of mysteries and thrillers. Academic librarians are, without a doubt, fans of "murder and mayhem." Of the 366 respondents who indicated that their favorite reading materials include works of fiction, 145 individuals (or 39.6 percent) mention some variation of the mystery genre, whether legal suspense novels, crime thrillers, or honest-to-goodness whodunits. "Many of the reference librarians are mystery fans," agrees Irene. "Part of the unwritten job description is that [one] buys the new Sue Grafton, another buys the new Janet Evanovich, etc. The novels are shared among the reference department." As further evidence of this popularity, Table 16 shows that 14 of the 41 authors (34.1 percent) whose works are cited by at least five librarians write either mysteries, suspense novels, or some variation of the thriller theme — Sue Grafton and Janet Evanovich among them. This sharing of books among librarians contributes to workplace collegiality, creating both personal affinities and conversational fodder.

We have already seen that reading mysteries can provide academic librarians with a much-needed source of stress-relief, with Lorna's escape to the Yorkshire Dales after a tough day at work being one such example. But mysteries and other crime-related readings have assisted respondents in providing reference service as well. Maud notes that all reading materials are of some benefit to the reference librarian —"even murder mysteries since often the techniques or setting offer information exposure." This has certainly proven to be the case for Mindy, who has a "3000+ volume personal mystery collection." "We have students in [a] multicultural class writing papers about authors who have heroes or heroines who are not WASPs," she explains. "Mysteries have lots of different types of heroes and heroines." With regard to her well-stocked personal library of mystery novels, Mindy adds that friends and family "have told me that I will probably die before I can read all of the books." In addition to student assignments, academic librarians have also recommended mysteries to patrons for leisure reading. In our discussion of readers' advisory service, we noted that Kurt recommended the works of Patricia Cornwell to a student-athlete. Similarly, Bruce notes that "[w]hen a patron asked for mysteries that were more 'on the edge' than Agatha Christie or Tony Hillerman, I was able to recommend Carol O'Connell's Mallory books."

The same diversity that characterizes academic librarians' use of mysteries also applies to religious books. Reading religious works has had a tremendous impact on their personal outlook and on their ability to relate to people. Colleen writes: "For me, religious materials provide a value system that has helped me in relating to patrons, faculty, and co-workers moment to moment." Conversely, another respondent observes that "[r]eading about historic aspects of the Bible convinced me that the Bible is folklore more than anything. It has no more to do with God than fairy tales. I don't waste time attending church any more. At one time, I was even a deacon." Librarians have also pointed to the utility of religious books at the reference desk. Paula recreates the following recent dialogue she had with a student:

> STUDENT: I need to find a book in the Bible. It's called the Book of Songs.
> ME: !
> STUDENT: I went to the Internet and looked at a lot of Bibles, and it had every book except that one.
> ME: Well, let's take a look at a Bible here on the reference shelves. (We got to the shelves; look through, and of course there's no Book of Songs. I know something's amiss, but I can't place it yet.) What class is this for?
> STUDENT: It's for Humanities. We have to read a story and compare it to the Bible.
> ME: Well, if you're comparing it to the Bible, are you sure that what you need is the Bible?
> STUDENT: I think it's in the Bible; he (the teacher) said it was ... but it's a Chinese Bible or something.
> ME: (lightbulb flashes on over head) OH! You need the *Book of Songs*! It's a collection of ancient Chinese texts translated by Arthur Waley. I READ IT A LONG TIME AGO.
> STUDENT: That must be it! We've been reading the Bible in this class, so I thought that this was a book of the Bible, but now I get it.

In addition to being able to untangle reference queries, academic librarians have also helped patrons by directing them to various sources on religious topics. One respondent assisted a student who "needed information on Protestant theology in conflict with Calvinism. She was having difficulty because she did not understand some of the terminology." Chuck explains, "I read many books about the Creation-Evolution debate. I have answered several questions in which knowledge gained in this area has helped me. Last month I was able to help a student develop a bibliography in this area. The knowledge I gained by outside reading of this material greatly assisted me in providing a more detailed answer for the student." Jordan was able to recommend *Occidental Myth* by Joseph Campbell to "a student trying to uncover the meaning behind elements in Buddhist sculpture."

The advice that Kara passes on from her graduate school reference instructor is consistent with various experiences that academic librarians have shared here about the effect that reading nonfiction and fiction during their free time has had on their work. The idea that the reference librarian should "READ EVERYTHING" does not signify that academic librarians need to alter their reading tastes to mesh with the needs of their patrons or the focus of their library. In fact, the opposite is true. As respondents point out again and again, the reference queries they receive are so varied as to preclude the option of "prepping" for work, by reading specific fiction and nonfiction titles. It is precisely this diversity that supports the idea that any book can have a significant impact, whether a scholarly text on a historical topic or a novel with a historical theme. As we have seen, academic librarians have put both to good use. The importance of reading outside of work extends beyond the information contained in individual books to include the librarian's ability to apply these various pieces of information, to develop a "reader's mind" that can "connect the dots" across various topics and disciplines, and to help patrons make similar connections. "I think that all reading helps a reference librarian," Shelley concludes. "Since any topic can come up, it helps a reference librarian to read widely, simply to be aware of the world, including the world of ideas and opinions, in as many fields or across as many disciplines as the individual librarian can manage to take an interest in." At the same time, Shelley points out yet another benefit for the academic librarian: "Reading makes one aware of all that is available to be known and even should suggest how much one does not know, since humility also helps a reference librarian's work."

5

You Can Lead Librarians to Knowledge, But You Cannot Make Them Think

Factors affecting how, and how much, academic librarians read

In this chapter we ask whether librarians want to read more outside of their working hours. We also examine the various environmental and psychological factors that prevent them from reading as much as they would like. Keeping in mind these factors and the stories that respondents tell of their actual work experiences, we then examine academic librarians' responses to the question of whether they would be able to provide better quality reference service if they were given paid work time to read the various materials that they choose to read during their free time.

Would librarians like to read more outside of their working hours?

As Table 21 shows, 76 percent of academic librarians would like to read more during their free time. The mere prospect of reading more elicited such enthusiastic responses as "Absolutely," "Always," "Oh, heaven, yes," and one librarian's resounding "YESYESYESYESYES!!!!" Yet, the responses of the 115 (21.5 percent) librarians who indicate that they do not want to read more outside of their working hours are equally emphatic, including one individual's heartfelt plea, "No. Please. No." Debunking the assumption expressed by one librarian in the "yes" camp that "I would think that almost anybody would" want to read more during their free time, a number of librarians explain that they already spend an adequate amount of time — or even too much time — reading. For some, reading an adequate amount is a direct result of their finding the time to read at work. "You have to understand that the Reference Desk is twenty feet from the Periodicals Browsing area," one respondent comments. "I read anything I'm interested in on my lunch or dinner hour. This is the reason I don't subscribe to many periodicals at home; they're readily available at work." Similarly, Hugh observes that "I occasionally

115

have the opportunity to scan the *New York Times, Los Angeles Times, Wall Street Journal,* [and] *The Globe & Mail* while at the reference desk."

Table 21. Would academic reference librarians like to read more outside of work? (Question 16 in Appendix A)

Response	No. of librarians (n = 534)*
Yes	406 (76%)
Possibly	13 (2.4%)
No	115 (21.5%)

* Percentages do not add to 100% because of rounding.

Other respondents explain that they already read a sufficient, if not excessive, amount outside working hours: any additional time spent reading would be at the expense of other aspects of their lives. Allison writes, "Actually, I think I get to spend enough time reading (which makes me pretty lucky). I could probably spend more, but I think my husband would be upset by that (as he is sometimes upset by the amount of time I currently spend reading since he doesn't get to read nearly as much as I do)." In addition, many activities already occupy their free time. Kit explains that there is "[n]ot enough time because of other commitments (family and household). Also, I do watch television programs in the evening so time is limited for reading." Gloria "would like to participate more in social activities with other people as well as do volunteering."

The challenge of allocating free time both for reading and other activities is evident in the responses of the 13 librarians who are somewhat ambivalent about wanting to read more. These individuals weigh what they identify as the relative advantages and disadvantages of dedicating more of their free time to reading. Not surprisingly, the most often mentioned disadvantage is lack of time to pursue other interests. Alice's ambivalence is representative: "Yes, because I love to read," she explains, and "no, because I have other things in my life that I enjoy doing." Another librarian comments along the same lines: "Yes, but I'd like to have more time [for] many more different activities in addition to reading." Eleanor, who also provides a "Yes and no" response, makes an interesting distinction between the act of reading and the end result of reading. "I wish I already knew more, so I wouldn't have to read so much," she muses. "There is just so much to learn in this world of ours. How about a computer chip in the brain that instantly gives us a library of information. Or, being able to absorb all the information in the books as I just look at the closed books on the shelves." In other words, Eleanor construes reading not only as a leisure-time avocation, but as a means of achieving the specific goal of increasing her knowledge. Her comments also suggest that, if she really could learn through some form of computer-chip osmosis, she would be inclined to spend her leisure time on other activities and interests.

The idea of reading to gather information, as opposed to reading as a hobby, underscores the responses of those librarians who do want to spend more time reading outside of work. Among these 406 respondents, 55 specify the *type* of material to which they would like to devote more reading time. As Table 22 illustrates, 60 percent of these 55 individuals would like to spend more time reading nonfiction, while 50.9 percent mention fiction. More time for reading newspapers and magazines is a somewhat lower priority, cited by only 27.3 percent of librarians. Interesting patterns emerge when these percentages are compared with what respondents had identified earlier as their favorite reading materials. For instance, the academic librarians who want to spend more time reading nonfiction are almost evenly divided between self-identified nonfiction readers and those who prefer to read fiction or newspapers and magazines. In contrast, of the 28 librarians who would like to read more fiction, 78.6 percent are already dedicated fiction readers, while only 21.4 percent favor other reading materials. These ratios are reversed in the case of newspapers and magazines: while 28.6 percent of respondents who want to dedicate more time to reading newspapers and magazines already count these as favorite reading materials, the remaining 71.4 percent prefer to read nonfiction or fiction.

Table 22. Materials that academic reference librarians would like more time to read

Type of material	No. of librarians (n = 55)*	No. of librarians for whom this material is a departure from current reading preferences	No. of librarians for whom this material is consistent with current reading preferences
Nonfiction	33 (60%)	17 (53.1%) (n = 32)[†]	15 (46.9%) (n = 32)[†]
Fiction	28 (50.9%)	6 (21.4%) (n = 28)	22 (78.6%) (n = 28)
Newspapers and magazines	15 (27.3%)	10 (71.4%) (n = 14)[†]	4 (28.6%) (n = 14)[†]

*Numbers do not add to *n* and percentages do not add to 100% because librarians cited multiple materials.
[†]Not all librarians indicated their current reading preferences in their survey responses.

Arguably, the desire to read materials that diverge from current preferences and practices is another way that academic librarians strive to be culturally and intellectually well-rounded. One respondent even comments that he would like to read "not necessarily more, but more variety." Rather than simply wanting to increase the quantity of books, newspapers, and magazines they read, academic librarians want to spend more time reading in order to fill what they recognize as gaps in their knowledge, or simply to pursue a reading plan that differs from more frequently traveled paths. Kayla, who in general favors "specific women writers," wants to focus attention away from the "fiction by Southern Africa women writers" that she has spent much of the past year reading and toward "more how-to-do-it or do-it-yourself books." While Jared is "interested in pop culture" and subscribes "to approximately 20 magazine titles," he remarks, "I would like to read more fiction/nonfiction but don't have the time." Kate admits that "[o]bviously, my reading is not well-balanced because of all the crime fiction. I would like to read more magazines and nonfiction." Olivia, whose favorite reading material outside of work is "Inspirational/Christian fiction," writes that "I would like to read more nonfiction, but I find fiction more relaxing."

Olivia's comments point to an inherent tension between what academic librarians want to read and what they feel they should be reading. This tension is especially evident in the case of respondents who would like to read either more fiction or fewer news sources. As one librarian who wants to read more "fiction or natural history and art books" comments, "I read newspapers to be informed about local events (I am the college archivist). But I do not read newspapers for pleasure." Likewise, Gary wants to read more "fiction and nonfiction" because he is "bottomed out on newspapers and magazines." And while some librarians explain that they simply do not want to read more newspapers or magazines, others confess that they feel they *should* read more news sources. For the most part, these individuals are regular fiction readers. "I feel that I should read the newspaper religiously, but when I do have time to read, I prefer to read fiction and try to relax," Shauna observes, adding that reading "scholarly books" and newspapers "feels too much like work. My job involves a lot of research, so I get enough of that kind of reading on the job. I want to escape with fiction when I'm home." This notion of escape, also evident in Olivia's observation that reading fiction is "more relaxing," points to the clearly defined role that academic librarians assign to reading fiction. Indeed, academic librarians' discussion in Chapter 4 of how fiction provides a release from workday stress is also a likely explanation of why 78.6 percent of respondents who want to read more fiction are already fans of this material.

Life beyond books: Why academic librarians do not read more during their leisure time

Considering that over 75 percent of librarians would like to read more newspapers, magazines, fiction, or nonfiction, what is preventing them from reading more outside of work? Based on comments such as "there are only so many hours in the day" and "I have little spare time, period," the main answer to this question is time. Of the 459 librarians who indicate why they do not read more, 423 (92.2 percent) cite the fact that free time is a scarce resource: there is not enough time in the day for everything that they need and want to accomplish. Carving time for reading out of busy schedules thus becomes an increasingly difficult task. Some ascribe this problem to their own "lack of discipline" or "bad time management," admitting that they "don't set [reading] time aside on a regular basis" or that they "don't make reading as much of a priority" as they feel they should. For the majority, however, not finding the time to read is considered an inevitable part of contemporary life. As one person laments, "I used to be an avid reader as a child, but real life gets in the way."

Table 23. Activities that compete with reading
(Question 17 in Appendix A)

Activity	No. of librarians (n = 423)*
Family/household responsibilities	205 (48.5%)
Hobbies/projects/other interests	123 (29.1%)
Television	51 (12.1%)
Work (extra hours, second job, bringing work home)	33 (7.8%)
Continuing education	25 (5.9%)
Commuting	13 (3.1%)

*Numbers do not add to *n* and percentages do not add to 100% because respondents cited multiple categories.

Academic librarians paint a vivid picture of the myriad aspects of "real life" that compete for their free time. As Table 23 shows, family and household responsibilities play the lead role in shaping reading habits, with 205 respondents describing how these responsibilities determine the amount of time spent reading outside work hours. Cynthia writes, "I don't have time!!! I have a house to take care of, with things constantly going wrong in it; my husband and I have four sets of parents between us all demanding our time, not to mention siblings and grandparents, and I don't like having to put a book down for days at a time, so I'm not likely to start one if I don't think I can finish it soon." Sue explains that "work and commuting time take 11.5 hours each day. The few hours left each evening are spent cooking, cleaning, and doing laundry or some other chore. If I do have any leisure time, I use it to catch up on the many UFOs (unfinished objects) in my sewing room."

There is a palpable sense of frustration in the voice of these librarians—frustration stemming from the onslaught of claims for their time and attention. Consider Frank's comments: "There are only 24 hours in a day. I only have two eyes. I have a life. A wife. Two sons. A dog. A cat. A house to maintain. Solicitations to throw away. %$#&**! phone to answer." Tim, too, would like to read more, but sees this happening only in his dreams, along with "a clean house, a mowed lawn, automobiles in perfect running order, 8 hours sleep, and supper with my wife and kids."

Compounding the difficulty of balancing household responsibilities and reading time is the sheer number of hours spent working. As Table 23 shows, 33 librarians note that work encroaches upon free time. While five of these individuals regularly work extra hours at the library, 11 librarians have second, part-time jobs to supplement either part-time or full-time library work, as is the case with Dolores, who holds "two part-time jobs in addition to a full time job." In another example, Miriam explains that "I am the mother of four children (all boys) aged 15, 13, 10 & 4. The 10-year old is handicapped. The workload at home is substantial. Despite the fact that I work part-time (i.e., 60 percent), my job is demanding and I often work extra hours. My husband runs a business from the home. I work with him. These two jobs, plus the family responsibilities, leave little leisure time."

For 17 of the 33 academic librarians who cite work as a reason why they do not read more during their free time, coming home does not mean leaving the office behind. In some instances, professional literature has supplanted pleasure reading. In other cases, librarians have to complete work at home — a practice that respondents note has become increasingly common. Jeremy attributes this to the fact that Internet access is becoming ubiquitous in North American households. "The number of non-working hours keeps shrinking," he sighs. "Part of this is involuntary and due to the growth of work on computerized projects. Since these can be 'taken home' via the Internet they inevitably are." As another respondents wryly comments, "21st century librarianship keeps me too busy to read."

Of course, not all claims on free time are as onerous as household chores or work-related tasks. Table 23 also shows that 123 librarians (29.1 percent) divide their time among a variety of hobbies and projects. There are church activities to attend, scout troops to lead, genealogical research to conduct, crafts to make, sports teams to coach, bridge games to play, exercise regimes to maintain, movies to see, books to write, and, for at least one respondent, "[t]oo much social and sexual activity" to enjoy. Tom watches "automobile racing on TV and sometimes live[s] at the track," in addition to completing "crossword puzzles in bed before sleeping." Charlene places responsibility for not reading more outside of work squarely on her horse, noting, "I spend a great deal of time at the stables." Additionally, Table 23 shows that 25 librarians are furthering their education, taking classes that range from English literature to conversational Spanish. While all of these educational pursuits necessitate spending time in a classroom, those enrolled in degree-granting programs also point out that a heavy load of reading assignments determines what they read outside of work hours, with little time left for recreational reading.

Guilt trip

The multiple claims on academic librarians' time result in two perspectives on the issue of balancing reading with either domestic responsibilities or hobbies and interests. For some, this is simply a non-issue. In fact, they consider reading to be less of a priority than other facets of their lives, freely admitting that there are other things they would rather be doing with their free time. This viewpoint is nicely summarized by one librarian's observation that "[t]here is more to life than reading." Claudia is "an avid crossword puzzle solver" who has "chosen to work on them instead of read." Emanuel writes that he would "rather surf, play computer games, or hang out with my wife." Indeed, librarians frequently mention personal relationships in the context of "other things in my life besides books." Carlos "prefer[s] to visit with family and friends," while Stephanie explains that "[s]pending time with my family is more important to me than personal reading."

For other librarians, the multiple claims on their time results in feelings of guilt for spending time reading. This is the case with Carol, who explains that "[o]nce I start a book I don't put it down, so I start neglecting other things I need to do." Joyce notes that "I have 4 cats to deal with, a home to maintain, a daughter in college to worry about, financial/estate/investment matters to deal with. Frankly, I sometimes feel guilty when I spend hours reading." Barbara's preference for novels heightens her sense that she should be spending her time on other tasks. "It makes me feel guilty to read so much fiction," she confesses. "I read when I should be doing other things like housework."

Interestingly, academic librarians do not attribute these guilty feelings to spending time reading current-events related materials such as newspapers. Rather, they make a distinction between spending time reading a newspaper and spending time reading materials construed as "pleasure reading." We have already seen that some librarians would like to read more fiction during their free time precisely because they "do not read newspapers for pleasure." As one librarian bluntly states, "Reading the newspaper is not recreational, it is to keep me informed on current events." For others, reading the newspaper is tantamount to work or household responsibilities. "I read the *New York Times* every evening at home," Helen writes. "That plus cooking dinner, grocery shopping, yard work, etc. fills up my evening. My only real chance to read books is on lunch hour, which is needless to say my favorite hour of the day!!!" Another individual who chides herself for a "lack of discipline" in setting aside time to read suggests that she "could read another newspaper a day instead of a novel."

When librarians associate works of fiction with pleasure reading—an association not made in the case of newspapers and magazines—the enjoyment that these books provide is simultaneously tinged with feelings of guilt that respondents' time should be spent on other things. The term "pleasure reading"—regardless of the materials to which this label is applied—is therefore problematic. There is a tendency to create a psychological barricade separating anything classified as "pleasure reading" from anything considered "useful" in terms of work. As one librarian remarks, "Current events are much more important than reading for pleasure." Yet, we have seen how reading popular novels—the material most often associated with pleasure reading—not only enables librarians to relax after work, but assists them in other facets of their work, including reference service. The many stories recounted by academic librarians have shown that anything they read can have a positive impact, and that even "pleasure reading" can be applied and valued not only personally, but also professionally.

Television

As with the notion of pleasure reading, television viewing is another factor that elicits both unapologetic and remorseful comments from respondents. Fifty-one librarians (12.1 percent) mention television as a reason they do not have more time for reading outside of work (see Table 23). Their responses reveal a spectrum of roles that television plays in their lives—roles that are projected to grow for the general adult population over the first decade of the 21st century. According to the United States Census Bureau, 98.2 percent of all households in 1999 had at least one television, with an average of 2.4 television sets per home. Additionally, 67.5 percent of households with televisions also had cable television. The average person spent 1,588 hours in 1999 watching programs on both broadcast and cable stations—an amount that is expected to increase to 1,595 hours by 2004. To put this in perspective, the average person spent 154 hours in 1999 reading a daily newspaper, 91 hours reading consumer books, and 81 hours reading consumer magazines.[1]

The discrepancy between the amount of time dedicated to reading and the amount of hours spent watching television serves as a backdrop for the comments of academic librarians who discuss their television viewing habits. For many, their comments amount to proclamations of guilt, riddled with the phrase "too much" or introduced with the word "unfortunately": "I probably watch too much television," writes one academic reference librarian, while another cites "time constraints caused by ... unfortunately watching too much television." There is the unmistakable sense that respondents use these terms both to acknowledge and to apologize for behavior they feel deviates from an expected norm. In effect, the apologetic tone of their responses stems from the same feeling one "voracious reader of historical romances" expresses: "gasp! I know we aren't supposed to acknowledge such lowbrow interests." At the same time, academic librarians explain that, like a good mystery or romance novel, watching television enables them to unwind after work—something they cannot do by reading more "serious" material. One person describes watching television as "too easy of an escape," while another mentions that it is "often easier to choose television and be a couch potato." Similarly, Denise admits to feeling "so stressed that usually I just want to vegetate in front of [the] television."

Of course, not all of the academic librarians who spend their free time in front of the television instead of behind a book, newspaper, or magazine are apologetic about this decision. In fact, some feel that watching television is a preferable alternative to reading. For some of these individuals, television programming such as the evening news — or the Discovery, History, and Travel channels on cable — is treated as a source of information. Others mention watching both news and entertainment programming. Brian responds to the question of why he does not read more by listing "*The Sopranos, Sex and the City, Masterpiece Theater, Mystery!, Nova* and *National Geographic* specials, C-SPAN, [and] Discovery Channel nature programming." Televised sports also occupies many librarians' viewing hours. For one baseball fan who spends most of his "leisure time watching games on TV," this means reading only "[d]uring the off-season."

In addition to stress relief, librarians suggest that television viewing allows them to multi-task. Describing reading as both "a solitary activity" and one that occupies a person's full attention, they approach television viewing as something that can be done in conjunction with other activities, including housework. The idea of being able to divide one's attention between television and other activities also applies to spending time with family members. Academic librarians invoke images that reflect what Robert Putnam refers to as the concept of "television as an 'electronic hearth' that would foster family togetherness."[2] Jennifer explains that "[i]n the hour or two after my children go to sleep in which my husband and I remain awake, we either discuss issues or most often watch television…. I feel like we are spending time together more if we're watching TV than if we're reading separate things." Renée also feels that "[r]eading is a solitary endeavor whereas watching TV is a way of spending time with one's spouse/family."

Time is not the only issue

Time is not the only factor that determines whether a librarian reads outside of working hours. Factors related to the specific nature of academic librarianship and respondents' work environment also come into play. For example, 72 respondents (15.7 percent) say that they are simply too tired to read when they get home at night (see Table 24). June summarizes this predicament as feeling "too tired to do much of anything by the time one gets home at 6:00 p.m. every night Monday — Friday" and not being able to "stay up late reading books if you have to be at work at 8:00 a.m. the next day." In addition, 18 of these 72 librarians suffer from eyestrain, including Emanuel, who notes that "I stare too much at print during work. Period, I need to give my eyes a break." Computer use has also taken its toll, as Elizabeth explains: "I 'skim' information constantly at work, usually on-line; my eyes are often too tired to read extensively in the evening." In addition to physical fatigue, there is mental fatigue, with eight respondents citing the problem of information overload. One librarian notes that "spending all day in the midst of reading materials" can be a strong disincentive to read at home. "Believe it or not, I get tired of looking at books," admits another individual. "I truly enjoy being a librarian and reading, [but] there is just a limit [to what] I can take in in a day." Leonard comments that "after looking at print in some form throughout the day, I find picking up a book or newspaper [far] down on my list."

Another environmental factor that impacts the amount of time that academic librarians spend reading at home is the sedentary nature of their work. Seventeen librarians (3.7 percent) explain that, because they spend all day indoors and behind a desk, they want to be physically active (and preferably outdoors) during non-working hours. Diane remarks that "[l]ibrarianship is largely an indoor sedentary profession. During my off-hours, I prefer to engage in more active pursuits." Alan likewise remarks: "I sit long enough at work behind my desk, so I feel that at home I should limit the amount of time I spend being sedentary." For some individuals, this means working out at a gym; for others it means spending "almost all of my entire free time outdoors."

Table 24. Factors other than time that impact reading outside of working hours (Question 17 in Appendix A)

Factor	No. of librarians (n = 459)*
Fatigue	72 (15.7%)
The need to be less sedentary	17 (3.7%)
Alternate sources of information (excluding television)	11 (2.4%)
Availability of materials	10 (2.2%)
Information overload	8 (1.7%)
Lack of interest	6 (1.3%)
Being a "slow reader"	5 (1.1%)

*Numbers do not add to *n* and percentages do not add to 100% because not all librarians cited these additional factors. The *n* represents the total of the 459 librarians who stated reasons for not reading more. Percentages are calculated based on *n* = 459 so as not to overstate results. This table should be read in conjunction with Table 23. Some respondents cited multiple reasons.

The fact that librarians spend "all day in the midst of reading materials," coupled with the fatigue of looking at print sources all day and the sedentary nature of their work, makes non-print sources of information appealing alternatives. We have already seen that some respondents spend time watching televised news programs; in addition, 11 respondents discuss their preferences for non-print news sources, including radio programming. For Karen, listening to National Public Radio (NPR) has supplanted newspapers as a daily information source: "I typically don't make time for reading. Also, if it were not for my almost daily listening to of NPR (morning news) I think I would feel that I needed to read the national and city newspapers to stay aware of what is going on in the world. Perhaps I depend too much on this medium to obtain my national and international news information." Gerald links his listening to NPR at home to the fact that he has access to print sources at work. "I listen to most of my news on National Public Radio (a few hours per day)," he explains. "It feels like a great waste of paper to get print subscriptions to anything (especially since I work in a library)." For Sue, the issue is timeliness: "I don't read more newspapers because I listen either to NPR or CNN. By the time the newspaper arrives, it is 'old' news!"

Gerald's comments regarding access to newspapers and magazines at work relate to another issue that academic librarians mention in their discussions of why they do not read more during their free time: the availability of materials. While access to materials at work shapes Gerald's reading behavior at home, the 10 respondents who cite availability of materials as a factor do *not* have access to the materials they would want to read outside of work hours. They explain that, on the one hand, the reading materials that appeal to them are not collected at either the library at which they work or at their local public libraries. On the other hand, buying these materials for themselves is precluded by the prohibitive prices of books and magazines. John prefers to read "books and journals that contain articles about [his] current interests," but notes that "nearby libraries don't hold the items I'd like to read. I don't want to pay the price to purchase an item." Others comment that "[o]ur library doesn't stock much fiction, and it's too much money to buy," or that there is "[l]ittle money with which to buy my own books, so I rely on a rather limited public library selection."

The additional factors we have examined thus far that determine whether academic librarians can or want to read more during their free time stem from the nature of their work and their work environment: too much information, tired eyes, and sedentariness. The final two categories listed in Table 24, however, present a different story of why some librarians do not read more outside of working hours. Five respondents describe themselves as "slow readers" who have difficulty completing books. As one of these individuals explains, "First of all, I don't sit down very much. And I've learned that I don't read very fast." For the six librarians in the "lack of interest" category, reading is simply not an appealing option. In some cases, the problem is that the respondent is an admittedly finicky reader who can find "only a few books to my liking." Another describes himself as "an impatient reader who gives up quickly on poor or disjointed writing — I start many more books than I finish," while two other librarians cite a "poor attention span" as contributing to their attenuated interest in reading. For Betty, there is "not enough personal satisfaction/reward in reading books, except for self-help books such as *Seven Habits of Highly Effective People*. I've always found reading difficult."

Paid work time for reading

In Chapters 3 and 4, academic librarians ascribe a number of benefits to reading books and periodicals outside of work — benefits that not only improve the quality of the reference service they provide, but also help in numerous other aspects of their job. In this chapter, we have seen many academic librarians stress that they would like to read more, but that "real life gets in the way." There are only so many hours in a day, households and personal relationships need to be maintained, and other activities play important roles in their lives. They work long hours, in some cases at more than one job, or are continuing their education, and when they come home their bodies and minds are tired; sometimes, as one respondent phrases it, the "boob tube seems more inviting" than a book, magazine, or newspaper.

The fact that so many librarians have experienced first-hand the ways in which reading during free time helps them at work, coupled with their lack of free time, makes their responses to the question of whether they feel that the quality of their reference service would improve if they were paid to read at work somewhat surprising. As Table 25 shows, only 27 percent of respondents feel that paid reading time would result in better reference service, while 17.1 percent see no benefit to being paid to read at work. Librarians who answered "no" to this question took issue with not only the concept of paid reading

Table 25. Do academic librarians think that reference service would improve if they had paid work time to read newspapers, magazines, nonfiction, or fiction? (Question 19 in Appendix A)

Response	No. of librarians (n = 526)
Yes	142 (27%)
Possibly	192 (36.5%)
No	90 (17.1%)
Already paid to read	102 (19.4%)

time, but also the nature of the materials that we suggested librarians might read. One librarian writes that the paid-reading-time proposition "[s]ounds silly to me — paid time to do personal/leisure reading? Give me a break! Paid time for scholarly/library science materials, yes. Other stuff, insane." Another respondent exclaims that this approach "would set librarianship back several years. Librarians need much more computer knowledge and more general knowledge, but little additional knowledge on current events and no more knowledge on fiction."

Even librarians who consider paid work time for reading to be "a great concept" express disbelief that it would actually be implemented in their libraries. "Of course," Jessica responds with regard to the question of whether paid time would improve the quality of her reference service, while also commenting, "[Y]ou are a dreamer." Similarly, Kurt feels strongly about the potential connection between paid reading time and improved reference service, but quips: "Hell hasn't frozen over yet, has it?" For one respondent, this type of skepticism comes from direct experience. Her library implemented a reading system, but she explains that it was "not viewed positively by those outside the reference department."

Yet, as Table 25 shows, 102 academic librarians (19.4 percent) state that they already have some form of paid work time to read. As Phyllis notes: "I already have paid time to do such reading. I am not expected to simply sit and read books all day (a common misconception held by people outside the library), but I am expected to use my worktime to read materials which pertain to my areas of responsibility — like librarianship and theology. So, whenever there is time while at the Ref. Desk or as I work in my office on a project, I read materials that help." Kendall points out that he is granted plenty of leeway in deciding not only how to use his time at work, but also, should he choose to read, which materials would be appropriate to read: "As a bibliographer/reference librarian, I have a great deal of freedom in deciding the most appropriate way of spending my work hours, including reading articles in current journals and magazines, web sites that provide current news and reports and other formats." Indeed, a number of librarians who have paid time to read at work see this as an opportunity to keep abreast of current events. "I don't feel bad about taking half an hour each morning to read the *New York Times* or *Chicago Tribune*, and check out CNN.com," Florence remarks. "I figure someone on the premises should keep alerted to recent developments in Israel or the [2000 presidential] campaign."

Table 26. Issues concerning the question of whether academic librarians should have paid work time for reading ($n = 526$)*

	Lack of time	Professional responsibility	Guidelines	Constraints	Propriety
Yes	4	1	8	0	0
Possibly	16	8	7	2	2
No	18	14	0	3	3
Already paid	9	0	0	0	0
Total	47 (8.9%)	23 (4.4%)	15 (2.9%)	5 (1%)	5 (1%)

*Numbers do not add to n and percentages do not add to 100% because not all librarians provided rationales for responses to the question of paid work time for reading. Percentages are calculated based on $n = 526$ so as not to overstate results.

Most academic librarians, however, express ambivalence about the usefulness of being paid to read at work. Only 192 respondents (36.5 percent) feel that being paid to read at work might improve the quality of the reference service they provide, and they were reluctant to endorse this concept wholeheartedly. Overall, they raise five separate issues in their discussions: lack of time; professional responsibility; guidelines; constraints; and propriety. Interestingly, librarians who are enthusiastic about or dismissive of the paid work time concept cite these same issues. Table 26 presents both a summary of these issues and a breakdown of the number of librarians who address each of these issues from the four viewpoints listed in Table 25.

Professional responsibility

We begin with the issue of professional responsibility, which addresses academic librarians' philosophical concerns with the concept of paid work time for reading. The 23 respondents (4.4 percent) who raise this issue emphasize that they essentially are already paid to read — or, more specifically, paid to be informed and knowledgeable individuals — since this knowledge is an integral part of their professional responsibility as academic librarians. As one librarian summarizes, "As a professional, I feel that I have an obligation to be well informed as part of the background I bring to my job." Donna sees this professional obligation in terms of being informed generally, as well as being knowledgeable about her library's collection. "It is my job to know the collections I must use and understand," she explains. "I already am 'paid' to read and understand and serve the public with my knowledge of our collections, its use, and the scope of its coverage."

Some respondents also feel that academic librarians are already keeping up with library collections and current events while at work, without having to specifically designate paid time to do so. Noting that "[p]rofessional librarians have the responsibility of staying well informed and should use their time accordingly," David adds that "[p]rofessionals are not hourly employees and should not count their time this way." What David is suggesting, then, is that there are already opportunities for academic librarians to read at work, but whether they take advantage of these opportunities depends upon their own initiative.

In fact, there are numerous examples of academic librarians who take this initiative and find the time to read at the reference desk. Grace finds that "the reference desk provides time to browse newspapers, magazines, and sometimes, new books." Others point out the role that online sources can play in staying informed at the reference desk. According to one such individual, the concept of "on-the-job reading seems a little redundant and unnecessary ... for reference librarians in an online environment." In fact, Marjorie believes that "reference librarians are already spending work time reading newspapers and online magazines at their desktops." She observes that, "[s]ince everyone now has their own PC, it is not obvious what they're working on, but I know my staff read cnn.com, salon, slate and newspapers on work time." Dale agrees with Marjorie's assessment, describing the use of online sources as "simple and unobtrusive information gathering that can be done on-the-job....": "I just enjoy reading extracurricularly and would hope that other librarians suffer from the same information-gathering habit. If they don't, then hopefully they find other ways to stay informed — like reading newspapers online while at the reference desk in between questions.... I always make a habit of pulling up cnn.com, time.com, nytimes.com, abcnews.com, etc. on the desk — all the while remaining approachable and friendly, of course!"

What Dale describes as his "hope that other librarians suffer from the same information-gathering habit" that he does introduces another component of the relationship between reading and professional responsibility. While some academic librarians cite personal initiative in relation to their professional responsibility to be informed and knowledgeable individuals, they also feel that this initiative is not something that can be produced or bolstered with paid time for reading. As Yolanda explains, "People are either readers or they are not"— a sentiment supported by Calvin, who adds that "folks who are inclined to read will find a way to do so — without paid time at work." Some librarians were adamant about this point, providing blunt assessments of librarians who do not fall into the category of "readers." Consider, for example, Vincent's comments.

> I read part of the newspaper at work — during my break and lunch hours. Anyone who is not motivated enough to find time to read a daily, quality newspaper at some point in the day is not a serious academic-type person and probably should not be doing academic reference work. A librarian who takes pride in his or her work needs to know what is going on in the world and be able to speak with people on an intelligent level. If money has to be offered as incentive to read a newspaper, it can probably be assumed that the librarian is neither self-motivated, nor does he/she have much interest in current events or keeping relevant.

While Vincent uses this argument to express the opinion that paid time for reading would not be of any benefit, others who use similar reasoning hold more conflicted views on the issue. They raise the question of whether the reference service provided by an individual not self-motivated to read in the first place would improve simply because this librarian was suddenly paid to read. Dina identifies herself as "a BIG BELIEVER in the value of outside reading," but wonders whether "asking librarians to read, if they are not naturally inclined to do so ... will result in tangible benefits." Citing the adage "You can lead a horse to water, but you can't make him drink," she theorizes that "[p]eople who have a love of learning and knowledge will make time to read. They don't need to be paid. I often hear people say, 'Oh, I wish I had more time to read.' These are the same people who mindlessly channel surf, or sleep until noon on weekends, or make plenty of time for gardening, crafts, etc. That is perfectly fine ... they are making time for what they value.... And if you don't have a real interest in reading, I doubt that you are really going to retain a high percentage of what you read."

Guidelines and constraints

The question of whether librarians will be able to retain, and therefore apply, what they read at work relates to another issue concerning the concept of paid work time for reading. As Table 26 shows, 15 librarians (2.9 percent) feel that there should be guidelines of some sort should a library choose to implement this type of system. More than half of these 15 individuals are librarians who endorse the 'paid work time for reading' concept in the first place. Some respondents who answered either "yes" or "possibly" to the question of whether having time to read at work would benefit reference service express concern that the system "would be grossly abused." Daniel explains, "I have been on many personnel evaluation committees over the years. The people who are motivated enough to keep learning do it, whether given time or not. For some this means an hour a day, for others every free moment they have.... Others, if given the time, would merely squander it, to no obvious benefit to the organization." For this reason, he proposes the following: "The concept is fine and I would fully endorse it, but only for folks that are already proven to be highly skilled as reference librarians. (They are already doing this on their own or they would not be highly skilled as reference librarians.) Use it as a reward, not a right, or accept the unpleasant reality that some will waste the time and money." In fact, he cites the same adage as Dina — that "you can lead a horse to water, but you cannot make it drink," adding that this principle "holds true when it comes to human learning. Only those thirsty will learn, no matter what time is spent on the activity."

What librarians see as "the potential for abuse in such a system," and the resulting waste of both time and money, prompts a variety of suggestions for guidelines that libraries could implement. While Daniel proposes using paid time for reading as a type of reward system, Grant feels that libraries should specify the amount of time and the materials that librarians could spend reading per work day, suggesting that "librarians could each be given 30 minutes a day to read books from their collections." Lauren also advises that libraries set guidelines for what type of materials could be read, noting, "I don't think that I would be able to provide better reference service to the library users if my library paid me to read, unless they also specified that I had to read a certain number of books, articles, etc. in particular subject areas." More than half of the respondents who believe that guidelines are necessary stress that the nature of the materials librarians could be paid to read is paramount. Sheila strongly supports the concept of paid time "BUT ONLY IF I restricted my reading to nonfiction in the subject areas related to my work environment." Josh also see the value of this concept "[a]s long as it has some relevancy," adding, "I don't see how reading articles on car racing would help me as a medical librarian. However, an interview with the Minister of Health might be relevant."

Of course, the determination of what is relevant to an academic work environment differs from librarian to librarian. While one individual identifies "reading material [that] pertains to my work" as "technology and health sections of newspapers, library journals, etc.," another comments that the focus should be "fiction and nonfiction books and journals, as that is perhaps more pertinent to our situation than newspapers and magazines." Others emphasize what they feel should *not* be considered as appropriate or beneficial materials, including Joyce, who feels that "unfocused reading for pleasure of novels, poetry, history, etc. ... would be of limited usefulness."

The idea that their reading habits could be hindered, or even monitored, through institutional guidelines leads some librarians to question whether paid time for reading would have a positive impact on reference service. As Table 26 shows, five individuals believe that the paid work time concept might become a constraint that would make reading feel, as one respondent puts it, "like homework." Matt notes, "[sh]ould I be paid to read, I would feel pushed to do it. It would remind me of all those readings I had to do when in high school, college, or university." Librarians express concern that this sense of being forced to read would eliminate the pleasure they get from their current leisure-time reading. "I read because I enjoy it. If it suddenly became part of work, I wonder if some of the enjoyment would go out of it," Ashley muses, adding, "I never set out to read specifically to help with my work." Ashley's comment harkens back to observations made by academic librarians in Chapter 4, where some librarians describe the benefits that reading books outside of work has brought to reference service while explicitly mentioning that they do not select reading materials with work in mind.

Meagan provides further insight into what some academic librarians see as the limitations of purposively selecting reading materials to fit their work environment: "I would feel constrained to 'apply' such reading to work, to select it with that in mind, if I were paid to read it during work, and that would spoil some of my pleasure in being free to read anything I want to on my own time. I really like having a job where virtually all of my interests are useful eventually, but I like the serendipity of how this happens." Meagan's viewpoint presents an interesting contrast to the guidelines proposed by other respondents; it also suggests that specifying what a librarian could read based on predictions of what will be useful at the reference desk would curtail not only the serendipity of finding relevant information, but also the librarian's ability to make connections among various information sources— something that many respondents have described again and again in previous chapters as vital to their work.

Propriety

The "relevancy" issue that librarians raise in the context of proposed guidelines also relates to the notion of propriety. Rather than being concerned that the materials librarians read at work are relevant to a given library, five respondents caution that reading at work would give the wrong impression to patrons. As one individual explains, "When I am on the reference desk and not helping a patron, I try to read professional literature in the library field. I don't think it looks 'right' to read magazines such as *Time*, etc., even though they might be more interesting!" Respondents are adamant about this when it comes to reading novels, with Sharon writing, "I especially feel that paid time to read fiction is inappropriate." This focus on fiction ties into concerns that the image of librarians reading at work would reinforce negative stereotypes of the profession.

Cathy remarks that "patrons will begin to think that the only thing that the librarians do is sit around all day in cushy chairs reading their favorite cook book or romance novel. That is a stereotype that needs to be broken." She also points out another way in which reading *anything* at the desk might be inappropriate: "The patrons will probably be apprehensive to address the librarian for help because they (the patron) feel that the librarian is too busy reading."

Lack of time

Finally, we come to the issue of time, or lack thereof, as a hindrance to the concept of paid work time for reading. As Table 26 shows, this issue is raised by 47 academic librarians (8.9 percent), who cover all four of the listed viewpoints on the utility of paying librarians to read. There are, on the one hand, respondents such as Kyle, who answered yes to the question of whether being paid to read at work would improve reference service, but then asks, "[W]hen would I get the rest of my work done?" On the other hand, there are librarians such as Lucy, who repeat Kyle's concerns but who do not endorse the concept of paid time for work: "If I took work time to do this reading, I would never get anything else done, e.g., collection development, government documents work, committee work, creating documentation...." Much like the respondents who raise the issue of professional responsibility, these respondents stress that paid time is beside the point and that pay cannot really function as an incentive to read. Here, however, the problem is not self-motivation, but rather the fact that there is too much to do in too little time in the average working day. As Kerry points out, "You cannot buy time.... [There is] too much we want to do at our jobs!" or, as Drew remarks, too much that needs to be done.

> [Y]ou must be realistic. Time is not something you can just say, here, take one hour each day and read what you like and I will pay you. You are going to have to provide someone else to do the work that I would be doing when you release me to read. When you add another activity, even if I love it, you have increased my work load. Most libraries have limits on the number of staff members who are expected to complete all the work. I'm certain we could all improve our work practices, but please don't add any more tasks I have to account for.

The idea that, even if librarians were paid to read, there would not necessarily be time to do so is discussed by the nine individuals who are already paid to read but who find that "reading is always the lowest priority." As Larry explains, "Technically, I already have paid time to do such reading; practically, it doesn't always happen because of time constraints," or as Desmond puts it, because of "the press of other work."

The idea that reading would, or, in the case of those who already have paid time, does "always fall to the bottom of the 'Things to do list'" reflects the reality of understaffed and underfunded libraries. Yet it also reflects the predominant outlook of librarians and, to a larger degree, the institutions at which they work. Of course it is impossible "to buy time"—to suddenly carve out free time for librarians from their already busy workday—without something else having to give. But Dina raises an interesting point when she suggests that "[p]eople who have a love of learning and knowledge will make time to read." Whether people read or pursue other interests, says Dina, they "are making time for what they value." So the question becomes: What does the library as an institution value? Could not the principle of making time for what is truly important be applied on a larger scale? Could not libraries send the message that reading is an important and valued component of the work of academic librarians by giving them paid time to read?

The stories in Chapters 3 and 4 suggest that the reading academic librarians do outside of work *is* an important part of what they do at work. These stories supply ready answers to the arguments made by librarians like Lucy, who feels that "[i]f I took work time to do this reading, I would never get anything else done, e.g., collection development, government documents work, committee work, creating documentation...," or Jocelyn, who insists that reading at work "would serve little purpose other than to take away time from preparing instruction sessions, teaching online database searching, participating in university committees, staffing the reference desk, developing new programs, etc." As we have seen, the experiences of numerous academic librarians demonstrate that reading newspapers, magazines, and books gives them the ability to answer difficult reference questions. In fact, Lucy herself provided the example we cite in Chapter 4 of being able to answer a patron's query on "U.S. interference in African government and politics" based on her reading of *The Poisonwood Bible* by Barbara Kingsolver. Reading also provides search examples for bibliographic instruction — examples that both entertain and inform students. Is this not a means of "preparing instruction sessions"? Likewise, reading book reviews in newspapers and magazines, not to mention reading the books themselves, is a crucial component of collection development. Librarians also identify reading as a source for programming ideas. And librarians explain that they are singled out to serve on university committees because of their proven knowledge and acumen — traits that they ascribe to reading extensively in specific subject areas.

Academic librarians, and especially library administrators, should dispense with the notion that reading newspapers, magazines, fiction, and nonfiction is a self-contained task. Rather, they should recognize that it permeates and informs all aspects of academic librarianship. In this sense, setting aside 30 minutes a day to read at work is no different from making time for any other component of the busy working day of the academic reference librarian.

III. Public Library Reference Staff

In this section we consider how awareness of current events affects the work of public reference staff members. We begin our investigation with the same issue that concluded the previous chapter: should librarians have paid work time to read? When we posed this question to academic librarians, we asked whether they thought they could provide improved reference service to their patrons if they had paid work time to read newspapers, magazines, nonfiction, or fiction. In the case of public library reference staff members, we move from probabilities into realities, focusing on whether or not they are currently paid to read print and electronic versions of local newspapers, national newspapers, or magazines.

Only 86 public library reference staff members (20.8 percent) are allocated paid time at work to read newspapers and magazines, with 79.2 percent not having paid time ($n = 414$). Individuals with paid time to read do so anywhere from one to two hours per week, to one to two hours per day, to upwards of 15 hours per week. Some are under no time constraints whatsoever. Noelle, for instance, observes that at her library "it is not specified how much time should be spent on this reading," adding that "[w]e are just expected to keep up with news and trends in our specific subject area, as well as general news and trends. We are expected to use our own judgment on time amounts for these things." Kendrick comments that "there is no time limit. We are encouraged to keep up with current events on the local, national, and international level."

Other reference staff members who are paid to read at work state that the library guidelines focus on the nature of the materials, rather than the amount of time spent reading. They cite the emphasis that is placed on reading local newspapers. "We are encouraged to read the local newspapers in order to better help our patrons," Crystal remarks. "This newspaper reading takes about an hour per week, since the local papers are printed only three times a week for one, and one a week for the other." At the same time, she also points out that "[a]s far as national newspapers, nothing is said about keeping up with national news. I believe we are expected to be cognizant of the major issues on our own time." As a library director, Zack stresses that his "[e]ntire staff subscribes to and reads the local paper every day before coming to work," adding that "[p]aid time is important to help staff answer questions."

There is a general consensus among respondents who are given paid time to read

133

that this system helps in reference work. One individual observes that "off-desk time" for reading has recently been implemented at his library, and the results so far have led him to conclude that "[o]ff desk time for reference work is essential. If a reference librarian is not up to date on events they are not providing quality service. It is essential that reference librarians have time to read current newspapers and periodicals." Isabelle concurs, observing that "[i]n thirty years experience it has been demonstrated to me on a more than ample basis, that a successful reference librarian must have a quizzical mind. As such, those staff read and study all the time. Those who don't usually fall by the wayside and leave the profession or at least the reference aspect of the profession."

Isabelle's viewpoint is shared by the majority of the 79.2 percent of public library reference staff members who are *not* granted paid time to read at work. Laverne describes the concept of paid time for reading as "useful," noting, "I live in another city than in the one I work so I frequently feel out of touch with local happenings and am unfamiliar with local personalities." Another respondent muses, "I think it would be useful to have at least 3 full time people asked to read both national newspapers for current events and at least one popular cultural magazine." Not everyone who comments on the need to keep abreast of current events, however, feels that paid time at work is an ideal solution. As with academic librarians, some public library reference staff members feel that they themselves should take the initiative in reading newspapers and magazines and that it is not "my employer's responsibility to keep me up to date and informed."

There are two components to how public library reference personnel take the initiative to keep "up to date and informed." In Chapter 5, we saw how academic librarians avail themselves of the opportunity to follow current events while at the reference desk—for example, by having reading news-related web sites—thereby rendering moot the issue of paid time. Reference personnel at public libraries agree with their academic counterparts, with 63 respondents stating that, while their library does not have a formal paid reading policy, most of their colleagues read "on the fly between questions at the reference desk." These individuals express doubt "that paid time would help much." Caleb elaborates: "We're not provided specific time to do those things, but it would not necessarily be frowned upon if we wanted to catch up on news through the Internet. If I'm not busy at the reference desk, I'll surf the Net and read the news and I think some of the other librarians do as well." Speaking from the perspective of a library director, Tovah adds: "In one sense we do not provide paid time for staff to keep up on current events. In another sense, there is plenty of opportunity to do this kind of reading when they are on the reference desk and it is not busy. Also, their time off the desk is not policed. They are expected to accomplish certain things (book selection, weeding, program planning), but if they spend some time reading current events there is nothing to prevent this from happening." Indeed, the practice of catching up on news at the reference desk does not constitute some form of institutional "don't ask, don't tell" policy. Instead, public library reference staff members repeatedly comment that they are "encouraged to explore web sites during slow periods," for example, or that, while not "paid by specific duties," they "do whatever we feel is necessary to stay abreast of things."

While accommodating reading time in busy work schedules is one way that public library reference personnel take the initiative to stay informed about current events, another approach is to read newspapers and magazines, whether in print or online, during their free time. Like academic librarians, many public library reference staff members who feel that paid time is unnecessary firmly believe that reading these materials is simply part of their professional responsibility. The comments of Estelle are representative of this school of thought: "I consider this reading to be my professional responsibility and something to be done on my own time. I am salaried, not an hourly worker on a time clock. Inasmuch as I purchase all the adult nonfiction, adult reference, adult videos, spoken audio and music — and all the reading for reviews for this is also done on my own time — the extensive reading of newspapers that I do daily is vital to all my responsibilities. 'Read newspapers' is the single most important piece of advice I can give to aspiring reference librarians in the public arena." While some stress professional responsibility, others write that staying informed of local, national and world events is an integral part of their "responsibility as a citizen." From one perspective, "professional responsibility" is indistinguishable from "citizen responsibility" for many public library reference personnel — a viewpoint that goes to the heart of what it means to work at a public library, where an important aspect of professional responsibility is the ability and willingness to be a responsible (i.e., informed) citizen.

Nonetheless, the idealism that underscores this concept of personal and professional responsibility is occasionally challenged by the reality of what some respondents have witnessed in their workplaces. One individual writes, "[I]n the past I felt it was the responsibility of staff members to keep up to date and read off the job. I read several papers a day and several magazines a week, but I'm finding this is the exception. So, I guess I may be changing my thoughts in this matter." Yet, having the opportunity to read at work does not mean that staff members will take advantage of it — the point that academic librarians stressed using the adage "you can lead a horse to water, but you cannot make him drink." Stan is the perfect embodiment of this conundrum: "The library director does provide me with paid time to read the local newspapers. However, I do not avail myself of this time because the local papers are poorly written and focus on parochial rather than national/international news."

In the next chapter, we take a closer look at how, and whether, public library reference staff members take the initiative to stay informed about current events on their own time, as well as the effects of this initiative on reference service. We concentrate on the news sources that public library reference personnel use to follow current events, including print and online newspapers, print and online magazines, and television and radio news programs. We then turn our attention to the impact of these various media on their ability to assist patrons both at the reference desk and in other aspects of their work.

6

Being a Jack-of-All-Trades

*How staying current affects the work of public
library reference staff members*

According to one public library reference staff member, staying abreast of current events is an occupational hazard. "There is one patron who lives for the news and the reference staff is collared by him every day to talk about the news," Crystal explains, jesting that "we manage to keep up that way if by no other." In fact, Crystal herself admits to being a news devotee, emphasizing, "I read on my own for my own fulfillment. I have always been a huge reader, like most librarians, I guess. I tend to know a little something about everything that comes across the reference desk."

Most public library reference staff members share this outlook, applying the information found in the pages of newspapers and magazines, as well as on television and radio news programs, in their role as what two respondents refer to as "a jack-of-all-trades" at the reference desk. Indeed, they have witnessed first-hand the beneficial effects of various general-interest media when it comes to providing reference service. As Table 27 shows, 78.8 percent of respondents have found that reading newspapers and magazines, either in print or online, has helped them in reference work, while 59.4 percent comment on how watching or listening to current affairs programs has assisted them. Public library reference personnel who have not noticed any connection between reading newspapers and magazines argue that "a general knowledge of how to find any information is preferable to filling one's head with stuff that may never be needed" and that only relatively few questions can be addressed with current newspapers and magazines. One individual suggests that her patrons "are either very clued in on current events or simply do not pick our brains for any story." Others assert bluntly that "[a]pathy about politics, current events, and science is quite striking" among their patrons. Vanessa, for instance, is "shocked at the lack of current events questions we get at our main library," estimating that "[i]n over a year working full-time here, I don't think I've ever had a current events question! I'm serious."

Public library reference personnel were ambivalent about the contribution that listening to or watching news programs has on the delivery of reference service. For some, it is not that television and radio are not applicable to their work, but rather that they consider television and radio to be less applicable than newspapers and magazines. Com-

Table 27. The impact of various media sources on reference work for public library reference personnel (Questions 9 and 13 in Appendix B)

	Has reading print or online newspapers and magazines helped in reference work? (n = 386)	Has watching or listening to current affairs or news programs helped in reference work? (n = 360)
Yes	304 (78.8%)	214 (59.4%)
No	82 (21.2%)	146 (40.6%)

menting that he "can't think of any specific examples" where television or radio programs have aided him in answering reference queries, Mitch ranks the various media as follows: "I'd say it is more likely that what I read in print or online is useful to answer reference questions than what I see on TV or hear on the radio. It is more likely that I get useful information from the radio ... than from TV." Clyde remarks, "I can't think of an example of news shows helping me with reference questions. That is not to say it doesn't help. I'm just not sure if I can get the most useful information from print or broadcast sources." Other respondents dismiss outright any potential contributions that television and radio news programming could make, considering such programming to be "just an amusement." One individual scoffs: "News? Not even when I was listening to NPR [National Public Radio] did a situation come up where the info was more than just after-dinner conversation."

The dual ideas that patrons generally do not pose current events-related questions and that current affairs programming more appropriately belongs to the category of entertainment rather than news points to the unique role that mainstream print and broadcast media play in the lives of public library patrons. As we will see in this chapter, the experiences of public library reference staff members highlight the fact that patrons do not just turn to newspapers, magazines, radio, and television to be informed about "hard news" current events. Rather, they depend on these media to learn about issues and events that affect them and their community on a more personal level. Take, for example, one respondent's observation that "the biggest help has not been the newspaper, but just shopping and eating out in the community." She continues: "Most of the librarians live outside the area, so I am pretty much the authority ... although I've only lived here four years—go figure." In other words, while the concept of current events encompasses global issues, it also signifies issues that are prevalent or popular at the local level. Staff members who discuss the positive impact of reading newspapers and magazines and watching or listening to radio and television programs on reference service emphasize the same point: that knowledge of one's community—the people who live there, their concerns and interests—makes for better reference service, and that accumulating this store of knowledge begins with reading, watching, and listening to the same information sources as their patrons.

Before we turn to the work experiences of public library reference staff, we focus on how these individuals accumulate community knowledge, examining the various news sources they regularly follow. We turn our attention first to the newspapers and magazines that they read during their own time, in both print and online formats. We then look at the range of radio and television current affairs programming that they tune into, and how often. After a discussion of how public library reference staff members have applied these media in answering questions at the reference desk, we conclude this chapter by looking at the other aspects of public library work that benefit when public library reference personnel read newspapers and magazines on their own time.

Newspapers and magazines

"I have never not been a newspaper reader, at least since the age of 10 or so," Mabel reminisces. "I grew up in the house of a newspaper publisher and editor. One of my brothers is a newspaper editor; my mother, another brother and sister are newspaper editors and I cannot imagine a day without reading a paper before going to work. I would feel at sea." The idea that newspapers or magazines serve as bearings for navigating the workday is shared by the majority of public library reference staff members (see Table 28). The fact that 81 percent of respondents take the time to read such sources daily is in stark contrast to the comments of the few staff members who never read newspapers and magazines outside of work. "No, I really hate the news and the media," avows one. "It is the same old crap every day and I find it very depressing." For others who never read print periodicals on their own time, the fundamental issue is not the nature of the materials, but how they choose to spend their free time: "When I'm on my own time, it is just that — MY time."

Table 28. Frequency with which public library reference personnel read newspapers and magazines on their own time (Questions 7 and 8 in Appendix B)

	Print newspapers & magazines (n = 416)	Online newspapers & magazines (n = 416)
Daily	337 (81%)	105 (25.2%)
Two to five times per week	43 (10.3%)	89 (21.4%)
Once a week at most	2 (.5%)	25 (6%)
Never	34 (8.2%)	197 (47.4%)

Far more representative of the views of public library reference staff members on reading current newspapers and magazines is the perspective provided by Enid: "I try to stay current and up-to-date by reading a wide variety of magazines and newspapers on my own time. I probably spend about ten hours a week doing this. I read local newspapers, national magazines (*Time, Newsweek*, etc.), entertainment magazines (*Entertainment Weekly*, etc.), and 'surf' the Internet for information." Enid's comments are typical on numerous levels. First, public library reference personnel, like their academic counterparts, strive through their selection of print materials to achieve a balance among local, national, and international news. Like Enid, some achieve this balance through a combination of daily local newspapers and weekly national newsmagazines or weekend national papers. Carl reads "everything local, current, national, and the Sunday *NY Times* for decent world news." Margot's reading schedule includes "the local, regional, and state newspaper daily," in addition to "[w]eekly magazines and several newspapers and columnists from other parts of the country." The emphasis public library reference staff members place on local news also extends to magazines. Ron, for instance, reads the "*Del Rio News Herald, San Antonio Express News, Texas Monthly, Texas Highways*, [and] *Texas Parks and Wildlife*," as well as *Newsweek* and *Reader's Digest.*

In addition to maintaining a balance between geographical diversity and regional knowledge, the newspapers and magazines that public library reference staff members read on their own time both reflect and bolster their professional identity as a "jack-of-all-trades." One individual remarks, "I want to be a generalist in my role as a public reference librarian, not a specialist." In order to maintain a broad knowledge base, they read many different magazine types. The big three newsmagazines—*Time, Newsweek*, and *U.S. News and World Report*—are only the tip of the iceberg. They read progressive and alternative publications such as *The Nation* and the *Utne Reader*, peruse *Harper's* and *The Atlantic Monthly*, but also turn their attention to "women's magazines" such as *Ladies Home Journal* and *Redbook*; home, gardening and cooking publications such as *Martha Stewart Living* and *Taste of Home*; and business magazines, including *Money, Kiplinger's Personal Finance*, and *Individual Investor*. Interestingly, *The New Yorker*, the third-most often cited magazine by academic librarians (see Table 11), is one cultural feature publication not mentioned regularly by public library reference staff members. Despite one person's comment that "*The New Yorker* seems to be the most topical" of the magazines to which she subscribes and "often engenders great and lively debates at the library," only two public reference staff members mention this publication.

The biggest difference between the current magazines most often cited by academic librarians and those mentioned by public library reference staff members, however, is in the category of celebrity, movie, and television publications. Magazines such as *Entertainment Weekly, People*, and *Premiere* collectively did not top academic librarians' reading agenda, with this category being the 10th most popular overall (see Table 10 in Chapter 3). Conversely, entertainment-based publications are a top priority for public library reference staff. As Gertrude remarks, "My 'joke' is that *People* magazine would be a great source for librarians to read religiously." In fact, public library staff members equate entertainment magazines with more news-oriented publications in terms of both priority and perceived value at the reference desk. Cicely explains that she reads *Entertainment Weekly* in order to "keep up with the youth culture questions." Crystal notes, "I read *People* on Mondays," indicating that this is the publication that launches her workweek. In some cases, the desire to stay in tune with youth culture prompts staff members to examine teen-oriented publications as well as celebrity magazines. Marianne observes that, in addition to reading *Smithsonian, Time*, and *Newsweek*, she will "also skim through *Seventeen, Teen, YM, People*, and *TV Guide* to keep up with Teen Trends," adding, "I have a teen of my own, so we get those at home for her." In fact, many respondents select newspapers and magazines to read on their own time that they foresee will be of use at the reference desk.

While many enjoy print newspapers and magazines, public library reference staff members are less enthusiastic about spending their free time reading newspapers or magazines online. As Table 28 shows, only 25.2 percent of respondents read online materials on a daily basis, as compared to 81 percent in the case of print materials, while 47.4 percent never read online sources during their free time. A number of factors contribute to this apparent disinterest in online materials, beginning with their perception that reading newspapers and magazines online is a distinctly work-related, rather than leisure-time, activity. With regard to print materials, Joel remarks: "A good librarian is a well-read librarian.... I read a lot on my own time. Because I have to? No, because I want to." He also comments, however, that he reads no papers or magazines online. In a particularly vivid example, Leonore details her subscriptions to the Canadian national newspaper *The Globe and Mail*, the Sunday *New York Times*, and the magazines *Canadian Living* and *People*, noting that she reads "the daily local [newspaper] carefully and purchase[s] one Sunday British newspaper," picks up *"Vanity Fair* to keep up on popular culture and ... *Municipal World* and *The Beaver* to keep up on Canadian information." Yet when asked if she reads online sources at home, this same individual writes: "Absolutely not. I refuse to use any of my personal home time to help the library."

In addition to making a distinction between reading print newspapers and magazines for personal enjoyment and edification and online sources for work, many public library reference personnel express a general aversion to reading online. While some admit a "basic dislike of reading for reading's sake from a computer screen," others cite what they see as the comparative benefits of print materials. Winnie explains that "the computer is a work tool. It is not a medium for regular whole-issue perusal when the paper version is so much easier to remember the basics of where we saw [an article] (sometimes even to the part of a page of XYZ publication), something that rarely happens when we are online." Trudy also avoids online newspapers, stating that "they do not add information to what is found in regular print." Other staff members explain that, rather than read online newspapers on a regular basis, they will periodically check web sites if there is a "breaking news story." Not surprisingly, staff members use the example of tracking the 2000 presidential election saga. "I don't read newspapers online so much on a daily basis but rather on an as needed basis," Brendan comments. "Take for instance the current presidential election debacle here in the States ... I find myself checking out the *Miami Herald* and other Florida newspapers regularly." Carmela consults the web sites of local television stations "if there is an issue going on that I think we need to be aware of, like the ongoing presidential thing."

Of course, another factor that affects whether respondents read online newspapers during their own time is the availability of Internet access. Some respondents mention having Internet access at home, including Randy, who writes that his "library system subscribes to ProQuest, which is also available to all county residents via home Internet access." He continues, "ProQuest provides us with electronic versions of the *NY Times*, *Washington Post, Wall Street Journal, Christian Science Monitor* and *LA Times*. I read from these papers through ProQuest two or three days per month for perhaps two hours at a stretch, generally tracing down articles on a particular topic and tracing them across publications and time." Although 41.5 percent of U.S. households had Internet access in August 2000,[1] Randy's situation appears to be anomalous for our respondents. Without home Internet access, the primary means of reading materials online during their own time is at work, either during breaks or at lunch. The amount of time available for online reading is therefore circumscribed. But, to judge from the comments of Leonore, even if reference staff members had home Internet access, they might not want to spend time staring at a computer screen at home.

The 219 public library reference staff members who do read newspapers and magazines online during their free time — whether once a day or once a week (105 + 89 +25; Table 28) — consult a variety of sources. In addition to major national papers such as the *Washington Post, New York Times*, and *Christian Science Monitor*, they also regularly visit the sites of Internet-exclusive publications such as *Salon* and the *Drudge Report*. Others focus their attention on "web sites not affiliated with a specific paper," preferring instead the general news and information sites of CNN, Reuters, and the Associated Press, to name but a few. This preference reflects the online information gathering habits of the general adult population. According to *Brill's Content*, of the five most popular online news and information sources based on the number of visitors between 2000–2001— about.com, msnbc.com, weather.com, cnn.com, and nytimes.com — just one is affiliated with a print publication.[2]

By the same token, some respondents use their free time to visit specialty or primary source web sites rather than news sites. "For current event news I also often will go straight to the source," Randy explains. "I've spent time reading on the Commission on Presidential Debates web site, ... the site for the European Union, WTO, the UN, other US Federal government sites, Catholic Information Network and the Vatican's site." Zack checks out "Lithuanian websites once a week or so for background information on travel and art, and to keep up with my Lithuanian reading proficiency," while Hubert visits "sites such as Intellicast for radar weather information." Others undertake online reading so as to anticipate likely reference questions. "I spend more time with book review sites though than with current event sites," Celeste explains. "My reference questions are more often 'what do I read next,' or 'what's a good book on the history of...' than 'who won the election in W. Germany last month.'"

In cases where respondents do cite specific newspapers that they read online, an interesting pattern emerges. We have seen that public library reference staff members tend to read local newspapers daily and national newspapers and news magazines on a weekly basis. While they read local daily papers in print, they use the Internet to scan either major national newspapers or dailies from different regions. Tyrone reads "the local paper everyday and *The Birmingham News*, the largest newspaper in the state on Sundays" in print, but will "also check the *International Herald Tribune, New York Times, London Times*, and Atlanta [papers] occasionally" online. Dion reads his local paper in print, but "will frequently go to the *London Times, Washington Post*, and a San Francisco paper" web site, in addition to perusing his "hometown paper, the *Times-Picayune* from New Orleans" online while at work. Some staff members use the Internet to catch up on their "hometown paper." For one of these individuals, home is Germany, which points to another factor in how respondents approach online versus print news sources. While some mention international publications in the context of print papers, including Italy's *Corriere Della Serra* and the *South China Morning Post*, for others, reading international publications is an excusively online activity, with the Internet providing timely access to international coverage that might not be readily available, or would be prohibitively expensive, in print.

Television and radio

As Haynes Johnson observes, a favorite topic of media pundits is the role that online information sources plays in the "fragmentation of the broad audience major TV networks and newspapers used to reach."[3] The result is a battle between old media and new media, where the object is to draw the attention of an audience that increasingly displays what Frank Rich describes as the "postmodern news-grazing habits of the young, who turn to antiestablishment sources as the Internet ... for their information fix."[4] We have seen that, when it comes to keeping up with current events on their own time, public library reference personnel generally prefer the "old media" format of print newspapers to "new media" online information sources. What are their preferences when it comes to two other "old media" sources: television and radio news programs?

Table 29. Frequency with which public library reference staff members tune into television and radio news shows on their own time (Questions 11 and 12 in Appendix B)

	TV news shows (n = 412)	Radio news shows (n = 401)*
More than three shows on a regular basis	69 (16.7%)	32 (8%)
Between one and three shows on a regular basis	194 (47.1%)	155 (38.7%)
Occasionally	54 (13.1%)	59 (14.7%)
Never	95 (23.1%)	155 (38.7%)

* Percentages do not add to 100% because of rounding.

As Table 29 shows, almost one quarter of respondents (23.1 percent) never turn to television programming as a source of current affairs information. A few of these individuals state that they would "prefer to listen to the radio" or "would rather read the newspaper." Another asserts, "Main media does not interest me." As one individual puts it, "I am not a television watcher, period!" At the other end of the spectrum, only 16.7 percent of respondents tune into more than three televised news shows on a regular basis. A plurality of public library reference staff members elect to watch between one and three news programs on a regular basis (47.1 percent), while 13.1 percent watch television news occasionally.

The ambivalence toward television news programs suggested by these figures is expressed in respondents' comments about their television-viewing habits. For the most part, they would concur with Rich, who points out that the declining viewing audience for these primetime programs is attributed not only to the choices presented by the Internet and the "500-channel cable-satellite media universe," but also to "the content and nature of the broadcasts themselves."[5] Rich quotes evening broadcast icon Walter Cronkite: "Those feature stories—Eye on America, your kitchen and mine, your back porch and mine, your garbage pail and mine—it's not bad stuff. But not, for God's sake, in the national news! Not on the front page! They're taking that time from the major news they should be covering."[6] Public library reference staff members allude to what they see as the less than stellar news coverage of televised news programs, most often in terms of the sensationalized content and presentation of the shows. Lilly comments, "The only regular show I watch is *Masterpiece Theatre*. Many of the news shows have become quite depressing. Seem to revolve around people having been thrown in jail for some crime or other that they did or didn't do. Or, how the government is cheating us in some way or other." And Sidney explains, "Almost every morning I flip on *CNN Headline News* as I get ready for work. I used to watch other news shows but they have turned to more sensational trash than true news reporting." Individuals who either occasionally or regularly turn to network news programs "watch out of habit more than of any intellectual curiosity." Caitlin writes, "Generally, I do not watch any TV newscast as you get little information, but I confess to watching *60 Minutes* and the *Today Show* (daily)."

Media watchers see this type of viewer ambivalence as the death knell of network evening news. As Rich observes, the "No. 1 cliché among media critics that we're watching the 'last hurrah' of network news anchors as we have known them for nearly half a century."[7] The numbers seem to support this assertion. Rich notes that, in 1981, NBC, ABC, and CBS "collectively commanded 84 percent of the viewing audience," while twenty years later, "the triumvirate of [Tom] Brokaw, [Peter] Jennings, and [Dan] Rather garner only 43 percent of the pie."[8] According to Nielsen Media Research statistics published in *Brill's Content*, "the combined ratings (percentage of all TV households) for the ABC, CBS, and NBC evening news have dropped" between the years 1970 and 2000, while the ratings for evening news programming on the cable networks, with the exception of CNN, have been increasing since 1991.[9]

Table 30. Types of television news programming watched by public library reference personnel

Category	Examples	No. of staff members (n = 317)*
Network evening news	*ABC Evening News; NBC Nightly News*	102 (32.2%)
Network current affair shows	*60 Minutes; Face the Nation*	101 (31.9%)
Cable news programming	*CNN Headline News; Larry King Live*	74 (23.3%)
Morning network news	*Good Morning America; The Today Show*	28 (8.8%)

* Numbers do not add to *n* and percentages do not add to 100% because not all staff members cited specific television programs in their responses. Percentages calculated based on *n* = 317 so as not to overstate results.

Yet, while public library reference personnel are not exactly impressed by the quality of network programming, their television viewing habits hardly point to the demise of the network evening news. To be sure, a few respondents, such as Sidney, have become cable news converts, choosing to receive all of their televised information from CNN, MSNBC, and Fox News. But there are others who "[a]lways watch the nightly news with Peter Jennings on ABC," or who steadfastly "rely on NBC for televised news—*The Today Show* in the morning, *NBC Nightly News*, and *Meet the Press*." As Table 30 shows, more respondents specifically mention watching the network evening news (local or national) than any other news programming. An almost identical number watch network current affairs shows, including primetime fare such as *48 Hours*, *Dateline*, and *20/20*, and what one individual refers to as "Sunday morning chatterboxes"—programs such as *Meet the Press* and *Face the Nation*. Interestingly, two reference staff members cite *Oprah* as a form of news programming, with one of these individuals explaining that she occasionally tunes in since "authors or issues that are discussed become patron requests." Speaking of current affairs programs in general, another observes: "These aren't particularly helpful in answering reference questions, but do help with chit chat to break the ice with patrons. In this regard, Jay Leno and other late night programs have their place."

In addition to being the second most popular form of news programming, current affairs programs engender the most commentary, both favorable and unfavorable, from public library reference staff members. On the one hand, there are respondents like Becky, who watches "as many of the current affairs programs as possible — *60 Minutes, Dateline, 48 Hours, 20/20*. I love them!" Vivian has the same tastes, remarking, "I like current affairs programs and watch those the most of anything on TV. This includes *Prime Time, Dateline, 20/20*, and *Larry King Live*." On the other hand, some reference staff members characterize current affairs programs, especially the network primetime news magazines, as too sensationalistic — the same diagnosis given to network news. "If an ad catches my eye I might watch one of the current affairs programs, but for the most part I don't watch them," writes one individual, concluding that "[a]ll too often I've found them to be more sensational than newsworthy." Evelyn agrees, commenting, "I consider the television newsmagazines to be too fluffy and sensationalized to be considered anything but entertainment," while Bobbie Jo describes these programs as "more alarmist than informative."

Although public library reference staff members cite network current affairs programs (both the primetime newsmagazines and, in the words of one respondent, "the Sunday talking heads type shows") at almost the same rate as network evening news broadcasts, they tend to watch these current affairs programs occasionally, rather than regularly. Some individuals point out that they decide whether to watch current affairs programs on a given week based on the stories the shows will cover. Suzanne explains, "I don't watch the 'news magazine' format programs every week, but watch the one whose subjects interest me." A notable exception is the CBS Sunday evening program *60 Minutes*, which one person describes as "the only current affairs show I feel is not overly sensationalized." Sixty-nine of the 317 reference staff members who watch televised news programs (21.8 percent) make a point of tuning in to *60 Minutes*. While some of them are occasional viewers, the majority are loyal followers— a fact that reflects the enduring popularity of this program with the general adult viewing public. Among the various statistics, milestones, and accolades recounted on the *60 Minutes* web site, the 34-year-old program currently holds the record for consecutive Nielsen Top 10 rankings, covering 22 television seasons between 1977 and 1999.[10]

The popularity of *60 Minutes* notwithstanding, the idea that public library reference personnel tune in to current affairs programs based on the content of a given week's episode is indicative of respondents' overall television viewing habits. As Table 30 shows, they watch network evening newscasts (32.2 percent) and network current affairs programs (31.9 percent) at roughly the same rate, with a slight decline in the rate at which they watch cable programming (23.3 percent) and a sharp decline in the rate at which they watch morning news programs (8.8 percent). Mornings may be an especially hectic time for public library reference staff members, but the relatively even distribution of responses across the first three types of programming suggests that they try to accommodate as wide a variety of television news programming as time allows. For example, listing "CNN, MSNBC, PBS and network stations" as sources that she turns to for televised news, Julianna explains, "I am not loyal to any. I try to get a rounded view by watching a variety." At the same time, the fact that some respondents "do a lot of channel surfing on all of the night time news programs and end up watching a little of all of them" is less indicative of dissatisfaction with any of the shows than of the specific roles that reference staff members have assigned to the different networks and programs in their quest for information. Maris, for instance, likes to "watch all the national newscasts," but prefers "ABC for overall coverage and foreign news, CBS for science news, [and] NBC for political news." Zack tunes into NBC while he gets ready for work, watches the "*CBS Evening News*, *Dateline*, *60 Minutes*, and *20/20* regularly," but notes that if "there is something of particular interest developing in the world, I watch MSNBC after the network news." Alma watches *CNN Headline News* "when major stories break" and the local news only "when we are expecting a hurricane."

In Chapter 5, we noted that, in 1999, 98.2 percent of American households had at least one television set (with an average of 2.4 television sets) on which the average American watches 1,588 hours per year of televised programming.[11] Like television viewing but unlike newspaper reading, Americans will spend more time listening to the radio in the years to come. In 1999, the average number of hours spent twirling the dial was 967; this is expected to increase to 1,012 hours per person by 2004.[12] Certainly, there is no lack of opportunity to listen to the radio: in 1998, 99 percent of American households had an average of 5.6 radios.[13] But public library reference personnel are less likely to get their news via radio than from television. As Table 29 shows, 38.7 percent of respondents never listen to news radio programming during their free time, compared to 23.1 percent who never watch television news shows and 8.2 percent who never read print periodicals (see Table 28).

There are many reasons why radio news is less of a priority for reference personnel. First, some individuals explain that they spend their commute listening to books on tape instead of radio news. Dora, who listens "to audiobooks during my commute to keep up with readers' advisory," notes that "[a]ll of my information about the news comes from staff members, and they don't bring up much so I don't think they are any better off than I am." Others prefer to "channel hop for good songs" while they drive. Max, however, lives by the adage "silence is golden": "I like a lot of silence so I am not the kind of person who likes a radio on in the background," he explains, adding, "I do a lot of reading, ... and I like it quiet when I am reading."

While 38.7 percent of public library reference staff members never listen to news shows on the radio, another 38.7 percent indicate that they listen to between one and three shows on a regular basis. No matter the number of news shows they follow, many are commuter listeners only — a fact that necessarily decreases the amount of time they spend listening to radio programs. One individual recounts, "I used to listen to various programs on NPR on the way home from work, when I used to have an hour and a half commute. Now that I live much closer to work, I rarely find myself listening to the radio." Observing that she will "listen in the car when I can to *Morning Edition* and *All Things Considered* [on NPR]," Shari describes her listening time as "irregular because my work hours do not have me in the car when these programs are broadcast."

Table 31. Sources of radio news programming listened to by public library reference staff members

Source	No. of staff members (n = 246)*
National Public Radio	109 (44.3%)
Canadian Broadcasting Corporation	24 (9.8%)
Local radio stations	18 (7.3%)
Syndicated, conservative talk radio shows	6 (2.4%)
Catholic Family Radio	2 (0.8%)

* Numbers do not add to *n* and percentages do not add to 100% because not all staff members cited specific radio programs or stations in their responses. Percentages are calculated based on *n* = 246 so as not to overstate results.

Not all radio listeners are commuter listeners. In fact, public library reference personnel have idiosyncratic listening rituals designed to fit not only their schedules, but also their individual proclivities. Hanna remarks, "I do not listen to the radio in the car, as I enjoy thinking and planning"; instead, she turns on the radio "in the morning while doing the dishes, and while doing the dinner dishes." In much the same way, Caitlin does "not listen to news on the radio unless I am in the kitchen baking on my days off." While these individuals tend to listen to news programs in conjunction with specific tasks, some respondents, like Bernice, are all-day listeners, listening "almost every waking hour, before and after work." In contrast to Max's preference for quiet, Leonore has the radio tuned to the Canadian Broadcasting Corporation [CBC] "always, even when I am working on my home PC or reading."

In fact, the concept of "always" having the radio on is not merely a figure of speech, but instead signifies that the respondent literally listens to the radio—and in many cases one station in particular—"all the time, usually 7 or 8 hours a day," as another loyal CBC listener explains. This means that some public library reference staff members listen to the radio even at work. As Norma states, "I have NPR on at the library all day and on in the car almost all the time. It is probably one of my main sources of news, particularly *All Things Considered.*"

While public library reference personnel might have different preferences about when and where they listen to news programs, there is not much discrepancy about their favorite programs and stations. As Table 31 shows, 44.3 percent of respondents who listen either occasionally or regularly to radio news cite NPR programs, including *All Things Considered, Morning Edition, Fresh Air, Science Friday,* and *The World.* As one devoted fan writes, "I wake up to NPR, I listen only to NPR when I have the radio on. I listen to all shows and consider NPR to be my primary source of information about current events." For many, NPR is their preferred source not only for radio news, but for news in general — eloquent testimony about the primary role of radio programming in keeping them abreast of current events. Describing herself as "an NPR junkie" who listens "whenever I can get away with it," including by tuning into the radio at her desk at work or by visiting the NPR web site, Winnie notes that the NPR programs "give regional, national, and especially international news [in] greater depth than I ever got on TV (including CNN)." Likewise, Belinda prefers *Morning Edition* "to any other news program — television, online, or print."

Not everyone is as enthusiastic. Finding that he listens to NPR less frequently than in the past, Felix concludes that "the last couple of years their bias on particular issues had cost them my reliance on their programs for informative data." Others, however, make a point of seeking out biased programming. Indeed, six respondents listen to syndicated, conservative talk radio personalities such as Rush Limbaugh, Dr. Laura, and Michael Savage to hear what one respondent describes as "the other side of things." While one individual quips that, while listening to conservative talk radio, "I find myself yelling at the radio too often," some reference staff members like Fay note that Rush Limbaugh and Michael Reagan, "although both very conservative and biased ... still provide an interesting forum for political ideas." More generally, the idea of talk radio—conservative or otherwise—as a forum for ideas prompts respondents such as Tyrone to listen to as many programs as possible. He explains, "I listen to a number of 'talk shows' when I can—everything from local sports shows to Dr. Edell to Limbaugh and Paul Harvey.... I have found that knowing what is on these shows helps answer questions. I have had to find poems and quotes and information on subject matter that first appeared on these shows. I usually do this in the car or when I am working on a project at home and just half listen, but it paid off too many times to stop." The decision to listen to specific radio shows based on their relevance to patron queries applies to local news programs as well. As Jenna remarks, "I listen to the local news radio station each morning as I'm getting ready to come to work. I find this is one of the best ways to learn about organizations and services in the area."

The early bird gets the ice worms in Antarctica: How following various media sources helps in reference work

While public library reference personnel express preferences for how they stay abreast of current events, are there differences in how these various media—newspapers and magazines, online sources, television currents affairs programs, and radio news shows—come into play at the reference desk? At the beginning of this chapter, we noted that 78.8 percent of respondents have discovered that reading print or online newspapers and magazines has helped in their reference work, compared to 59.4 percent who cite the benefits of watching or listening to current affairs or news programs (see Table 27). Despite this discrepancy, respondents ascribe particular advantages to following the news on radio or television, one of which is the ability to track a story as it develops. Adam, recalling his ability "to find information on the Seagram purchase [for] a patron because I had heard the details of the purchase on the radio," notes that he has "used the radio to assist with ... late breaking economic and political stories." Not surprisingly, public library reference staff members frequently mention how television and radio enabled them to follow the serpentine path of the presidential election 2000, which, in turn, made them more adept at answering queries. "I watched election returns on MSNBC and then followed the story," one respondent wrote during the vote-counting. "We have been getting daily inquiries as to how the situation is changing, and watching the news has allowed me to stay informed. I am able to name the principles involved and where the voting recount currently stands."

Like radio and television news, staff members also mention that online publications can supply them with up-to-the-minute news that they can pass on to their patrons. As a resident of Florida, Cicely observes that "hurricanes are always popular reference questions. The *Orlando Sentinel* has all the major links and satellite imaging." Public library patrons also want to know about late-breaking international developments that are too recent for print newspapers and magazines. Becky remembers how "[w]e once needed a map of Bosnia when the war was going on. Print sources were not current enough. CNN had shown a graphic on TV that morning so I went to the CNN website and found exactly what the patron needed."

Reference personnel also identify the role played by various types of television and radio programming. Terrance focuses on current affairs radio and television shows in his comments, explaining that "listening to or watching discussions of issues (e.g., on the topic of biotechnology/genetic engineering) helps me to understand the different points of view on issues and to provide balanced information when I receive a reference request on the topic." Hazel, who works in a public library in Canada, feels strongly that information can be gleaned not only from the television or radio program itself, but also from commercials. She recalls the following incident: "Recently I had a question about Advil. I had seen this product advertised on American television commercials so I was aware of it and recognized the name. The question posed by my patron was: Is Advil available in Canada? Checking the Internet, Advil did in fact appear on several sites. I didn't have to go through the verification process so often necessary when one is not familiar with certain aspects of reference questions."

Reference personnel are clearly aware that television and radio cannot be disparaged as sources of information. They understand that snippets of information from unlikely sources can inspire important inquiries. In this sense they might identify with Anthony Harris, director of the Criminal Justice Program at the University of Massachusetts, Amherst.[14] Harris is credited with showing that the most significant factors in keeping the homicide rate down are not policies like "zero tolerance" policing, but rather "something much more practical: faster ambulances and better care in the emergency room." How did he come up with his insight? By watching television — and not even television news. As Ryan Lizza reports, Harris had his epiphany "while watching an emergency-room reality TV show that featured the story of a man stabbed in the head with a huge knife. Despite horrendous injuries, E.R. doctors saved the man's life. Instead of a homicide, the patient became an aggravated-assault victim." Murder rates, Harris subsequently discovered, are being "artificially suppressed because thousands of potential homicide victims each year are now receiving swift medical attention and surviving."

While our respondents describe advantages of print and online newspapers and magazines, radio, and television in terms of answering reference questions, they also explain that these various sources complement each other. As Jesse comments, "In our society, we get news from every angle. I read the newspaper headlines, watch the nightly news, read a magazine or two a week and look at online news sources multiple times throughout the day. I often forget which source it was ... [from which] I gleaned the information. Often it appears in multiple sources." The fact that the same stories are covered in multiple sources, coupled with the idea that there are advantages to relying on certain sources in certain situations at the reference desk, creates a type of synergy when it comes to answering patron queries. For example, Winnie shares her experiences answering queries about dinosaurs in Antarctica, a topic that she "first heard on NPR, later saw in a newsmagazine article, [and] a month or so later in *Scientific American*." As a result, "[w]hen patrons came in for science stuff on fossils and wanted new dinosaur info I had something I could go to quickly that was 'hot,' as well as the NPR news online having background support info that lead us to tons of other fabulous things." Kendrick was able to direct a patron to both print and online information about treatment for Alzheimer's disease. The patron's query, Kendrick notes, "was asked a day or so after I had read about the treatment in the *San Francisco Chronicle*" and after he "had also heard a similar report on NPR *Morning Edition*." In another example of the intersection of various media, Cicely recalls that she was able to answer a patron's query that was based on a question from the television game show *Who Wants to Be a Millionaire?* The question was about a comedy film, put together by the White House staff for members of the press corps, which featured President Bill Clinton doing laundry. Cicely "was able to answer the question immediately," not because she had watched the game show that featured the original question, but because she had read about the film in a magazine article.

Table 32. How following various media sources helps with reference queries for public library reference personnel (Questions 9 and 13 in Appendix B)

	Print or online newspapers and magazines (n = 304)*	Television and radio news or current affairs programs (n = 214)*
Increasing background knowledge	89 (29.3%)	86 (40.2%)
Directing patrons to specific articles/information	62 (20.4%)	7 (3.3%)
Being aware of specific authors/titles	15 (4.9%)	33 (15.4%)
Identifying new or alternate resources	9 (3%)	2 (0.9%)
Selecting search terms/ understanding terminology	5 (1.6%)	2 (0.9%)

* Numbers do not add to *n* and percentages do not add to 100% because not all staff members cited specific examples in their responses. Percentages are calculated based on *n* = 304 and *n* = 214, respectively, so as not to overstate results. The *n*'s in Table 27 and Table 32 differ because not all the people who answered Question 9 provided concrete examples that could be further categorized. Some respondents mentioned more than one area.

Further evidence of synergy among various news sources can be found in the general themes that characterize the experiences of reference staff members when they discuss how reading newspapers and magazines, as well as listening to or watching news programs, helps them in providing reference service. These five themes— Increasing one's background knowledge, Directing patrons to specific articles or information, Being aware of specific authors and titles, Identifying new or alternate resources, and Selecting search terms and understanding terminology — are summarized in Table 32. Not only do these themes transcend the boundaries between various media formats, but they reiterate issues that were raised by academic librarians, including the notion that awareness of current political, social, and economic events is essential to providing quality reference service. We discuss each of these themes in the following sections.

Increasing background knowledge

Like academic librarians, public library reference personnel explain that the various media sources they consult during their free time contribute to their general background knowledge, which, in turn, allows them to improve reference service. The 89 respondents (29.3 percent) who describe the contribution of print and online newspapers and magazines note that reading these publications "gives you a little edge so that you won't have to tackle a question cold." Gordon characterizes this "edge" as the familiar "frame of reference" which is constructed by reading current newspapers and magazines. Like academic librarians, public library reference personnel discuss how they depend upon this frame of reference to identify the key players, geographical locales, and timeframe of events at the local, state, national, and international levels. Deanna observes that "having a broad range of reading tastes gives me a general familiarity with most topical fields so even if I am not an expert in the field of inquiry that a patron brings up, I usually know what topical terms, areas and resources to use to find their information. In other words, I know what they want and how and where to look for it." Knowing how and where to find this information gives Deanna the assurance that she "won't be caught 'off-guard' when asked about" disparate topics. Indeed, Eunice suggests that many of her colleagues have, in fact, been "caught off-guard" at the reference desk. "I am often the only one who has any idea of what the patron is talking about," she laments. "Most staff have very poor common knowledge."

Like Deanna, some public library reference personnel discuss how reading newspapers and magazines, either in print or online, helps them pinpoint what, exactly, a patron "wants to know." "It has helped me to be able to ask the patron the right questions and to get specific information that they are asking for," Naomi writes. "Sometimes, they only need very general information, [and so] I would use a different source than if they wanted very specific information on the same subject." Identifying patrons' needs is central to negotiating the reference interview, and respondents explain that reading outside of work enables them to ask discerning questions. Naomi provides such examples as: "Does the information need to be very current? Is it important that it be from a reliable source? If a student is doing a biography on Liszt, does he need to include a picture, a piece of his music?" In addition, respondents again stress that the frame of reference that they construct by reading newspapers and magazines is crucial for filling in gaps or correcting misinformation in patron queries. As Seth summarizes, "Patrons don't always remember things accurately or [they] misunderstand what they heard, so a reference librarian needs to be able to translate or let the patron think one has a crystal ball."

Once they have established just what information the patron is seeking, public library reference personnel state that having read about various topics in newspapers and magazines also helps in identifying relevant sources or in answering the question directly without recourse to additional sources. "By being aware of the scope of reporting in print or online newspapers and magazines I can more effectively offer appropriate resources to patrons," Marilyn writes, adding, "I'm also more familiar with the parameters of the discussion, lexicon, etc." Carrie agrees, remarking, "Being current helps me to know what sources to use when looking for answers to a reference question." Reference personnel point out that the ease with which they can determine exactly what information the patron is seeking and subsequently identify the most likely relevant sources means that they expend less time on each query — an important consideration, given "the fast-food needs of today's library users." In fact, Bea feels that the primary way that reading newspapers and magazines assists with reference service "is in the speed of relating to the context of the question," observing, "I think any of the other librarians would find as good or complete an answer, but it may take them just a little longer to get to it if they are not as familiar with the context."

Three respondents have a somewhat different interpretation of what it means to be familiar with relevant sources, asserting that, by reading the newspaper on a regular basis, they become familiar not only with the reported events, but also the organization of the pages themselves. As one respondent explains, "Sometimes patrons will ask about a specific article and just being familiar with the layout of the paper helps. For example, regional information is usually in the B section of the newspaper and entertainment information is in a special Thursday section." Elena also notes that reading various newspapers online has made her "aware of their page format." For Leonore, the benefit is knowing not only which sections will have relevant articles, but also which days these sections appear: "the important city information is put in the local paper on Saturdays" and "the upcoming cultural events are always in Thursday's issue."

Underpinning the comments of public library reference personnel is the idea that reading newspapers and magazines does not simply increase their general knowledge of events, but also helps them, as one respondent phrases it, "to recognize breaking news stories and issues, and to get a sense of what people are reading and thinking about." Public library reference personnel are, in essence, reading between the lines of current news stories, taking note of issues and events that will, in all probability, have a direct impact on their patrons. This was an idea first introduced in responses to the question of which newspapers and magazines academic librarians spend their free time reading. In Chapter 3, academic librarians also adopted a proactive approach to reference work, specifically by foreseeing queries about Supreme Court decisions and being sure to read the relevant articles in national newspapers. The importance of taking a proactive approach, however, forms an even stronger undercurrent in the responses of public library reference personnel, especially when it comes to local news. "When there are local issues in the local paper, it prompts us to realize we will get asked questions, such as those relating to town ordinances, or teacher's salaries, etc.," Trudy explains. "We have these statistics at the reference desk." Reggie provides the following example of news items at the state level that prompted patron queries: "Our state has recently changed the law regarding driver license renewal. Someone was in and asked about the three requirements of identification for renewal. It had been in the *Daily Oklahoman* and we had clipped the article knowing someone would want to know about [the requirements.]"

Of course, being alert to news items that will generate patron queries applies to reading magazines as well as newspapers. Winnie recalls a recent run on volcano-related materials at her library, describing how "an entire 6th grade class had to do a 3-d project on volcanoes, because the science teacher had seen that the current issue of *National Geographic* had a nifty article on South Pacific volcanoes." In fact, Winnie has tracked the type of publications that are most likely to inspire school assignments, and cause mad rushes for books that would rival the hunt for the hottest toys during holiday shopping seasons. "Magazines that usually kick the teachers' salivating mechanism are the weekly newsmagazines, *National Geographic*, *Readers Digest*, *People*, and *Biography*," she writes, adding, "I wish they'd pay more attention to *Scientific American* (especially the short pieces), *Atlantic Monthly*, *Smithsonian*, and *Civilization* magazines instead of the nearly totally pop-culture focus they seem to go for lately."

In Chapter 4, academic librarians discussed the assumption that librarians who work in an academic setting and are therefore part of an academic community should be familiar with the various subjects that their patrons—i.e., students—are studying. A similar dynamic shapes the role of public library reference personnel. In this case, the assumption is that individuals working in the information professions will be informed about the community of which both they and their patrons are part. As Seth remarks, "Especially in small libraries, patrons look to the staff to know what is going on in the community, nation, and world. Many think that the librarian knows everything. We don't—quite—but know where to find it. Patrons like to chat while they're checking out materials and they seem to have more confidence in the librarians who know what is going on and are well read. The patrons are more apt to ask their reference questions of the librarians who are knowledgeable about things."

While many of the examples in which public library reference personnel take a proactive approach to reference work involve local news events, respondents like Seth stress that patrons want library personnel to help them situate these issues within the larger arena of national and world events. Respondents note that there are often instances where "breaking local news stories ... became national."

With Election 2000 unfolding as librarians responded to our survey, examples of how local news impacts national and international events were readily at hand. Results (contested or otherwise) from local elections determine national leadership not only at the executive level, but within the legislative branches as well. Votes from one county can affect the outcome of an election for a seat in the House of Representatives, which, in turn, can tip the balance of power in Congress. Local ballot initiatives that are passed and implemented affect how other states treat similar issues. Judicial decisions handed down in county courts may subsequently be appealed to district courts, courts of appeal, and, ultimately, the Supreme Court. School board decisions—a topic mentioned by many respondents—can similarly affect, and be affected by, education issues at the national level. Public library reference personnel recognize these connections and, by keeping up with current affairs through newspapers and magazines, provide the information that their patrons need to be informed citizens.

Estelle summarizes this process: "I am rather unconsciously scanning all the print sources that come before my eyes, categorizing and filing it away, often with particular patrons in mind. I proactively call patrons re new information.... I irritate my husband by asking him his sources when he makes provocative comments with information I wish similarly to store. Effective current awareness retrieval is a core skill of a public service librarian." And although "current awareness retrieval" begins with current awareness knowledge in newspapers and magazines, 40.2 percent of respondents describe how they have gained background knowledge of current events or socio-cultural issues through radio or television news and current affairs shows.

The popularity of using television and radio to develop one's background knowledge points to the key role that these media play in the lives of public library patrons. As a result, using television and radio programs to augment one's knowledge of current events becomes all the more important. Public library reference staff members state how watching or listening to news programs helps them "feel better informed and more able to converse about what is happening on the local level, the state level, and national level" much in the same way as reading print and online newspapers and magazines does. Respondents apply this knowledge not only in terms of knowing where to find information for specific queries, but also in terms of conveying information that they recognize would be beneficial to patrons. For example, Marianne notes that "just very recently, I watched on TV (either *Dateline* or *20/20*) a segment [about] the Allstate Insurance company coming under fire for telling accident victims unsound legal advice, getting them to sign settlements that saved the company money. A few days later, a lady came in and said that a car had hit her and the driver's insurance company told her to sign this settlement and that she did not need a lawyer. I mentioned the segment and she was going to check with a lawyer anyway." The knowledge that respondents have gained from such programs has also enabled them to directly answer questions on topics ranging from red tide to the safety ratings of automobiles.

Because television and radio programs often form an integral part of patrons' queries, public library reference personnel must be especially cognizant of radio and television programming. As Joy explains, "Patrons often frame their questions with 'I saw this on such and such news program.' Keeping up with at least some of the news shows keeps me in context even though it is, of course, impossible to watch every show that patrons mention." This also applies to radio programs. As Christine observes, "Many of our readers also listen to NPR and having heard the same reviews and features they have heard assists me in ... answering questions." While respondents note that patrons do refer to specific newspaper articles when seeking information, by far the vast majority of patrons refer to television and radio shows, suggesting that, while reference personnel may rely on newspapers and magazines, patrons primarily get their current events information from television and radio. Earl's comment regarding his use of print and online sources at the reference desk summarizes this phenomenon. Public library reference personnel, he explains, are "asked everyday for information that has appeared in print news *almost as often* as for information that has been broadcast on TV or radio" (emphasis added).

Respondents provide diverse examples of cases where "people refer to segments on news shows." Hope recalls two such incidents: "PBS aired a special on the Rockefellers one evening and two days later a gentleman came in wanting to find the Rockefellers' family tree. I was able to trace it with ease after viewing the show." She also remembers when a radio station "did a small piece on the background of Kit Kittredge," the latest doll in the American Girl Collection. "As the day went on I found the website for Kit after I was asked to provide a picture of the doll and biographical information on her." Wayne remembers how he "had a question just the other day about Megatranspac, a walking tour of ... Africa that was featured on NPR." He comments, "Without having heard about this in advance, I wouldn't have had much of a clue about what it was or where to find more information about it."

As Hope and Wayne's examples demonstrate, radio and television programs often prompt patron queries that fall outside the realm of current "hard-news" events. They also reflect the very specific nature of the information requests that patrons derive from such programs. On the one hand, it could be argued that the specificity of these requests and their connection to a particular news programs would make finding additional information for patrons easier. Indeed, two respondents note that in some cases they simply contacted the radio station or visited the web site of the program that hosted the segment. On the other hand, the same difficulty applies to radio and television requests as to print and online queries: patrons do not always remember key details. As one respondent observes, "We look for information on news stories that appeared on TV almost daily.... Sensational murders are frequent topics on the news shows, and we have several patrons who are fascinated with true crime. They never seem to remember the exact details, so it's important to find someone on staff who may have seen the show." Another respondent remembers how "I was able to help a patron find a book about job hunting that she had heard on NPR, even though she had the title completely wrong, because I heard the same broadcast." The specificity of the queries that television and radio programs generate thus poses unique challenges if reference staff members did not see or hear the program in question.

While both academic and public reference personnel describe the serendipity of having just read an article about a topic and then being able to respond to a query on that same topic, that sense of serendipity gives way to more concrete anticipation in the case of questions based on television and radio programs. Public library reference personnel recognize that "the public hears the same things we do," and, more significantly, that patrons "often come in after hearing a story wanting more information." As was the case with print and online newspapers and magazines, respondents take a proactive approach that will ensure that they will be able to fulfill these information requests. One individual explains that, when she listens to the radio or watches news programs, she generally keeps pen and paper nearby to jot down information she knows people will ask for. Maura recounts: "When the Alaska Airline jet went down off California, I got the web site for the passenger list from television news. I posted that web site at work, so [patrons] could access it if they wanted to. Most of the time when I use online, print, TV and radio information for reference, I usually come upon information and make a note of it (usually mental) in the event someone asks. Or I present the information I find out before I'm asked for it, like with the Alaska Airlines list."

In fact, a number of reference staff members stress not only the importance of watching or listening to news broadcasts with probable queries in mind, but also the idea of making information available to the public before requests are made. Like Maura, these individuals will hear a story on the news, follow up on the story by going to the station's web site to print out the complete information, and make this printout available at the reference desk. Hector recalls that a local television station "issued a statement about a recall for dip-tubes in water heaters, which needed to be replaced. We were able to find complete details from their web site because I heard it on the news." For these library staff members, anticipating requests becomes a community service.

In addition to providing information, respondents state that recognizing stories relevant to the community served by the library also involves debunking misinformation. In the following example, Felton recalls that the misinformation he corrected concerned the library itself: "I happened to hear the other day that [there was going to be] satellite voting for the Presidential Election at all Polk County libraries. I knew this was not true, as I am director of one of them, so I called the appropriate office and told them they needed to correct their information. This helped me to prepare for the onslaught of mad people who were going to come to vote. I informed the staff of how to prepare, got together all the information of where and what to tell people." The result, he explains, is that "[w]e managed to come out of it smelling pretty good." Felton stresses that "we were prepared simply because I keep abreast of news."

Directing patrons to specific articles or information

As Table 32 shows, 62 public library reference personnel (20.4 percent) have used their reading of newspapers and magazines to direct patrons to specific articles. Echoing the comments of academic librarians in Chapter 3, one public library reference staff member observes, "It seems I am constantly pulling out past copies of the newspapers to find an article I remember reading yesterday, last week or even last month." Says Delia, "During this past election, there was a series of questions relating to the revision of our city charter. The questions were complex and required careful reading and analysis. The issue was very politically charged. Of all the reference librarians, I am the only one who lives in [the city] and who has been following the issue closely. The day before the election people came to ask for information on the questions. I remembered that the questions had been published in the paper and was able to quickly refer people to the article." Likewise, Greta assisted a student who "was doing a report on home schooling.... I recalled that a few months ago *Newsweek* had a cover story on home schooling that clearly explained the topic, provided lots of statistics, etc. The student was very happy to get the article."

Library staff members also note that reading current newspapers and magazines increases their ability to evaluate which sources will best meet their patrons' information needs. In one example, Fay points out that following the 2000 presidential election in both print and online sources allowed her to determine which newspapers and magazines provide the best coverage of various candidates and issues. She discovered that *The Hartford Courant* had "great articles on [Senator Joe] Lieberman that were more specific than any ... of the national magazines" and that "the state newspaper worked better than the national." She has had ample opportunity to apply this knowledge: "I have had success helping several students with projects on the presidential elections by staying on top of which magazine and news sites had stronger pieces [and] [l]ocating information on the vice presidential candidates and their respective positions on the issues." In the same vein, Felix directed patrons with queries on "the curiously structured Electoral College" to an article in *Time* that he determined "has been helpful to folks who just want the basic facts and not a dissertation" on the subject.

Like academic librarians, public library reference personnel stress that recent articles, as well as articles in local newspapers and regional publications, are often not indexed. Without having read these articles, they would not have been able to recommend valuable resources to patrons. Wallace gives an example: "Since I regularly read *Newsweek*, I knew that they had recently done a cover story about children with autism. A patron was looking for some current articles and this was not yet indexed."

Crystal's preference for recommending articles directly from her own reading stems not only from practical considerations concerning the use of indexes, but also from the added value that these personal suggestions bring to the reference interview. Noting that she has "many, many examples," she relates the following story: "There was a patron whose daughter was doing a research paper on disabilities and she wanted some information on Christopher Reeve's disability. I remembered a cover story [in] *Redbook* about him and I pulled the back issue for her.... In my opinion, this is much faster than searching databases and provides the personal touch that is lacking in our society. Nothing's wrong with database searching, but when it comes from your own knowledge it is more satisfying somehow." Much like the academic librarians in previous chapters, Crystal has realized the importance of showing unfeigned interest in patron queries. Not only are patrons suitably impressed, but reference staff members themselves derive job satisfaction from the encounter because they have been able to rely on their "own knowledge."

In contrast to the numerous examples in which public library reference personnel directed patrons to specific print or online articles that they themselves had read, only seven respondents (3.3 percent) stated that they were able to direct patrons to information that came from television and radio news that they had watched or listened to. One respondent notes that "[i]f a patron has a general request about a topic I can say that there was a newsclip/program about the topic." Isaac reports, "I've had people come in with consumer questions and while I show them books to assist, I was also able to direct them to consumer advocates on local radio and TV shows as well ... for additional help." Generally, directing the patron to news programs means visiting a corresponding web site and downloading information or transcripts. As Fay explains, "A teacher had asked a question that I was able to refer to a PBS *Nova* special. *Nova* had done a program on the subject. We went to PBS.org, searched the topic and were able to download the entire program transcript for the teacher who was then able to take it to his class." Ivy recalls, "I once had a question about a home in Canada for girls with anorexia and remembered that a couple of years before that I had seen a show on *20/20* about that very home. I looked up the show on *20/20's* website and found the information for the patron (even after two years)."

Being aware of specific authors and titles

In Chapter 4, academic librarians explain that they become aware of specific authors and titles by reading fiction and nonfiction outside of work. As Table 32 shows, the primary way of finding out about new authors and titles for public library reference personnel is by listening to the radio and watching television. "Many times over the years I have watched or listened to interviews with authors of fiction or nonfiction books, and was later asked about either the author or the topic," Terrance recalls. "Having heard the interview helped me to answer the reference question." This is also the case with print and online periodicals. Darius comments that "patrons have come in to request very new titles. Newspapers and some periodicals give reviews of the most recent so I immediately can know what they are talking about." Yet, while 33 respondents (15.4 percent) cite television and radio programming, only 15 individuals (4.9 percent) mention the benefits that reading print and online newspapers and magazines brings to this aspect of reference work.

One of the 15 public library reference staff members who provided an example of how she used print sources to increase her awareness of recent publications hints at an explanation for this discrepancy: "A patron wanted the book that a contestant on *Who Wants to Be a Millionaire* had written. I had read in *People* the week before about how the book became a bestseller after he appeared on the show, so I got the magazine and found the book title that way." In other words, while reference staff members themselves might learn of new authors and titles primarily through print or online general-interest publications, their patrons often first hear about books through television or radio. We witnessed a similar dynamic when reference personnel drew upon knowledge of current events and popular culture that they had gained from radio and television programs when faced with queries based on these same programs. Both situations lead to a similar conclusion: reference service is improved when library reference personnel draw upon and can relate to the same sources of knowledge as their patrons do. As one respondent summarizes, "Knowing what our patrons are listening [to] and watching can only help us do our jobs better."

Many public library reference staff members use the Oprah Book Club as an example of how it is imperative for them to keep abreast of what "patrons are listening and watching" and, ultimately, reading. "People like to request books that are popular in the media," Elena comments. "Oprah's picks are pretty popular, so if I watch when she announces a new book, we can anticipate the rush or answer questions about which book it is, the plot, etc." Respondents also stress the role that listening to the same programs as their patrons can play in filling in the gaps "[w]hen a patron can't remember a specific name or title." As Yvonne explains, "I often remember what they're talking about and help them to find it."

Reference personnel also refer to the way in which author interviews on television and radio-based talk shows influence the questions they receive and their own awareness of authors and titles. Becky has found that "[w]hen authors appear on the *Today Show*, it's a sure bet that we'll get called to see if we have whatever book they're pushing." Greta recalls how she was able "to help a patron find a book about job hunting that she had heard about on NPR, even though she had the title completely wrong, because I heard the same broadcast." Simon makes a similar point about the necessity of being familiar with NPR. "The popular authors are easy to find, but we do not carry many books discussed on NPR," he explains. "Trying to find them is very challenging unless it is a program that I've listened to." In addition to author identification, Elena notes that hearing writers interviewed on these shows "gives me more of their background, helping [me] pass that along to patrons," with the result that she feels "better equipped to answer book-related questions." Tuning into radio or television interviews also heightens awareness of the library's collection. As Gene points out: "Having heard a panel discussion on NPR on the current upheaval in Israel, I recognized the author of a recent book on our new book shelf and could recommend it to a patron who was looking for the point of view that the author had voiced when on the air."

Identifying new or alternate resources and selecting search terms

Newspapers, magazines, television, and radio are also used to identify new or alternate resources. Most of the stories in this area focus on print newspapers and magazines as the predominant means of identifying new and additional resources. Roxanne has used information originally read in newspapers to identify "Medicare telephone numbers, housing contacts, New York Childcare Plus link for families in need of health insurance, unclaimed property contacts, local legislatures telephone numbers, [and] web sites." Just as academic librarians discovered that the web sites they read about in newspapers and magazines often exactly matched the information needs of their patrons, public library reference staff members note the high level of correspondence between web sites they read about in general-interest periodicals and the reference requests which are ultimately met using these web sites. Noelle referred a patron to "a new website sponsored by the state where people can look for local jobs" that she had first read about in her local newspaper. Marianne recalls that a "North Carolina newspaper offered some information on Internet sites for African American History Month that came in useful fielding questions from kids doing their projects." Ideal resources can also be found on television and radio. Hanna writes, "I had a student come to the library wanting help finding a 'wacky law'— anything on the books that was ridiculous and outdated. I remembered hearing on the radio the disc jockey talking about dumb ordinances. I called the radio station to ask where they came up with them. He told me of a web site called dumblaws.com. It was just what my patron was looking for."

Moreover, seven public library reference staff describe situations where they selected search terms first identified through either reading print or online newspapers and magazines, or listening to or watching radio and television news programs. Selma recalls, "A couple of weeks ago I was asked about a treatment for liver disease and recently read something about it in a local paper. It was enough to supply me with the name of the drug so I could find more about it in other sources." While the idea of identifying key search terms by reading articles on specific topics is familiar from the experiences of academic librarians, public library reference personnel state that radio and television programs also aid them in selecting likely search terms. Muriel recounts the following story: "Often patrons will ask for more information on topics they have heard about or seen on television. The last one I helped a patron on was locating information on [the] spread of germs and bacteria because of the reuse of water at dental offices. I remembered a news program or exposé (*20/20* or *48 Hours*) that I had seen late summer and recalled the term 'closed water systems' being used. That got me to the information that the patron wanted more quickly than I would probably have gotten to it with the terms the patron used."

The broad range of community information needs

Our discussion so far has focused on the various ways in which public library reference personnel apply what they read, listen to, or watch when providing reference service. The notion that public library reference staff members are, in the words of two respondents, "jacks-of-all-trades," however, is less a reflection of the variety of benefits that they derive from these materials—the ability to answer questions directly, for example, or to identify search terms—than it is a reflection of the variety of queries to which they apply these benefits. We have seen some indication of this variety in the stories that illustrate each of the categories presented in Table 32. Yet, these experiences alone do not give a complete picture of the usefulness of newspapers and magazines to public library reference work. To get that complete picture, we have to look at the diverse social and human contexts in which questions are asked. Accordingly, we have categorized the 143 responses in which respondents either mention the topics of the queries to which they have applied their reading of newspapers and magazines (e.g., "Information read in *Newsweek* helped answer a question about the Human Genome Project") or cite specific questions (e.g., "A patron wanted to know where Hillary Clinton was born").

Table 33. Subject areas of queries to which public library reference staff members responded based on their reading of print or online newspapers and magazines

Subject area	No. of staff members (n = 143)*
Local events	58 (40.6%)
Health/Science	31 (21.7%)
Arts/Entertainment/Popular Culture	24 (16.8%)
National events	22 (15.4%)
Biographies/Obituaries	14 (9.8%)
Business	7 (4.9%)
Domestic	5 (3.5%)
Education	5 (3.5%)
International events	3 (2.1%)
History/Religion	2 (1.4%)

*Numbers do not add to *n* and percentages do not add to 100% because respondents cited multiple queries.

As shown in Table 33, public library reference personnel respond to queries on a broad range of subject areas, from business to education, from health matters to popular culture, as well as to questions about the various personalities at the center of current events. From a socio-cultural perspective, this suggests that public library reference personnel play a key role in their communities, not the least because they know about the intimate and less intimate habits, tribulations, joys, quirks, and frustrations of numerous patrons. For example, 14 individuals mention patrons who pose questions revolving around people in the news, either by requesting biographical information or obituaries. One respondent explains that she has "a very regular patron who has a hobby of collecting famous people's obituaries. By reading *People* magazine and watching *Entertainment Tonight* this helps me to be aware of who has recently died." Another respondent notes that what begins with an interest in an obituary can often develop into a request for broader biographical information, explaining that "stories of celebrity deaths ... may lead to an interest in their writings or biographies." Patron interest in cognate information is also reflected in the questions that fall within the broad category of Arts/Entertainment/Popular culture. Not only do reference staff members field requests for further information on specific authors, books, or films, but they also respond to queries on such diverse topics as beauty pageants, time capsules, and Frank Gehry buildings. Russell recalls a patron who "was looking for information on that 'new museum that sort of looks like a ship'" and instinctively "was able to direct [him] to an article on the new museum in Bilbao that was in *Architectural Record*." And Thelma comments, "Surprisingly enough, I am most often helped by *People* magazine. I don't have children and that is often the only exposure that I have to the pop music groups and stars." She provides the example of "a specific question dealing with henna dye patterns ... that I was able to find from an article that I had read earlier in that magazine."

While Thelma has found entertainment magazines to be extremely useful, Hedy depends on different sources to help with what she terms "domestic queries." "Oddly enough," she writes, "it is the women's magazines that help me answer some of my reference questions. I get quite a few that I would call 'domestic' queries. I recall one time having read an article in *Parents* magazine that helped me to answer a question on costumes for Halloween." In another holiday-related example, Hope explains, "I had an experience where someone wanted to make a chocolate turkey for her centerpiece for Thanksgiving and I had remembered seeing the instructions in the November issue of *Martha Stewart Living*."

Among the list of subjects that are of great concern to patrons are those related to personal health issues and science. As Table 33 shows, 31 public library reference staff members report that they have been able to deal successfully with patron queries on topics ranging from "the discovery that blueberries aid memory" to chronic fatigue syndrome, from tagging butterflies to "ice worms in Antarctica," because of the newspapers and magazines they read during their free time. The responses of public library reference personnel to such queries necessitate not only a broad frame of reference that comes with reading widely on various topics, but also a sensitivity in applying this accumulated knowledge. Reflecting on her experiences at the reference desk, Sibyl recalls that "[s]everal years ago a lady brought her children into the library. She had just found out from the doctor that she only had a short time to live and she needed material on how to tell her children and help them to understand and be able to cope. Years later, the children came in and told us thanks for the help." In another example, Ramona observes that "just this week a patron came in who had been diagnosed with diabetes. She was looking for current information. I had read the Sunday paper, which had started a series of articles on diabetes to be run in three or four parts. I gave her the articles to help her out." In fact, Ramona herself has diabetes, and she drew on her personal experiences to direct the patron to additional information sources that she herself had found most helpful when she first received her diagnosis.

Respondents most frequently apply their reading of newspapers and magazines to queries about local events, from homecoming parades to road projects, from local crimes to holiday store closures. By reading local publications, reference personnel have been able to inform patrons on how to reach their Congressional representatives, where they can receive flu shots, and where school test scores can be located. Elections in particular give rise to a host of questions about local news and information. Typically, public library reference personnel explain to patrons how their home state splits its electoral vote, direct them to polling locations, and help them to decipher local candidates' stands on various issues. Because a trip to the polls usually entails registering opinions on state referendums, public library reference staff members are involved in explaining these convoluted issues. Evelyn answered questions on a "specific problem related to the legal status of game farms in Montana"; she notes that articles from the *Billings Gazette* and *Montana*

Stockgrower were helpful. And while Americans were heading to the polls in a general election in November 2000, it was business as usual for city and town councils. In addition, patrons never stop needing to know about the times, locations, and agendas of council meetings.

Although media coverage makes it difficult to believe otherwise, the passing of seasons is marked by events other than elections and politicking: individuals and communities set their calendars by holidays and sports seasons. Some public library reference staff members describe how they use local newspapers and magazines to inform patrons about designated trick-or-treat times and pumpkin displays. With regard to sports events, Jack has responded to queries on "who the Indiana Pacers will be playing against and when," while Audrey "was asked who the new [coach of the Cincinnati] Bengals was and remembered that from reading the Sunday paper the day before."

National events–based queries are less commonplace. While 40.6 percent of respondents gave one or more examples of local events questions, only 15.4 percent did so in the case of national events questions. Not surprisingly, the term "national events" is often a synonym for "political events," and, in the context of the 2000 presidential election, public library reference personnel were asked repeatedly about the mechanics of the Electoral College, as well as the national itineraries of candidates. In other election cycles, other issues would likely predominate. International questions are even less common than national questions, with only three respondents (2.1 percent) citing instances of these questions. And two of these three respondents explain that these questions generally come from students working on class assignments. Although such questions are few and far between, they do cover an impressive number of subjects and "big issues," including cloning, WTO demonstrations, the death penalty, and the Ebola virus in Uganda. The dearth of international questions could reflect *which* experiences respondents chose to report, rather than a disinterest of international affairs on the part of patrons. At the same time, the fact that 40.6 percent of respondents provide examples of local events questions, compared to 2.1 percent of respondents in the case of international events, ties into general information-gathering trends. As Sarah Wildman reports in *The New Republic*, the Pew Research Center "released a study of 3,002 Americans that showed only 6 percent had noticed the coup in Venezuela or the rise of right-wing French presidential candidate Jean-Marie Le Pen. Only 5 percent had paid attention to the economic and political upheaval in Argentina. Even the nuclear tension between India and Pakistan drew only 23 percent. And 49 percent said they occasionally follow international news—the same percentage documented in 2000."[15] While Americans feel "that they *should* care about the rest of the world" (original emphasis), this honest intent does not always translate into actual reading (or watching or listening) behavior.[16]

The discrepancy between intent and behavior has two implications for public library reference personnel. On the one hand, patrons' obvious interest in the local events that have a more immediate impact on their lives means that reference staff members must read the local sources that impart this information. On the other hand, keeping abreast of international news even though patrons may not pose many international events questions allows reference personnel to inform patrons of issues *before* those issues metamorphose into national and local concerns.

Community reading: How reading newspapers and magazines helps public library reference staff members in other aspects of their work

Does the reading of print and online newspapers and magazines help public library reference personnel in non-reference aspects of their job? The response was overwhelmingly positive: 310 individuals (82.2 percent) could recall some instance where their reading of such materials had a positive impact on other facets of their work ($n = 377$). These positive responses were categorized according to the 10 aspects of librarianship presented in Table 34: collection development; being well-rounded; keeping abreast of library issues; community awareness; conversing with patrons; readers' advisory services; outreach and programming; bibliographic instruction; personal and professional development; and bibliographic control.

Table 34. Other aspects of public library work that are improved by reading newspapers and magazines (Question 10 in Appendix B)

Aspect of public library work	No. of reference staff members ($n = 310$)*
Collection development	88 (28.4%)
Being well-rounded/increase in general knowledge	68 (21.9%)
Keeping abreast of library issues	27 (8.7%)
Community awareness	23 (7.4%)
Making conversation	16 (5.2%)
Outreach and programming	12 (3.9%)
Readers' advisory services	11 (3.5%)
Personal/professional development	9 (2.9%)
Bibliographic instruction	5 (1.6%)
Bibliographic control	1 (0.3%)

*Numbers do not add to *n* and percentages do not add to 100% because not all respondents provided examples. Percentages are calculated based on $n = 310$ so as not to overstate results.

At first glance, the majority of these aspects are familiar from the stories that academic librarians shared in Chapters 3 and 4. For example, in the case of bibliographic instruction, public library reference personnel, like academic librarians, cite the usefulness of reading newspapers and magazines when selecting topics for instruction sessions. One respondent explains that she uses newspapers to demonstrate to "6th graders that there is more to research than using the encyclopedia," mentioning an assignment she designed where the students "are required to pick a nation and find articles on that nation." And just as academic librarians used the general-interest periodicals that they read outside of work to tailor their instruction sessions to the scholarly pursuits of university students, public library reference personnel seek topics to which their patrons can relate. This is the case with Wanda, who uses "topics such as Cooking and Recipes" in her Internet search class, noting that she finds "reviews of websites in popular magazines that help me prepare" for these classes.

Although both academic librarians and public library reference personnel point to numerous non-reference aspects that have been helped by reading general-interest periodicals, they do so at different rates. While bibliographic instruction was cited by 14.3 percent of academic librarians (see Table 13), it was mentioned by only 1.6 percent of public library reference personnel. Obviously, bibliographic instruction is a more important component of the daily working life of the academic librarian than the public library staff member. By the same token, some categories assume a special meaning that reflects the reality of the public library environment. Consider the category "Making conversation," mentioned by 5.2 percent of respondents. Unlike the academic librarians who related "Making conversation" stories, public library reference personnel do not feel pressured to make cocktail conversation or to prove their mental mettle at faculty luncheons. Instead, the idea of making conversation within the realm of public libraries focuses almost exclusively on patrons. As Shari explains, "Many people who come into the library come for more than books. They come to visit or talk, sometimes they are just lonely looking for social contact. Since the library is essentially a 'community center' for them, it's nice to be able to discuss the news and world happenings." In fact, Paulette argues that the "biggest benefit" of reading periodicals during one's free time "is not in the reference aspect of it." Rather, she continues, "it helps us develop a relationship with our patrons. In our community patrons come to the library to find out about things, it's true, but they come more because they like the staff and the relationships that we've developed with them over the years, even with passing comments on current events. We can provide a great reference service but it wouldn't do us a bit of good if we didn't have relationships with people!"

The focus on patrons— understanding, anticipating, and responding to their information needs— underscores the experiences of public library reference personnel in virtually every aspect of library work listed in Table 34. It also addresses the paramount idea of community awareness— the notion that public library reference personnel are more than mere information providers, that they are, for better and worse, full participants in the life of a specific community in a specific time and place.

We now trace this theme of community focus by looking at how reading print and online newspapers and magazines helps public library reference personnel in the following areas: collection development; being well-rounded individuals; keeping abreast of library issues; outreach and programming; and, finally, community awareness itself.

Collection development

Public library reference staff members see an innate connection between reference service and collection development, with one respondent describing collection building "as the handmaid of reference work." It is therefore not surprising that respondents cite collection development as the primary aspect of librarianship outside of reference work that benefits from reading newspapers and magazines. The relationship between collection development and reference work is strengthened by the similar approach that public library reference personnel take in performing these respective duties. Just as respondents are proactive in anticipating reference requests when reading, listening, or watching various current affairs sources, they also read newspapers and magazines with an eye toward "what the customers will be rushing in the door for next."

A wide variety of periodicals help in anticipating and meeting the expectations of patrons, ranging from national newsmagazines to specialized publications. Ray notes that "*Newsweek's* discussion about new books has helped me buy materials for the library to meet patron's needs," while Adrienne uses "*Romantic Times* for selection of romance titles most frequently." Entertainment publications also serve as a bellwether in predicting patron interest. Vivian explains, "*People Magazine* has interesting book and film reviews. They also regularly publish chapters from celebrity biographies. This is one place to measure the level of interest in a new book or film." Cicely points out, "Reading *Entertainment Weekly* gives me the popular culture background necessary ... to know what sorts of purchases to make." General-interest periodicals are also used to guide purchasing decisions for non-print collections. Leila, who describes herself as "an OLD librarian," notes that she "read about Bryn Terfyl in *Opera News* and bought that CD for the collection." Three reference staff members use movie reviews from various newspapers to select videos.

Public library reference personnel develop purchasing ideas not only from reviews, but also from general articles. Randy observes that he "frequently will find a book mentioned in an article on current events and proceed from there to find a review and then to purchase. For instance, I read a discussion of certain trends in globalization in the *Economist*, which mentioned Daniel Yergen's book *The Commanding Heights*. Based on Yergen's reputation, the discussion in the *Economist*, and the review I was able to find, I purchased the book for the library. Under other circumstances, I might not have been aware of it." Leila recalls a similar experience in which she "read an article in *The New Yorker* about [the] adoption of Romanian children and went out and bought the book mentioned in the article." At the same time, the contextual information contained in feature articles informs reference personnel not only of the "who" or the "what" of book selection, but also the "why"— the benefit, as one respondent phrases it, of "understanding why a topic or author is of interest."

Other respondents describe the usefulness of newspaper and magazine feature articles not only in terms of selecting specific titles, but also in identifying trends that will have an impact on patrons or that will simply pique their interest. Cognizance of these trends, in turn, informs the collection decisions reference personnel make. Gene remarks, "When eBay was featured in newspaper articles, I added more works on collectibles to the reference area." While this example focuses on national trends, materials are also purchased based on local events. Noting that the area where he works "is an evolving rural to bedroom community," Scott explains that issues mentioned in the local newspaper "concerning open land and the creation of land trusts" resulted in the purchasing of "relevant books about the subject." In another example, Rhonda comments that her library "set up a small business collection in our reference room due to the profusion of small businesses cropping up in the community as documented in our local papers."

These examples point to the limitations of professional library reviewing tools. Some reference staff members explain that reviewing tools are not as timely as general-interest publications in informing them of new materials that their patrons expect to find in the library's collection. Nell observes, "I can't even begin to count the number of times that newspapers or magazines have alerted me to new books that are coming out that the regular selection tools have either missed or are terribly late in reviewing." Nell's comment regarding "missed" books also highlights the fact that general-interest newspapers and magazines often carry "reviews of books and videos not covered in library publications." Many of these overlooked materials focus on local issues. Myrtle explains that reading general-interest publications "[h]elps me keep up on current trends and fads, which helps me … purchase materials on subjects of current interest. Many things are never mentioned in the review journals because they are of local interest only or are too much of a fad to receive recognition in 'legitimate' review sources." In addition, two respondents point out that the concept of "local interest" includes books by local authors, which in all likelihood would also be overlooked by professional reviewing publications.

The idea of using general-interest newspapers and magazines to identify new materials also needs to be examined in terms of the large number of patron queries that are based on author interviews from television or news programs. Brendan remembers the following incident.

> I had someone in the library just the other day seeking information on David McCullough's next book. The patron thought it might be on John Adams and Thomas Jefferson but we were unable to find any info in the professional journals for reviews, books in print or forthcoming books in print, or on the web at Amazon.com, for example. Then the following Sunday I was reading the *Boston Sunday Globe* magazine and lo and behold there was a story on David McCullough and his forthcoming book on John Adams … due out in the spring of 2001. Both the patron and I were thrilled to have the answer right in front of us so quickly in the end.

While Brendan notes that he saw McCullough's book referred to in a newspaper, where did the patron first hear about it? The query could have been generated by an author interview broadcast on radio or television, or it is equally probable that the patron was alerted about McCullough's book in a general-interest newspaper or magazine. Considering the limitations of professional reviewing tools with regard to both content and timeliness, public library reference personnel need to consult general-interest publications to keep pace with what their patrons are reading about. As one respondent observes, "I read the paper and magazines to get ideas for books to order…. Patrons read magazines and they see the ads from book clubs. They want to read these popular books. I feel great when I know that our library owns them all."

Being well-rounded

Like academic librarians, 68 public library reference personnel (21.9 percent) stated that reading newspapers and periodicals outside of work contributes to their sense of being well-rounded individuals, bolstering confidence that their background knowledge will aid them in various work responsibilities. While some define well-roundedness in terms of their ability "to hold a reference dialogue with a patron" and "to intelligently know what he is talking about"— in other words, the ability to escape what one individual calls the "mouth hanging open in an I have no idea mode"— their experiences center on how this knowledge results not only in finding the information sought by the patron, but also in relating to the patron as a person. This is readily apparent in the comments of Crystal, who explains that reading newspapers and magazines "helps me to relate to a patron who is looking for a book on seasonal affective disorder when I have just read an article on this subject. I KNOW the gist of their problem and can deal with it more empathetically. This is not to say that I am an expert, but I know enough to know that it's a medical and psychological problem."

Reference staff members also note that "[b]eing well-read helps you see the whole picture." As one respondent remarks, "Reading newspapers keeps me up-to-date with what is going on, which is a must for reference work. It helps me to make connections I otherwise would not have made if I hadn't read the current events." For some, seeing the whole picture and making connections means exploring areas that are beyond their usual purview. Maris observes that reading general-interest newspapers and magazines "[g]ives me a broader outline about topics I would never usually investigate, like technology." Greta comments, "Even though I do not do any online trading of stocks, reading about it in print and online has at least helped familiarize me with the general idea. I was talking with a co-worker, who does not read magazines or newspapers at all and does not even own a TV, and I mentioned online trading, and he said, with all seriousness, 'What's that?' I consider this sort of ignorance to really hamper one's job performance." And Denton states that reading newspapers helps him "resist the temptation to be too literary."

The broader mental horizons that are a result of being a well-rounded individual often extend into the realm of popular culture and quotidian pursuits. Letty has observed that "[c]rafts and hobbies are very popular" in her community, adding, "I am often able to help patrons by locating specific information for them because I am familiar with the different aspects of what they are trying to accomplish." Likewise, Cicely reads *Entertainment Weekly* not only to assist with collection development, but also to be exposed to "the popular culture background necessary to relate to the kids" that come into her library. "I find the Internet supplement especially useful," she writes. "It helps me stay on top of the hip websites and the trends in electronic gaming." Respondents again emphasize that, by tracking trends that are of importance to their patrons, they can alert them to information even before any requests are made — another example of the proactive approach of many public library reference personnel. "One of the great delights for reference librarians who like their work is the ability to scoop folks by bringing [to their] attention things that relate to their ongoing interests," another individual writes. Patrons thus come away from the library "knowing that library staff are really savvy and perspicacious FOR THEM and their needs."

Keeping abreast of library issues; outreach and programming

The 27 individuals (8.7 percent) who discuss the role that reading newspapers and magazines plays in helping them keep abreast of library issues explain that these materials provide them with ideas for introducing new services and improving existing policies. While eight respondents note that newspapers and magazines alert them to new technologies, others cite issues such as budgeting and marketing. "We are always looking for ways to improve our services to our patrons," explains Marshall. "Many ideas on ways to run small businesses and customer services can be found by following the example, or avoiding the mistakes, of other businesses." Indeed, reference personnel look to newspaper articles as a source not only for ideas, but also for guidance in decision-making, based on reports of what other libraries have succeeded (or failed) to accomplish. As Trevor remarks, "I can keep up with issues facing other libraries and how they are being handled and make my decision on how I would handle them if they arose."

One issue that arises frequently in respondents' experiences is Internet filtering. Noting that reading newspapers and magazines "keeps me abreast of trends, so the library can be proactive instead of reactive ... specifically in regard to 'filtering' and 'e-books,'" Felix describes how he and his colleagues "took care of our response before they became hot items" using ideas contained in general-interest publications. Mattie recalls how she justified the library's position on filtering to a patron: "I had to discuss with a parent a situation wherein his minor child had accessed inappropriate material on the Internet. Although our security level is high, I was able to explain why reading patrons' computer information is illegal, and that not every site can be blocked regardless of security level. Having read information on this subject, I could state my case with some authority."

In addition to policies and procedures, public library reference personnel also discover programming ideas from the newspapers and magazines they read during their free time. "Reading a variety of publications helps me to place things in a broader context," Tyson comments. "It helps me to pick up on trends so I can better plan programs that will be relevant and popular with our public." Laverne planned "a local canine police demo based on an article from the paper about the unit." And Vivian recollects programs and displays that were intended to coincide with events and happenings reported by general-interest publications. "We did a Star Wars marketing display around the release of the new Star Wars movie last year," she recalls. "We have a display up about Steve Allen who recently died, and did a big display of Frank Sinatra, which included his music. When Martha Stewart does a holiday planning issue, it may be time for a display of holiday craft and decorating books."

Community awareness

We end this chapter by examining the idea, cited by 23 public library reference personnel (7.4 percent), that reading newspapers and magazines, especially local publications, results in a greater sense of community awareness. There are two interconnected components to this concept. On the one hand, reading local publications provides specialized background knowledge focusing exclusively on a specific community. "It just generally helps me to know what is going on in the local area," Noelle comments. "It makes me feel informed. It prepares me for questions that I think may be asked in the next few days." On the other hand, reading local publications enables reference personnel to better understand their patrons, enabling them to situate patrons within the context of the community as a whole. As Stacy observes, "Reading local newspapers, magazines (we have two), and newsletters is of great benefit to librarians. They are providers of knowledge about the community at large. We can better serve our patrons if we know more about how they live." By keeping "a pulse on the community," reference personnel are not only reading about their communities, but are also gathering information that allows them to read the community itself. Kellie emphasizes the importance of "knowing the illiteracy rate of your neighborhood, so when people forget their

glasses you may be sensitive to the fact that they need information." Decoding this scenario— and reacting appropriately and sensitively in this situation — would be considerably more difficult without the prior knowledge cited by Kellie.

We have noted throughout our discussion areas where the viewpoints of public
library reference personnel either echo or diverge from those of academic librarians. It
is also interesting to discuss one factor that appears to have little, if any, relevance for
public library reference staff members: maintaining or increasing their credibility. In
Chapters 3 and 4, academic librarians documented their struggles and successes in establishing their scholarly credentials with university departments. This notion of credibility as something that one needs to fight to establish is not emphasized in the public library
realm. Instead, reference personnel stress that, because they are the first line of defense
for their patrons, they must learn to accept a wide array of crucial responsibilities and
treat these responsibilities with the utmost seriousness. As Tammy remarks,

> Yes, I read and read often. Reading affects and influences every part of my life. I live in a
> community where 43 percent of the people have not graduated from high school and are
> illiterate. I used to have people volunteer in the library and ... I would find post-it notes
> on the shelves with ABCs on them because these goodhearted people did not have the liter-
> acy skills and they used the post-it notes as reminders of how to shelve the books. That was
> scary to me, but it drove the point home of how many people out there do not have literacy
> skills. I make sure that I read because most of the people in my county do not. They come
> and ask me because I am the first person they see when they walk in the library.

Public library reference personnel have described instances where they have helped students with their school projects, have let parents know when they can take their children
trick-or-treating, and have alerted community members as to when and where they can
get winter flu shots. One respondent helped a patron make stock purchases; another
helped a patron build just the right type of birdhouse for attracting martins. Still another
directed a patron to "information on a convicted murderer on Florida's death row" that
was used by this patron "to discourage a friend interested in marrying the convict." Handling a mind-boggling array of questions and resolving untold situations, public library
reference personnel serve as indispensable jacks-of-all-trades for their communities.
Reading newspapers and magazines goes a very long way in helping them maintain their
role as the first line of defense for public library patrons who are confronted with untold
problems, perplexing situations, unique bewilderments, thorny dilemmas, or insatiable
curiosities— in short, for all of us.

IV. Professors and Academic Librarians

In the previous chapters, we focused on what academic librarians and public library reference personnel told us about how reading newspapers, magazines, and books helps them in all aspects of their work. We saw that reading such materials helps immeasurably during reference transactions, collection development, the formulation of search strategies, and during university social occasions.

We now turn to what professors in the humanities and social sciences think about the state of reference service at academic libraries. In other words, while the previous chapters presented the perspective of librarians and reference staff members, the next chapter will focus on how users perceive the contribution that reading may, or may not, bring to the reference transaction. Do users also think that reading helps reference librarians be better reference librarians?

Professors are, of course, a very special type of user (or patron) in the academic library environment. Extremely influential on different levels, they can portray the library either negatively or positively to their students and colleagues, can encourage or discourage others to consult with reference librarians by their words and actions. What professors think about reference service and reference librarians is an important aspect of how the library as an institution is positioned within the university or college.

As the next chapter will show, the type of reading that professors often expect or recommend that reference librarians do in order to help them is more academically oriented than the newspapers, general-interest periodicals, and popular fiction and nonfiction that many reference librarians told us helped them when dealing with student problems and queries. Professors expect librarians to read scholarly journals and monographs, and to know about recent research trends and developments. At the same time, a professor of English Literature told us how "after having a librarian introduce my freshman honors class to ways of researching historical materials related to the novel *Cold Mountain*, I would try and get the same person to do it next year. She focused the demonstration on specific topics that I had given her, such as Cherokee myths in the novel and the Civil War in North Carolina. In the old days the librarians tended to cover too much territory, leaving the students without concrete demonstrations concerning their areas of interest."

This story functions as a good example of how professors want reference librarians to be both generalists and subject-specialists, to be both broadly conversant with manifestations of popular culture and to concentrate more narrowly on certain specific areas of that broad cultural canvas. On the one hand, the professor is certainly glad that the librarian was conversant with *Cold Mountain*— a best-selling popular novel. Some claim can therefore be made that the librarian reads widely and keeps up with contemporary literature — that the librarian, is, in other words, a generalist. On the other hand, the professor appreciates the fact that the librarian did not cover "too much territory," that she spent a sufficient amount of time on selected topics such as Cherokee myths so that students received in-depth instruction that did not leave them swamped with too much information presented on too superficial a level. This concentration on a few selected areas of interest therefore suggests subject specialization.

This dual expectation — that academic reference librarians should be both generalists and subject-specialists— recurs often in the responses of professors in the humanities and social sciences. One way to understand this expectation is to place it within the context of interdisciplinarity — the scholarly practice of bringing in ideas from other fields and using these ideas in one's own field. When ideas from two fields are used in conjunction or juxtaposition, they can illuminate a specific phenomenon from a new and intriguing perspective. When a professor who is embarked on an interdisciplinary pursuit consults with a reference librarian, the professor wants the librarian to be aware of new developments and trends in a broad range of fields because such awareness will be useful for creating interdisciplinary connections. But the professor also wants the librarian to understand the base field — the field to which interdisciplinary knowledge is being applied. Otherwise, how can salient connections be made? In short, professors want reference librarians to be both generalists and subject-specialists. How to meet such high expectations?

As with our findings in Chapters 3 and 4 that librarians and reference personnel can meet (and surpass) the expectations of their patrons by reading an eclectic array of materials, the next chapter shows that professors believe that reference librarians who read a wide and diverse array of materials can meet their expectations both on the generalist and subject-specialist level.

7

Meeting the Expectations
of Professors

*The need for academic librarians to read and
think as if they were researchers*

We begin this chapter with an overview of the frequency with which professors in
the humanities and social sciences make use of the academic library reference desks of
their home institutions. As shown in Table 35, slightly less than half of the professors (46.2
percent) had asked four or more reference questions in the past year. Many professors relied
on research assistants for diverse kinds of help and therefore made use of library reference services only about once a year; nevertheless, some professors indicated that they had
asked 20, 30, or even 50 reference questions in the preceding two-year period.

Despite the varying rates at which they made use of academic reference services, a
majority of professors (62.3 percent) received satisfactory answers at least 75 percent of
the time at the reference desk. In some fields, this rate of satisfaction soared to 90 percent (Russian Literature), but it never dipped below 47.8 percent (East Asian History).
Moreover, 130 professors (55.1 percent) mentioned examples of being impressed with the
subject-specific knowledge of reference librarians, while only 64 professors (27.1 percent) recalled instances when they had been disappointed with the extent of such subject-
specific knowledge. Professors in North American History (76.5 percent) and Women's
Studies (76.2 percent) had the greatest number of impressive experiences to recount;
professors in European History (50 percent) and French Literature (50 percent) related
the largest number of examples of disappointing reference service.

When it came time for them to go to the reference desk of their academic library,
116 professors (49.2 percent) made a point of consulting with a preferred reference librarian. This percentage accords almost exactly with the data obtained when professors were
asked how they would rate the subject-specific knowledge of academic reference librarians. While 19.1 percent rated such knowledge as excellent and another 25.8 percent rated
it as very good or informed, 19.9 percent of responding professors rated it as only adequate or fair, with 10.6 percent labeling it as weak or minimal and a further 8.9 percent
calling it terrible or non-existent (see Table 36). Accordingly, 44.9 percent of professors
(19.1 percent + 25.8 percent) viewed the subject-specific knowledge of reference librar-

ians in a very positive light; in fact, if the replies of professors who gave an answer of "can't say" or "don't know" are discounted, this percentage rises to 52 percent (106 out of 204). In addition, the figure of 49.2 percent is very close to the figure of 55.1 percent, which represents the percentage of responding professors who mentioned examples of being impressed with the subject-specific knowledge of reference librarians (see Table 35). It is therefore logical that professors would go out of their way to seek out a specific librarian at approximately the same rate at which they believe that certain librarians had excellent or very good subject-specific skills.

Table 35. How professors in the humanities and social sciences view service provided by academic reference librarians

Field	Professors who asked four or more reference questions in the past two years	Professiors who indicated that they received satisfactory answers at least 75% of the time	Professors who mentioned examples of being impressed by subject-specific knowledge of librarians	Professors who mentioned examples of being disappointed with subject-specific knolwedge of librarians	Professors who typically spoke to a preferred reference librarian
American Literature (n = 19)	8 (42.1%)	13 (68.4%)	10 (52.6%)	3 (15.8%)	7 (36.8%)
Anthropology (n = 15)	9 (60%)	8 (53.3%)	8 (53.3%)	5 (33.3%)	11 (77.3%)
Archaeology (n = 22)	9 (40.9%)	12 (54.5%)	13 (59.1%)	8 (36.4%)	10 (45.5%)
East Asian History (n = 23)	9 (39.1%)	11 (47.8%)	12 (52.2%)	5 (21.7%)	13 (56.5%)
European History (n = 20)	10 (50%)	12 (60%)	10 (50%)	10 (50%)	11(55%)
French Literature (n = 12)	7 (58.3%)	8 (66.7%)	8 (66.7%)	6 (50%)	7 (58.3%)
Linguistics (n = 19)	4 (21.1%)	10 (52.6%)	4 (21.1%)	1 (5.3%)	6 (31.6%)
North American History (n = 17)	8 (47.1%)	11 (64.7%)	13 (76.5%)	4 (23.5%)	11 (64.7%)
Psychology (n = 22)	13 (59.1%)	14 (63.6%)	12 (54.5%)	0 (0%)	8 (36.4%)
Russian Literature (n = 20)	11 (55%)	18 (90%)	11 (55%)	4 (20%)	9 (45%)
Sociology (n = 8)	5 (62.5%)	7 (87.5%)	4 (50%)	2 (25%)	6 (75%)
English Literature (n = 18)	8 (44.4%)	10 (55.6%)	9 (50%)	7 (38.9%)	8 (44.4%)
Women's Studies (n = 21)	8 (38.1%)	13 (61.9%)	16 (76.2%)	9 (42.9%)	9 (42.9%)
Total (n = 236)	109 (46.2%)	147 (62.3%)	130 (55.1%)	64 (27.1%)	116 (49.2%)

One striking aspect of these results is their conformity with the so-called 55 percent rule. Study after study in the field of LIS has demonstrated that patrons are satisfied with library service at a rate of about 55 percent. But what about the other 45 percent of patrons? What would make them satisfied? Is it possible that this substantial minority is not satisfied because reference librarians lack subject-specific knowledge that would allow them to understand fully all the implications and ramifications of any individual question? If the professors surveyed here received satisfactory answers 75 percent or more of the time at a rate of 62.3 percent, if they remembered examples of impressive subject-specific knowledge on the part of reference librarians at a rate of 55.1 percent, and if they judged that librarians had excellent or very good subject-specific knowledge at a rate of either 44.9 percent or 52 percent (depending on the method of calculation), is it possible that the presence or absence of subject-specific knowledge is an important determining factor in whether professors in the humanities and social sciences view reference librarians in a positive or negative light?

Table 36. How would you rate the overall subject-specific knowledge of academic reference librarians at your campus in your broad subject field?

Field	Excellent or impressive	Very good or or above average or informed or knowledgeable	Average moderate or OK or fair or acceptable	Weak or minimal	Bad or terrible or non-existent	No need for subject specific knowledge	Can's say or don't know or no answer
American Literature (*n* = 19)	5	4	5	1	1	1	2
Anthropology (*n* = 15)	2	3	3	4	1	2	0
Archaeology (*n* = 22)	4	4	8	3	2	0	1
East Asian History (*n* = 23)	2	8	3	4	1	0	5
European History (*n* = 20)	4	6	2	1	3	0	4
French Literature (*n* =12)	1	4	3	3	0	0	1
Linguistics (*n* = 19)	1	4	5	3	0	1	5
North American History (*n* = 17)	4	5	5	0	1	0	2
Psychology (*n* = 22)	5	3	5	0	4	1	4
Russian Literature (*n* = 20)	3	10	2	0	3	0	2
Sociology (*n* = 8)	2	1	2	1	1	0	1
English Literature (*n* = 18)	4	5	3	2	1	0	3
Women's Studies (*n* = 21)	8	4	1	3	3	0	2
Total (*n* = 236)	45 (19.1%)	61 (25.8%)	47 (19.9%)	25 (10.6%)	21 (8.9%)	5 (2.1%)	32 (13.6%)

Certainly, there could be other explanations for this confluence of figures around the 55 percent mark, or it could be completely coincidental, but it is nevertheless intriguing to speculate that a major reason for the dissatisfaction of library patrons when asking questions at the reference desk is the lack of subject-specific knowledge on the part of the person answering the question. What if reference librarians were not only taught all the latest information technology, retrieval, and storage skills in LIS institutions, but were also initiated into the importance of gaining, through a variety of means, a solid background in one or more subject areas? What if the expertise and confidence to satisfy demanding academic reference patrons came from a concerted effort to be well-informed and knowledgeable about the important issues and trends in one or more fields— the kind of knowledge gained from engaging in scholarly activities such as discipline-based and interdisciplinary reading?

In examining more closely the opinions and words of advice of the 236 humanities and social science professors who completed this survey, the answer to the question about the central importance of subject-based knowledge for academic reference librarians will, inevitably, be ambiguous. Some professors are extremely strong proponents of the viewpoint that librarians should possess such knowledge; others bluntly assert that what they expect from librarians is not subject-based knowledge, but the ability to locate diverse items of information in a timely and efficient manner.

No matter their points of view, there is enough overall evidence in their responses to suggest that professors value and respect highly the academic reference librarian who displays genuine interest in, as well as has some knowledge of, the issues and trends associated with a specific scholarly subject, discipline, or field. In a large number of cases, the more subject-based knowledge that a librarian is able to display, the more impressed a professor becomes.

We do *not* claim that information technology, retrieval, and storage skills should *not* be an important component of the education of academic reference librarians. Rather, these skills should be set in the wider context of a program devoted to ensuring that librarians gain, or improve their level of, subject-based knowledge. Just as, in the previous chapters, we saw that the relatively simple act of reading general-interest newspapers, magazines, fiction, and nonfiction had a positive effect on the ability of academic and public library reference personnel to answer reference questions from students and members of the general public, so, in this chapter, it will become apparent that reading the eclectic contents of academic publications— both in English and in foreign languages— is of great help in satisfying the expectations of professors in the humanities and social sciences.

Characteristics of impressive reference service

As shown in Table 37, the characteristic most frequently mentioned by professors as being indicative of high-quality reference service was knowledge of specialized, nonstandard information sources. Forty-eight professors touched upon this theme in their open-ended answers to the question "Can you tell me about one or two instances where you were really impressed with the subject-specific knowledge of an academic reference librarian when you asked a question in your subject area?" The second-most frequently mentioned theme — which occurred in 30 answers — was more general in nature: professors simply stated that the level of subject-based knowledge displayed by a librarian had, in fact, been high. Often, however, these two themes intermingle and overlap, not only with each other, but also with other themes listed in Table 37. Although it is useful to extract individual themes from the open-ended responses of professors, it is just as useful to remember that one thematic aspect frequently intersects with other aspects, thus providing, when all is said and done, a broader perspective on what is, and what is not, impressive in the eyes of professors when they consult academic reference librarians.

Table 37. Why were professors in the humanities and social sciences impressed with service received from academic reference librarians? (*n* = 130)*

Reason	Count
Good knowledge of a wide range of specialized sources (not just standard sources)	48
Good subject specific knowledge	30
Good and persistent searching skills	26
Keeps up with technological advances	20
Found something obscure	18
Good teaching skills	18
Made proactive suggestions or took proactive steps	17
Knows the collections of home institution very well, as well as other collections	14
Foreign language skills	10
Keeps up with what my department is doing	6
Impressed, with no specifics	4
Took an active interest in my research	4
Evidence of own scholarly interests	3
Was able to answer interdisciplinary questions	2
Networking	1
Total thematic units	221*

* The *n* of professors does not equal the total of thematic units because some professors indicated multiple reasons for being impressed with reference librarians.

The following comment from a professor of English Literature is a good example of this overlapping. We start with this particularly rich example so as to give a sense of the many factors involved in the definition of impressive academic reference service.

My contact with the head librarian is often informal (we chat about my research, about classes I'm teaching, about electronic resources for those classes, etc) when we run into each other on campus, which happens a couple of times a month. Recently I found him picking basil outside of one of our cafeterias; we began to talk about a course I was teaching on Arthurian Literature, which had a website; the librarian admired the website, and made some specific comments for electronic resources which might be linked to it; he then proposed that I participate in a seminar on teaching and techno-pedagogy to be held soon at a nearby college ... this is how things tend to work here, oddly enough. Another librarian, who manages an electronic database in my field, regularly astonishes me with her knowledge of medieval French and Italian texts. Generally, when I suggest a book which we should acquire, she has already done so.

Beyond the idyllic image of intellectual and basil-picking communal life at a small liberal arts institution offered here lies a revealing portrait of mutual collegial support and interaction. First, the head librarian is very much aware of course offerings by the English department; after all, he knows that the professor in question is teaching a course about Arthurian Literature and that the course has a web site. It is likely that the head librarian also knows about course offerings in other departments, either through visiting their web sites or through direct contact with various instructors. Clearly, he makes a point of acquainting himself with the curricular offerings of various faculty members, perhaps anticipating informal meetings with faculty or their students where advice and recommendations can be exchanged: "this is how things tend to work here, oddly enough." More importantly, he not only has a few words of praise for the Arthurian Literature web site, but he is able to offer detailed suggestions about valuable hyperlinks that the professor has overlooked or not considered. These detailed suggestions imply that the head librarian knows a little something about Arthurian Literature, or, at the very least, that he has taken the time to find out something about the subject. In either case, he adopts a proactive approach, confident in his ability to make a meaningful contribution to the English professor's work. In addition, judging from the fact that he urges the English professor to participate in a seminar about electronic teaching, he appears to be cognizant of new developments in pedagogical techniques and a key participant in the intellectual life of the immediate region. Not only has he already networked and built bridges to another area college, but he is now extending the network to include the English professor. The head librarian, however, is not the only one who deserves high praise. At the same time, hovering in the background, is another librarian who has "astonishing" knowledge of medieval French and Italian texts, so much so that she is always buying the most important new books in the field and managing subject-based electronic databases.

Present in this vignette is a combination of subject-specific knowledge, ability in foreign languages, a decided comfort level with new technologies, familiarity with specialized sources, demonstrated networking skills, close contact with the teaching and research agenda of various faculty members, and a ready confidence to make proactive suggestions. Little wonder that the English professor is suitably impressed. Yet, from one perspective, the unifying feature linking all the components of the English professor's story is the central role played by subject-based knowledge. Without such knowledge, it is doubtful whether, taken as a whole, the conversation with the head librarian would have been as detailed or as extensive as it was. It is the head librarian's knowledge of and interest in Arthurian Literature — together with his awareness that Medieval Literature as a whole is a research area for the English professor — that was the instrumental factor in generating this scholarly and productive conversation. Similarly, we can imagine the English professor running into the second-mentioned librarian — the one with an excellent knowledge of medieval French and Italian texts — on another occasion elsewhere on campus. Because of their mutual interests and common knowledge base, the chances for a fruitful academic exchange between them are just as high as in the case of the fortuitous meeting with the head librarian.

To be sure, not every example of impressive reference service is as eloquent and inclusive as the above episode. However, knowledge of specialized — as opposed to standard — sources typically goes hand-in-hand with some degree of subject knowledge. Consider the following instance of high-quality reference service noted by a professor of Russian Literature: "On a question relating to St. Petersburg, the reference librarian was able to direct me to a directory (book) of place/street names that I didn't know existed. It was obvious to me that not only did she know 'of' this book, but that she had actually perused it herself." Or this example from an East Asian history professor: "I was looking for information about Chinese local gazetteers and found that the librarian had a special interest in the subject and could help me find what I was looking for." Finally, a professor of Archaeology recalls trying "to track down sources on elephants—Asian elephants. One reference librarian was indispensable in helping me locate sources in various areas of the library. We had to look through classical texts as well as Buddhist and Hindu literature." In all three cases, foreign language skills are a crucial element in reference service success, but there is something more: intellectual curiosity on the part of the reference librarian. This intellectual curiosity can manifest itself in different ways, most obviously in the knowledge of specialized resources. But this knowledge of specialized sources can also be related to the pursuit of a librarian's own scholarly and personal interests, the furthering of which leads, in turn, to the discovery of additional specialized resources that can then be shared with others.

Foreign language skills, on the part of librarians, are valuable in other ways too, since such skills permit the resolution of seemingly minor issues that are, nevertheless, significant for the patron involved. A professor of Linguistics gratefully remembers the time when "I had some word in French spelled wrong, and the librarian knew it was wrong." A professor of East Asian history felt very comfortable asking about "how to find some books in Russian (which I don't read) when I have an imperfect romanization of the title and some confusion about the name of the author." A professor in Women's Studies recounts the following incident:

> I was glad when a librarian understood a common issue having to do with the search for a German periodical which my library has on microfilm. The periodical is called *Der Teutsche Merkur*, but since libraries don't alphabetize European language titles under articles (Der, the), I didn't know whether it would be listed as Teutsche Merkur, which is nonsense in German, or Teutscher Merkur, which is correct.... I found a librarian who knew enough German to understand the problem, and much more important, who followed up on my search for the microfilm, notifying me later of his findings.

Obviously, there is no way of telling whether these three librarians were fluent in French, Russian, and German, respectively, or whether they knew only a few rudiments of the language, but what is obvious is the palpable relief experienced by the three professors in having access to professional help for non–English reference questions. This is especially so in the case of the Women's Studies professor, who has finally found someone to understand her quandary and, because of this understanding, to take steps to resolve it. We can imagine that she might have experienced frustration, possibly going from one unilingual librarian to another, increasingly exasperated until she finally happens upon a librarian who, at the very least, has reading knowledge of German.

Something akin to such frustration likely happened to the professor of East Asian history as he approached librarians at his institution with a question about Chinese orthography. When the librarians could not help him, he turned to a member of the circulation staff, from whom he received a clear and erudite answer.

I was most impressed with a member of the circulation staff, with whom I had raised a query about a possible cataloguing error. He was very familiar with minor details of Chinese orthography, and relationship between traditional and simplified forms of Chinese character, and explained that two traditional forms have been simplified into a single form, leading to some confusion in the pronunciation of that character. In case you really want specific details, there is a book by a Taiwanese scholar named Chuang Yingchang called Lin-i-pu. When publications from the People's Republic of China refer to this book, they use a character for the 'i' that is usually pronounced 'pi' yielding the title 'Linpipu.' But in fact, of course, this is just an error, and the book was correctly cataloged under Lin-i-pu.

Foreign language skills for a librarian may seem like an esoteric requirement, but, on occasions when one least expects it, knowing a foreign language can make a difference as to whether professors and other patrons view library reference service in a positive or lackluster manner. In the three examples above, foreign language skills resolved cataloging or spelling questions. On a broader level, however, foreign language skills give librarians entry into a wider universe of specialized sources—both print and electronic—of potentially great interest to scholars exploring international or country-specific questions. In one sense, facility in foreign languages by librarians is an acknowledgment that not all books and reference tools are written in the English language, and that it is not enough to know only English-language resources. Whether they want to admit it or not, librarians who know only English are, for the most part, unnecessarily limiting themselves in the kinds of resources to which they can confidently point patrons.

On a broader level still, such skills position librarians as scholarly, informed, and well-read members of an academic community who can make real contributions to the advancement of knowledge. With increasing immigration to North America, with increasing economic activity between and among nations, and with an increasing realization of the importance of understanding political events in other countries from the indigenous perspective, universities and colleges will, inevitably, increase their emphasis on foreign cultures and languages. As students and professors pay more and more attention to such topics, librarians will, just as inevitably, have to deal with more and more questions on these same topics. In the future, academic librarians in North America who are competent only in the English language may not be seen as providing the kind of high-quality service that their patrons expect as a matter of course. For example, in describing a particularly adept reference librarian, a different professor of Women's Studies than the one mentioned above lists the outstanding qualities of this individual:

> Our reference librarian makes regular presentations to the department: faculty members, graduate students, sessional instructors. She draws attention to the new reference works received and any particularly interesting new journals and books. She speaks of particular areas of political concern, where cuts might be made for instance and advises on appropriate action. She knows in advance which journals are important to us. She speaks on our behalf to retain important journals and monograph budgets, and is energetically proactive when it comes to acquiring new databases and ensuring that internal initiatives to acquire reference material includes reference needs in humanities and women's studies. I have simply not been disappointed. She is outstanding. She speaks several languages, is incredibly knowledgeable, is always available and interested, and is able to translate the increasingly technical knowledge of libraries into the discourse of students & faculty members.

The fact that this reference librarian "speaks several languages" is just one part of what makes her so impressive. From the description offered here, she would likely be an excellent librarian even without her foreign language skills. But these language skills are an integral part of who she is and the service that she provides, and so the Women's Studies department has come to see her as the standard against which other types of library service are measured. After all, the field of Women's Studies does not only concern itself with privileging the voices of women, marginalized and otherwise, in North America; it is also interested in delving into the often difficult circumstances of women in Africa, Far Eastern Asia, Southeastern Asia, and South America. Based on the testimony of this Women's Studies professor, then, librarians should not only be able to help in translating the discourse of technology, but should also be capable of helping to facilitate access to foreign materials through their knowledge of foreign languages.

In many ways, knowledge of languages other than English is another way of saying that an academic librarian knows specialized, non-standard information sources: both skills enhance subject-based knowledge. Of course, subject-based knowledge can also manifest itself in other ways—for example, through the types of intellectual suggestions that a librarian makes to patrons. A professor of English Literature recalled, "I was looking for historical information on the 1840s in Ireland (esp. the time of the Great Famine). That information was shown to me quickly. What impressed me was the co-related suggestions about North American and Canadian Irish immigration patterns and their very real connections with the Famine." A professor of European History described asking "for information on new databases relating to German history. The response I received was very useful and could have been given only by someone familiar with German archives and libraries as well as the history of Germany." A professor of Psychology noted admiringly how "one of the librarians was able to answer a question on a topic area of neuropsychology that many faculty could not answer…. This person was able to refer me to several sources besides journals in this area." A Russian Literature professor was encouraged that the reference librarian knew "details of present developments in Russian culture [and had] knowledge of the contemporary state of Czech literature." A professor of Archaeology, seeking "a sense about the kinds of resources available to study ports in the ancient world" was delighted that the subject "happened to be an area of interest for one of the staff." In all these cases, the distinguishing feature that made the reference encounters impressive in the eyes of the respective professors was the scholarliness of the librarian's approach. Because the librarian has subject-specific knowledge, the professor is able to talk with the librarian as if he or she were a fellow departmental professor, thus creating a more equal interaction that benefits both parties and increases the esteem of professors for the library and librarians.

Note here the range of special interests possessed by the reference librarians: Irish immigration patterns; German history; neuropsychology; contemporary Czech literature; and nautical archaeology. How does one become knowledgeable about such diverse topics? Many professors commented upon the fact that reference librarians have advanced degrees in a specific field, linking the degree with the level of service received. For example, a professor of American Literature observed, "One of the reference librarians has I think an M.A. in English. He orders books for us in the department when money becomes available, tells us at department meetings about technical updates, polls us on use of journals, etc. When he works the desk, his answers are always impressive." An Anthropology professor attributes impressive library service at least partly to the fact "that several of our resource librarians have anthropology degrees." A Psychology professor fondly recalls the high level of service offered "in another library, where several of the librarians had Ph.D.s and knew a ton of stuff about the collections."

But having formal training in a subject area is not the only way to accumulate knowledge and gain the respect of professors. Consider the two following examples. A professor of American Literature writes that "once, while [I was] researching the 1906 Atlanta Riot, a special collections archivist brought out some letters that he had purchased for himself. They related directly to the events of the riot. I was amazed. He let me use them in the book, no questions asked." A professor of East Asian History, in the midst of compiling a section for an encyclopedia entry, describes how "our librarian knew of many sources and provided several more the next week. I am certain that she spent the interim researching the topic on her own." Here, both staff members seem to have scholarly interests of their own. The special collections archivist is obviously well versed in the intricacies of the Atlanta Riot, having gone so far as to start his own collection of primary materials, and it is possible that his interest in the 1906 Riot is an indication of a wider interest in racial relations in Georgia and other southern states. And the librarian mentioned by the East Asian History professor was apparently so interested in the topic of the professor's encyclopedia entry that she took the time, unasked, to research the question more thoroughly.

Judging from these examples, subject-based knowledge can be variously accumulated. Formal education is one way, but ongoing and active interest in an intellectual topic is just as useful and just as likely to result in praise for a job well done.

Characteristics of disappointing reference service

Equally informative about the needs and expectations of professors using the library are examples of what they consider disappointing reference service. Table 38 shows the reasons that professors in the humanities and social sciences thought that the service they received was poor. In many ways, Table 38 is similar to Table 37. While the presence of subject-specific knowledge and familiarity with specialized and obscure sources are the two top reasons for being impressed with reference service, it is the absence of subject-specific knowledge and the lack of familiarity with little-known sources that are the top two reasons for disappointment. Professors who were disappointed that librarians did not know foreign languages and foreign resources were also significantly represented. Seven professors mentioned a lack of foreign language skills, and another five talked about unfamiliarity with foreign language sources, which is probably due to not knowing foreign languages. Again, the concept of a foreign language source may very well be the same as a specialized source: foreign language sources are not standard sources. Somewhat surprisingly, a relatively large number of professors also complained that librarians did not know their own collections.

Table 38. Why were professors in the humanities and social sciences disappointed with service received from academic reference librarians? (*n* = 64)

Reason	Count
Lack of subject-specific knowledge	16
Lack of knowledge of specialized sources; used only standard sources	12
Lack of knowledge of own collection	7
Lack of foreign language knowledge	7
Lack of knowledge of standard sources	7
Not interested/didn't care	7
Lack of technological knowledge	7
Unable to satisfy general information need	6
Didn't know foreign language sources	5
Failure to follow through on something that had been promised or took a long time	4
Bad approach in teaching	4
Didn't listen to what I was really asking	2
Didn't know the kinds of courses offered by departments/lack of contact with faculty	2
Person was too busy	2
Unfriendly	2
Can't remember the details	1
Total thematic units	91*

* The *n* of professors does not equal the total of thematic units because some professors indicated multiple reasons for being disappointed with reference librarians.

As in the previous section, we want to start with a vignette that incorporates a number of these significant themes. A professor of American Literature contrasts the middling service received at the home institution with the exemplary service received at another library.

> The staff [here] are entirely laconic and don't give the impression they know anything about the collection or are even interested in it. You have to be completely prepared & informed. Elsewhere, definitely — the kind of thing where I come in and comb the card catalog for "vocabularies"— i.e., lists of words in both a European language and a Native American language — and when I bring the slips to the librarian, she says, oh, you should look under "glossaries" too, and I think that so and so's exploration narrative has some lists of words in it, have you seen that? That sort of thing, people who take an active interest in your research, who know the texture of their collections, who like "the thrill of the hunt." … I do however really wish that our Special Collections staff was not so unfriendly and uninformed. I wish they were a bit scholarly — I guess they're trained librarians, but frankly, all they do is take your slips of paper & vanish to retrieve things— I never have any sense that they're interested about anything, or even proud of their own collection, which actually has some pretty cool stuff. I think it's important that even the "desk staff" who are doing routine stuff be invested in serving the researcher.

Bluntly put, this is a searing indictment contrasting, on the one hand, scholarly individuals and, on the other hand, "trained librarians." What this professor would like to see — and what is not present at the home institution — are library staff who are prepared, informed, interested, gregarious, and research-oriented. In short, the professor wants to work with librarians and special collections staff who do not place the entire scholarly burden on the person coming into the library and using the resources contained therein.

Instead, the professor wants a little bit of subject knowledge and some suggestions based on an amalgam of erudition and ready acquaintance with the collections at hand. The professor, moreover, knows that such informed and knowledgeable help is available at other institutions: in the past, one librarian alerted him or her to the existence of bilingual vocabularies in out-of-the-way sources. But the use of the phrase "trained librarians"— and its association with poor service — suggests that the excellent service she or he received elsewhere is an exception worthy of particular mention. Possibly the professor is saying librarians at the home institution have been "trained" to be the way they are, namely, something less than scholarly.

Perhaps this is an overly harsh assessment of the matter. Yet the same types of complaints voiced by the above professor of American Literature reappear in the accounts of other professors, lending some credence to the negative connotations of the "trained librarian" analogy. With regard to a fundamental lack of subject expertise, an East Asia History professor writes, "I realized from the beginning that nobody at my institution has specialized knowledge regarding my field of study. Some did not even know whether I was talking about Asians in America or international relations between Asia and the United States." Another professor of American Literature expresses consternation after "ask[ing] a librarian about the co-existent hemispheric (north and south) development of American literature. This fellow didn't have a clue." A professor of European history is befuddled not only at dilatory service, but, more importantly, that a basic resource in the field is not even on the reference librarian's radar screen: "I asked a couple of years ago that the reference librarian ... help me compile a list of journals available on our campus and, secondly, to devise a list of what journals we might consider subscribing to or renewing subscriptions to. She managed to do this, but it took a week (whereas I browsed the online catalog and did it in an hour) and among the journals that our campus was not subscribing to was the leading, flagship journal for medieval studies: *Speculum*. It was not on her 'to get' list. She didn't even know it existed." An archaeology professor observes disparagingly that a reference librarian "thought archaeology was fossils, not the human past." Another archaeology professor, "trying to find out about our databases, subscriptions to databases, etc., for fauna globally," is referred to science librarians elsewhere in the university system, but even "they seemed largely unable to grasp the concept that we would have information related to whole organisms...." In these five examples, the exasperation of the professors is fueled by a disbelief that seemingly basic concepts and ideas are beyond the ken of academic reference librarians. All five of these professors might very well agree with the earlier assessment that "I wish they were a bit scholarly ... I never have a sense that they're interested about anything."

Professorial exasperation is particularly keen when it comes to the inability of reference librarians to operate in languages other than English. Take the following comment from a professor of French Literature: "Our frustrations came to a head several years ago when library staff insisted on sending us information about books for purchase that were all English volumes. We have found it very difficult to build our collection ... working with a staff who are not familiar with the fundamentals of a sound base in French." A professor of European History shares this frustration, noting that "our history bibliographer here had no idea how to find about books recently published in German history via the Internet (or any other way, it seems). When I asked the library to order two big books in European history for a course I'm teaching, no one had heard of the authors." And a Sociology professor, while condemning the disinclination to learn foreign languages and learn about foreign language sources, contextualized such disinclination as part of a larger problem.

> I am routinely disappointed by the librarians here.... I have tried to work with the librarian assigned to our area and she seems to have no interest in learning about what I think are important research concerns. Her main concern seems to "look good" to her administrative superiors. It took me many months to get her to provide me with searches for some of the journals we do not receive, and she seemed reluctant to investigate anything that is not in English. When I invite her to talk to students she gives examples that have nothing to do with the type of research we are training them to do despite the fact that I give her printouts of the assignments ahead of time. Either she does not have the motivation to learn more about the field, or there is some other problem that I truly do not understand.

On one level, lack of foreign language skills inhibits collection development, forcing libraries to rely overmuch on English-language books and journals. Multiple perspectives are lost, resulting in a uni-dimensionality of thought and voice that should be the antithesis of collection development practices. On a second level, disinterest in anything but English is somehow related, as the Sociology professor cogently observes, to an attitude of close-mindedness toward other aspects of library work. This librarian has "no interest in learning" about research issues in Sociology and "no motivation" to learn about the field of Sociology in general. Her contentment "with looking good to her administrative superiors" metaphorically parallels her contentment with being unilingual. As she limits herself in these ways, she also diminishes the possibility that she will ever provide adequate reference service and creates, for the Sociology professor, a climate of routine disappointment.

If the lack of subject-based knowledge and foreign language knowledge on the part of reference librarians is frequently cause for criticism among professors, so too is the lack of knowledge of specialized resources and even the lack of knowledge about the collections contained in the library as a whole. Professors, it is clear, do not want standard sources that, invariably, they already know about. A professor of European History states, "I have also had problems with different librarians who cannot cope with foreign language references and whose concept of a reference is to direct people to an encyclopedia." A professor of French Literature recalls that "on one occasion when [I was] looking for research materials on several Haitian writers in French, the reference librarian could only direct me to the standard French literature references, not those which might deal specifically with Caribbean French-language literature. She did not have any idea about materials outside the traditional sources." A professor of Russian Literature encountered a similar problem: "I was trying to find out some specific information about Russian religious philosophy and one of the reference librarians couldn't do more than point me to a general set of encyclopedias on religion." Again, lack of knowledge of specialized resources is a sign that a reference librarian is not interested in the intricacies of subject areas, is not, in other words, "invested in serving the researcher" by acquiring and developing an ever-increasing range of skills that would enable an in-depth knowledge of specialized resources. As we have noted before, knowledge of specialized resources is often connected with the kinds of specialized knowledge that come with facility in a foreign language or in-depth knowledge of a discipline.

Not knowing specialized resources sometimes is exacerbated by not knowing one's own collections. A professor of Anthropology observes:

> My work in First Nations ... needs contemporary media resources, background reference material, and access to archival materials (at my own institution and elsewhere). Our reference librarians have often had difficulty finding materials I know exist on First Nations points of view toward current political and cultural issues. I am also disappointed in the limited range of newspapers and magazines on aboriginal issues in our library. Reference librarians do not seem to know about stuff present in other departments of the library (e.g., special collections). I usually want a more integrated view of how to pursue a topic.

The key point here is the expressed need for an "integrated view." Reference librarians who do not have subject-based knowledge, foreign language knowledge, or knowledge about specialized, often obscure resources have very little chance to offer "a more integrated view of how to pursue a topic." If, in addition, they do not know their own collections, then the chances for adequate reference service diminish even further. Consider the plight of the English Literature professor who "needed to consult a guide to our microfilm holdings of 19th-century journals. No librarian even knew where it was, and [the staff] seemed entirely ignorant of the contents of these holdings." Or the case of the professor of North American History whose students were told by a reference librarian that "the library contained no works on the colonial history of New York, when in fact we have significant collections." Or, finally, the case of a professor in European History, who indicates "disappointment with a reference librarian not knowing I (and the institution) offered courses in pre-modern history and told me when I was preparing a list of reference items that we had 'nothing in that field' (she was wrong)." In these examples, the unfamiliarity of librarians with their own collections has detrimentally affected faculty research, student assignments, and the preparation of syllabi. While not as intellectually demanding as acquiring subject-based or foreign language skills, extensive and detailed knowledge of all aspects of one's own collection is a valuable and not-to-be-overlooked contribution to good reference service.

So far in our overview of what professors have identified as disappointing reference service, we have focused on the skills that some librarians simply do not have and that professors would like them to have. As shown in Table 38, these "knowledge lacks"—subject-specific, foreign language, specialized sources, own collections—predominate. In concluding this section, we want to draw even more connections among these themes by presenting a case where a reference librarian not only gave erroneous information, but discouraged others from pursuing research. A Women's Studies professor recounts how she devised an assignment in which students were to write the "social histories of feminist ethnographies (anthropological monographs) ... by collecting two kinds of materials: book reviews and citation rates for the ethnographies." A librarian specializing in Women's Studies proved to be "very knowledgeable" in this area, showing the professor, for example, "where indexes list their editorial boards, as well as their lists of publications that they index." However, when the professor subsequently approached a different librarian—one specializing in anthropology—with identical questions about the best resources to use for the assignment, the librarian identified a few, but very few (my students identified many more) and a number of which were quite inappropriate for the project (e.g., I wanted indexes that definitely indexed book reviews published in peer-reviewed journals, and he identified a number that in reality don't index these). Furthermore, the librarian, in demonstrating SSCI and AHCI to me and later to my class, kept emphasizing how "hard" and "mind-breaking" it was to do citation-rate research. Not only did I think that this was the wrong tone to set with students trying to learn a new skill-set, but I actually didn't think that the software or the hardcover editions were hard to use at all.

Clearly, the anthropology librarian has a weak command of reference tools such as indexes and procedures such as citation analysis. Yet, as the professor of Women's Studies asserts, students were able to locate applicable materials relatively easily, and the use of print and electronic tools to find citation rates also seemed relatively simple. Compared with the "very knowledgeable" service provided by the Women's Studies librarian on the same questions, the anthropology librarian stands out as someone who is not very interested in learning about new resources and meeting new challenges such as citation research. Worse, his negative attitude seeps into his teaching approach. He creates difficulties instead of surmounting them, perhaps causing students to be skeptical about their assignment instead of encouraging them in their own efforts with a professional and thoroughly researched presentation that validates the professor's carefully conceived assignment.

No one, of course, wants to "break their mind." But there is a difference between "mind-breaking" subject matter — typically associated with something difficult, vexing, and exhausting, as well as an undercurrent of futility — and subject matter that breaks open the mind, that is, intellectual discovery that frees the mind from its usual parameters and ways of thinking. Unfortunately, this Anthropology librarian does not display a willingness to make intellectual discoveries or to open himself up to new ways of thinking that might result, in this case, from an intellectual investment in citation research. In effect, he is closing his mind, much like the librarians who do not show evidence of subject-based knowledge, foreign language knowledge, or the knowledge of specialized resources that is often the result of subject-based and foreign language skills.

Characteristics of the preferred reference librarian

Emerging from these individual examples of impressive and disappointing academic reference service are the broad outlines of the ideal reference librarian. As shown in Table 35, when professors in the humanities and social sciences were asked whether they make a point of consulting with a specific reference librarian when they visit their library, nearly half (49.2 percent) said that they did so. And, as shown in Table 39, when asked what characteristics led them to choose that specific librarian, the answers they gave were, in general, consonant with their examples of impressive and disappointing service. The main reason (35) why professors opted for a preferred reference librarian was that the person was knowledgeable in the professor's field. An almost equal number of professors (29) stated that their academic departments had been assigned library liaisons — individuals who presumably have some subject expertise in the fields for which they are responsible — to whom they turned first. When these two categories are added, professors mentioned subject-based knowledge or field specialization as a key aspect of why they opted for a particular reference librarian a total of 64 times (32.7 percent).

Table 39. Characteristics of the academic reference librarian that professors in the humanities and social sciences would prefer to consult ($n = 116$)*

Characteristic	Count
Knowledgeable in my field because of background in this area (education, specialization)	35
Library has designated departmental liaisons/specialists	29
Good search process and technology skills	23
Someone with whom I have had positive experiences in the past	22
Displays a real interest in my question or area (intellectually curious)	18
Knowledgeable in general	15
Persistence; patience; never gives up	14
Good personality, friendly, cheerful, or good communication skills	9
Professional attitude; time consciousness; trustworthiness	9
Works well with students and has good teaching skills	5
Creative	4
Language skills	4
Proactive; keeps me informed without me having to ask	4
No reason given	4
Has "good connections"	1
Total thematic units	196*

* The *n* of professors does not equal the total of thematic units because some professors indicated multiple characteristics of their preferred reference librarian.

On its face, this is not surprising. Why should a professor consult with someone who doesn't know very much, if anything, about his or her area of study? Why should anyone consult with librarians—either academic or public—who are not well-read or intellectually curious and who do not keep their fingers on the pulse of issues important to their patrons? But the very simplicity and obviousness of this notion has often been forgotten as many LIS institutions devote increasing curricular space to and accentuate the discourse of technical issues such as electronic records, database design, and knowledge management, de-emphasizing the need for their graduates to expand their knowledge of (or acquire new knowledge of) one or two subject-based disciplines.

Yet professors are very much in favor of librarians having such subject-based skills. A professor of Anthropology writes that an "advanced degree in anthro ... determines my choice [of librarian]." A French professor chooses to go "to two [librarians] who have undergrad/grad degrees in lit studies and who came to library studies from that background." Another French professor notes, " I direct my questions to young energetic librarians who are not intimidated to work with titles and sources in French. I am put off by librarians who apologize for pronunciation, etc." A professor of European History consistently works with a person who "has a Ph.D. in European history, and [thus] a better sense of how to get European materials." A professor of Sociology consistently went to a specific librarian who had "a Ph.D. in History, but demonstrated a great deal of knowledge in sociology and criminology...." A professor of North American History consults with a librarian with "an MA in history, as well as library science." A professor of Women's Studies is very pleased to have the opportunity to work with a librarian who has "a doctorate in the history of women's education" and is therefore "the most knowledgeable person about resources for historical and interdisciplinary work in my field." An English professor typically uses "our liaison who has a Ph.D. in English and knows how research is done." Another English professor consults "the specialist in art history." An East Asian History professor gravitates towards a librarian who is "a former student in the History department and is familiar with the needs of historians herself from personal experience." Another East Asian History professor observes that he has a favorite reference librarian who holds a Ph.D.; "I usually go to him for all my questions [because] he is extremely knowledgeable and helpful." To be sure, some professors applaud the information retrieval and technology skills of reference librarians, but, again and again, the most heartfelt praise seems to be directed towards those librarians in whom they detect solid and extensive subject-based knowledge, who know the issues involved in field-specific research, who can make interdisciplinary connections, and who are confident in their abilities to work in more than one language.

In many academic libraries, especially smaller ones or those caught in the turmoil of restructuring, it is unlikely that every librarian will have an advanced degree symbolic of discipline-specific knowledge. However, as many professors observed, there is an alternative: wide-ranging general reading that is the result of sustained intellectual curiosity. For example, a professor of Russian Literature explains that he usually "looks for 'Joan' because I have often worked with her (she has done a lot of library orientation work with my classes and I like the way she assigns tasks to students that make learning about the library 'active' for them. Why I admire her work personally is that I know she reads a lot and has 'fingered' a lot of material. I find her name on many of the new books' circulation lists, so I know she is sampling avidly." A professor of European History speculates, "If I ever felt the need to consult a reference librarian, I would seek out a particular individual — seems to have had a good education and is himself intellectually curious." And an American Literature professor characterizes a preferred librarian as "the person [who] is an omnivorous reader, has an insatiable curiosity, loves to share tips about sources of information, and always has a supply of funny jokes."

Here, reading and intellectual curiosity operate in a kind of symbiosis, one fueling the other — and the result is a person whose steady appetite for new knowledge makes him or her that much more of a valuable reference librarian. Particularly suggestive is the example of the librarian referred to above as Joan, who is not only lauded for her broad reading habits, but also for her ability to generate "active" library assignments for students. Although there is no evidence that the former trait has bearing on the latter trait, the contrast between Joan and the Anthropology librarian who complained that citation research is "mind-breaking" is telling. Joan reads, and the Russian Literature professor who talks about her creates the impression of a vivacious woman who is, in large part, intellectually creative and enthusiastic because of her reading. The Anthropology librarian, on the other hand, is portrayed as displaying very little, if any, enthusiasm — as if he were not at all interested in the intellectual possibilities inherent his tasks, as if he were not willing to be intellectually curious. In many ways, reading — the kind described as "omnivorous" by the professor of American Literature above — is an index of intellectual vitality, a way in which librarians can both keep up with developments in a subject area and learn about new subject areas. In essence, general reading is the very hallmark of the subject-based knowledge that professors find so praiseworthy.

Advice to reference librarians from professors

If professors in the humanities and social sciences are impressed when reference librarians have subject-based knowledge, and if such discipline-specific knowledge is a central reason they prefer to deal with a specific librarian, what advice would these professors give to librarians so that they could improve service to people asking questions in various subject areas? Table 40 provides a detailed synopsis of the numerous recommendations, consolidated under three main headings: Library and Information Science (LIS) skills; Subject-based (SB) skills; and Department consultation (DC) skills. These groupings are arbitrary, and thus open to dispute from many viewpoints. But they represent an attempt to differentiate between the kinds of skills that can be applied to any library reference interaction (LIS skills) and the types of skills that are most useful in dealing with subject areas (SB skills). The sub-categories that make up the third category — DC skills—could arguably be included in the SB skills category because they involve keeping up-to-date about the various research and teaching agendas of faculty members in academic departments, but we grouped them into a distinct category for the purposes of transparency.

Table 40. What advice would you give to academic reference librarians so that they could improve service to people like you asking questions about your particular subject area?

	Literature Professors (n = 69)	History & Women's Studies Profs (n = 81)	Social Science Professors (n = 86)	Total (n = 236)*
Library & Information Science (LIS) skills				
Knowledge of information technology & retrieval	7	10	11	28
Reference interviewing and search process skills	8	8	10	26
Keep up with reference & bibliographic tools	12	8	5	25
Patience, care, and perseverance to find answer	5	4	6	15
No need for subject-based skills	4	3	4	11
Know collections in your library & other libraries	4	3	3	10
Cheerful and helpful attitude	4	3	2	9
Training others	3	2	3	8
Make people aware of what you know	2	1	1	4
Networking with other librarians	0	2	1	3
Thematic units for LIS skills	49 (57%)	44 (42.3%)	46 (43%)	139 (46.8%)

	Literature Professors (n = 69)	History & Women's Studies Profs (n = 81)	Social Science Professors (n = 86)	Total (n = 236)*
Subject-based (SB) skills				
Keep up with journals & books in the field by reading	6	6	16	28
Have real interest in or knowledge about the field	7	10	11	28
Know about interdisciplinary areas	3	5	6	14
Know foreign languages	9	5	0	14
Take or have taken courses in the field	2	5	5	12
Know electronic-based subject resources	0	4	5	9
Think "outside the box"	2	5	2	9
Attend professional meetings in the field	0	1	1	2
Thematic units for SB skills	29 (33.7%)	41 (39.4%)	46 (43%)	116 (39.1%)
Department consultation (DC) skills				
Consult with faculty to stay current	4	14	9	27
Keep track of research interests of faculty	3	4	5	12
Consult course outlines, syllabi, and assignments	1	0	1	2
Concentrate on political aspects of the job	0	1	0	1
Thematic units for DC skills	8 (9.3%)	19 (18.3%)	15 (14%)	42 (14.1%)
Total thematic units mentioned by professors	86 (100%)	104 (100%)	107 (100%)	297* (100%)

* The *n* of professors does not equal the total of thematic units because some professors gave more than one piece of advice.

The results show that 46.8 percent of all surveyed humanities and social sciences professors urge reference librarians to acquire one or more of the skills that fall into the category of LIS skills, including reference interviewing and search process skills, keeping up with bibliographical sources, and mastering information technology and retrieval concepts. At the same time, a significant percentage of professors (39.1 percent) recommended that librarians devote their time to one or more of the SB skills, including taking courses in a discipline-specific field, reading scholarly journals in the field, and attending professional meetings in the field. Finally, 14.1 percent of professors stressed the importance of DC skills such as consulting with faculty members to stay abreast of developments in a discipline and closely tracking the research interests of individual faculty. Thus, regardless of whether or not DC skills are included with SB skills, anywhere from 39.1 percent to 53.2 percent of professors in the humanities and social sciences consider SB skills to be a major component of good academic reference service. Of course, there is no suggestion here that LIS skills are not important. Instead, we propose that SB skills should be considered to be on an equal footing with LIS skills, and that SB skills should be encouraged and valorized in all reference librarians. (Table 41 contains a selection of some of the more creative recommendations made by professors.)

The leitmotif of this section, therefore, can be encapsulated in the following comment by a professor of American Literature: "Don't be so tech-inclined. Keep the focus on books, with computer assistance remaining just that: computer assistance." It is a simple enough piece of advice — almost Luddite on its surface — but it contains a wealth of insights that deserve further attention.

How, then, is this observation best understood and explicated? One way to approach its deceptive complexity is to set it alongside the very detailed recollections of a professor of French Literature who wrote as follows.

> I will give a very personal answer. What I found the more disturbing and sad is a certain attitude of total disinterest in your question. I can understand reluctance to listen to a long explanation when there is a line of people waiting for answers. No, I speak of coming at a time when I was completely alone to ask for help. You start explaining what you are looking for, give some details ... to facilitate the search. After a few minutes, you feel the person is not interested. She or he has looked quickly on the computer and said he found nothing. And it's obvious he is waiting for you to drop the subject and leave. Sometimes, if I really have time and patience, I will go on with my asking. Most of the time I will leave enraged and try to find by myself ways to obtain some results. It's very disappointing and sad to see this person missing an opportunity to learn — perhaps a little more about his job and the correct way to do it. So as I said before, I think we don't ask librarians to know everything in an area (we are the ones supposed to know more). But it will be really nice to feel that the person is ready to make his contribution by providing information on tools available, by listening to understand really what exactly you are looking for, and perhaps even sometimes, showing some initiative, some cleverness to imagine new ways of finding the needed information.

Taken together, these two quotes create an intriguing dynamic. The French Literature professor's reference librarian has not taken the advice of the American Literature professor, who wanted computer assistance to remain "just that: computer assistance," that is, a small part of the panoply of assistance that could be provided by reference librarians. According to the French Literature professor's account, the librarian conducted himself as if all the answers were contained on the computer screen. Computer assistance has become more than just computer assistance. It has become the entire universe of possible assistance, with the result that the French Literature professor's librarian showed disinterest, was unwilling to learn, and was disinclined to make any intellectual contribution whatsoever. To repeat the words of the French Literature professor, the librarian was bereft of initiative, cleverness, and imagination. No wonder the professor left enraged.

Table 41. Creative advice from professors in the humanities and social sciences for academic reference librarians about how to improve service

1. Aside from taking a degree in the discipline, they might consult course outlines and/or essay assignment sheets on a semi-regular basis for a range of courses in the discipline. This way, the librarians could learn first hand what the students are being asked to research. For the faculty's specialized interests, just a basic acquaintanceship with the most important bibliographies... is crucial.

2. One of the problems in my area is that it's so interdisciplinary. I have to check indexes in literature, history, anthropology, linguistics... and a lot of people in English depts. are in the same boat .... Librarians need to ask what sort of answer we're seeking, what level, detail, etc.... and

also should take the opportunity, if they're serious "research" librarians, of setting out to learn something about the current state of fields, not just what they were like when they were in university. They should ask faculty members more questions, they need to consult more with our department.

3. I've got a bit more used to [our librarians], but if folks could suggest a few more concept-level searches. For instance, in looking how the body is socially inscribed, philosophy will be key, as will be history. When I have asked for help in the past, they remained so focused on the topic that these concept kinds of approaches never came up.

4. It would help if they took a mini-term course in introductory anthropology or archaeology, or read a good introductory textbook. This would introduce them to the various [sub]fields and the general subject matter covered.

5. Take as many diverse classes in college as possible; look over the course catalog and see if you can reasonably note the general content of each course offered.

6. A reverse internship. Get the college/university to buy out some teaching time of experienced faculty so they can spend a few hours a week in the libraries working with the librarians.

7. To think completely "outside the box" and not waste a lot of time with sources that, although perhaps more familiar to them, are not usually that helpful for my particular field. In other words, to be willing to learn about the many and varied reference tools for my field, which are so highly specialized that they would not likely have come across them before. Too often, I've had reference librarians rely on more familiar tools that inevitably steer me in directions that are not helpful.

8. To learn as many languages as possible; to talk to faculty in appropriate fields; to read newsletters of major professional organizations.

9. Our bibliographer is a psychologist. Her training has helped our department tremendously. She knows what we need often before we ask. I think hiring individuals with advanced degrees in the social sciences would be helpful.

10. Knowledge of the Table of Contents of edited books, which do not show up on many searches. Knowledge of different areas of anthropology and its overlap with archaeology and Native American history. Requires a multidisciplinary perspective.

11. Train themselves "as if" they were researchers in the areas they represent. In my case this means acquiring foreign languages and knowledge of European history.

12. Librarians should have training in the reading of at least two languages other than their mother tongue.

13. Generally, know your disciplines and your patronage. Librarians of all sorts do well for themselves whenever they invest significant amounts of time and energy in becoming friends/colleagues with the teaching and research faculty. Doing that certainly reinforces the image of the reference librarian as a valued, learned colleague rather than some wimpy servile type for whom answering a question is a chore of the first water.

14. Read through recent journals and book reviews. Familiarize yourself with the kinds of work academic historians are doing at present — read their footnotes. Start a discussion with the faculty members asking questions and learn what sorts of things they do and what sorts of sources they use, what journals they read regularly. Work with grad students or faculty members to find out which internet sites are useful.

15. I think specialization in a field (or a few fields) of study is necessary. Also, someone who is personable and likes to talk with faculty about their research becomes very in tune and hence helpful, often directing us to references before we find them.

Now, what if the French Literature professor's librarian had understood reference work in the same manner as the professor of American Literature: that is, that computer assistance is only a small part of reference, that the focus should be on books, and by extension, the intellectual content therein contained? Attention to the intellectual content of books— in other words, reading — might have allowed the French Literature professor's reference librarian to engage more fully the professor's question, might have sparked some original thinking that would have allowed him to take the initiative and imaginatively contribute to the resolution of the problem at hand. Certainly, the French Literature professor admits that "we don't ask librarians to know everything in an area (we are the ones supposed to know more)," but the syntax of the professor's sentence implies an expectation that librarians know something about a subject area so that they can realistically contribute to answering a question even as they learn from the professor who, inevitably, "know[s] more." We are therefore back to the fundamental importance of subject-based knowledge for reference work that shows initiative and imagination; and, according to the professor of American Literature, a central way to bring about improved and imaginative reference service is to "keep the focus on books" and subject-related reading.

Beyond the desire for imagination and initiative, why are professors insistent that librarians possess the kind of in-depth subject-related knowledge that is available in books? The answer is connected with the notion that they believe librarians should be anticipating queries, preparing for them before they occur. If a librarian has been thinking about and studying discipline-based matters as a general part of her or his daily tasks, it becomes that much easier to display imagination and initiative. As a professor of Archaeology explains, reference librarians "need to remain current in the trends a field is taking in order to know what subject areas are going to be of interest to faculty and graduate students." But knowing about current trends in a field can only occur if one knows the general contours of that field. Thus, as another Archaeology professor suggests, "it would help if they took a mini-term course in introductory anthropology or archaeology, or read a good introductory textbook [because] this would introduce them to the various [sub-]fields and the general subject matter covered." A professor of North American History urges libraries to "hire people with a background in history [because] without this knowledge, it would be extremely difficult to understand the needs of individuals in the field." Still another Archaeology professor says that it is important to "have a look at some of the recent general publications of discussions in journals about the field [to] comprehend the breadth of the field and its interdisciplinary nature." A professor of Russian Literature recommends that librarians "really handle the books, etc. yourself ... read! (even if only a little of as many books that you can). Certainly know the various indices available and how to use them [and] keep track of their interests/research and point out new things as they become known to you."

In sum, the successful academic reference librarian must know — either through courses, books, journals, or personal contact with faculty — three things: the foundations of a field, its contemporary trends, and its interdisciplinary breadth. And knowing these three things will be an important factor in librarians being able to anticipate and prepare for possible queries— preparation that will result in imaginative contributions to solving reference queries and the development of an initiative-based culture of reference help.

Possessing subject-based knowledge allows the librarian to anticipate queries from both students and faculty. With regard to student questions, an American Literature professors observes that "aside from taking a degree in the discipline, they might consult course outlines and/or essay assignment sheets on a regular basis for a range of courses in the discipline. This way, the librarians could learn first hand what the students are being asked to research." An Archaeology professor concurs: "Take as many diverse classes in college as possible; look over the course catalog and see if you can reasonably note the general content of each course offered." Why is familiarity with course outlines and syllabi an advantage for reference librarians? Simply put, it permits them to understand the intellectual context in which a question is asked. It allows them to get a structural overview of the course, to know how a particular topic in a course is being positioned vis-à-vis other topics, to see what connections and relationships a professor wants students to draw from the choice of subject matter, and to weigh the relative importance that the professor attaches to certain topics based on their inclusion or exclusion from the syllabus.

When librarians combine their subject-based knowledge of a particular topic — the type of knowledge they get from "taking a degree in the discipline" or taking "as many diverse classes in college as possible"— with an awareness of the curricular requirements for specific courses, the level of service provided to students necessarily increases. What student would not like to be in the position of the previously described English professor who, while seeking historical information on life in Ireland during the Great Famine of the 1840s, was presented with "co-related suggestions about North American and Canadian Irish immigration patterns and their very real connections with the Famine" by a reference librarian? In addition, paying attention to course outlines, syllabi, and assignments is another way of keeping up with trends in a field because syllabi from a specific department, taken collectively, function as a proxy indicator of major developments and salient research interests for that field. Syllabi and course assignments often contain extensive and up-to-date reading lists, as well as statements about an individual professor's philosophical approach to, and assumptions about, the topic at hand — all of which can be used by the prescient reference librarian to direct students to appropriate resources, make pertinent and innovative suggestions, and to improve or update the librarian's own knowledge of the field. Not knowing about the issues and sub-issues in a field — in short, not knowing the intellectual context of a query — creates a situation where reference librarians, as an English Literature professor put it, "fall into the habit of having one pet reference tool you refer everyone to, whether it is appropriate or not."

Anticipation of possible queries and areas of interest is equally important when dealing with professors. A professor of Psychology writes that "our bibliographer is a psychologist. Her training has helped our department tremendously. She knows what we need before we ask. I think hiring individuals with advanced degrees in the social sciences would be helpful." A professor of Women's Studies states, "I think specialization in a field (or a few fields) of study is necessary. Also, someone who is personable and likes to talk with faculty about their research becomes very in tune and hence helpful, often directing us to references before we find them." And a professor of European History urges librarians "to train themselves 'as if' they were researchers in the areas that they represent, [which] in my case ... means acquiring foreign languages and knowledge of European history." Here, perhaps, is the crux of the issue: librarians should train and educate themselves "as if they were researchers in the areas that they represent" so that they can know what patrons— in this case, professors—"need before [they] ask." To do this properly, of course, is hard work: it often means acquiring an extensive set of skills, including foreign languages and in-depth subject knowledge of one, or preferably more, fields.

Yet such research-oriented skills are becoming increasingly vital because of the growing interdisciplinarity of all academic fields. For example, a professor of English Literature advises reference librarians to be prepared for anything, since "I have colleagues who are researching on the following: alien abduction narratives; politics and poetry in Northern Ireland; cyborgs and robots in literature; the modified English language of Caribbean and African writers .... The list could go on." A professor of Women's Studies wants reference librarians to "update information re: ethnic studies generally as interdisciplinary and cross disciplinary course and how to do research in these areas." Another professor of American Literature explains that one of the problems with that area of study is its interdisciplinary nature: "I have to check indexes in literature, history, anthropology, linguistics ... and a lot of people in English depts. are in the same boat .... Librarians need to ask what sort of answer we're seeking, what level, detail, etc. ... and also should take the opportunity, if they're serious 'research' librarians, of setting out to learn something about the current state of fields, not just what they were like when they were in university. They should ask faculty members more questions, they need to consult more with our department." A professor of Anthropology says it would be nice "if folks could suggest a few more concept-level searches. For instance, in looking how the body is socially inscribed, philosophy will be key, as will be history. When I have asked for help in the past, they remained so focused on the topic that these concept kinds of approaches never came up." And a professor of Archaeology, after suggesting that librarians pay attention to acquiring a "knowledge of the Table of Contents of edited books which do not show up on many searches," emphasizes that they should have "knowledge of different areas of anthropology and its overlap with archaeology and Native American history. Requires a multidisciplinary perspective."

How can reference librarians gain such interdisciplinarity and multidisciplinarity? One answer is to work side-by-side with professors on a daily basis. A professor of Archaeology recommends "a reverse internship [whereby] ... the college/university buy[s] out some teaching time of experienced faculty so they can spend a few hours a week in the libraries working with the librarians." Under this plan, professors would presumably supply the subject-based knowledge that reference librarians lack, teaching them about current trends in various fields. Thus, as more and more professors from different departments participate in the reverse internship program, reference librarians would accumulate an array of discipline-specific knowledge as well as insight about how these disciplines intersect and inform each other.

Another intriguing way to enhance interdisciplinary understanding is contained in the comments of a professor of European History and an English Literature professor. The European History specialist advises librarians to "read through recent journals and book reviews. Familiarize yourself with the kinds of work academic historians are doing at present — read their footnotes." In much the same way, the English Literature specialist believes that librarians should "skim the main journals in my field (*Victorian Studies, Victorian Literature and Culture, Nineteenth-Century Literature*, as well as *ELH* and *Representations*) in order to see what kinds of resources are being footnoted."[1]

Why would anyone want to make a study of footnotes? We can almost hear the librarian who lamented about the "mind-breaking" nature of citation-rate research sighing about the equally mind-numbing nature of careful footnote study. Yet footnotes are not only an incisive record of the research sources that support the argument of a scholarly article or book, they also reflect the intellectual path that the author(s) took to arrive at the argument. Examining footnotes can provide information about what kinds of sources from what kinds of disciplines are being used to what extent in a field at a particular time. Using this information, reference librarians can track broad trends in the evolution of a field, noting, for example, that an anthropologist who has written an article on how the body is socially inscribed has made use of sources that are traditionally thought to pertain to the fields of philosophy and history. Reference librarians can then familiarize themselves more closely with those same philosophical and historical sources, recreating in a general sense the scholarly journey of the author(s) of the article or book by making the same intellectual connections and deducing the same relationships. And they can even go one step further, putting themselves in the place of an anthropology professor researching a new issue, asking himself or herself: what sources in such cognate fields as history, philosophy, psychology, or art are germane to my problem?

In short, the astute study of footnotes is a rich source of knowledge about interdisciplinary trends, allowing reference librarians to educate themselves in detail about field-specific issues and to act "as if they were researchers in the areas they represent." The new knowledge thereby created — whether manifested by an increased awareness of specialized sources, fruitful insights into important current research questions, or a better understanding of the ways that fields can intersect and overlap — helps to give reference librarians additional intellectual tools to anticipate reference queries.

If the footnote analysis described here seems esoteric, a similar sort of familiarity with current discipline-specific trends and the research concerns of individual professors can be achieved through close and regular consultations with academic departments. Such consultation — or "working relations," as an Anthropology professor puts it — will help reference librarians to anticipate questions. But, as a professor of Women's Studies warns, it is not enough to have departmental liaisons. Instead, librarians must make the commitment "to visit each department to make faculty *individually* aware of their services — rather than relying on a liaison [because] I am the liaison here for our faculty, and I am about the only one here the librarian ever talks with" (emphasis added). A Linguistics professor also stresses the need for individual contact: librarians should "visit each professor and meet them personally, if possible. Ask that each send an email message describing main research and teaching interests. Send regular email correspondence and updates so that they know you are available."

Of course, there is no single formula for such individualized contact between librarians and discipline-specific faculty. For instance, an English Literature professor recalls how "the librarian in charge of English & American Literature sent me a letter after I was hired offering to tell me about special collections, and asking whether I had any special desires. This seems exemplary to me, and I would recommend that other librarians do the same." A French Literature professor advises librarians "to get to know the faculty [by] go[ing] to department meetings so people can see you and hear what you have to offer." A professor of Women's Studies suggests that, after meeting "with new faculty as they come in to find out what they do ... and become familiar with their work," librarians should "set up a few keywords that always are highlighted with someone's work and keep them informed on what is coming out on those topics (including new databases that would be appropriate, books, journals, electronic search mechanisms, etc.)." A Sociology professor describes a system where librarians have developed "descriptions of individual research concerns and ... constantly scan available resources in search of titles that may be of interest to particular researchers [and] faculty members. Copies of titles pages of books or Table of Contents are regularly sent to our faculty with cover pages asking whether the full text of a particular writing should be made available." Finally, a professor of European History not only offers a full-scale program designed to ensure close working contact between faculty and librarians, but also observes that these good working relationships benefit students.

> Sit down and meet with faculty (1 hour with each one, e.g.) and ask them to provide in advance or arrive prepared with a list of things they'd like the library to get or what they use that the library has and how best the librarian can help with upcoming classes. Librarians should know what sort of classes the faculty member teaches, what seminar topics have been taught in the past three years and in the next three. Librarians should ask what presses are publishing the best monographs for that faculty member, and what journals and databases would be most useful for that faculty member. Knowing the content needs of faculty can help librarians work to make learning more enjoyable for students.[2]

One key point in all these examples is advanced planning and proactive service that anticipates research and pedagogical needs. But a subsidiary point is that such advanced planning — even to the extent of knowing curricular plans three years into the future — serves "to make learning more enjoyable," whether for students or for faculty members. Professors begin to feel that they are not alone in their research work, that one or two librarians actually care about the same discipline-based trends and issues that they care about, and that librarians and professors are embarked upon a common mission to make "learning more enjoyable" by being intellectually prepared for student questions and problems.

The approaches described so far are formal in nature — one gets the sense that they occur in someone's office, with a determined agenda — yet many survey respondents believe that there is a need for more informal contact between librarians and professors. An Archaeology professor imagines: "[If I were a librarian] I would go to lunch with ... faculty members once a year and have them tell me what was happening in the field, what was going on with particular journals, which presses were publishing the best lists, etc." An American Literature professor agrees, counseling librarians to "have lunch with some profs? Seriously, this would be really useful to everybody [since] we're all constantly scrambling. There are so many new research tools from week to week we don't know how to use, and they need to know where we're at."[3] An Anthropology professor recommends "cultivating relations with patrons outside of the context of the inquiry and beyond the library." Luncheon meetings and other meetings "beyond the library" can, of course, be just as formal as meetings in offices, but there is nevertheless the sense that individuals in such settings have stepped outside of their formal roles, that they are having a conversation that, while informative and beneficial to both sides, blurs the boundaries of their respective job titles, creating the possibility of enhanced personal and professional cooperation. Hinting at some of these benefits, a professor of North American History writes that "librarians of all sorts do well for themselves whenever they invest significant amounts of time and energy in becoming friends/colleagues with the teaching and research faculty. Doing that certainly reinforces the image of the reference librarian as a valued, learned colleague rather than some wimpy servile type for whom answering a question is a chore of the first water."

Still, the transformation from a "wimpy servile type" to a "valued, learned colleague" cannot be accomplished if the librarian is not learned or sincerely interested in the field of study represented by the professor. The use of the terms "friend" and "colleague" in this context implies someone with whom one can have an intelligent conversation about discipline-specific matters more or less as an equal, not someone who does not appear to be in the same intellectual "league" as the professor. Thus, librarians must have an existing subject-specific knowledge base as a prerequisite to any fruitful formal or informal exchanges between themselves and professors. In one sense, the greater a librarian's subject-based knowledge, the greater the chances that that librarian and discipline-specific faculty members will become valued and learned colleagues or friends. And the more they become friends and colleagues, the more that the librarian will begin to think as if he or she was a researcher, thus anticipating needs before they arise.

Reference librarians who do not have a strong educational background in a field and who do not think as if they were researchers in a field have very little opportunity to anticipate potential issues and concerns before they arise or to ask intelligent questions that show they really understand the basis of the patron's problem. Indeed, broad exposure to ongoing professorial research may help reference librarians, as a professor of East Asian History notes, "to think completely outside the box and not waste a lot of time with sources that, although perhaps more familiar to them, are not usually that helpful for my particular field. In other words, to be willing to learn about the many and varied reference tools for my field, which are so highly specialized that they would not likely have come across them before. Too often, I've had reference librarians rely on more familiar tools that inevitably steer me in directions that are not helpful." In addition, the more that librarians work, consult, and stay in touch with professors by dealing with their research concerns, the more they can assist students with innovative suggestions and possible directions of approach to a thorny problem. The current research interests of a professor are, in the near future, likely to underpin that professor's intellectual design of a course, inform his or her lectures, color the choice of research topics of his or her graduate students, and effect the types of assignments he or she gives to undergraduate students. As a professor of English Literature observes, "every successful new problem you solve expands your own usefulness to faculty and students."

Keeping up with changes and developments in various fields

By now many of the major recommendations that professors in the humanities and social sciences have for reference librarians are becoming clear. While not disputing the importance of LIS-based skills, professors repeatedly focus on the importance of subject-based skills and departmental consultation skills. When they were asked about examples of impressive academic service, they consistently mentioned librarians who had detailed discipline-specific knowledge and who were able to make innovative suggestions based on subject expertise. Conversely, when asked about examples of disappointing reference service, they pointed to librarians who had little, if any, subject-specific skills. In this section, we ask professors to imagine themselves as reference librarians trying to keep pace with constants changes and developments in an academic field of study. What would they, as individual librarians, do to keep up?

Table 42. If you were an academic reference librarian, what would you do to keep up with changes and developments in your broad field of study?

	Literature Professors (n = 69)	History & Women's Studies Profs (n = 81)	Social Science Professors (n = 86)	Total (n = 236)*
Library & Information Science (LIS) skills				
Knowledge of information technology & retrieval	8	11	11	30
Keep up with reference & bibliographic tools	5	7	6	18
Know collections in your library & other libraries	4	3	1	8
Networking with other librarians	1	7	0	8
Read LIS journals	3	2	2	7
Attend LIS conferences and continuing education classes	3	2	1	6
Problem-solving skills and creating sample searches	2	1	1	4
Subscribe to LIS discussion lists	2	1	0	3
No need for subject-based skills	1	1	1	3
Read publisher and book seller catalogs	2	0	0	2
Thematic units for LIS skills	31 (32.6%)	35 (24.6%)	23 (20.7%)	89 (25.6%)
Subject-based (SB) skills				
Read academic journals in the field	11	22	14	47
Attend discipline-based conferences & association meetings	3	17	11	31
Know electronic-based subject resources	9	10	7	26
Read book reviews	4	8	11	23
Subscribe to discussion lists in the field	4	7	4	15
Read newsletters of associations in the field	2	4	8	14
Read in general	2	6	5	13
Knowledge of trends in field from own study	4	4	5	13
Read general-interest journals	4	4	1	9

	Literature Professors (n = 69)	History & Women's Studies Profs (n = 81)	Social Science Professors (n = 86)	Total (n = 236)*
Attend public lectures or courses in the field	2	3	2	7
Keep abreast of conference proceedings & grants	1	1	3	5
Do research or teach in the field	1	3	0	4
Know interdisciplinary topics	3	1	0	4
Know foreign languages	2	1	0	3
Read books	0	0	3	3
Thematic units for SB skills	52 (54.7%)	91 (64.1%)	74 (66.7%)	217 (62.4%)
Department consultation (DC) skills				
Consult with faculty/syllabi to stay current	9	13	13	35
Know research interests/read publications of faculty	3	3	1	7
Thematic units for DC skills	12 (12.6%)	16 (11.3%)	14 (12.6%)	42 (12%)
Total thematic units mentioned by professors	95 (100%)	142 (100%)	111 (100%)	348* (100%)

* The *n* of professors does not equal the total of thematic units because some professors gave more than one piece of advice.

From one perspective, this question is much like the previous one where professors were asked to give advice to reference librarians in general about how to improve service. But in the previous question, much of the advice turned on the need for librarians to have subject-specific and interdisciplinary knowledge in order to anticipate queries and problems. Certainly, some professors discussed strategies about how to acquire and enhance such knowledge, but the central emphasis remained on the fact that such subject-based knowledge was necessary. On the other hand, this question assumes the fact of constant change in a field of study and shifts the focus away from reference librarians in general to the shoulders of individual professors and librarians and their own strategies to become more knowledgeable in subject areas.

Again, as in Table 40, Table 42 groups responses into three main categories—LIS-skills, SB-skills, and DC-skills—and then further sub-divides them. As shown in Table 42, 62.4 percent of professors opted for various SB-skills to keep up with changes and developments in their field of study, while 25.6 percent of professors listed LIS-skills and 12 percent mentioned DC skills. In the SB-skills category, the two most frequently discussed methods were reading field-specific academic journals (47) and attending field-specific conference or association meetings (31).

If all six sub-categories that speak about reading (reading academic journals; reading general-interest journals; reading book reviews; reading books; reading in general; and reading newsletters of associations) are combined, we find that professors consider some form of subject-based reading to be far and away the most important activity (mentioned 109 times) that they would do as librarians. As an American Literature professor summarized, "'The short answer, of course, is read [because] in a field of study as broad as English, there are constant developments, currents, countercurrents." And, because all fields of study are broad, this advice applies, as it were, broadly across all fields. A professor of European History bluntly suggested that librarians "[r]ead, read, read!!! Especially journals and book reviews as well as professional journals in my field that relate to teaching and research." A professor of East Asian History noted that librarians should "regularly read all the major journals in the field, especially the book reviews." In short, reading is something that professors expect librarians to do frequently. (Table 43 contains a selection of some of the more creative recommendations made by professors.)

Did professors give more details about the types of reading that librarians should undertake? Most certainly yes. We present the following advice from a professor of American Literature as an example of what one individual recommends that librarians read:

> PMLA and similar bibliographies. The essential journals in the field: *American Literature, Cambridge Quarterly, Modern Fiction Studies, Shakespeare Quarterly,* etc.... The latest trends in the discipline, as gleaned from the *Times Literary Supplement, The New York Review of Books, London Review of Books, New York Times Book Review,* and so on. Any kind of digest that features abstracts or summaries of book reviews and articles. These could be supplemented by an ongoing acquaintanceship with the primary materials, the novels published every year, for example, and the secondary ones, studies that break new ground, make headlines, and so on.

Of course, the titles mentioned deal specifically with English and American Literature, but what we want to draw attention to here is the *structure* of the recommended reading program, as well as its obvious extensiveness. The structure is particularly important because it can be applied to other fields as well. Accordingly, reading starts with knowledge about research studies that "make headlines" and about "the latest trends in the discipline." Where to find such information? Popular newspapers and journals are a key source: in the field of literature, such publications as *The New York Review of Books* and the *Times Literary Supplement* are necessary starting points. But the field of literature is not the only one that is covered by the popular press, and it is not the only field where professors recommended that reference librarians begin the task of acquainting themselves with recent trends by reading mainstream publications. In this respect, the comments of an Anthropology professor are instructive: "Actually, reading the popular press, such as *Archaeology* magazine, is a fairly easy way to keep on top of things." Important, too, is the emphasis placed on the word "ongoing" by the American Literature professor. New developments, discoveries, and interpretations occur on a daily basis, so it is logical that a reference librarian should have an "ongoing" knowledge of current issues—the type of "ongoing-ness" that is conveniently provided by popular press publications. As well, ongoing knowledge of a field can be frequently gained from newsletters and bulletins of professional associations—a fact mentioned by 14 professors.

Table 43. Creative advice from professors in the humanities and social sciences for academic reference librarians about how to keep up with changes in various fields of study

1. Invent puzzles to solve: locate biographical information on lesser-known figures, find manuscripts for a number of literary works, begin to create bibliographies for literary criticism on particular topics. Practice using the library.

2. The short answer, of course, is read. In a field of study as broad as English, there are constant developments, currents, countercurrents; you can take the temperature of some of these by reading at least the title pages of major journals like PMLA. I would also ... try to keep abreast of the research interests of faculty in the field; who's working on gender theory? ... on post-colonialism? ... on textual criticism?

3. Peruse the journals, read the articles and as many book reviews as possible, for starters. Then go into the books themselves.

4. Read current journals, attend conferences, participate (where possible) in the intellectual life of the campus—attending talks, speaking with faculty about classes and research.

5. Attend the national conferences of [various] fields. Look at citation indexes to get a feel for what kinds of journals publish what kinds of articles; subscribe to the professional association newsletters; read selected book reviews in 3–4 of the major journals.

6. Actually, reading the popular press, such as *Archaeology* magazine, is a fairly easy way to keep on top of things. Also, if new literature databases come out, this would be helpful to know about.

7. The best way is to network. Get to know the other librarians, scholars in the field. Find out who is publishing, who is teaching. The big conferences (American Asian Studies, American Slavic Studies) are great for getting to know what's up. Again, there has to be a commitment from the institution to get their librarians there. I guess as a librarian, you would have to have an interest in it—so pick up one or two fields and make those your specialty. (This may already go on in library school, I have no idea.)

8. Read, read, read!!! Especially journals and book reviews as well as professional journals in my field that relate to teaching and research.

9. Since the most interesting research is being done in what used to be considered non-mainstream areas—I'm thinking of studies of trauma, transcultural representations, etc.—I would seek to learn which tools—most likely interdisciplinary—can yield the best and most reliable information. In my experience from adjudicating and supervising, students are increasingly directing their own research toward such areas. There will be increasing need for access to non-traditional formulations of disciplines and research areas that will require different tools.

10. Review conference programs and proceedings; study grant agency funding lists and funded project topics. Survey UMI listings of dissertation titles.

11. I would take field trips to the "big" universities, visiting their libraries and exploring their collections. I'd set up a mentoring system within my home library.... Part of the job description should be taking time to explore the resources at hand ... to better recommend them to others.

12. I would read the *Times Literary Supplement*, which is broadly-based, weekly, and up-to-date. I would talk to the people in the English dept. who publish and are active.... I would attempt to gain a basic knowledge of literary periods (Romantic vs. Victorian, e.g.), and of standard editions.... Knowledge of this kind builds confidence and enthusiasm, I think, between librarians and academics.

13. In addition to what I was taught in a librarian graduate program, I would pay attention to on the edge curriculum issues in universities and newly developed areas such as women's studies and ethnic studies.

14. Attending classes, taking independent studies, getting a certificate or higher degree in the field ... consulting with professors in the field.

15. The emphasis on cultural studies means that literary scholars will need help finding material that used to belong to other disciplines (or to no discipline at all, i.e., popular culture).

Another reason that professors may have for recommending popular press sources is that these sources provide a context for academic debates that are often abstruse, esoteric, and directed at initiates. Reference librarians who read about these debates in venues such as *Archaeology* or the *New York Times Book Review* will better understand the subtleties of the debates when they come across them in academic journals and book reviews than will the librarians exposed to these debates without a background overview. To be sure, as the American Literature professor quoted above recognizes, popular publications are only a precursor to further reading; they must be supplemented by journals, digests, bibliographies, and primary materials of various kinds. But even here there is a hierarchy, as noted by a professor of Anthropology, who suggests that librarians "[p]eruse the journals, read the articles and as many book reviews as possible, for starters. Then go into the books themselves." Just as an article in the popular press may lead a reader to have a better sense of a topic before he or she tackles an academic article on that topic, the academic journal article or book review can also stimulate further interest in a subject area, and this interest often leads to reading a more in-depth treatment of the subject in book form, which, in turn, may cause interest in other topics discussed in the book, or at least an awareness of and acquaintance with them. Taken as a whole, then, the knowledge that results from reading "builds confidence and enthusiasm ... between librarians and academics," according to a professor of English Literature.

While reading is a central activity, it should not be a complete substitute for hands-on involvement in intellectual life and scholarly debate. A number of professors viewed reading as a part of a package of activities designed to make the reference librarian what could well be described as a "scholar-librarian." Reading is vital, they agreed, but reading should also be supplemented by a variety of public actions—attending conferences and departmental colloquia, taking advanced degrees, presenting papers, organizing conferences, keeping up with funding bodies—that position the librarian as a credible force in the wider academic community. For example, a professor of Anthropology wrote: "Read current journals, attend conferences, participate (where possible) in the intellectual life of the campus—attending talks, speaking with faculty about classes and research." A professor of North American History was adamant that librarians must "[r]ead extensively in the field of history, and develop one's own research agenda." Another professor of North American History recommended that a librarian "might belong to several of the professional associations and attend their annual meetings ... routinely read the major journals, especially the book review section ... [and] pick the brains of faculty members so as to keep abreast of changing trends." A Women's Studies professor recommended, "Look regularly at the journal *Signs*, look at the new reference works being produced ... about women writers.... I would also recommend trying to attend one or two of the regular colloquia sponsored by the departments for which that librarian is especially responsible." Another Women's Studies professor was of much the same opinion: "I would read a lot, talk to those who call on the library for services, attend conferences of librarians and academics, give papers, organize conferences." A professor of European History advises "[r]eading some of the major scholarly journals (especially the book reviews) [and] [a]ttending some of the talks by invited speakers to that university in that area of study." Finally, a professor of Anthropology urges librarians to "attend the national conferences of [various] fields. Look at citation indexes to get a feel for what kinds of journals publish what kinds of articles; subscribe to the professional association newsletters; read selected book reviews in 3–4 of the major journals." In other words, professors believe that the private act of reading and the act of public participation in intellectual activities inform each other, making each all the more richer and valuable.

Conferences were especially praised as important public activities. One reason is that they facilitate networking, in effect becoming an extension of the librarian's local network and allowing librarians to gather a great deal of information in a relatively short period of time. As well, they provide an impetus for in-depth study of a field. A professor of East Asian History summarized the value of conferences as follows:

> The best way is to network. Get to know other librarians, scholars in the field. Find out who is publishing, who is teaching. The big conferences ... are great for getting to know what's up. Again, there has to be a commitment from the institution to get their librarians there. I guess as a librarian, you would have to have an interest in it — so pick up one or two fields and make those your specialty. (This may already go on in library school, I have no idea.)

Conferences are seen as places where librarians can develop, or enhance, knowledge of subject specialties.

It is interesting to note that this professor of East Asian History assumes that subject specialization may exist at LIS schools. Some LIS schools do in fact encourage such specialization by offering dual degrees: witness, for example, San Jose State University (combined MLIS degrees with MA degrees in Latin American Studies or History); Southern Connecticut State University (combined MLS degrees with MS degrees in Chemistry, English, or Foreign Languages); the Catholic University of America (combined MSLS degrees with MA degrees in Greek and Latin, Musicology, or Biology); Indiana University (combined MLS degrees with MA degrees in Art History, Comparative Literature, Music, or Russian and East European Studies); the University of Oklahoma (combined MLIS degree with MA in History of Science); the University of Wisconsin–Milwaukee (combined MLIS degree with MS in Urban Studies); and the University of Southern Mississippi (combined MLS degree with MA in Anthropology). Most LIS schools, however, do not.[4] If professors are keen to deal with reference librarians who are, for all intents and purposes, scholar-librarians invested in the intellectual life of the field, subject-specific conferences are invaluable, especially in filling the lacunae in subject-specific education evident at some LIS institutions. Another way to fill in the subject-specific gaps of LIS education may be through "attending classes, taking independent studies, getting a certificate or higher degree in the field ...," as recommended by a professor of Women's Studies. A professor of Archaeology advises librarians to "[r]ead the latest texts or sit in on an intro course." In effect, going to conferences, reading, and taking subject-specific course work function as diverse forms of continuing education that many professors are convinced that reference librarians should engage in.

Of course, many librarians are unable to attend subject-specific conferences, but that does not mean that they cannot participate in the intellectual life of their chosen field through processes and actions that serve as proxies for the conference experience. For instance, a professor of Linguistics urged librarians to "[r]eview conference programs and proceedings; study grant agency funding lists and funded project topics [and] survey UMI listings of dissertation titles." Another American Literature professor offered advice along the same lines: "Check the MLA and American Studies databases to see what presentations are being delivered at the field's conferences." A Psychology professor would "do a weekly scan of the relevant literature and at least keep up with the terminology and the most prominent authors." Through concerted attention to conference programs, conference proceedings, dissertation titles, and grant agency funding lists, a reference librarian can thus keep close to recent developments and directions in a field when he or she is prevented from traveling to conferences.

Noteworthy, too, was the fact that some professors mentioned that reference librarians should spend more time getting to know both their own library and the resources of larger libraries. For example, a professor of American Literature suggested that librarians "[i]nvent puzzles to solve: locate biographical information on lesser-known figures, find manuscripts for a number of literary works, begin to create bibliographies for literary criticism on particular topics. Practice using the library." A professor of Russian Literature thought that librarians should "take field trips to the 'big' universities, visiting their libraries and exploring their collections. I'd set up a mentoring program within my home library.... Part of the job description should be taking the time to explore the resources at hand ... to better recommend them to others." Another professor of Russian Literature had much the same idea, observing that it was important to "be aware of the contents of collections of other major libraries especially in the areas where my collection is weaker."

Why are all these methods of keeping current important? As we saw in the previous section, the increasing emphasis on interdisciplinarity means that scholars are looking for an ever-wider range of materials from an ever-wider range of primary and secondary sources. Reference librarians who can make connections across disciplines—whether through private reading that contributes to their subject knowledge, public participation at conferences, or a detailed familiarity with sources held by their home institution or elsewhere—will be better able to guide and help professors in their research. As a professor of English Literature stated, "The emphasis on cultural studies means that literary scholars will need help finding material that used to belong to other disciplines (or to no discipline at all, i.e., popular culture)." Or, as a professor of French Literature put it, "since the most interesting research is being done in what used to be considered non-mainstream areas—I'm thinking of studies of trauma, transcultural representations, etc.—I would seek to learn which tools—most likely interdisciplinary—can yield the best and most reliable information." In other words, as formerly non-mainstream subject areas become mainstream subject areas—and as these subject areas increasingly become fertile ground for numerous scholars—reference librarians will need to approach their jobs in a way that forces them to think across traditional disciplinary boundaries.

Eventually, such interdisciplinary and cross-disciplinary thinking will become the norm, just as it has for scholars. And just as scholars have had to read extensively and think in new ways to gain knowledge about new disciplines and to forge connections across disciplines, reference librarians too can benefit from extensive reading and familiarity with new subject areas so as to make needed connections across fields—something that will allow them to assist professors and students in meaningful and innovative ways. In so doing they will become both generalists and subject-specialists, equally adept at creating new connections among fields and applying that newly gained knowledge to a specific aspect of a particular field. In many respects, the future model for reference work may very well not be defined by ever-increasing technological prowess and acumen on the part of reference librarians, but rather by ever-increasing scholarship manifested as broad exposure to ideas gained through reading and the application of that reading to challenging intellectual problems and queries. When all is said and done, reference librarians will be compelled to think as if they were researchers, and in so doing they will *become* researchers. And if there is anything that a researcher must do in order to retain her or his intellectual edge, it is to read as much as possible so as to gain as much general and subject-specific knowledge as possible.

In many ways, the ideal academic reference librarian is very much like a modified version of the German *Referenten* of the 1950s and 1960s, as Fred Hay reminds us.[5] Surveying the history of the subject specialist in academic libraries, he describes how the *Referenten* — a subject bibliographer who possesses a Ph.D. and two years of library education and has passed a state-administered exam — not only contributes to superior collection development, but, in the course of performing reference work, brings about a situation where "the library is more likely to be viewed by the faculty as a genuinely scholarly enterprise.... The professor will tend to have more confidence in the library staff member who is his academic equal."[6] We are thus reminded of the English Literature professor who observed that reading — and, by extension, the subject knowledge that results from such reading — "builds confidence and enthusiasm ... between librarians and academics." Such confidence furthers research and teaching, making the academic reference librarian a truly integral part of university life.

Two final examples are instructive in this regard. When asked about instances of impressive service at the reference desk, a professor of East Asian History remembered "ask[ing] about a couple of journals in the field of Asian studies, which are not necessarily well known, and he [the librarian] knew more about them than I did." And a professor of European History recalled how "they tried to help me find out about journals on the subject of the history of the Orient published in Germany between about 1880 and 1930. They found books I didn't know of, and even better, called a local expert in who helped me even more." In both cases, the reference librarians exhibit traits of researchers, not only knowing about obscure journals but also about other experts working in the area. In both cases, they "know" more than the professors themselves. Here, reference librarians have become researchers; in many respects they have even surpassed the professors whom they were called upon to help. As we have seen in this chapter, reading and developing subject-specific skills can aid in this process.

8

Reading as a Species of Intellectual Capital

The theories of Pierre Bourdieu provide some insights about the processes of change in library reference work.[1] Bourdieu formulated the notion of "field," defined as a "social microcosm" or a "configuration of objective relations between positions." There are numerous "fields" in society, and each follows "specific logics." For instance, the world of economics is a field, as is the world of art, religion, or literature. At the same time, however, the limits of a field are fluid and "always *at stake in the field itself*" (original emphasis). A field, Bourdieu believes, can be compared to a "game," with the difference that a field follows "rules, or regularities, that are not explicit and codified." In addition, a field has "stakes which are for the most part the product of competition between players." Each participant or player has one or more "species of capital" (knowledge of a certain skill, for example) that can be deployed during the competition. For Bourdieu, it is the "species of capital" that is "efficacious in a given field, both as a weapon and as a stake of struggle." Whoever has capital can wield power and influence. In a sense, capital allows an individual "to *exist,* in the field under consideration, instead of being considered a negligible quantity" (original emphasis). Accordingly, it is "the state of relations of force between players that defines the structure of the field." To clarify his point, he compares "species of capital" with tokens of different colors. The position of each player within the field thus depends not only on the number and arrangement of that individual's tokens, but also on "the *evolution over time* of the volume and structure of this capital" (original emphasis). More important, individuals can decide to play in order to transform, partially or completely, the immanent rules of the game. They can, for instance, work to change "the relative value of tokens of different colors" through strategies aimed at discrediting the form of capital upon which the force of their opponents rests (e.g., economic capital) and to valorize the species of capital they preferentially possess (e.g., juridical capital). A field is therefore dynamic; it is a "*field of struggles* aimed at preserving or transforming" the configuration of "potential and active forces" within it (original emphasis). Because the field is "a structure of objective relations between positions of force," participants within the field attempt to "impose the principle of hierarchization most favorable to their own products."[2]

If librarianship is considered to be a field in Bourdieu's terms, it is possible to understand it as a "field of struggles" in which one form of capital — subject knowledge of a diverse array of topics—is in the process of being discredited. Another form of capital—ready acceptance of any form of technological innovation—is being valorized. Patricia Madoo Lengermann, Jill Niebrugge-Brantley, and Jane Kirkpatrick, using the sociological theories of Dorothy Smith's *The Everyday World as Problematic* and *The Conceptual Practices of Power*, locate the library as the "mediator between the sphere of the extralocal apparatus of ruling" (defined as the sphere shaped by "capitalism and patriarchy" and including such "documents of control" as laws, contracts, news reports, media portrayals, etc.) and the "sphere of the local actuality" (defined as possessing a feminine consciousness insofar as it is concerned with the "dailiness" of living, personal relationships and concrete coping activities).[3] As the technology-driven information revolution marketed by "the extralocal apparatus of ruling" is enforced as a new "textual revolution" to which all must submit, the library—a place inscribed with a feminist notion of professional service — is faced with numerous challenges to remain "a supportive environment focused on the needs of individuals in the local actualities of lived experience."[4] In effect, reference librarians are in danger of allowing their field to be defined by external forces that are making technology-based solutions the primary "species of capital" in an effort to "impose the principle of hierarchization most favorable to their own products."[5]

Reference librarianship is undergoing profound changes. On both symbolic and practical levels, there is competition to lay claim to the field of reference librarianship, to make it conform more closely to the interests of one group of players who feel that they are currently in the ascendant: the proponents of digital reference models. There are of course many definitions and models of digital reference service, some of which are summarized by Gobinda Chowdhury.[6] As she explains, a wide range of entities, including publishers, public and university libraries, search engines, and subject experts, can provide digital reference services. These services have such names as Askme, AllExperts, Ask Jeeves, Ask a Librarian, 24/7 Reference Project, the Collaborative Digital Reference Service (CDRS) of the Library of Congress, and SIFTER, a project based at Indiana University that relies on "information agents that would perform a number of functions such as culling information from complex resources residing in diverse locations, and conducting analysis, synthesis and customization according to the requirements of the user."[7] But, as Chowdhury concludes, "one of the major problems of a digital search environment is the absence of human intermediaries who play a major role in traditional online search services."[8] She quotes an editorial from a special issue of *Information Processing & Management* in 1999, which states that, while "[a]ccess services that facilitate search and browsing have been central to digital library research thus far, there is a great need for attention to reference and question-answering, on-demand help, and fostering of citizenship and literacy and mechanisms to simplify participatory involvement of user communities."[9] And, to judge from her definition of digital reference services, Marilyn Domas White also wants to see human intermediaries play a greater role in these services. She emphasizes that, in digital reference services, "knowledgeable individuals answer questions, and responses are transmitted via electronic means. Interim search processes need not involve electronic devices although they often do. There may even be interim contact with questioners via telephone or electronic means if questions require clarification."[10]

On the surface, then, there is recognition that digital reference models should include human participation. But, as we saw in Chapter 1, writers such as Steve Coffman, Matthew

Saxton, Chris Ferguson, and Susan McGlamery included human intermediaries in their proposals, but these human intermediaries are part of a call center model characterized by strict productivity goals, routinization, and regimentation. On the one hand, this is a form of human participation; on the other hand, it is not. Also revealing is the type of language, taken from systems analysis, that is being used to evaluate digital reference services (DRS). Consider the following example: "The framework ... is based on systems analysis, with the emphasis on identifying key elements associated with client input: the throughput (i.e., the processing of the query by the system) and system output (i.e., communications from the DRS, usually in the form of responses to queries)."[11] From a rhetorical point of view, what is most telling here is that, while clients are expressly invoked, no other humans appear. Instead, there is "throughput" and the "system," mentioned twice. Presumably, system throughput is facilitated by human intervention, but the lack of emphasis on human presence in such throughput may be an indication that human presence is not as highly valued and as central as other aspects of the system. The human reference staff member, while indeed present, is conceived of as just another element in the overall functioning of the system. The system matters; the humans who make it run do not. And, no matter how well-intentioned and central the human presence may have originally been within a system or systems, all systems invariably face financial and performance-based pressures. Even if the digital reference service model implemented by public and academic libraries is characterized by the type of quality-oriented workflows identified by Phil Taylor, Gareth Mulvey, Jeff Hyman, and Peter Bain,[12] managers and administrators of systems will find themselves confronted with the need to cut costs and increase productivity — pressures that will intensify and regiment working pace and conditions such that there will be very little difference between digital reference services and quantity-oriented call centers.

To use Bourdieu's terms, advocates of digital reference services are deploying their "species of capital"— their belief in the efficacy of technological innovation as represented by the call center model — in order to render less valuable the "species of capital" of reference librarians whom they accuse of being concerned only with "'reviewing the professional literature' and other odd tasks" such as "keeping kids quiet, scheduling staff, ordering supplies, presiding over children's story times, checking books out, and other details of managing the building."[13] However, these supposedly valueless tasks go a long way toward creating "a supportive environment focused on the needs of individuals in the local actualities of lived experience"[14] and privileging in-depth subject knowledge about a wide variety of topics. From the perspective of Bourdieu, this is a strategy "aimed at discrediting the form of capital upon which the force of [an] opponent rests"[15] and emphasizing the superiority of an opposite species of capital. The end result is that the "relative value of tokens of different colors"[16] has changed in the field of reference librarianship. Technological innovation has become a weapon allowing one group of individuals to exert power and influence on their own behalf while marginalizing the contributions of those who are skeptical of the ultimate value of such technological advances. It allows this first group of players to paint themselves as innovators in the profession, and it renders the second group a "negligible quantity."[17] In one sense, technological innovation is being construed as a synecdoche for progress, which in turn will allow the field of reference librarianship to survive. The terms of the debate thus permit any skeptic of technological innovation to be branded an opponent of progress and thus an impediment to the field's survival.

Equally disturbing is the fact some of the same proponents of unmitigated technological innovation in reference service (i.e., the digital call center model described previously) are also marshalling evidence to suggest that the education and experience levels of library reference personnel have virtually no effect on the quality of reference service outcomes. Consider, for example, Matthew Saxton and John Richardson Jr.'s *Understanding Reference Transactions: Transforming an Art into a Science*.[18] Deploying a sophisticated battery of statistical tests, they argue[19] that the main factor in determining three reference outcomes (patron's rating of the degree of completeness of the information received; patron's rating of the degree of usefulness of the information received; and patron's rating of the degree of satisfaction with the information received) for 696 reference transactions that were judged to be easy (mean rating of 1.36 on a 7-point Likert scale, with a value of 1 representing the easiest type of question)[20] is the behavior of the individual librarian, where behavior is defined as being "concerned with optimizing the quality of communication between the librarian and library user."[21] Aspects of behavior are encapsulated within the *Guidelines for Behavioral Performance of Reference and Information Service Professionals* developed by the Reference and User Services Association (RUSA)—approachability, interest, listening/inquiring, searching, and follow-up—and operationalized in Saxton and Richardson's book as patron ratings about the degree to which a library reference staff person was "ready to help me," was "interested in my question," "understood my question," and "made sure I found what I wanted."[22] Other variables such as a librarian's education and experience had no predictive power on these three reference outcomes.[23] A fourth reference transaction outcome—accuracy of the information received, where accuracy was assessed by a panel of external judges—was not predicted by the individual behavior of the librarian; indeed, "[t]he only variable that was found to predict the accuracy of the librarian's response was the difficulty of the query [insofar as] [t]he responses provided to users by librarians for difficult queries were less likely to exhibit a high degree of accuracy than responses provided to users posing simple queries."[24]Accordingly, they suggest that only "utility measures" such as the degree of completeness and usefulness of information received should be considered as "critical outcome measure[s] for assessment of reference services.[25] In other words, there is very little need, if any, to pay attention to the accuracy of information received in assessing reference services in the future, especially because most queries received are easy ones and, besides, accuracy goes down when the query becomes more difficult. Finally, in educating students "specializing in reference work," they want to shift the emphasis away from "a series of electives that specialize in the literature and resources of some subject area" so that "more emphasis needs to be placed on developing ... behavioral skills in more than one course...."[26]

What are we to make of all this? Quite simply, a very intriguing act of sleight-of-hand has been performed by Saxton and Richardson. For all intents and purposes, the logic of their argument is as follows. Because most reference queries are simple ones, because patrons say that they find the information provided for these simple queries to be complete, useful, and satisfactory, and because the behavior of reference staff members is by far the best predictor of successful reference outcomes, reference personnel should be concentrating on perfecting these behaviors—behaviors which, from one perspective and up to a certain point, are generic and could be applied to all types of service encounters: "acknowledge[ ] the presence of the patron through smiling...," "face the patron when speaking and listening," "maintain [ ] ... eye contact," and "communicate[ ] in a receptive, cordial, and encouraging manner"[27]—rather than spending time on increasing their educational level and taking courses that specialize in diverse subject areas. Moreover, insofar as these behaviors cannot predict accuracy, reference departments should only keep "utility measures" for reference assessment purposes. The notion that the information received in a reference transaction should be accurate is thus positioned as an old-fashioned idea that is no longer relevant. And, by associating the idea of accuracy with difficulty, then dismissing the need to consider the idea of accuracy all together, they surreptitiously dismiss the idea of educated librarians with graduate degrees who display subject-specific knowledge and who would therefore be equipped, by virtue of this type of graduate education, to deal with difficult reference queries with a great deal of accuracy.

Inevitably, one of the consequences of their attempt to transform the art of reference service into a science—their act of legerdemain—is to hasten and legitimize the deprofessionalization of reference work. If a librarian's education and years of experience do not much matter when it comes to providing complete, useful, and satisfactory reference service—and if most reference queries are not that difficult to begin with—it is easy to see how Saxton and Richardson could suggest that it is financially unproductive and wasteful for public library systems to employ and retain well-paid professional librarians with graduate degrees to answer reference queries. If we follow the logic of their argument to the very end, they imply that the same reference service levels, or even improved reference service levels, could be achieved by training inexperienced paraprofessionals with no graduate degrees and no specialized knowledge of subject areas to follow the RUSA *Guidelines for Behavioral Performance.* Accordingly, the type of ideal workforce that they envision for public library reference work is very close to the model of the call center, with its constant turnover of poorly paid and highly stressed employees trained to mechanistically follow pre-determined scripts in dealing with customer service (reference) queries. And, because data about the accuracy of the dispensed information are not being collected—recall that only "utility measures" are considered to be valid assessments for the overall functioning of information centers—administrators of these call centers can point to the fact that they are indeed providing quality service, thus justifying the perpetuation of the call center model.[28] Public library systems would thus save money—money that could then be invested in advanced digital reference systems, which would mean even fewer in-person reference interactions with highly educated librarians possessing subject-specific knowledge.

Is this overstating matters? Perhaps not. Recall, from Chapter 1, that it was Steve Coffman and Matthew Saxton, who, in presenting their vision of the future of reference work, expressed the belief that, because anywhere from 50 percent to 80 percent of all reference questions "might not require" professional librarians, "a large percentage of the 67 staff needed to operate the networked reference service [at the County of Los Angeles Public Library system] would not require professional degrees nor would they require professional salaries."[29] Further, they note that, because most of the 116 staff currently providing reference service do have professional degrees, the "potential cost savings of a centralized service staffed with a high percentage of paraprofessionals could be substantial."[30] Finally, they enthuse that "[r]educing the average question length by just 22 seconds, from 172 seconds to 150, would reduce staff requirements by over 10 percent from 67 to 60 positions."[31] In other words, what they want is fewer employees working faster and faster. But, as we have seen, what they describe as a "centralized service" is a convenient euphemism for the type of service that has very many of the characteristics of call center work, with all its negative implications. Coincidentally or not, we are thus faced with a situation where advocates of "centralized reference centers" staffed by ever-decreasing numbers of paraprofessionals answering questions at a fast pace are part of the same group of individuals who have concluded that education and experience levels of public library reference personnel have very little, if any, effect on positive reference service outcomes.

The specter of deprofessionalization of the reference function looms ominously. An increasing percentage of reference questions is being offloaded to paraprofessionals working in settings that resemble call centers, which are notorious for low pay, high turnover, lack of advancement opportunities, and stressful working conditions. As reference functions become more and more automated through call center interactive voice-response systems and automated call distribution systems, the intellectual component traditionally associated with reference librarianship becomes increasingly etiolated. Indeed, the kind of subject knowledge gained from an intensive program of reading is fast becoming an endangered "species of capital." It may seem trivial to suggest that reading newspapers, magazines, academic journals, and books can help to re-intellectualize reference work and re-establish a "species of capital" that could be "efficacious in a given field, both as a weapon and as a stake of struggle."[32] But, as the examples discussed in the previous chapters suggest, there is real value for reference work in reading newspapers, magazines, academic journals, and books. Although few would discourage reference librarians from reading intensively and extensively in diverse subject areas, by the same token, such reading is not, for the most part, encouraged and valorized as a vital component of reference work. Were it to be so encouraged and lauded, such inherently deprofessionalizing proposals as digital reference call centers, with their implications of labor market segmentation and the feminization of "bad jobs," might prove to be unnecessary.

As technological skills become widespread among a larger segment of the population, reference librarians should consider how best to develop a unique knowledge niche that would allow them to differentiate themselves from potential library users— to position themselves as market leaders instead of followers. In today's frenetic world the key to preservation of the reference librarian and the reference function in North America may lie in forging a reputation as a profession whose individual members are repositories of accumulated knowledge. Only a strong and concerted commitment to a program of in-depth, time-consuming, and painstaking reading in diverse subjects can achieve this goal. Long-term success should be measured not by how frantically one strives to emulate and adopt reigning paradigms of whatever sort, but by creating a service that is of lasting value to the growing legions of ultra-connected and time-pressed individuals. Ultimately, a service profession such as librarianship thrives not by offering what others already have, but by providing something that others lack— in this case, a wealth of subject knowledge accumulated through an ongoing program of focused and purposive reading.

Are there practical ways for academic and public librarians to embark on a concerted program of reading? One model is provided by the medical community, which has long had informal institutions called journal clubs to help doctors keep up with the steady stream of medical literature about various subject areas. In essence, journal clubs are venues for continuing education that, according to Mark Linzer, can be traced back to the middle 1800s at St. Bartholomew's Hospital in London, England.[33] Because the library at St. Bartholomew's was small and lacked a reading room, "some of the self-select of the pupils, making themselves into a club, had a small room over a baker's shop near the Hospital gate where we would sit and read the journals and where some, in the evening, played cards."[34] In North America, the first recorded example of a journal club was in 1875 at McGill University, in Montréal, Canada, where Sir William Osler, aghast at the high cost of medical publications, formed a club "for the purchase and distribution of periodicals to which he could ill afford to subscribe as an individual."[35] The idea was then exported, in 1889, to the Johns Hopkins Hospital in Baltimore, Maryland.[36] Here, journal clubs were typically associated with individual medical departments, with both experienced and less-experienced physicians gathering together to read and discuss articles on a specific medical topic or to review developments in a broad field. At Johns Hopkins, departmental journal clubs "usually met on a monthly basis at members' homes in the evening, but in the 1920s and 1930s the Department of Medicine journal club had an 'open meeting' for faculty and housestaff during the regular work day."[37] Although all participants hoped to increase their general medical knowledge and hence improve patient care, each attendee looked to the journal club to meet specific goals. For the junior staff member, the goal was "an introduction to the systematic use of the medical literature"; for senior staff, it was "a convenient method for surveying the literature."[38]

Contemporary journal clubs are usually thought of in relationship to medical residency programs, where they serve the goal of developing critical reading and critical thinking skills for physicians in training, especially in light of the trend toward evidence-based practice.[39] As Patrick Alguire observes, while early journal clubs "served to help practitioners stay abreast of scientific developments ... more recently they have been used as a vehicle to teach critical appraisal skills, research design, medical statistics, clinical decision theory, and clinical epidemiology."[40] Surveying recent literature about the effect of reading clubs, Alguire concluded, in 1998, that "well-designed educational trials have demonstrated that it is possible to improve basic knowledge in clinical epidemiology and biostatistics, but not critical appraisal skills, using a journal club format."[41] Nonetheless, he notes that "residents exposed to critical appraisal techniques in journal club report paying more attention to the methods and becoming more skeptical of the author's conclusions."[42] In 2001, after conducting a meta-analysis of research articles about journal clubs, Jon Ebbert, Victor Montori, and Henry Schultz wrote that "one randomized controlled trial found an improvement in knowledge of clinical epidemiology and biostatistics, reading habits, and the use of medical literature in practice, but no improvement in critical appraisal skills," while "six less methodologically rigorous studies found possible improvements in critical appraisal skills."[43] There is evidence, then, that journal clubs contribute to increasing the knowledge base of medical residents.

In the 1990s, journal clubs expanded beyond residency programs. Medical undergraduates,[44] perioperative nurses,[45] nursing teachers,[46] family physicians,[47] and medical reference librarians at both universities and hospitals[48] established journal clubs. They became so popular in the medical community that "how-to-start-a-successful-journal club" articles appeared in well-respected academic publications.[49] In addition, the Medical Library Association (MLA) not only published detailed guidelines about starting both in-person and electronic journal clubs, but offered incentives to librarians who actively participate in such clubs.[50] MLA established so-called journal club article series, consisting of 6–12 articles per series. Club members select a given series of articles –"all articles must concern a single topic, area or theme"— and meet six times over a six-month period. To earn points for membership in the Academy of Health Information Professionals—"a professional development and career recognition program"—librarians must contribute to the ongoing discussion about articles. For example, in electronic journal clubs, "each participant must post two or more responses to at least five and preferably all six discussions to receive credit for participation."[51]

In effect, a journal club becomes a community with a shared interest to develop and expand knowledge in new areas, or to deepen existing knowledge about a specific topic. Why should librarians be interested in forming such a community? One answer is provided by an initiative that some business schools are adopting in order to "make business students better 'integrative' thinkers."[52] The initiative is to form "reading communities" so as to go "beyond the traditional silos of business education strategy and find[ ] those common elements for effective managers to make decisions."[53] Business professors have discovered that such seemingly unlikely books as Irma Rombauer's *Joy of Cooking*, Michael Beschloss's *The Crisis Years: Kennedy and Khrushchev, 1960–1963*, Rohinton Mistry's *A Fine Balance*, Michel Foucault's *Madness and Civilization* and *The Birth of the Clinic*, and Jean Baudrillard's *America* and *The Perfect Crime*, among others, have made a large positive effect on their thinking and professional success.[54] Accordingly, they have created a list of these books with an eye to encouraging students to become eclectic readers who are keen to increase their knowledge and creativity levels. As one professor puts it, "[H]aving a broad approach to reading is the key to integrative thinking for the business leader of tomorrow."[55] Compiling a wide-ranging book list and working systematically through that book list "allows you to push back the boundaries so you can have wider access to learning new things. The broader you think, the better you solve problems down the road."[56]

Journal clubs and reading communities are thus one way for academic and public librarians to learn more about new subject areas or to keep up with developments in a chosen field of interest. Clubs could be formed among academic librarians to read about, study, and discuss any number of disciplines, sub-disciplines, or emerging interdisciplinary areas so that individual members could "better … solve problems down the road." Unfortunately, there does not seem to be much precedent for this type of activity within librarianship. One exception is a reading group about critical literary and cultural theory that was established at George Washington University (GWU).[57] Realizing that their subject knowledge about literary theory was weak — "several librarians … expressed concern over our ignorance in one important area of subject specialization: contemporary critical theory"[58]— eight librarians established a reading circle to study and discuss such seminal thinkers as Roland Barthes, Jürgen Habermas, Jacques Lacan, Richard Rorty, and Julia Kristeva. They were particularly concerned about gaps in this aspect of their knowledge because "[f]aculty members would speak to us about deconstruction, new historicism, or Bakhtin, but often we were unable to define these movements or the thinkers associated with them."[59] Here, then, is one type of situation that professors in Chapter 7 complained about: reference librarians who have very little idea about basic theories in a rapidly expanding field, or librarians who are unable to think laterally across fields. The librarians at GWU, however, decided to do something about their avowed lack of knowledge, perhaps embarrassed that they were not providing a sufficiently high quality of reference service to professors in the humanities and social science who wanted to know about these key thinkers and apply them to their own fields. The reading circle that they formed was entirely self-directed and allowed members — including support staff in the club's second year — to pick literary and cultural theorists or schools that were most applicable to their own work. Each reading assignment included a brief definition of the person or school in question, an important primary text from that person or school, and an interpretation of a literary passage or cultural phenomenon using the primary text. Participants in the reading group naturally increased their knowledge about the cultural and literary theorists under study. But, as described by Scott Stebelman, there were additional benefits.

> We expected to become more knowledgeable about the critics, but we did not expect to interact in new invigorating ways with one another. Most of our daily work as librarians involves rather practical and mundane issues, such as determining which books to order, or how to access a new database. We do not ordinarily see ourselves as "intellectuals," capable of analyzing highly abstract systems and coming forward with fresh insights about why they are important and how they might even be relevant to developments within our own profession; however, that in fact occurred on many occasions, and with an excitement that was galvanizing. We were stretching ourselves in unconventional ways, but ways that would be just as productive and important for us professionally as if the content had focused on traditional functional skills.[60]

Learning about specific subject areas turned out to be both intellectually and psychologically stimulating, not to mention fun. Moreover, it would be logical to suppose that the quality of reference service that these librarians and support staff members provided to both professors and students after the reading group experience increased substantially. After all, members of the reading group had learned to analyze highly abstract systems and to develop fresh insights — exactly the type of qualities that professors demand in reference librarians. In other words, librarians had learned to think as if they were researchers. They were now capable of making interdisciplinary connections, recognizing, for instance, that Habermas is important to sociologists, that Lacan's theories are employed by art historians, that Bakhtin is used by professors in faculties of education, and that Jacques Derrida is cited widely by psychologists.

In addition, GWU librarians began to understand how very little they knew about many things and, presumably, how much more interesting their work could be when they had solid subject-based knowledge on which to fall back on. Stebelman concludes: "We decided to continue our work indefinitely [because] [t]he critics and schools we touched upon represented only a fraction of the reading that still needed to be done.... The excitement that has grown out of this group has spawned discussion about reading groups in other disciplines, such as one exclusively for librarians in the social sciences."[61] In short, academic librarians discovered that, in order to improve reference service, they did not so much have to know about the very latest in technological innovations and database algorithms. Rather, they had to know a great deal about subject-based topics so that they could not only understand and cope with the reference questions asked of them, but also make the kind of intellectually demanding interdisciplinary connections that professors and students increasingly expect when they consult reference librarians. They also discovered that reading is the central way to gain such knowledge and insight. In the GWU case, librarians read about difficult concepts and scholarly thinkers. But, as we saw in Chapters 3–4, many of the questions that academic librarians deal with come from students researching recent social, cultural, and political issues and phenomena, and so it is important for librarians not only to read about academic theories and theorists, but also to delve into general-interest publications that contain informative overviews and detailed explorations of diverse general topics of contemporary interest.

The same sort of reading group or journal club could be useful for public library reference staff members. As we saw in Chapter 6, many of the questions fielded by reference personnel deal with current international, national, and local issues, and it was those staff members most attuned to and aware of such issues who could provide the best reference service. How could a reading group help in public libraries?

Recall that librarians at GWU implemented their idea after they concluded that they were receiving many questions about a specific subject area—critical literary and cultural theory—and that they were having trouble with such questions. An analogous process could occur in public libraries. Reference personnel may note that they receive numerous queries in which patrons ask for more background information about current popular films; or they may observe that, when certain political and social issues are dealt with on network news broadcasts or radio call-in shows, many questions about these topics are received at the reference desk. If this is the case, reading groups could be formed about likely future topics of interest. These topics could be identified from detailed perusal of newspapers and magazines, which typically identify and cover important occurrences before television and radio.

For instance, the cover story on the front page of the November 29, 2002, issue of *USA Today* was entitled "Hollywood goes to Epic Proportions."[62] Providing an extensive overview of Hollywood's rediscovery of a long-neglected film genre — historical epics— that was slated to reach its peak in the summer of 2003 and early 2004, the article cited the general subject areas of the upcoming films and gave a useful historical timeline placing the events in chronological perspective. Films dealing with Ancient Greece and Rome were very popular, with *Troy* retelling the story of the Trojan War and *The 300 Spartans* recounting the Battle of Thermopylae. There were also movies about Alexander the Great and Hannibal. How is this relevant? The films, even if not wildly successful at the box office, will generate interest in the underlying historical events. Public library reference staff members could anticipate this interest by reading books—individually or in reading groups—that cover these events. If they chose to form a reading group, it would be relatively easy to assign each individual the general historical topic of one of the 11 upcoming epic films reported by *USA Today*. At meetings, the historical events could be summarized and discussed for the benefit of all attendees, and a supplementary recommended reading list could be circulated. In this way, many reference staff members could benefit from the accumulated knowledge and reading of each reading group participant.

Of course, this is only one example. Political issues could also form the basis of a reading group. After the 2002 mid-term elections in the United States, the *New York Times* published a long article entitled "Corporations Revise Wish Lists" that outlined seven areas— energy, insurance, health care, banking, communications, automobiles, and taxes— where it was almost certain that there would be much legislative, administrative, and corporate action in the form of committee hearings, lobbying, bills, political commentary, and executive orders.[63] These seven areas would affect almost all Americans in some way and thus could provide ready subject material for a reading group, with each participant reading about, summarizing, and facilitating a discussion about one issue.

While these two examples may be appropriate for some public libraries, they may not be useful for others. But reading groups can be formed to discuss a virtually endless number of subjects. The main point here is that public library reference personnel should recognize — as did their academic colleagues at GWU — that reading groups can have a beneficial effect on all aspects of their work. The knowledge gained from reading groups— or from reading in general — not only assists them in answering specific reference questions, but also gives staff members added confidence in their ability to provide the type of insightful, thoughtful, and wide-reaching help that can only come from a broad exposure to the world of ideas. As Stebelman noted, librarians who participated in a reading group became excited that they "were stretching ourselves in unconventional ways, but ways that would be just as productive and important for us professionally as if the content had focused on traditional functional skills."[64]

When all is said and done, the desire and willingness to read is a matter of personal responsibility. Even in the GWU example, about two-thirds of the professional librarians chose not to participate in the reading group during its first year of operation. Perhaps these individuals read extensively on their own; perhaps they do not. As we saw in Chapter 5, there are numerous reasons why librarians do not read, or do not increase the amount of reading they do. After all, the range of leisure time options is astoundingly large, many librarians have other important commitments, and time pressures have a way of multiplying instead of dissipating. Yet, for academic librarians, reading newspapers, magazines, and books on their own time has demonstrated value in such areas as selecting appropriate search terms, helping students with the topics of their assignments, and increasing their background knowledge of subject-specific areas. Our respondents also stated that reading such materials provides significant help when it comes to collection development, bibliographic control, bibliographic instruction classes, discovering new web sites, maintaining credibility with peers, outreach and programming, and so on. And, as shown in Chapter 7, demanding users want librarians who have extensive subject-based knowledge and the ability to make intellectual connections among fields. Reading is equally valuable for public library reference personnel. As we discussed in Chapter 6, various media sources such as newspapers and magazines have helped public library reference staff members in better understanding patrons' requests, specifying terminology, increasing their awareness of specific articles and titles, and becoming a highly valued and highly dependable member of the community served by the library.

If reading newspapers, magazines, and nonfiction and fiction books for both subject-specific and general knowledge is such a valuable contribution to work-related tasks, it would seem natural that library administrators and managers would encourage staff members to devote time and energy to reading materials that, at first glance, are not functionally oriented, but that nevertheless contribute a great deal to the delivery of library services. Some administrators do, in fact, encourage such pursuits by building paid time for reading into the schedules of staff members. Nonetheless, some respondents worried that a renewed emphasis on reading newspapers, magazines, and books would perpetuate the stereotype of the librarian who sits at the reference desk and reads. This concern about the professional image of librarians is perfectly understandable, but it approaches the issue from a skewed perspective. The real question to ask is: why has the act of reading become something that is not encouraged, and to a certain extent is even frowned upon? Who benefits from portraying reading as not equated with, or part of, legitimate professional activity? We have seen throughout this book that reading material that is typically looked upon as *not* contributing to the professional responsibilities of a librarian — general-interest newspapers, general-interest magazines, popular and specialized nonfiction, and fiction — does indeed help librarians carry out those professional responsibilities at a very high level. If this is so, such reading should be rewarded and made a regular and paid part of the library workday. Some respondents, of course, noted that the concept of paid time for reading was problematic, yet instituting such paid time would, at the very least, serve as symbolic recognition that reading is a valuable professional activity that can add real value in many areas of library work.

Intensive reading by librarians and other staff members should be viewed as a significant component of the intellectual capital present in public and academic libraries. Intellectual capital — an "elusive intangible asset" and resource possessed by the human individuals that constitute an organization — has been conceptualized by Nick Bontis as consisting of human capital, structural capital, and relational capital.[65] The essence of human capital is intellect —"the tacit knowledge embedded in the minds of ... employees,"[66] and the more of this intellect that there is, the better. In addition, Bontis, building on the work of William Hudson, explains that two key components of human capital are education and experience, broadly defined. In the business world, these components could be manifested as "brainstorming in a research lab, daydreaming at the office, throwing out old files, reengineering new processes, improving personal skills, or developing new leads in a sales representative's 'little black book.'" [67] In the world of libraries, and especially in the world of library reference departments, reading — all kinds of reading — should be formally included as an important aspect of human and intellectual capital. It should be encouraged, accounted for, and quantified as a performance measure insofar as reading is a type of individual learning, and individual learning "is a prerequisite for organizational learning" and organizational success.[68] Librarians who actively and extensively read should once again become the bedrock of library culture. Library administrators and managers have an important role to play in the development of such a library culture because culture —constituting the set of "beliefs, values, and attitudes pervasive in the organization [that] result[ ] in a language, symbols, and habits of behavior and thought"— is increasingly accepted "as the conscious or unconscious product of senior management's belief."[69]

In a book entitled *Valuating Information Intangibles*, Frank Portugal discusses four ways to measure the contribution of librarians and information professionals to organizational success.[70] One of these ways is intellectual capital valuation. Yet, among his extensive "intellectual capital valuation metric set," [71] which contains such useful items as the annual turnover of full-time permanent library or information center employees, average years with unit of full-time permanent library or information employees, and number of women library or information center managers, there is no recognition of the positive impact that employee reading can have on a library's ability to deliver a wide range of services—especially reference services, but also such other services as collection development and bibliographic instruction—at a very high level. Just as other aspects of intellectual capital can be quantified in Portugal's system — e.g., percentage of library or information center managers with masters' or doctoral degrees in library or information science, or in other professional areas—the extent of employee reading can, and should, be measured and thus justifiably valorized as a significant part of library culture that leads to organizational success.

Reading is a profoundly intellectual activity, but, as Lorna Peterson remarks, North American librarianship, "with its roots in nineteenth century reverence for efficiency and scientific methods, can be said to be anti-intellectual."[72] Thus it is no surprise that the concept of reading as a legitimate and highly valued professional activity for librarians is suffering. Instead, professionalism is defined as cognizance of and facility with digital concepts that "reduce the size of our information ... and increase the sophistication of subject retrieval."[73] Knowing how to retrieve a piece of information frequently passes for knowledge, and librarians are rarely encouraged to accrue knowledge about anything else except functional procedures and about ways to make such procedures faster and more powerful. In the end, as Peterson laments, "we neglect that it is the time spent with materials in reflection and applying intelligence and imagination that creates knowledge."[74]

Academic and public library reference personnel should therefore spend time reading general-interest newspapers, magazines, specialized journals, and nonfiction and fiction books, and then reflecting upon the content of such publications. In this way, they can move one step toward the creation of real knowledge—knowledge that will ultimately be more useful to patrons and the library itself than fleeting technological skills with short-term expiry dates.[75] Library administrators who are concerned about the lasting professionalism of their staff members should do all that they can to promote and encourage the type of reading discussed in this book. The worrisome stereotype is not that of the librarian who reads at the reference desk; rather, the worrisome stereotype should be the one of the librarian who only engages in mechanical search procedures without any awareness or knowledge of the underlying content. If public and academic library personnel commit themselves, whether individually or as a group, to read extensively and widely in diverse subject-specific areas, then librarianship would not have to be concerned so much about issues of deprofessionalization because it would be confident that it was resting on a solid intellectual foundation.

Appendix A

Methodological Notes and Text of Survey Questions Sent to Academic Reference Librarians

Preliminary information

This survey was sent to randomly chosen academic reference librarians in the United States and Canada during October and November 2000 by 53 students enrolled in FIS 1310 Information Resources and Services, Faculty of Information Studies, University of Toronto. The instructor for FIS 1310 was Juris Dilevko. This survey was one of five assignments (including an exam) for the class. The instructor provided each student with an electronic version of the survey questions, as well as with electronic versions of the letters that were sent to academic reference librarians as introductory messages. Each student was asked to send out about 20 surveys in the hopes of getting about seven to ten completed and returned surveys.

Each student was asked to create an EXCEL spreadsheet in which all the answers of the respondents were entered. The student copied the answers directly from the respondent's returned e-mail message into the EXCEL spreadsheet. All respondents were assigned a letter or number. The name of the respondent's home institution was also entered into the spreadsheet. Home institution information was subsequently converted into "size of library" information by the authors and their research assistant, following the definitions used and explained in Appendix D (under "Definitions for Independent Variables: Library Size"). The types and distribution of the institutions at which responding academic reference librarians worked is presented below.

Information about the number of years

Library size	Definition	# of respondents from this type of library (n = 539)
Very small	Masters Colleges and Universities I and II with FTE enrollments below 1000; Baccalaureate Colleges—Liberal Arts and General with FTE enrollments below 1000; all Associate Colleges	46 (8.5%)*
Small	Masters Colleges and Universities I and II with FTE enrollments between 1000 and 2500; Baccalaureate Colleges—Liberal Arts and General with FTE enrollments above 1000	143 (26.5%)*

Library size	Definition	# of respondents from this type of library (n = 539)
Medium	Masters Colleges and Universities I and II with FTE enrollments above 2,500	166 (30.8%)*
Large	All institutions classified by the Carnegie Foundation as Doctoral/Research Universities— Intensive	60 (11.1%)*
Very large	All institutions classified by the Carnegie Foundation as Doctoral/Research Universities— Extensive	124 (23%)*

* Percentages do not add to 100% because of rounding.

respondents had been providing academic reference service was also collected. This information is summarized in the table below.

Experience in providing academic reference service	No. of responding academic librarians (n = 537)
Less than one year	5 (0.9%)
One to three years	71 (13.2%)
Four to seven years	105 (19.6%)
Eight to ten years	71 (13.2%)
Eleven to twenty years	166 (30.9%)
More than twenty years	119 (22.2%)

As part of the assignment, each student was asked to indicate the total number of academic reference librarians to whom he or she had sent the survey questions. The assignment then asked each student to analyze the responses of his or her individual set of returned surveys in an essay of no more than 1,000 words. When submitting work for this assignment, each student submitted his or her written analysis, as well as his or her completed spreadsheet in print form. Individual written analyses were graded and returned to students. Submitted spreadsheets were retained, and our research assistant subsequently created electronic word-processing and spreadsheet files containing all the data from the 539 surveys. This omnibus data then became the basis for the results presented in Chapters 3, 4, and 5 of this book, as well as the statistical analyses discussed in Appendix D.

An introductory letter informing academic librarians that they had been randomly selected to complete the survey was sent before the actual survey questions were sent to them. Academic reference librarians could choose to decline to receive the survey questions by sending a return message to that effect. If they did not decline to receive the survey questions within a period of three days, an e-mail message containing the survey questions was sent to them. The survey questions were contained in the body of the e-mail message; they were not appended as an attachment file. Librarians were instructed to reply to the survey simply by hitting the "reply" button in their e-mail software and typing in (keying in) the answers to the questions directly in the e-mail message. If reference librarians who had been sent survey questions had not replied within two weeks, a reminder message was sent.

Five hundred and thirty-nine surveys were completed and returned by academic reference librarians. Some students had better success rates than others. For example, one student sent out 35 surveys and received 21 completed surveys; another student sent out 28 surveys and received 14 completed surveys. Others did not fare so well. For instance, one student sent out 21 surveys and received only 7 completed surveys. Another student sent out 38 surveys and received only 12 completed surveys. Still another student sent out only nine surveys, but received five completed surveys. In total, 1,164 surveys were sent out, with a response rate of 46.3 percent. However, a few students did not specifically state how many surveys they sent out. In these cases, we arbitrarily assumed that they had sent out 20 surveys, and used this number in calculating the above response rate. Thus, if these students had really sent out more than 20 surveys, the response rate indicated above would decrease.

While the relatively low response rate means that the results presented in Chapters 2–5 should be treated with caution, an impressive number of academic reference librarians from a wide variety of institutions did respond to this survey. The results are thus a reasonable snapshot of the reading habits of academic librarians in the United States and Canada, as well as a reasonable snapshot of whether academic reference librarians think that their reading has helped them in their reference work.

How were the reference librarians selected?

Each student was assigned 35–40 pages in the *American Library Directory* (Volumes 1 and 2) covering the United States and Canada. Students were then instructed to arbitrarily pick, within their assigned pages, about 10–15 libraries marked as "college or university libraries" (i.e., those marked with a C). They were asked to write down the names of these institutions. They were then asked to find the home pages of these institutions on the Web, and then to locate the main library home page. They were then asked to explore the main library home page, with concentration on the reference department. They were then asked to collect the names and e-mail addresses of librarians who are listed as working in the reference department and/or the names of librarians

who seemed to have jobs that involved some sort of reference work. (They were also told that some libraries may not provide such information, or that such information may be hard to locate. In these cases, they were asked to move on to their next selected institution.) In total, they were asked to collect and write down the names of 60–70 reference librarians from their 10–15 institutions. Each librarian was assigned a number. From this list of 60–70 reference librarians, each student was asked to select, at random, 20 names. Two random selection methods were given: putting equal-sized pieces of paper (each of which contained a number corresponding to the name of one of the 60–70 librarians) into a hat, picking out 20 pieces of paper, and then matching the numbers on the pieces of paper with the numbered librarian list; or using a random-number generator in a spreadsheet package. The 20 selected individuals were then contacted as described above and asked to participate in the survey. Some students contacted more than 20 individuals; some students contacted fewer than 20 reference librarians.

Finally, each student was asked to keep, in a separate file or list, the names of all reference librarians who returned completed surveys. On the class day that this assignment was submitted, each student wrote down the names of his or her responding librarians on individual strips of paper. All strips of paper were placed into a hat, and three names were drawn. The three selected librarians each received $50 USD. The source of this prize money was the personal funds of Juris Dilevko.

Text of the survey questions

Could I ask you to take a few minutes of your time today or tomorrow to answer the questions and to send me back your answers as quickly as possible. Remember, all results will only be reported in the aggregate, and your responses will remain completely anonymous. Don't forget also about your eligibility for one of three prizes of $50 USD if you return your answers by [insert date].

The first four questions ask you about basic data about you and your library department. Starting with Question 5, the questions all deal with various aspects of your reading habits and whether your reading habits help in answering reference queries or other aspects of your job.

Question 1. How many professional librarians (full-time equivalents) work in your library providing reference service on a regular basis during any given week? Include all those librarians who exclusively provide reference service AND those who have other duties in addition to their reference desk duties.

Question 2. How many years have you personally been providing reference service on a regular basis?

Question 3. How many hours per week do you personally spend providing online, telephone, or in-person reference service?

Question 4. What is your favorite type of reading material outside of your work hours?

Question 5. How often do you read your LOCAL daily newspaper (print or online) outside of your work hours? A local paper is defined as one that is published in the town/city in which you live or in the next biggest town/city from your place of residence. A local paper concentrates mostly on local events. You can choose from such options as:

daily;
two or three times per week;
once a week;
once a month;
once every two months or so;
never;
or you can be more precise, if you wish.

Question 6. How often do you read a NATIONAL daily newspaper (print or online) outside of your work hours? Examples of NATIONAL daily newspapers are: *New York Times, Washington Post, Wall Street Journal, USA Today, (The Globe and Mail* in Canada), or any other paper that is NOT published in your immediate geographical locality and is distributed widely on a national basis. You can choose from such options as:

daily;
two or three times per week;
once a week;
once a month;
once every two months or so;
never;
or you can be more precise, if you wish.

Question 7. Which newspaper or newspapers, both LOCAL and NATIONAL, do you read at least once a week outside of your work hours? Please provide a list of all these newspapers.

Question 8. How would you characterize the way you MOST OFTEN read newspapers? This question tries to get at the distinction between: skimming headlines; glancing at an article by reading only the first three or four paragraphs; and reading an article carefully from start to finish. You can choose from among the following:

I skim the headlines in most sections of the paper;
I read carefully most of what is in the entire paper from cover to cover;
I glance at the first two or three paragraphs of most articles in the newspaper;
I skim the headlines or glance at the first two or three paragraphs of most articles in the paper, and then, only if a particular article interests me, do I read that article carefully;
I read carefully all the articles in certain sections of the paper, whether they in-

terest me or not, and skim or glance at the remaining sections of the paper.

Or you can offer your own assessment, if you wish.

Question 9. How often do you read magazines (print or online) outside of your work hours? By magazine, this question means publications such as *Time, Newsweek, The New Yorker, Business Week, Harper's, Scientific American, Discover.* DO NOT include sports, car, cooking, or fashion magazines when answering this question; also DO NOT include publications such as *TV Guide* or the *National Enquirer.* You can choose from such options as:

daily;

two or three times per week;

once a week;

once a month;

once every two months or so;

never;

or you can be more precise, if you wish.

Question 10. How would you characterize the way you most often read magazines such as *Time, Newsweek, Business Week, Harper's, Scientific American,* or *The New Yorker?* You can choose from among the following:

I read the magazine carefully from cover to cover;

I read a little bit from each article, and if it catches my interest, then I go on and read the entire article;

I only read the first 3 or 4 paragraphs of each and every article.

Or you can offer your own characterization of your reading style of these magazines.

Question 11. Which magazine or magazines do you read on a regular basis (at least 6 times per year) outside of your work hours? Please include ALL magazines, including sports, car, cooking, and fashion magazines.

Question 12. How many FICTION books have you read in the last 12 months

outside of your work hours? Include novels of any genre, books of poetry, and plays. Do not include children's books.

Question 13. Could you tell me the titles (and, if possible, the authors) of two or three recent FICTION books (novels, poetry, plays) that you have read? Do not include children's books.

Question 14. How many NONFICTION books have you read in the last 12 months outside of your work hours? Some examples of nonfiction are: history and social-history books of all types; political books; biographies; art books; travel books, etc. Do not include self-help books, advice books, or how-to books.

Question 15. Could you tell me the titles (and, if possible, the authors) of three recent NONFICTION books that you have read? Do not include self-help books, advice books, or how-to books.

Question 16. Would you like to read more (newspapers, magazines, fiction, nonfiction) outside of your working hours?

Question 17. What are some of the reasons that you don't read as much as you would like to outside of your working hours? Please be as specific as you possibly can, and provide all reasons that may apply.

Question 18. In general, do you think that any of the types of reading material mentioned so far (newspapers, magazines, fiction, nonfiction) could somehow help you to provide better quality reference service when dealing directly with questions asked by users of your library? If so, in what way?

Question 19. Do you think you would be able to provide better quality reference service to your library users if you were given PAID work time to read newspapers, magazines, nonfiction, or fiction? You can choose from such answers as:

very strong yes;

lukewarm yes;

it would help only on rare occasions;

it would not serve any purpose at all;

I already have paid time to do such reading;

or you may choose to provide your own answer.

Question 20. Can you give any concrete examples of how your READING OF NEWSPAPERS OR MAGAZINES outside of your working hours has helped you in your reference work by helping you to answer a reference query? Be as specific as you possibly can. What was the reference question or reference problem, and how did your reading of newspapers or magazines outside of your working hours help you to resolve the situation?

Question 21. Has your reading of NEWSPAPERS OR MAGAZINES outside of your working hours helped you in any another aspect of your job besides directly answering reference queries? Be as specific as you possibly can by giving a concrete example.

This is the second to last question [Question 22]: Can you give any concrete examples of how your READING OF NONFICTION OR FICTION BOOKS outside of your working hours has helped you in your reference work by helping you to answer a reference query? Be as specific as you possibly can. What was the reference question or reference problem, and how did your reading of fiction or nonfiction outside of your working hours help you to resolve the situation?

This is the very last question [Question 23]: Has your reading of NONFICTION OR FICTION BOOKS outside of your working hours helped you in any another aspect of your job besides directly answering reference queries? Be as specific as you possibly can by giving a concrete example.

THANK YOU AGAIN FOR PARTICIPATING!!!!!!!!!!!!

Appendix B

Methodological Notes and Text of Survey Questions Sent to Public Library Reference Staff Members

Preliminary information

The survey was sent to randomly chosen public reference staff in the United States and Canada during the month of November 2000 by 53 students enrolled in FIS 1310 Information Resources and Services, Faculty of Information Studies, University of Toronto. The instructor for FIS 1310 was Juris Dilevko. This survey was one of five assignments (including an exam) for the class. The instructor provided each student with an electronic version of the survey questions, as well as with electronic versions of the letters that were sent to public library reference staff as introductory messages. Each student was asked to send out about 20 surveys in the hopes of getting approximately seven to ten completed and returned surveys.

An introductory letter informing public library reference staff members that they had been randomly selected to complete the survey was sent before the actual survey questions were sent to them. Public library staff members could choose to decline to receive the survey by sending a return message to that effect. If they did not decline to receive the survey questions within a period of three days, an e-mail message containing the survey questions was sent to them. The survey questions were contained in the body of the e-mail message; they were not appended as an attachment file. Public library staff members were instructed to reply to the survey simply by hitting the "reply" button in their e-mail software and typing in (keying in) the answers to the questions directly in the e-mail message. If public library staff members who had been sent survey questions had not replied within two weeks, a reminder message was sent.

Each student was then asked to create an EXCEL spreadsheet in which all the answers of the respondents were entered. The student copied the answers directly from the respondent's returned e-mail message into the EXCEL spreadsheet. All respondents were referred to either by letter or number. The name of the respondent's home institution was also entered into the spreadsheet. Home institution information was subsequently converted into "size of library" information by the authors and their research assistant, according to the definitions used by the American Council of Learned Societies (ACLS). ACLS uses these definitions when setting subscription prices that various academic libraries have to pay for ACLS

Library size	Definition	# of respondents from this type of library (n = 419)
Small	Institutions serving a population of less than 10,000 individuals	22 (5.3%)
Medium	Institutions serving a population of between 10,000 and 49,999 individuals	118 (28.2%)
Large	Institutions serving a population of between 50,000 and 499,999 individuals	159 (37.9%)
Very large	Institutions serving a population of above 500,000 individuals	120 (28.6%)

products and services. See www.historyebook. org/pricingsubscriptions.html (accessed April 9, 2002). The types and distribution of the institutions at which responding public library reference staff worked is contained in the table above.

Of the 419 respondents, 418 provided information about their professional status: 275 respondents had an ALA-accredited degree (65.8 percent); 126 respondents did not have such a degree (30.1 percent); and 17 individuals indicated that they were in the process of working towards an ALA-accredited degree (4.1 percent). Percentages are based on n = 418. Information about the number of years respondents had been providing reference service was also collected. This information is summarized in the table below.

Experience in providing reference service	No. of responding reference staff members (n = 414)
Less than one year	6 (1.4%)
One to three years	49 (11.8%)
Four to seven years	84 (20.3%)
Eight to ten years	64 (15.5%)
Eleven to twenty years	105 (25.4%)
More than twenty years	106 (25.6%)

As part of the assignment, each student was asked to indicate the total number of public library reference staff members to whom he or she had sent the survey questions. The assignment then asked each stu-

dent to analyze the responses of his or her individual set of returned surveys in an essay of no more than 1,000 words. When submitting work for this assignment, each student submitted his or her written analysis, as well as his or her completed spreadsheet in print form. Individual written analyses were graded and returned to students. Submitted spreadsheets were retained, and our research assistant subsequently created electronic word-processing and spreadsheet files containing all the data from the 419 surveys. This omnibus data then became the basis for the results presented in Chapter 6 of this book.

Four hundred and nineteen surveys were completed and returned by public library reference staff members. Public library staff members' response to this survey was not as enthusiastic as academic reference librarians' response to the survey they received (see Appendix A). Thus, many students made contact with many more public library staff members than initially planned in order to get six or seven completed surveys. Some students had better success rates than others. For example, one student sent out 15 surveys and received 13 completed surveys; another student sent out 18 surveys and received 12 completed surveys. Others did not fare so well. For instance, one student sent out 50 surveys and received only 9 completed surveys. Another student sent out 45 surveys and received only 7 completed surveys. Still another student sent out 53 surveys, but received only 9 completed surveys. In total, 1,558 surveys were sent out with a response rate of 26.9 percent. However, some students did not specifically state how many surveys they sent out. In these cases, we arbitrarily assumed that they had sent out 20 surveys, and used this number in calculating the above response rate. Thus, if these students had really sent out more than 20 surveys, the response rate indicated above would decrease.

While the relatively low response rate means that the results presented in Chapter 6 should be treated with caution, an impressive number of public library reference staff members from a wide variety of institutions did respond to this survey. The results are thus a reasonable snapshot of the ways in which public library staff members stay current, and a reasonable snapshot of their feelings about whether these methods help them in their reference work.

In Chapter 6, we analyze the answers to survey questions 5–13. Answers to survey questions 14–19 will be discussed in subsequent work.

How were the reference staff members selected?

Each student was assigned 35–40 pages in the *American Library Directory* (Volumes 1 and 2) covering the United States and Canada. Students were then instructed to arbitrarily pick, within their assigned pages, about 20 libraries marked as "public libraries" (i.e., those marked with a **P**) that also had e-mail addresses for named individuals, especially those designated as reference librarians or reference staff members. They were asked to write down the names of these libraries and staff members and their e-mail addresses. In total, they were asked to collect and write down the names of 60–70 libraries and staff members who had e-mail

addresses listed in the *American Library Directory*. Each staff member was assigned a number. From this list of 60–70 staff members, each student was asked to select, at random, 20 names. Two random selection methods were given: putting equal-sized pieces of paper (each of which contained a number corresponding to the name of one of the 60–70 librarians) into a hat, picking out 20 pieces of paper, and then matching the numbers on the pieces of paper with the numbered staff member list; or using a random-number generator in a spreadsheet package. The 20 selected individuals were then contacted as described above and asked to participate in the survey. Some students contacted more than 20 individuals; some students contacted fewer than 20 reference staff members. Because many public libraries only had general e-mail addresses with no personal name designations, or because many smaller public libraries do not have clearly demarcated reference specialists, a paragraph was included in the introductory e-mail message acknowledging that the e-mail message might reach the wrong person. This paragraph read as follows: "If you yourself don't wish to complete this survey, could you forward it to as many others within your public library who might be willing to complete this survey. And could you ask these other people to send me their e-mail addresses so that I can send them the survey?"

Finally, each student was asked to keep, in a separate file or list, the names of all public library staff members who returned completed surveys. On the class day that this assignment was submitted, each student wrote down the names of his or her responding staff members on individual strips of paper. All strips of paper were placed into a hat, and three names were drawn. The three selected staff members each received $50 USD. The source of this prize money was the personal funds of Juris Dilevko.

Text of the survey questions

The first four questions ask you about basic data about you and your library department. Starting with Question 5, the questions all deal with various aspects of your reading habits and whether your reading habits help in answering reference queries or other aspects of your job. Remember, you can be EITHER a professional librarian OR a para-professional who provides 10 or more hours of reference service each week at your library.

Question 1. How many professional librarians AND non-professional staff work in your public library providing reference service on a regular basis during any given week? Include all those individuals who exclusively provide reference service AND those who have other duties in addition to their reference desk duties.

Question 2. Do you hold an ALA-accredited degree which allows you to identify yourself as a professional librarian?

Question 3. How many years have you personally been providing reference service on a regular basis?

Question 4. How many hours per week do you personally spend providing online, telephone, or in-person reference service?

Preamble to the remaining questions

Many of the reference questions that are asked at public library reference desks are related to current issues and events such as medical discoveries, social and cultural trends, political developments, international affairs, and technological advances. Patrons also ask about new or proposed local, state, or national laws and regulations. The purpose of this survey is to find out how reference workers at public libraries keep up on all these issues "so that they can anticipate patron needs and have a better understanding of the context for questions."

Question 5. Does your library provide you with paid time specifically to read the PRINT VERSIONS of local newspapers, national newspapers, and magazines OR to read the ELECTRONIC online versions of local newspaper, national newspapers, and magazines on web sites? If yes, how much paid time per week? If no, do you think paid time for this activity would be useful to you in answering patron reference questions?

Question 6. Does your library have PRINT newspapers and magazines in the staff lounge as a way of helping you "keep up" with current events? If yes, please give as many details as possible.

Question 7. Do you take it upon yourself to read PRINT newspapers and print magazines on a regular basis ON YOUR OWN TIME as a way of helping you "keep up" with current events? If yes, please give as many details as possible, such as which print newspapers and print magazines you read on a regular basis and how much time you spend doing so.

Question 8. Do you take it upon yourself to read ONLINE NEWSPAPERS, that is, local, national, and world news web sites ON YOUR OWN TIME as a way of helping you to "keep up" with current events? If yes, please give as many details as possible, such as which web sites you visit on a regular basis and how much time you spend doing so.

Question 9. Can you give any concrete examples of how your reading of PRINT OR ONLINE NEWSPAPERS OR MAGAZINES has helped you in your reference work by helping you to answer a reference query? Be as specific as you possibly can. What was the reference question or reference problem, and how did a newspaper or magazine help you to resolve the situation?

Question 10. Has the reading of PRINT OR ONLINE NEWSPAPERS OR MAGAZINES helped you in any another aspect of your job besides the very specific task of answering reference queries asked by patrons? Be as specific as you possibly can by giving a concrete example.

Question 11. Do you watch a national television newscast (e.g., CNN, CBS in the United States or CBC in Canada) or television current affairs programs (e.g., *60 Minutes*) on a regular basis? If so, give as many details as possible. Which show(s)? How often?

Question 12. Do you listen to a national news or current affairs shows on the radio (e.g., NPR in the United States or CBC in Canada) on a regular basis? Which show(s)? How often? If so, give as many details as possible.

Question 13. Can you give any concrete examples of how watching or listening to current affairs or news shows on TV or the RADIO has helped you in your reference work by helping you to answer a reference query? Be as specific as you possibly can. What was the reference question or reference problem, and how did TV or RADIO help you to resolve the situation?

Question 14. Does your library have a method(s) of providing ongoing CURRENT AWARENESS SERVICES to all reference staff members? A current awareness service helps all reference staff keep up on current reference resources and alerts them to new developments and issues which might be the subject of future reference questions. Some methods of providing a current awareness service could be: staff meetings, printed newsletters or memos, bulletin boards, or e-mail. If your library does provide such a service to reference staff, please describe in as much detail as possible any of the methods that your library uses for this.

Question 15. Can you give any concrete examples of how a CURRENT AWARENESS SERVICE (of the types mentioned in the previous question) provided by your library has helped you in your reference work by helping you to answer a reference query? Be as specific as you possibly can. What was the reference question or reference problem, and how did the current awareness service help you to resolve the situation?

Question 16. Do you engage in SHELF-STUDYING the print sources in your general reference section either during working hours or on your own time? By "shelf-study" this question means the act of physically taking down a reference book from the reference collection, and paging through it in order to see, and hopefully remember, the type and extent of content that is contained in that book. Shelf-study is done when there is no specific reference question that impels you to consult a particular book; rather, it is an exploratory type of browsing activity in order to gain information that could POTENTIALLY assist you in answering reference questions in the future. If you do engage in "shelf-study," how often do you do so?

Question 17. Can you give any concrete examples of how SHELF-STUDY OF THE PRINT REFERENCE COLLECTION has helped you in your reference work by helping you to answer a reference query? Be as specific as you possibly can. What was the reference question or reference problem, and how did SHELF-STUDY help you to resolve the situation?

Question 18. Do you engage in ON-LINE BROWSING of web sites (such as governmental, statistical, legal, scientific web sites, etc.) that could be POTENTIALLY useful in your reference work during your working hours or on your own time? By "online browsing" this questions means going to a governmental or statistical web site, for example, and clicking through it in order to see, and hopefully remember, the type and extent of information that is contained there. This is done when there is no specific reference question that impels you to consult a web site; rather, it is an exploratory type of browsing activity. In many respects, online browsing is the ELECTRONIC VERSION OF SHELF-STUDY. If you do engage in this type of online browsing activity, how often do you do so? And what are some typical sites that you visit?

Question 19. Can you give any concrete examples of how the type of ONLINE BROWSING OR ELECTRONIC SHELF-STUDY mentioned in the previous question has helped you in your reference work by helping you to answer a reference query? Be as specific as you possibly can. What was the reference question or reference problem, and how did ELECTRONIC SHELF-STUDY OR ONLINE BROWSING help you to resolve the situation?

THANK YOU VERY MUCH FOR PARTICIPATING IN THIS SURVEY!!!!!!!!
GOOD LUCK IN THE DRAW!

Note: Some of the ideas for the survey questions were drawn from Elizabeth Thomsen's book *Rethinking Reference: The Reference Librarian's Practical Guide for Surviving Constant Change* (New York: Neal-Schuman, 1999).

Appendix C

Methodological Notes and Text of Survey Questions Sent to Professors in the Humanities and Social Sciences

Preliminary information

This survey was sent to randomly chosen university professors in the broad fields of humanities and social sciences in the United States and Canada during the months of September through November 2001 by 13 students enrolled in FIS 2131, The Literature of the Humanities and Social Sciences, Faculty of Information Studies, University of Toronto. The instructor for FIS 2131 was Juris Dilevko. This survey was one of four assignments (including an exam) for the class. The instructor provided each student with an electronic version of the survey questions, as well as with electronic versions of the letters that were sent to university professors as introductory messages. Each student was asked to send out about 80–100 surveys in the hopes of getting approximately 30–40 completed and returned surveys.

Students were asked to follow these steps: choose a broad field of study within the humanities and social sciences that was of personal interest to them; select at random the names of 40–50 institutions in the United States and Canada using alphabetical web-based lists of universities and colleges arranged by state or province; determine whether their selected institutions had departments in the field of study of interest to them; and send e-mail inquiries to about 80–100 professors in their selected field asking them whether they would fill out a questionnaire. As part of the assignment, each student was asked to indicate the total number of professors to whom he or she had sent the survey questions.

An incentive was offered in an attempt to increase the response rate. Professors were told that if an overall response rate of 50 percent was achieved, i.e., if each student received 40 or more responses, then a donation of $500 USD would be made to the American Indian College Fund to aid the educational aspirations of Native Americans as they pursue higher education at colleges and universities in North America. The donation was offered in the name of Juris Dilevko. Although the response rate target was not met, the $500 USD donation to the American Indian College Fund was nevertheless made. Personal funds of Juris Dilevko were used to make this donation.

An introductory letter informing professors that they had been selected to complete the survey was sent before the actual survey questions were sent to them. Professors could choose to decline to receive the survey questions by sending a return message to that effect. If they did not decline to receive the survey questions within a period of three days, an e-mail message containing the survey questions was sent to them. The survey questions were contained in the body of the e-mail message; they were not appended as an attachment file. Professors were instructed to reply to the survey simply by hitting the "reply" button in their e-mail software and typing in (keying in) the answers to the questions directly in the e-mail message. If professors who had been sent survey questions had not replied within two weeks, a reminder message was sent.

Each student was asked to create an EXCEL spreadsheet in which all the answers of the respondents were entered. The student copied the answers directly from the respondent's returned e-mail message into the EXCEL spreadsheet. All respondents were assigned a letter or number. Each student compiled the results for his or her particular field and made a class presentation about the most interesting findings for that field. The results reported in Chapter 7 are, however, based on an overall compilation of returned surveys across all 13 fields. Open-ended responses were entered into a spreadsheet software package, content analyzed, and classified into thematic units that form the basis of the discussion in Chapter 7.

In total, students sent 1,540 initial e-mail inquiries to various professors in the humanities and social sciences. Completed questionnaires were received from 236 professors in 13 broad fields of study as follows: American Literature; Anthropology; Archaeology; East Asian History; English Literature; European History; French Literature; Linguistics; North American History; Psychology; Sociology; Russian Literature; and Women's Studies. The response rate for this survey was 15.3 percent. While the low

response rate means that the results presented in Chapter 7 should be treated with caution, the wide range of academic settings and specialties represented in these results nonetheless provides a degree of confidence that the opinions expressed are a reasonable snapshot of prevailing academic thinking about reference service at universities and colleges in the United States and Canada.

Of the 236 responses, 96 (40.7 percent) were from full professors, 86 (36.4 percent) from associate professors, 49 (20.8 percent) from assistant professors, and five (2.1 percent) from lecturers. The student enrollments at the institutions where responding professors were employed ranged from about 1,000 to more than 45,000, and the highest degree granted at these institutions ranged from the B.A. to the Ph.D.

Text of the survey questions

The survey consists of only 11 descriptive questions and four brief preliminary questions about you and your institution.

Here are the four preliminary questions. Insert your answers directly after each question.

A. What is your broad field of study?

B. What is your specialty within this broad field of study?

C. Are you an assistant, associate, or full professor?

D. What is the highest degree that your college or university awards?

Here are the eleven descriptive questions. Insert your answers directly after each question.

Question 1. About how many times in the previous two years can you remember having asked a reference question related to your field of study at the reference desk of your college or university library?

Question 2. What percentage of the time do you estimate that you have received an answer that was personally satisfactory to you?

Question 3. In overall terms, how would you rate the subject-specific knowledge of academic reference librarians at your campus in your broad subject field? Use any two phrases or adjectives of your own choosing.

Question 4. Can you tell me about one or two instances where you were really impressed with the subject-specific knowledge of an academic reference librarian when you asked a question in your subject area? Please provide as many details as possible.

Question 5. Can you tell me about one or two instances where you were really disappointed in the subject-specific knowledge of an academic reference librarian when you asked a question in your subject area? Please provide as many details as possible.

Question 6. Thinking back to the incident(s) that you mentioned in the previous question, do you think that the reference librarian *should have been* able to answer the question that you asked? Why or why not?

Question 7. When you go to your academic library and you have a specific reference question that you would like to ask, do you make a special point of going to one particular librarian to ask your question? If yes, what specific qualities does this person have that make you trust her or him more than the other reference librarians? Provide as many details as possible.

Question 8. What advice would *you* give to academic reference librarians so that they could improve service to people like you asking questions about your particular subject area? Give as many details as possible.

Question 9. If you were an academic reference librarian, what specific sources (both print and electronic) in your broad field of study would you make very sure that you were very familiar with? I would really appreciate it if you would list between 5–10 such sources.

Question 10. Again, if *you* were an academic reference librarian, what would you do to keep up with changes and developments in your broad field of study? Be as specific as possible.

Question 11. Can you give me one or two real questions dealing with your scholarly and research subject area that you have asked at anytime in the past at the reference desk of your college or university library *and* for which you received a reply that was not satisfactory to you? That is to say, where the reference staff member did not know how to get you the information that you required or steered you in the wrong direction.

THANK YOU AGAIN FOR TAKING TIME FROM YOUR BUSY SCHEDULE TO COMPLETE THIS SURVEY.

JUST PRESS THE REPLY BUTTON ON YOUR E-MAIL SOFTWARE AND SEND YOUR COMPLETED ANSWERS BACK TO ME.

YOUR EFFORTS HAVE BEEN VERY INSTRUMENTAL IN TRIGGERING A DONATION OF $500 USD TO THE AMERICAN INDIAN COLLEGE FUND.

Appendix D

Statistical Analyses of Selected Variables from the Survey Sent to Academic Reference Librarians

Logistic regression analysis was performed to answer a series of research questions. These questions are presented below, and are discussed in groups of four.

Research Question 1: Is there a significant relationship between the amount of reading that academic reference librarians do and instances where the reading of newspapers or magazines has helped them in providing reference service?

Research Question 2: Is there a significant relationship between the amount of reading that academic reference librarians do and instances where the reading of newspapers or magazines has helped them in other aspects of their job?

Research Question 3: Is there a significant relationship between the amount of reading that academic reference librarians do and instances where the reading of nonfiction and fiction books has helped them in providing reference service?

Research Question 4: Is there a significant relationship between the amount of reading that academic reference librarians do and instances where the reading of nonfiction and fiction books has helped them in other aspects of their job?

The following variables and data structures were used in the statistical tests.

Independent variables

IV-1. Library size (LIBSIZE): 5 levels (1 = very small; 2 = small; 3 = medium; 4 = large; 5 = very large)

IV-2. Years worked (YEARSWORK): 5 levels (1 = less than one; 2 = one to three; 3 = four to seven; 4 = eight to ten; 5 = eleven to twenty, or more)

IV-3. Read local paper (LOCPAP): 5 levels (1 = never; 2 = once a month or less; 3 = once a week; 4 = two to five times per week; 5 = daily)

IV-4. Read national paper (NATPAP): 5 levels (1 = never; 2 = once a month or less; 3 = once a week; 4 = two to five times per week; 5 = daily)

IV-5. Read magazines (MAGAZINE): 5 levels (1 = never; 2 = once a month or less; 3 = once a week; 4 = two to five times per week; 5 = daily)

IV-6. Read fiction (FICTION): 7 levels (1 = zero; 2 = one to five; 3 = six to ten; 4 = eleven to twenty; 5 = twenty-one to fifty;

6 = fifty-one to one hundred; 7 = more than one hundred)

IV-7. Read nonfiction (NONFICTION): 6 levels (1 = zero; 2 = one to five; 3 = six to ten; 4 = eleven to twenty; 5 = twenty-one to fifty; 6 = fifty-one to one hundred or more)

IV-8. Library profile (PROFLIB): 5 levels (1 = one to five; 2 = six to ten; 3 = eleven to twenty; 4 = more than twenty)

Definitions of independent variables

Library size (LIBSIZE)

The five definitions follow the classifications determined by the American Council of Learned Societies (ACLS) when setting subscription prices that various academic libraries have to pay for ACLS products and services. See www.historyebook.org/pricingsubscriptions.html (accessed April 9, 2002). The categories are based first on the Carnegie Classification of Institutions of Higher Education, 2000 edition, and subsequently on enrollment figures for full-time and part-time students.

Very small: Masters Colleges and Universities I and II with FTE enrollments below 1000; Baccalaureate Colleges—Liberal Arts and General with FTE enrollments below 1000; all Associate Colleges.

Small: Masters Colleges and Universities I and II with FTE enrollments between 1000 and 2500; Baccalaureate Colleges—Liberal Arts and General with FTE enrollments above 1000.

Medium: Masters Colleges and Universities I and II with FTE enrollments above 2,500.

Large: Institutions classified by the Carnegie Foundation as Doctoral/Research Universities—Intensive.

Very Large: Institutions classified by the Carnegie Foundation as Doctoral/Research Universities—Extensive.

Years worked (YEARSWORK)

Number of years respondent self-reported that he or she has been providing reference service on a regular basis.

Read local paper (LOCPAP)

Frequency with which the respondent self-reports that he or she reads a local newspaper (print or online) outside of work hours. A local paper is defined as one that concentrates mostly on local events and is published in the town/city in which the respondent lives or in the next biggest town/city from the respondent's place of residence.

Read national paper (NATPAP)

Frequency with which the respondent self-reports that he or she reads a national newspaper (print or online) outside of work hours. The following national newspapers were provided as examples: *New York Times*, *Washington Post*, *USA Today*, *The Globe and Mail* (Canada), or any other paper that is NOT published in respondent's immediate geographic locality and is distributed widely on a national basis.

Read magazines (MAGAZINE)

Frequency with which the respondent self-reports that he or she reads magazines outside of work hours. By magazines, this question means publications such as *Time*, *Newsweek*, *The New Yorker*, *Business Week*, *Harper's*, *Scientific American*, and *Discover*. Does not include sports, car, cooking, or fashion magazines, nor such publications as *TV Guide* or *National Enquirer*.

Read fiction (FICTION)

Number of fiction books that respondent self-reports as having read in the last 12 months outside of work hours. Includes novels of any genre, books of poetry, and plays. Does not include children's books.

Read nonfiction (NONFICTION)

Number of nonfiction books that respondent self-reports as having read in the last 12 months outside of work hours. Includes history and social-history books of all types; political books; biographies; art books; travel books; etc. Does not include self-help books, advice books, and how-to books.

Library profile (PROFLIB)

Number of professional librarians (full-time equivalents) that the respondent reports work at his or her home institution providing reference service on a regular basis during any given week. Includes those librarians who exclusively provide reference service and those who have other duties in addition to their reference desk duties.

Dependent variables

DV-1. Answers to Question 20 of the Academic Library Survey: 2 levels (yes, no)

The "yes" level includes respondents whose replies were originally grouped into the following categories: "yes"(with or without an example); "often" (with or without an example); "sometimes" (with or without an example). The "no" level comprises those respondents who stated that reading newspapers or magazines has not helped them in providing reference service.

DV-2. Answers to Question 21 of the Academic Library Survey: 2 levels (yes, no)

The "yes" level consists of respondents who mentioned any job-related activity that has been helped by reading newspapers or magazines. The "no" level comprises those respondents who stated that reading newspapers or magazines has not helped them in other work-related areas.

DV-3. Answers to Question 22 of the Academic Library Survey: 2 levels (yes, no)

The "yes" level includes respondents whose replies were originally grouped into the following categories: "yes" (with or without an example); "often" (with or without an example); "sometimes" (with or without an example). The "no" level comprises those respondents who stated that reading nonfiction or fiction books has not helped them in providing reference service.

DV-4. Answers to Question 23 of the Academic Library Survey: 2 levels (yes, no)

The "yes" level consists of respondents who mentioned any job-related activity that has been helped by reading nonfiction or fiction books. The "no" level comprises those respondents who stated that reading nonfiction or fiction books has not helped them in other work-related areas.

Data screening and assumptions

Initial screening procedures were performed to ensure that the assumptions underlying the logistic regression model were satisfied. The ratio of cases to variables was satisfactory. Multicollinearity between predictors was not present. Four outliers were identified and removed from the analyses; these cases all had Delta Deviance and Delta chi-square statistics that were high in comparison to other cases. The assumption of expected frequencies—all cells should have a minimum of expected frequencies—was partially violated; a remedial procedure was thus undertaken. All variables were tested in pairs to determine adequate expected frequency counts. If a cell did *not* have the required expected frequency, the levels of the various independent variables were changed. Two changes were made. **YEARSWORK**, which was initially made up of six levels, was reduced to five levels. **NONFICTION**, which was initially made up of seven levels, was reduced to six levels. An analysis was also performed to verify that the dependent variables did not all "tap" the same construct. If the dependent variables were all measuring something similar, they would be highly correlated. If, however, their correlations are relatively small, they are each measuring something different. Phi coefficients— which represent the correlations between each pair of dependent dichotomous variables— are reported below.

DV Pair	Phi Coefficient
Q1 * Q2	0.2609
Q1 * Q3	0.3142
Q1 * Q4	0.2103
Q2 * Q3	0.2208
Q2 * Q4	0.3273
Q3 * Q4	0.3375

While the dependent variables do display some overlapping variance, there is no statistical evidence that they are measuring a similar construct. Dependent variables should be eliminated only if they were correlated at 0.90 to 0.95, or higher. All four dependent variables were therefore used in the regression analyses.

Research question 1

Is there a significant relationship between the amount of reading that academic reference librarians do and instances where the reading of newspapers or magazines has helped them in providing reference service?

In other words, which of the eight independent variables best predicts the dependent variable (Answers to Question 20 in Appendix A)?

The number of total cases used for this analysis was 457 (408 "yes" responses and 49 "no" responses). Seventy-eight cases were deleted from the analysis because of missing data on one or more of the variables. A test of the full model with all eight predictors (independent variables) against a constant-only model was statistically significant (χ^2 = 42.9112, $p < .0001$, $df = 8$), indicating that the predictors, as a set, were able to reliably distinguish "yes" and "no" responses on the dependent variable. The variance explained by the independent variables was 8.96 percent ($R^2 = .0896$). Using the present model, 76 percent of cases were correctly classified. The two best predictors are **LOCPAP** (χ^2 = 14.3041, $p < 0.0002$, $df = 1$) and **NONFICTION** (χ^2 = 13.1517, $p < 0.0003$, $df = 1$). All other independent variables are not statistically significant.

Research question 2

Is there a significant relationship between the amount of reading that academic reference librarians do and instances where the reading of newspapers or magazines has helped them in other aspects of their job? In other words, which of the eight independent variables best predicts the dependent variable (Answers to Question 21 in Appendix A)?

The number of total cases used for this analysis was 464 (400 "yes" responses and 64 "no" responses). Seventy-one cases were deleted from the analysis because of missing data on one or more of the variables. A test of the full model with all eight predictors (independent variables) against a constant-only model was statistically significant (χ^2 = 29.3572, $p < .0003$, $df = 8$), indicating that the predictors, as a set, were able to reliably distinguish "yes" and "no" responses on the dependent variable. The variance explained by the independent variables is 6.13 percent ($R^2 = .0613$). Using the present model, 69 percent of cases were correctly classified. The two best predictors are **NATPAP** ($\chi^2 = 7.888$, $p < 0.005$, $df = 1$) and **NONFICTION** ($\chi^2 = 4.4504$, $p < 0.0349$, $df = 1$). **LOCPAP** ($\chi^2 = 3.7435$, $p < 0.0530$, $df = 1$) was marginally significant. All other independent variables are not statistically significant.

Research question 3

Is there a significant relationship between the amount of reading that academic reference librarians do and instances where the reading of nonfiction and fiction books has helped them in providing reference service? In other words, which of the eight independent variables best predicts the dependent variable (Answers to Question 22 in Appendix A)?

The number of total cases used for this analysis was 462 (353 "yes" responses and 109 "no" responses). Seventy-three cases were deleted from the analysis because of missing data on one or more of the variables. A test of the full model with all eight predictors (independent variables) against a constant-only model was statistically significant ($\chi^2 = 39.3413$, $p < .0001$, $df = 8$), indicating that the predictors, as a set, were able to reliably distinguish "yes" and "no" responses on the dependent variable. The variance explained by the independent variables was 8.16 percent ($R^2 = .0816$). Using the present model, 68.7 percent of cases were correctly classified. The best predictor for this model is **NONFICTION** ($\chi^2 = 23.0410$, $p < .0001$, $df = 1$). All other independent variables are not statistically significant.

Research question 4

Is there a significant relationship between the amount of reading that academic reference librarians do and instances where the reading of nonfiction and fiction books has helped them in other aspects of their job? In other words, which of the eight independent variables best predicts the dependent variable (Answers to Question 23 in Appendix A)?

The number of total cases used for this analysis was 451 (366 "yes" responses and 85 "no" responses). Eighty-four cases were deleted from the analysis because of missing data on one or more of the variables. A test of the full model with all eight predictors (independent variables) against a constant-only model was statistically significant ($\chi^2 = 18.2396$, $p < .0195$, $df = 8$), indicating that the predictors, as a set, were able to reliably distinguish "yes" and "no" responses on the dependent variable. The variance explained by the independent variables was 3.96 percent ($R^2 = .0396$). Using the present model, 64.2 percent of cases were correctly classified. The best predictor for this model is **NONFICTION** ($\chi^2 = 9.5940$, $p < .0020$, $df = 1$). All other independent variables are not statistically significant.

Summary

The independent variable **NONFICTION (reading of nonfiction)** is statistically significant in all four logistic regression models. The more that academic reference librarians read nonfiction books, the more these same librarians answer positively to Academic Library Survey Question 20 (yes = 408; no = 49). The more that academic reference librarians read nonfiction books, the more these same librarians answer positively to Academic Library Survey Question 21 (yes = 400; no = 64). The more that academic reference librarians read nonfiction books, the more these same librarians answer positively to Academic Library Survey Question 22 (yes = 353; no = 109). The more that academic reference librarians read nonfiction books, the more these same librarians answer positively to Academic Library Survey Question 23 (yes = 366; no = 85). Thus, **NONFICTION (reading of nonfiction)** is the best predictor of all four dependent variables, taken one at a time.

The independent variable **LOCPAP (reading of local newspapers)** is statistically significant or marginally statistically significant on two logistic regression models. The more that academic reference librarians read local newspapers, the more these same librarians answer positively to Academic Library Survey Question 20 (yes = 408; no = 49). The more that academic reference librarians read local newspapers, the more these same librarians answer positively to Academic Library Survey Question 21 (yes = 400; no = 64).

The independent variable **NATPAP (reading of national newspapers)** is statistically significant in one logistic regression model. The more that academic reference librarians read national newspapers, the more these same librarians answer positively to Academic Library Survey Question 21 (yes = 400; no = 64).

Variables **LIBSIZE, YEARSWORK,** and **PROFLIB** were held constant; their influence was thus partialled out.

Alternate research questions

In the previous models, eight predictors (independent variables) were used to answer each research question. We were also interested in finding out whether models with fewer predictors (independent variables) would provide different results. We slightly modified our approach, taking into account that the "yes-no" values for DV-1 and DV-2 were specifically based on a question asking only about "newspapers and magazines" and that the "yes-no" values for DV-3 and DV-4 were based on a question asking only about "nonfiction and fiction books." Modified research questions are presented below. Data screening and assumptions remain the same as above.

Research question 1a

Is there a significant relationship between the amount of reading of newspapers and magazines that academic reference librarians do and instances where the reading of newspapers or magazines has helped them in providing reference service? In other words, which of six independent variables (excluding **FICTION** and **NONFICTION**) best predicts the dependent variable (Answers to Question 20 in Appendix A)?

The number of total cases used for this analysis was 470 (424 "yes" responses and 46 "no" responses). Sixty-one cases were deleted from the analysis because of missing data on one or more of the variables and an additional eight were deleted because an analysis of residuals showed these eight cases to be outliers. A test of the six-predictor model (six independent variables) against a constant-only model was statistically significant ($\chi^2 = 33.9795$, $p < .0001$, $df = 6$), indicating that the predictors, as a set, were able to reliably distinguish "yes" and "no" responses on the dependent variable. The variance explained by the independent variables was 6.97 percent ($R^2 = .0697$). Using the present model, 71.8 percent of cases were correctly classified. The two best predictors are **LOCPAP** ($\chi^2 = 13.696$, $p < 0.0002$, $df = 1$) and **MAGAZINE** ($\chi^2 = 5.143$, $p < 0.0233$, $df = 1$). All other independent variables are not statistically significant.

Research question 2a

Is there a significant relationship between the amount of reading of newspapers and magazines that academic reference librarians do and instances where the reading of newspapers or magazines has helped them in other aspects of their job? In other words, which of six independent variables (excluding **FICTION** and **NONFICTION**) best predicts the dependent variable (Answers to Question 21 in Appendix A)?

The number of total cases used for this analysis was 475 (416 "yes" responses and 59 "no" responses). Fifty-five cases were deleted from the analysis because of missing data on one or more of the variables and an additional nine were deleted because an analysis of residuals showed these nine cases to be outliers. A test of the six-predictor model (six independent variables) against a constant-only model was statistically significant ($\chi^2 = 46.4046$, $p < .0001$, $df = 6$), indicating that the predictors, as a set, were able to reliably distinguish "yes" and "no" responses on the dependent variable. The variance explained by the independent variables is 9.31 percent ($R^2 = .0931$). Using the present model, 75.6 percent of cases were correctly classified. The two best predictors are **NATPAP** ($\chi^2 = 15.9207$, $p < 0.0001$, $df = 1$) and **MAGAZINE** ($\chi^2 = 9.508$, $p < 0.002$, $df = 1$).

Research question 3a

Is there a significant relationship between the amount of reading of nonfiction and fiction books that academic reference librarians do and instances where the reading of nonfiction and fiction books has helped them in providing reference service? In other words, which of five independent variables (excluding **LOCPAP**, **NATPAP**, and **MAGAZINE**) best predicts the dependent variable (Answers to Question 22 in Appendix A)?

The number of total cases used for this analysis was 476 (366 "yes" responses and 110 "no" responses). Fifty-eight cases were deleted from the analysis because of missing data on one or more of the variables and an additional five were deleted because an analysis of residuals showed these five cases to be outliers. A test of the five-predictor model (with five independent variables) against a constant-only model was statistically significant ($\chi^2 = 44.4436$, $p < .0001$, $df = 5$), indicating that the predictors, as a set, were able to reliably distinguish "yes" and "no" responses on the dependent variable. The variance explained by the independent variables was 8.91 percent ($R^2 = .0891$). Using the present model, 68.8 percent of cases were correctly classified. The best predictor for this model is **NONFICTION** ($\chi^2 = 30.9026$, $p < .0001$, $df = 1$). All other independent variables are not statistically significant.

Research question 4a

Is there a significant relationship between the amount of reading that academic reference librarians do and instances where the reading of nonfiction and fiction books has helped them in other aspects of their job? In other words, which of five independent variables (excluding **LOCPAP**, **NATPAP**, and **MAGAZINE**) best predicts the dependent variable (Answers to Question 23 in Appendix A)?

The number of total cases used for this analysis was 461 (380 "yes" responses and 81 "no" responses). Seventy cases were deleted from the analysis because of missing data on one or more of the variables and an additional eight were deleted because an analysis of residuals showed these eight cases to be outliers. A test of the full model with all eight predictors (independent variables) against a constant-only model was statistically significant ($\chi^2 = 21.3484$, $p < .0007$, $df = 5$), indicating that the predictors, as a set, were able to reliably distinguish "yes" and "no" responses on the dependent variable. The variance explained by the independent variables was 4.53 percent ($R^2 = .0453$). Using the present model, 65.2 percent of cases were correctly classified. The best predictor for this model is **NONFICTION** ($\chi^2 = 14.9671$, $p < .0001$, $df = 1$). All other independent variables are not statistically significant.

Summary

The more that academic reference librarians read magazines, the more these same librarians answer positively to Academic Library Survey Question 20 (yes = 424; no = 46). The more that academic reference librarians read magazines, the more these same librarians answer positively to Academic Library Survey Question 21 (yes = 416; no = 59). The more that academic reference librarians read local newspapers, the more these same librarians answer positively to Academic Library Survey Question 20 (yes = 424; no = 46). The more that academic reference librarians read national newspapers, the more these same librarians answer positively to Academic Library Survey Question 21 (yes = 416; no = 59). The more that academic reference librarians read nonfiction books, the more these same librarians answer positively to Academic Library Survey Question 22 (yes = 366; no = 110). The more that academic reference librarians read nonfiction books, the more these same librarians answer positively to Academic Library Survey Question 23 (yes = 380; no = 81).

Variables **LIBSIZE**, **YEARSWORK**, and **PROFLIB** were held constant; their influence was thus partialled out.

Notes

Preface

1. Stephen Karetzky, *Reading Research and Librarianship: A History and Analysis*. Westport, CT: Greenwood, 1982 (p. xv).

2. Janice A. Radway, *Reading the Romance: Women, Patriarchy, and Popular Literature.* Chapel Hill, NC: The University of North Carolina Press, 1991 (pp. 102, 211, 213); Catherine Sheldrick Ross, "Finding without Seeking: The Information Encounter in the Context of Reading for Pleasure," *Information Processing & Management* 35 (1999): 793–795.

3. Stephen Krashen, *The Power of Reading: Insights from the Research.* Englewood, CO: Libraries Unlimited, 1993; Burke, Jim. *I Hear America Reading: Why We Read, What We Read.* Portsmouth, NH: Heinemann, 1999.

Part I

1. See, for example, Jon Lee Anderson, "Who Needs Saudi Arabia when You've Got Saõ Tomé?" *The New Yorker* (October 7, 2002): 74–86; Norimitsu Onishi with Neela Banerjee, "Chad's Wait for Its Oil Riches May Be Long," *New York Times* (May 16, 2001): A1, A11; and Rachel L. Swarns, "Oil Abounds, Misery Too: A Case Study," *New York Times* (January 14, 2001): Section 4, p. 6.

2. Norimitsu Onishi, "A Corner of Africa Where Dreams Gush Like Oil," *New York Times* (July 28, 2000): A4.

3. Stephen Levy, "The World According to Google," *Newsweek* 140 (December 16, 2002): 46–51 (p. 47).

4. See, for example, Joseph Janes, "Why Reference is About to Change Forever (But Not Completely)." In R. David Lankes, John W. Collins III, and Abby S. Kasowitz (Eds.), *Digital Reference Service in the New Millennium: Planning, Man-*agement, and Evaluation (pp. 13–24). New York: Neal-Schuman, 2000 (p. 22).

5. Stephen Levy, "The World According to Google," *Newsweek* 140 (December 16, 2002): 46–51 (p. 49).

Chapter 1

1. John V. Richardson, Jr., "Question Master: An Evaluation of a Web-based Decision-support System for Use in Reference Environments," *College & Research Libraries* 59 (January 1998): 29–37.

2. *Ibid.*, p. 29.

3. Ronald J. Heckart, "Machine Help and Human Help in the Emerging Digital Library," *College & Research Libraries* 59 (May 1998): 250–259.

4. *Ibid.*, pp. 251–254.

5. Chris D. Ferguson, "Shaking the Conceptual Foundations, Too: Integrating Research and Technology Support for the Next Generation of Information Service," *College & Research Libraries* 61 (July 2000): 307.

6. *Ibid.*, p. 308.

7. *Ibid.*, p. 308.

8. Steve Coffman and Matthew L. Saxton, "Staffing the Reference Desk in the Largely-digital Library." In C.D. Ferguson (Ed.), *From Past-present to Future-perfect: A Tribute to Charles A. Bunge and the Challenges of Contemporary Reference Service* (pp. 141–163). New York: Haworth Press, 1999 (p. 148).

9. Susan McGlamery and Steve Coffman, "Moving Reference to the Web," *Reference & User Services Quarterly* 39 (Summer 2000): 381–382.

10. *Ibid.*, p. 382.

11. *Ibid.*, p. 382.

12. *Ibid.*, p. 382.

13. Roma M. Harris, *Librarianship: The Ero-*

sion of a Woman's Profession. Norwood, NJ: Ablex, 1992 (p. 123).

14. Roma M. Harris and Victoria Marshall, "Reorganizing Canadian Libraries: A Giant Step Back from the Front," *Library Trends* 46 (Winter 1998): 570.

15. *Ibid.*, pp. 570–571.

16. Steve Coffman and Matthew L. Saxton, "Staffing the Reference Desk in the Largely-digital Library." In C.D. Ferguson (Ed.), *From Past-present to Future-perfect: A Tribute to Charles A. Bunge and the Challenges of Contemporary Reference Service* (pp. 141–163). New York: Haworth Press, 1999 (p. 143).

17. *Ibid.*, pp. 143, 154.

18. *Ibid.*, p. 154.

19. See, for example, Roma M. Harris, *Librarianship: The Erosion of a Woman's Profession.* Norwood, NJ: Ablex, 1992; see also Susan Hildenbrand, "Ambiguous Authority and Aborted Ambition: Gender, Professionalism, and the Rise and Fall of the Welfare State," *Library Trends* 34 (Fall 1985): 185–198.

20. Steve Coffman and Matthew L. Saxton, "Staffing the Reference Desk in the Largely-digital Library." In C.D. Ferguson (Ed.), *From Past-present to Future-perfect: A Tribute to Charles A. Bunge and the Challenges of Contemporary Reference Service* (pp. 141–163). New York: Haworth Press, 1999 (p. 153).

21. *Ibid.*, p. 153.

22. *Ibid.*, p. 153.

23. *Ibid.*, pp. 154–155.

24. *Ibid.*, p. 155.

25. *Ibid.*, p. 157.

26. Susan McGlamery and Steve Coffman, "Moving Reference to the Web," *Reference & User Services Quarterly* 39 (Summer 2000): 385.

27. *Ibid.*, p. 385.

28. Roma M. Harris and Victoria Marshall, "Reorganizing Canadian Libraries: A Giant Step Back from the Front," *Library Trends* 46 (Winter 1998): 578.

29. *Ibid.*, p. 577.

30. *Ibid.*, p. 579.

31. *Ibid.*, p. 579.

32. Sue Fernie and David Metcalf, *(Not) Hanging on the Telephone: Payment Systems in the New Sweatshops.* Working Paper 891, Centre for Economic Performance. London: London School of Economics, 1998.

33. Lester C. Thurow, "Regional Transformation and the Service Activities." In Lloyd Rodwin and Hidehiko Sazanami (Eds.), *Deindustrializa-tion and Regional Economic Transformation: The Experience of the United States* (pp. 179–198). Boston: Unwin Hyman, 1989.

34. Ranald Richardson, Vicki Belt, and Neill Marshall, "Taking Calls to Newcastle: The Regional Implications of the Growth in Call Centers," *Regional Studies* 34 (June 2000): 358.

35. Ginger Conlon, "The Human Side of Call Centers," *Sales & Marketing Management* 150 (October 1998): 92–94.

36. Mark Higgins, "Life on the Line: Call Centers are Pretty Exciting, Unless You're Actually Handling the Calls," *Marketing Magazine* 101 (March 18, 1996): 8.

37. David Menzies, "Last Call: In Which Our Intrepid Reporter Delves Into the Inner Sanctum of the Call Center Business," *Marketing Magazine* 104 (September 27, 1999): 14–17.

38. Ruth Buchanan and Sarah Koch-Schulte, *Gender on the Line: Technology, Restructuring and the Reorganization of Work in the Call Centre Industry.* Ottawa: Status of Women Canada Research Directorate, 2000. Retrieved November 2, 2000, from www.swc-cfc.gc.ca/publish/research/001010-0662281586-e.html

39. Joan McFarland, "Many are Called, but What are the Choices: Working in New Brunswick's 1-800 Call Centres," *New Maritimes* 74 (July/August 1996): 10–19. A slightly updated version of this article appears as Joan McFarland, "Call Centres in New Brunswick: Maquiladoras of the North?" *Canadian Woman Studies/Les Cahiers de la Femme* 21/22 (July/August 2002): 65–70.

40. Bruce Bryant-Friedland and John Finotti, "Low-paying Call Center Jobs Have Fueled Jacksonville's Back-office Boom," *The Florida Times-Union* (January 12, 1998): A1.

41. *Ibid.*, p. A1.

42. Ranald Richardson, Vicki Belt, and Neill Marshall, "Taking Calls to Newcastle: The Regional Implications of the Growth in Call Centers," *Regional Studies* 34 (June 2000): 362.

43. Angela Karr, "One in Three Agents Walk." *Teleprofessional Magazine* 12 (October 1999): 18–19.

44. Ranald Richardson, Vicki Belt, and Neill Marshall, "Taking Calls to Newcastle: The Regional Implications of the Growth in Call Centers," *Regional Studies* 34 (June 2000): 364.

45. James Curtis, "Call Centers Must Adapt their Ways," *Marketing* [United Kingdom] (December 2, 1999): 33–34, 37.

46. Ruth E. Thaler-Carter, "Why Sit and Answer the Phone All Day?" *HR Magazine* 44 (March 1999): 104.

47. Ginger Conlon, "The Human Side of Call Centers," *Sales & Marketing Management* 150 (October 1998): 92.

48. *Ibid.*, p. 92.

49. Ruth E. Thaler-Carter, "Why Sit and Answer the Phone All Day?" *HR Magazine* 44 (March 1999): 104

50. James Curtis, "Call Centers Must Adapt their Ways," *Marketing* [United Kingdom] (December 2, 1999): 33–34, 37.

51. Phil Taylor, Gareth Mulvey, Jeff Hyman, and Peter Bain, "Work Organisation, Control and the Experience of Work in Call Centres," *Work, Employment and Society* 16 (March 2002): 135.

52. *Ibid.*, p. 134.

53. *Ibid.*, p. 136.

54. *Ibid.*, p. 141.

55. *Ibid.*, p. 148.

56. *Ibid.*, p. 149.

57. Steve Coffman, "Building Earth's Largest Library: Driving into the Future," *Searcher* 7 (March 1999), 34–37, 40–47.

58. *Ibid.*, p. 47.

59. Mark Leibovich, "At Amazon.com, Service Workers Without a Smile," *Washington Post* (November 22, 1999): Al, A14.

60. *Ibid.*, p. A14.

61. *Ibid.*, p. A14.

62. Mike Daisey, *21 Dog Years: Doing Time @ Amazon.com*. New York: The Free Press, 2002 (p. 61).

63. Mark Leibovich, "At Amazon.com, Service Workers Without a Smile," A14.

64. Daisey, *21 Dog Years*, p. 78.

65. *Ibid.*, p. 75.

66. *Ibid.*, p. 79.

67. *Ibid.*, p. 79.

68. Nick Guyatt, "What's Going on at Amazon.com?" Princeton University Campus Greens, Labour and Free Trade Working Group, 2001. Retrieved March 1, 2000, from http:// www.princeton.edu/~greens. See also WashTech, "Amazon.com to Begin Outsourcing Customer Service Operations to India." 2000. *WashTech News.* Retrieved March 1, 2001, from http://www.washtech.org/amazon/090700_india.php3

69. WashTech, "Amazon.com to Begin Outsourcing Customer Service Operations to India." 2000. *WashTech News.* Retrieved March 1, 2001, from http://www.washtech.org/amazon/090700_india.php3

70. Steven Greenhouse, "Unions Pushing to Organize Thousands of Amazon.com Workers," *New York Times* (November 23, 2000): C1, C3.

71. Steven Greenhouse, "Amazon.com is Using the Web to Block Unions' Efforts to Organize," *New York Times* (November 29, 2000): C1, C2.

72. Ruth Buchanan and Sarah Koch-Schulte, *Gender on the Line: Technology, Restructuring and the Reorganization of Work in the Call Centre Industry.* Ottawa: Status of Women Canada Research Directorate, 2000. Retrieved November 2, 2000, from www.swc-cfc.gc.ca/publish/research/001010-0662281586-e.html, pp. 9–10, 16–19. See also Ranald Richardson, Vicki Belt, and Neill Marshall, "Taking Calls to Newcastle: The Regional Implications of the Growth in Call Centers," *Regional Studies* 34 (June 2000): 359–361.

73. Ruth Buchanan and Sarah Koch-Schulte, *Gender on the Line: Technology, Restructuring and the Reorganization of Work in the Call Centre Industry.* Ottawa: Status of Women Canada Research Directorate, 2000. Retrieved November 2, 2000, from www.swc-cfc.gc.ca/publish/research/001010-0662281586-e.html, pp. 15–16.

74. *Ibid.*, p. 15.

75. *Ibid.*, p. 14.

76. *Ibid.*, pp. 48–51.

77. *Ibid.*, p. 53.

78. *Ibid.*, p. 53.

79. Steven Ellis, "Data Entry and the Economy of Offshore Information Production," *Library Resources & Technical Services* 41 (April 1997): 112.

80. *Ibid.*, pp. 117, 119.

81. Ruth Buchanan and Sarah Koch-Schulte, *Gender on the Line: Technology, Restructuring and the Reorganization of Work in the Call Centre Industry.* Ottawa: Status of Women Canada Research Directorate, 2000. Retrieved November 2, 2000, from www.swc-cfc.gc.ca/publish/research/001010-0662281586-e.html, p. 53.

82. Ewart C. Skinner, "The Caribbean Data Processors." In Gerald Sussman and John A. Lent (Eds.), *Global Productions: Labor in the Making of the Information Society* (pp. 57–88). Creeskill, NJ: Hampton Press, 1998 (p. 83).

83. Joan McFarland, "Call Centres in New Brunswick: Maquiladoras of the North?" *Canadian Woman Studies/Les Cahiers de la Femme* 21/22 (July/August 2002): 70.

84. Quoted in McFarland, p. 70. The quotation comes from Swasti Mitter, *Common Fate: Common Bond: Women in the Global Economy.* London: Pluto Press, 1986 (p. 13).

85. McFarland, "Call Centers in New Brunswick," p. 70.

86. Lenny Siegel, "New Chips in Old Skins: Work and Labor in Silicon Valley." In Gerald

Sussman & John A. Lent (Eds.), *Global Produc-tions: Labor in the Making of the Information So-ciety* (pp. 97–110). Creeskill, NJ: Hampton Press (pp. 99–102).

87. Steve Coffman and Matthew L. Saxton, "Staffing the Reference Desk in the Largely-digi-tal Library." In C.D. Ferguson (Ed.), *From Past-present to Future-perfect: A Tribute to Charles A. Bunge and the Challenges of Contemporary Refer-ence Service* (pp. 141–163). New York: Haworth Press, 1999 (p. 143).

88. Roma M. Harris and Victoria Marshall, "Reorganizing Canadian Libraries: A Giant Step Back from the Front," *Library Trends* 46 (Winter 1998): 579.

89. Noah Kennedy, *The Industrialization of Intelligence: Mind and Machine in the Modern Age.* London: Unwin Hyman, 1989.

90. Antonio Gramsci, *Selections from the Prison Notebooks of Antonio Gramsci.* New York: International Publishers, 1971 (p. 323).

91. Ruth Buchanan and Sarah Koch-Schulte, *Gender on the Line: Technology, Restructuring and the Reorganization of Work in the Call Centre In-dustry.* Ottawa: Status of Women Canada Re-search Directorate, 2000. Retrieved November 2, 2000, from www.swc-cfc.gc.ca/publish/research/001010-0662281586-e.html, pp. 63–72.

92. Chris D. Ferguson, "Shaking the Concep-tual Foundations, Too: Integrating Research and Technology Support for the Next Generation of Information Service," *College & Research Libraries* 61(July 2000): 306.

93. *Ibid.*, p. 308.

94. *Ibid.*, p. 305.

95. *Ibid.*, p. 308.

96. Brenda Dervin, "From the Mind's Eye of the User: The Sense-making Qualitative-quanti-tative Methodology." In J.D. Glazier and R.R. Powell (Eds.), *Qualitative Research in Information Management* (pp. 61–84). Englewood, CO: Li-braries Unlimited.

97. *Ibid.*, p. 68.

98. *Ibid.*, p. 75.

99. Carol C. Kuhlthau, *Seeking Meaning: A Process Approach to Library and Information Ser-vices.* Norwood, NJ: Ablex, 1993 (p. 144).

100. *Ibid.*, p. 188.

Chapter 2

1. Frank Keller Walter, "In a Quiet Corner with a Little Book," *Collection Management* 6 (3/4), 28–35 (p. 31). Reprinted 1984; original article 1925.

2. *Ibid.*, p. 32.

3. *Ibid.*, pp. 32–33.

4. James Ingersoll Wyer, *Reference Work: A Textbook for Students of Library Work and Librar-ians.* Chicago: American Library Association, 1930 (pp. 120–121).

5. Margaret Hutchins, *Introduction to Refer-ence Work.* Chicago: American Library Associa-tion, 1944 (p. 103).

6. *Ibid.*, p. 103.

7. Shiyali Ramamrita Ranganathan, *Reference Service* (2nd ed.). London: Asia Publishing House, 1961 (p. 104).

8. *Ibid.*, pp. 349, 352.

9. *Ibid.*, p. 350.

10. Leigh Buchanan, "The Smartest Little Company in America," *Inc.* 21 (January 1999): 54.

11. Elizabeth Thomsen, *Rethinking Reference: The Reference Librarian's Practical Guide for Sur-viving Constant Change.* New York: Neal-Schu-man, 1999 (p. 32).

12. *Ibid.*, p. 34.

13. Shiyali Ramamrita Ranganathan, *Reference Service* (2nd ed.). London: Asia Publishing House, 1961 (p. 391).

14. Denis Joseph Grogan, *Grogan's Case Stud-ies in Reference Work. Volume 6: Biographical Sources.* London: Clive Bingley, 1987 (pp. 65–67).

15. Denis Joseph Grogan, *Grogan's Case Stud-ies in Reference Work. Volume 1: Enquiries and the Reference Process.* London: Clive Bingley, 1987.

16. *Ibid.*, p. 9.

17. *Ibid.*, p. 18.

18. *Ibid.*, p. 19.

19. Denis Joseph Grogan, *Grogan's Case Stud-ies in Reference Work. Volume 4: Periodicals and Their Guides.* London: Clive Bingley, 1987 (p. 94).

Chapter 3

1. National Opinion Research Center at The University of Chicago, "Codebook Variable: News." Available: http://www.icpsr.umich.edu (ac-cessed June 17, 2002).

2. Statistics Canada, "Canadians' Reading Habits." Available: http://www.statcan.ca (ac-cessed June 18, 2002).

3. Audit Bureau of Circulations, "Top 100 US Newspapers by Circulation," Audit Bureau of Cir-culations FAS-FAX Report, September 30, 1999.

4. Robert D. Putnam, *Bowling Alone: The Col-lapse and Revival of American Community.* New York: Simon & Schuster, 2000 (pp. 218–219).

5. *Ibid.*, p. 219.

6. *Ibid.*, p. 219.

7. Mediamark Research, "Fall 2000 Magazine Audience Estimates (Sorted by Adult 18+ Audience)." Available: http://www.mediamark.com (accessed June 18, 2002).

8. William L. Hamilton, "They've Got Your Numbers," *New York Times* (August 15, 2002): D1, D4.

9. The Tidal Basin Incident involved Congressman Wilbur Mills (Democrat—Arkansas) and a stripper whose stage name was Fanne Fox (the "Argentine Firecracker"). For more information, see http://www.washingtonpost.com/wp-srv/local/longterm/tours/scandal/tidalbas.htm (accessed November 17, 2002).

Chapter 4

1. *The Bowker Annual Library and Book Trade Almanac 2000* (45th ed.), edited by Dave Bogart (New York: Bowker), p. 637.

2. *The Bowker Annual Library and Book Trade Almanac 2001* (46th ed.), edited by Dave Bogart (New York: Bowker), p. 631.

3. *Ibid.*, p. 630.

4. *Ibid.*, pp. 618–620.

5. *Ibid.*, p. 638.

6. *The Bowker Annual Library and Book Trade Almanac 2000* (45th ed.), edited by Dave Bogart (New York: Bowker), p. 636.

7 *The Bowker Annual Library and Book Trade Almanac 2001* (46th ed.), edited by Dave Bogart (New York: Bowker), p. 625.

8 *Ibid.*, p. 619.

9 All Bill Bryson titles are counted as one title.

10. *The Bowker Annual Library and Book Trade Almanac 2001* (46th ed.), edited by Dave Bogart (New York: Bowker), p. 623.

11. *The Bowker Annual Library and Book Trade Almanac 2000* (45th ed.), edited by Dave Bogart (New York: Bowker), p. 626; *The Bowker Annual Library and Book Trade Almanac 2001* (46th ed.), edited by Dave Bogart (New York: Bowker), p. 622.

12. *The Bowker Annual Library and Book Trade Almanac 2001* (46th ed.), edited by Dave Bogart (New York: Bowker), p. 624.

Chapter 5

1. All figures in this paragraph taken from United States Census Bureau, *2001 Statistical Abstract of the United States*, pp. 704–705.

2. Robert D. Putnam, *Bowling Alone: The Collapse and Revival of American Community*. New York: Simon & Schuster, 2000 (p. 224).

Chapter 6

1. United Census Bureau, "Home Computers and Internet Use in the United States: August 2000," p. 1. Retrieved from www.census.gov/prod/2001pubs/p23-207.pdf (October 30, 2002).

2. *Brill's Content* (Fall 2001), p. 43.

3. Haynes Johnson, *The Best of Times: America in the Clinton Years*. New York: Harcourt, 2001 (p. 187).

4. Frank Rich, "The Weight of an Anchor," *New York Times Magazine* (May 19, 2002). Available http://www.nytimes.com (accessed October 26, 2002), par. 4.

5. *Ibid.*, par. 4.

6. *Ibid.*, par. 5.

7. *Ibid.*, par. 2.

8. *Ibid.*, par. 1.

9. *Brill's Content* (Fall 2001), p. 42.

10. CBS, "60 Minutes Milestones." Available: http://www.cbsnews.com (accessed October 24, 2002).

11. United States Census Bureau, *2001 Statistical Abstract of the United States*, pp. 704–705.

12. *Ibid.*, p. 704.

13. *Ibid.*, p. 705.

14. Ryan Lizza, "The Ambulance-Homicide Theory," *New York Times Magazine* (December 15, 2002): 66.

15. Sarah Wildman, "Tuning Out the World," *The New Republic* (September 9, 2002). Available: www.tnr.com (accessed September 7, 2002), par. 5.

16. *Ibid.*, par. 6.

Chapter 7

1. The comments of the English Literature professor are drawn from the professor's answer to the question: "If you were an academic reference librarian, what would you do to keep up with changes and developments in your broad field of study?" The comments are included here for thematic reasons, but are counted only in the appropriate table, in this case, Table 42.

2. The comments of the professor of European History are drawn as described in note 1.

3. The comments of the professor of Ameri-

can Literature and the professor of Archaeology are drawn as described in note 1.

4. This list is drawn from the web page of the Office for Accreditation & Committee on Accreditation of the American Library Association. The web address is http://www.ala.org/alaorg/oa/accreditation.html. Link to "Institutions Currently Offering Accredited Master's Programs." This link was accessed on November 8, 2002. Some of the universities listed in the present chapter have other dual degrees. The list presented here is intended as a select list.

5. Fred J. Hay, "The Subject Specialist in the Academic Library: A Review Article," *The Journal of Academic Librarianship* (January 1990): 11–17.

6. *Ibid.*, p. 15. Hay quotes J. Periam Danton, *Book Selection and Collections: A Comparison of German and American University Libraries.* New York: Columbia University Press, 1963 (pp. 37–38).

Chapter 8

1. Pierre Bourdieu and Loïc J.D. Wacquant, *An Invitation to Reflexive Sociology.* Chicago: The University of Chicago Press, 1992.

2. All quotations in this paragraph are taken from Bourdieu and Wacquant, *An Invitation to Reflexive Sociology*, pp. 97–101.

3. Patricia Madoo Lengermann, Jill Niebrugge-Brantley, and Jane Kirkpatrick, "Democracy, Technology, and the Public Library." In Donna Allen, Ramona R. Rush, and Susan J. Kaufman (Eds.), *Women Transforming Communications: Global Intersections* (pp. 83–94). Thousand Oaks, CA: Sage Publications, 1996 (pp. 84–85).

4. *Ibid.*, p. 93.

5. Pierre Bourdieu and Loïc J.D. Wacquant, *An Invitation to Reflexive Sociology.* Chicago: The University of Chicago Press, 1992 (p. 101).

6. Gobinda G. Chowdhury, "Digital Libraries and Reference Services: Present and Future," *Journal of Documentation* 58 (May 2002): 258–283.

7. *Ibid.*, p. 271.

8. *Ibid.*, p. 275.

9. *Ibid.*, p. 262.

10. Marilyn Domas White, "Diffusion of an Innovation: Digital Reference Service in Carnegie Foundation Master's (Comprehensive) Academic Institution Libraries," *The Journal of Academic Librarianship* 27 (May 2001): 173.

11. Marilyn Domas White, "Digital Reference Services: Framework for Analysis and Evaluation," *Library & Information Science Research* 23 (2001): 212.

12. Phil Taylor, Gareth Mulvey, Jeff Hyman, and Peter Bain, "Work Organisation, Control and the Experience of Work in Call Centres," *Work, Employment and Society* 16 (March 2002): 133–150. See discussion in Chapter 1.

13. Steve Coffman and Matthew L. Saxton, "Staffing the Reference Desk in the Largely-digital Library." In C.D. Ferguson (Ed.), *From Past-present to Future-perfect: A Tribute to Charles A. Bunge and the Challenges of Contemporary Reference Service* (pp. 141–163). New York: Haworth Press, 1999 (pp. 143, 154).

14. Patricia Madoo Lengermann, Jill Niebrugge-Brantley, and Jane Kirkpatrick, "Democracy, Technology, and the Public Library." In Donna Allen, Ramona R. Rush, and Susan J. Kaufman (Eds.), *Women Transforming Communications: Global Intersections* (pp. 83–94). Thousand Oaks, CA: Sage Publications, 1996 (p. 93).

15. Pierre Bourdieu and Loïc J.D. Wacquant, *An Invitation to Reflexive Sociology.* Chicago: The University of Chicago Press, 1992 (p. 99).

16. *Ibid.*, p. 99.

17. *Ibid.*, p. 98.

18. Matthew L. Saxton, and John V. Richardson, Jr. *Understanding Reference Transactions: Transforming an Art into a Science.* Amsterdam: Academic Press, 2002 (p. 100).

19. Saxton and Richardson hypothesize that "reference service performance is determined by some combination of the joint effects of the difficulty of the query; the education of the library user and the user's familiarity with libraries and library services; the service behaviors exhibited by the librarian during the transaction; the experience, education, and job satisfaction of the librarian; and the size and policies of the library" (p. 8). Sixteen independent variables were developed to measure the five elements of this hypothesis, as well as four variables measuring reference outcomes (completeness of the information received, as determined by the patron; usefulness of the information received, as determined by the patron; satisfaction level with information received, as determined by the patron; and accuracy of information received, as determined by outside assessors) (p. 67). Reference transactions at a number of California public libraries were examined, and information about each of the 20 variables was entered for each of the 3,520 reference queries. Only 696 of those transactions were

used in the final data analysis because of missing data, and even then "[t]he mean imputation method was employed to account for missing data" (p. 78). The degree of difficulty of these 696 reference transactions was rated by external judges to be very low (mean rating of 1.36 on a 7-point Likert scale), with accuracy rated very high (mean rating of 6.57 on a 7-point Likert scale) (p. 81). However, interrater reliability scores among the judges were quite low (0.5444 and 0.5545, after averaging Spearman-Brown correlations) (p. 80). Three of the four dependent variables (reference outcomes), namely, completeness, usefulness, and satisfaction, were "predicted by the individual behavior of the librarian" (p. 101), with such variables as user's familiarity and user's education level having low levels of predictive power.

20. Saxton and Richardson, *Understanding Reference Transactions*, p. 81.

21. *Ibid.*, p. 60.

22. *Ibid.*, pp. 60–61.

23. Towards the end of their book, Saxton and Richardson, puzzled as to the reasons why "measures of librarian experience and education fail to predict service outcomes," suggest that these variables might be "indirect predictors of the outcome variables." They ask: "To what degree does the librarian's experience and education predict the extent to which the librarian follows the behavioral guidelines" (p. 100)? But note that education is only valuable here as a predictor of behavior characteristics. Education is not being conceived as something that, for example, provides a great deal of subject-specific knowledge about diverse topics and areas.

24. Saxton and Richardson, *Understanding Reference Transactions*, p. 98.

25. *Ibid.*, pp. 99–100.

26. *Ibid.*, p. 101.

27. Reference and User Services Association, Guidelines for Behavioral Performance of Reference and Information Service Professionals, par. 1.3, 2.1, 2.2, 3.2. Available at http://www.ala.org/rusa/stnd_behavior.html (accessed May 18, 2002).

28. To be sure, Saxton and Richardson claim that "the distribution of scores for the accuracy outcome measure sharply contradicts the conventional finding that reference queries are answered correctly only just over 50 percent of the time. In this study, over 90 percent of the reference queries were judged to be completely accurate or partially accurate or provided the user with an accurate referral to another agency" (p. 95).

But, as we saw previously, there was very little agreement among judges about just what exactly constituted an accurate answer. In addition, most of the questions asked were relatively easy and even partially accurate answers, as well as referrals, are included in the "over 90 percent" figure.

29. Steve Coffman and Matthew L. Saxton, "Staffing the Reference Desk in the Largely-digital Library." In C.D. Ferguson (Ed.), *From Past-present to Future-perfect: A Tribute to Charles A. Bunge and the Challenges of Contemporary Reference Service* (pp. 141–163). New York: Haworth Press, 1999 (pp. 154–155).

30. *Ibid.*, p. 155.

31. *Ibid.*, p. 157.

32. Pierre Bourdieu and Loïc J.D. Wacquant, *An Invitation to Reflexive Sociology*. Chicago: The University of Chicago Press, 1992 (p. 98).

33. Mark Linzer, "The Journal Club and Medical Education: Over One-hundred Years of Unrecorded History," *Postgraduate Medical Journal* 63 (1987): 475–478.

34. *Ibid.*, p. 476.

35. *Ibid.*, p. 476.

36. *Ibid*, pp. 475–476.

37. *Ibid.*, p. 476.

38. *Ibid.*, p. 476.

39. Patrick C. Alguire, "A Review of Journal Clubs in Postgraduate Medical Education," *Journal of General Internal Medicine* 13 (1998): 347–353.

40. *Ibid.*, p. 347.

41. *Ibid.*, p. 351

42. *Ibid.*, p. 351.

43. Jon O. Ebbert, Victor M. Montori, and Henry J. Schultz, "The Journal Club in Postgraduate Medical Education: A Systematic Review," *Medical Teacher* 23 (2001): 455–461.

44. Richard Edwards, Martin White, Jackie Gray, and Colin Fischbacher, "Use of a Journal Club and Letter-writing Exercise to Teach Critical Appraisal to Medical Undergraduates," *Medical Education* 35 (2001): 691–694.

45. Alice T. Speers, "An Introduction to Nursing Research through an OR Nursing Journal Club." *AORN Journal* 69 (June 1999): 1232–1236. See also Evelyn I. Stelmach, "A Staff Journal Club as a Method of Continuing Education," *AORN Journal* 59 (May 1994): 1061–1063.

46. John Sheehan, "A Journal Club as a Teaching and Learning Strategy in Nurse Teacher Education," *Journal of Advanced Nursing* 19 (1994): 572–578.

47. Arnold Shmerling, "Journal Clubs for Gen-

eral Practitioners," *Australian Family Physician* 20 (June 1991): 814–816.

48. Brenda L. Seago, Lynne U. Turman, Andrea S. Horne, Philip Croom, and Karen Cary, "Journal Club with a Mission," *Bulletin of the Medical Library Association* 82 (January 1994): 73–74. See also Anne C. Tomlin, "From Dowdy to Dandy: Spiffing Up the Journal Club," *The One-Person Library: A Newsletter for Librarians and Management* 12 (April 1996): 1–3.

49. See, for example, Andrew J. Gibbons, "Organising a Successful Journal Club," *BMJ* 325 (7371; November 2, 2002): S137. Available at http://bmj.com/content/vol325/issue7371/ (accessed November 13, 2002).

50. Medical Library Association, "MLA Journal Club: Journal Club Guidelines," Available at http://mlanet.org/education/telecon/jcguide.html (accessed November 13, 2002).

51. *Ibid.*, "How Often do Clubs Meet or Interact Electronically."

52. Sue Toye, "The Business of Books: Rotman Students Say Broad Approach to Reading Key to Developing Good Business Skills," *The Bulletin: University of Toronto* (November 4, 2002): 5.

53. *Ibid.*, p. 5.

54. The full list of titles is available at http://www.rotman.utoronto.ca/readingcommunity.htm (accessed November 21, 2002).

55. Sue Toye, "The Business of Books: Rotman Students Say Broad Approach to Reading Key to Developing Good Business Skills," *The Bulletin: University of Toronto* (November 4, 2002): 5.

56. *Ibid.*, p. 5.

57. Scott Stebelman, "Taking Control of Continuing Education: The Formation of a Reading Group at George Washington University," *The Journal of Academic Librarianship* 22 (September 1996): 382–385.

58. *Ibid.*, p. 383.

59. *Ibid.*, p. 383.

60. *Ibid*, p. 384.

61. *Ibid.*, p. 384.

62. Scott Bowles, "Hollywood Goes to Epic Proportions," *USA Today* (November 29, 2002): A1, A2.

63. Mary Williams Walsh, "Corporations Revise Wish Lists," *New York Times* (November 7, 2002): C1, C5. This is an umbrella article followed by shorter pieces on the individual seven areas signed by Neela Banerjee, Joseph B. Treaster, Milt Freudenheim, Riva Atlas, Seth Schiesel, Danny Hakim, and David Cay Johnston.

64. Scott Stebelman, "Taking Control of Continuing Education: The Formation of a Reading Group at George Washington University," *The Journal of Academic Librarianship* 22 (September 1996): 384.

65. Nick Bontis, "Managing Organizational Knowledge by Diagnosing Intellectual Capital: Framing and Advancing the State of the Field." In Chun Wei Choo and Nick Bontis (Eds.), *The Strategic Management of Intellectual Capital and Organizational Knowledge.* New York: Oxford University Press, 2002 (p. 629).

66. *Ibid.*, pp. 629, 637.

67. *Ibid.*, p. 631.

68. *Ibid.*, p. 627.

69. *Ibid.*, p. 634.

70. Portugal, Frank H. *Valuating Information Intangibles: Measuring the Bottom-line Contribution of Librarians and Information Professionals.* Washington, DC: Special Libraries Association, 2000.

71. *Ibid.*, pp. 99–140.

72. Lorna Peterson, "Definitions of Personal Assistance in the New Millennium: Philosophical Explorations of Virtual Reference Service." In R. David Lankes, John W. Collins III, and Abby S. Kasowitz (Eds.), *Digital Reference Service in the New Millennium: Planning, Management, and Evaluation* (pp. 37–45). New York: Neal-Schuman, 2000 (p. 42).

73. *Ibid.*, p. 42.

74. *Ibid.*, p. 42.

75. See also the comments of William Wisner in his controversial book *Whither the Postmodern Library? Libraries, Technology, and Education in the Information Age*: "computers will not save education…. Only reading can save it" (p. 72).

Bibliography

Alguire, Patrick C. "A Review of Journal Clubs in Postgraduate Medical Education." *Journal of General Internal Medicine* 13 (1998): 347–353.

Anderson, Jon Lee. "Who Needs Saudi Arabia When You've Got Saõ Tomé?" *The New Yorker* (October 7, 2002): 74–86.

Audit Bureau of Circulations. "Top 100 US Newspapers by Circulation." Audit Bureau of Circulations FAS-FAX Report, September 30, 1999.

Bontis, Nick. "Managing Organizational Knowledge by Diagnosing Intellectual Capital: Framing and Advancing the State of the Field." In Chun Wei Choo and Nick Bontis (Eds.), *The Strategic Management of Intellectual Capital and Organizational Knowledge* (pp. 621–642). New York: Oxford University Press, 2002.

Bourdieu, Pierre, and Loïc J.D. Wacquant. *An Invitation to Reflexive Sociology.* Chicago: The University of Chicago Press, 1992.

Bowker Annual Library and Book Trade Almanac 2000 (45th ed.), edited by Dave Bogart. New York: Bowker.

Bowker Annual Library and Book Trade Almanac 2001 (46th ed.), edited by Dave Bogart. New York: Bowker.

Bowles, Scott. "Hollywood goes to Epic Proportions." *USA Today* (November 29, 2002): A1, A2.

Brill's Content (Fall 2001).

Bryant-Friedland, Bruce, and John Finotti. "Low-paying Call Center Jobs Have Fu-

eled Jacksonville's Back-office Boom." *The Florida Times-Union* (January 12, 1998): A1.

Buchanan, Leigh. "The Smartest Little Company in America." *Inc.* 21 (January 1999): 42–54.

Buchanan, Ruth, and Sarah Koch-Schulte. *Gender on the Line: Technology, Restructuring and the Reorganization of Work in the Call Centre Industry.* Ottawa: Status of Women Canada Research Directorate, 2000. Available at http://www.swc-cfc.gc.ca/publish/research/001010-0662281586-e.html (accessed November 2, 2000).

Burke, Jim. *I Hear America Reading: Why We Read, What We Read.* Portsmouth, NH: Heinemann, 1999.

CBS. "60 Minutes Milestones." Available at http://www.cbsnews.com (accessed October 24, 2002).

Chowdhury, Gobinda G. "Digital Libraries and Reference Services: Present and Future." *Journal of Documentation* 58 (May 2002): 258–283.

Coffman, Steve. "Building Earth's Largest Library: Driving into the Future." *Searcher* 7 (March 1999): 34–37, 40–47.

_____, and Matthew L. Saxton. "Staffing the Reference Desk in the Largely-digital Library." In C.D. Ferguson (Ed.), *From Past-present to Future-perfect: A Tribute to Charles A. Bunge and the Challenges of Contemporary Reference Service* (pp. 141–163). New York: Haworth, 1999.

Conlon, Ginger. "The Human Side of Call

Centers." *Sales & Marketing Management* 150 (October 1998): 92–94.

Curtis, James. "Call Centers Must Adapt their Ways." *Marketing* [United Kingdom] (December 2, 1999): 33–34, 37.

Daisey, Mike. *21 Dog Years: Doing Time @ Amazon.com.* New York: The Free Press, 2002.

Danton, J. Periam. *Book Selection and Collections: A Comparison of German and American University Libraries.* New York: Columbia University Press, 1963.

Dervin, Brenda. "From the Mind's Eye of the User: The Sense-making Qualitative-quantitative Methodology." In J.D. Glazier and R.R. Powell (Eds.), *Qualitative Research in Information Management* (pp. 61–84). Englewood CO: Libraries Unlimited, 1991.

Ebbert, Jon O., Victor M. Montori and Henry J. Schultz, "The Journal Club in Postgraduate Medical Education: A Systematic Review." *Medical Teacher* 23 (2001): 455–461.

Edwards, Richard, Martin White, Jackie Gray and Colin Fischbacher. "Use of a Journal Club and Letter-writing Exercise to Teach Critical Appraisal to Medical Undergraduates." *Medical Education* 35 (2001): 691–694.

Ellis, Steven. "Data Entry and the Economy of Offshore Information Production." *Library Resources & Technical Services* 41 (April 1997): 112–122.

Ferguson, Chris D. "Shaking the Conceptual Foundations, Too: Integrating Research and Technology Support for the Next Generation of Information Service." *College & Research Libraries* 61 (July 2000): 300–311.

Fernie, Sue, and David Metcalf. *(Not) Hanging on the Telephone: Payment Systems in the New Sweatshops.* Working Paper 891, Centre for Economic Performance. London: London School of Economics, 1998.

Gibbons, Andrew J. "Organising a Successful Journal Club." *BMJ* 325 (November 2,

2002): S137. Available at http://bmj.com/content/vol325/issue7371/ (accessed November 13, 2002).

Gramsci, Antonio. *Selections from the Prison Notebooks of Antonio Gramsci.* New York: International, 1971.

Greenhouse, Steven. "Amazon.com is Using the Web to Block Unions' Efforts to Organize." *New York Times* (November 29, 2000): C1, C2.

_____. "Unions Pushing to Organize Thousands of Amazon.com Workers." *New York Times* (November 23, 2000): C1, C3.

Grogan, Denis Joseph. *Grogan's Case Studies in Reference Work. Volume 1: Enquiries and the Reference Process.* London: Clive Bingley, 1987.

_____. *Grogan's Case Studies in Reference Work. Volume 4: Periodicals and their Guides.* London: Clive Bingley, 1987.

_____. *Grogan's Case Studies in Reference Work. Volume 6: Biographical Sources.* London: Clive Bingley, 1987.

Guyatt, Nick. "What's Going on at Amazon.com?" Princeton University Campus Greens, Labor and Free Trade Working Group, 2001. Available at http://www.princeton.edu/~greens (accessed March 1, 2001).

Hamilton, William L. "They've Got Your Numbers." *New York Times* (August 15, 2002): D1, D4.

Harris, Roma M. *Librarianship: The Erosion of a Woman's Profession.* Norwood, NJ: Ablex, 1992.

_____, and Victoria Marshall. "Reorganizing Canadian Libraries: A Giant Step Back from the Front." *Library Trends* 46 (Winter 1998): 564–580.

Hay, Fred J. "The Subject Specialist in the Academic Library: A Review Article." *The Journal of Academic Librarianship* (January 1990): 11–17.

Heckart, Ronald J. "Machine Help and Human Help in the Emerging Digital Library." *College & Research Libraries* 59 (May 1998): 250–259.

Higgins, Mark. "Life on the Line: Call Centers are Pretty Exciting, Unless You're Actually Handling the Calls." *Marketing Magazine* 101 (March 18, 1996): 8.

Hildenbrand, Susan. "Ambiguous Authority and Aborted Ambition: Gender, Professionalism, and the Rise and Fall of the Welfare State." *Library Trends* 34 (Fall 1985): 185–198.

Hutchins, Margaret. *Introduction to Reference Work.* Chicago: American Library Association, 1944.

Janes, Joseph. "Why Reference Is About to Change Forever (But Not Completely)." In R. David Lankes, John W. Collins III, and Abby S. Kasowitz (Eds.), *Digital Reference Service in the New Millennium: Planning, Management, and Evaluation* (pp. 13–24). New York: Neal-Schuman, 2000.

Johnson, Haynes. *The Best of Times: America in the Clinton Years.* New York: Harcourt, 2001.

Karetzky, Stephen. *Reading Research and Librarianship: A History and Analysis.* Westport, CT: Greenwood, 1982.

Karr, Angela. "One in Three Agents Walk." *Teleprofessional Magazine* 12 (October 1999): 18-19.

Kennedy, Noah. *The Industrialization of Intelligence: Mind and Machine in the Modern Age.* London: Unwin Hyman, 1989.

Krashen, Stephen. *The Power of Reading: Insights from the Research.* Englewood, CO: Libraries Unlimited, 1993.

Kuhlthau, Carol C. *Seeking Meaning: A Process Approach to Library and Information Services.* Norwood, NJ: Ablex, 1993.

Leibovich, Mark. "At Amazon.com, Service Workers Without a Smile." *Washington Post* (November 22, 1999): Al, A14.

Lengermann, Patricia Madoo, Jill Niebrugge-Brantley and Jane Kirkpatrick. "Democracy, Technology, and the Public Library." In Donna Allen, Ramona R. Rush, and Susan J. Kaufman (Eds.), *Women Transforming Communications:*

Global Intersections (pp. 83–94). Thousand Oaks, CA: Sage Publications, 1996.

Levy, Stephen. "The World According to Google." *Newsweek* 140 (December 16, 2002): 46–51.

Linzer, Mark. "The Journal Club and Medical Education: Over One Hundred Years of Unrecorded History." *Postgraduate Medical Journal* 63 (1987): 475–478.

Lizza, Ryan. "The Ambulance-Homicide Theory." *New York Times Magazine* (December 15, 2002): 66.

McFarland, Joan. "Call Centres in New Brunswick: Maquiladoras of the North?" *Canadian Woman Studies/Les Cahiers de la Femme* 21/22 (Spring/Summer 2002): 65–70.

_____. "Many Are Called, but What Are the Choices: Working in New Brunswick's 1-800 Call Centres." *New Maritimes* 74 (July/August 1996): 10–19.

McGlamery, Susan, and Steve Coffman. "Moving Reference to the Web." *Reference & User Services Quarterly* 39 (Summer 2000): 380–386.

Mediamark Research. "Fall 2000 Magazine Audience Estimates (Sorted by Adult 18+ Audience)." Available at http://www.mediamark.com (accessed June 18, 2002).

Medical Library Association. "MLA Journal Club: Journal Club Guidelines." Available at http://mlanet.org/education/telecon/jcguide.html (accessed November 13, 2002).

Menzies, David. "Last Call: In Which Our Intrepid Reporter Delves Into the Inner Sanctum of the Call Center Business." *Marketing Magazine* 104 (September 27, 1999): 14–17.

Mitter, Swasti. *Common Fate: Common Bond: Women in the Global Economy.* London: Pluto, 1986.

National Opinion Research Center at The University of Chicago. "Codebook Variable: News." Available at http://www.icpsr.umich.edu (accessed June 17, 2002).

Onishi, Norimitsu. "A Corner of Africa

Where Dreams Gush Like Oil." *New York Times* (July 28, 2000): A4.

_____, with Neela Banerjee. "Chad's Wait for Its Oil Riches May Be Long." *New York Times* (May 16, 2001): A1, A11.

Peterson, Lorna. "Definitions of Personal Assistance in the New Millennium: Philosophical Explorations of Virtual Reference Service." In R. David Lankes, John W. Collins III, and Abby S. Kasowitz (Eds.), *Digital Reference Service in the New Millennium: Planning, Management, and Evaluation* (pp. 37–45). New York: Neal-Schuman, 2000.

Portugal, Frank H. *Valuating Information Intangibles: Measuring the Bottom-line Contribution of Librarians and Information Professionals.* Washington, DC: Special Libraries Association, 2000.

Putnam, Robert D. *Bowling Alone: The Collapse and Revival of American Community.* New York: Simon & Schuster, 2000.

Radway, Janice A. *Reading the Romance: Women, Patriarchy, and Popular Literature.* Chapel Hill: University of North Carolina Press, 1991.

Ranganathan, Shiyali Ramamrita. *Reference Service* (2nd ed.). London: Asia, 1961.

Reference and User Services Association. *Guidelines for Behavioral Performance of Reference and Information Service Professionals.* Available at http://www.ala.org/rusa/stnd_behavior.html (accessed May 18, 2002).

Rich, Frank. "The Weight of an Anchor." *New York Times Magazine* (May 19, 2002). Available at http://www.nytimes.com (accessed October 26, 2002).

Richardson, John V., Jr. "Question Master: An Evaluation of a Web-based Decision-support System for Use in Reference Environments." *College & Research Libraries* 59 (January 1998): 29–37.

Richardson, Ranald, Vicki Belt and Neill Marshall. "Taking Calls to Newcastle: The Regional Implications of the Growth in Call Centers." *Regional Studies* 34 (June 2000): 357–369.

Ross, Catherine Sheldrick. "Finding without Seeking: The Information Encounter in the Context of Reading for Pleasure." *Information Processing & Management* 35 (1999): 783–799.

Saxton, Matthew L., and Richardson, John V., Jr. *Understanding Reference Transactions: Transforming an Art into a Science.* Amsterdam: Academic, 2002.

Seago, Brenda L., Lynne U. Turman, Andrea S. Horne, Philip Croom and Karen Cary. "Journal Club with a Mission." *Bulletin of the Medical Library Association* 82 (January 1994): 73–74.

Sheehan, John. "A Journal Club as a Teaching and Learning Strategy in Nurse Teacher Education." *Journal of Advanced Nursing* 19 (1994): 572–578.

Shmerling, Arnold. "Journal Clubs for General Practitioners." *Australian Family Physician* 20 (June 1991): 814–816.

Siegel, Lenny. "New Chips in Old Skins: Work and Labor in Silicon Valley." In Gerald Sussman and John A. Lent (Eds.), *Global Productions: Labor in the Making of the Information Society* (pp. 97–110). Creeskill, NJ: Hampton, 1998.

Skinner, Ewart C. "The Caribbean Data Processors." In Gerald Sussman and John A. Lent (Eds.), *Global Productions: Labor in the Making of the Information Society* (pp. 57–88). Creeskill, NJ: Hampton, 1998.

Speers, Alice T. "An Introduction to Nursing Research through an OR Nursing Journal Club." *AORN Journal* 69 (June 1999): 1232–1236.

Statistics Canada. "Canadians' Reading Habits." Available at http://www.statcan.ca (accessed June 18, 2002).

Stebelman, Scott. "Taking Control of Continuing Education: The Formation of a Reading Group at George Washington University." *The Journal of Academic Librarianship* 22 (September 1996): 382–385.

Stelmach, Evelyn I. "A Staff Journal Club as

a Method of Continuing Education." *AORN Journal* 59 (May 1994): 1061–1063.

Swarns, Rachel L. "Oil Abounds, Misery Too: A Case Study." *New York Times* (January 14, 2001): Section 4, p. 6.

Taylor, Phil, Gareth Mulvey, Jeff Hyman and Peter Bain. "Work Organisation, Control and the Experience of Work in Call Centres." *Work, Employment and Society* 16 (March 2002): 133–150.

Thaler-Carter, Ruth E. "Why Sit and Answer the Phone All Day?" *HR Magazine* 44 (March 1999): 98–104.

Thomsen, Elizabeth. *Rethinking Reference: The Reference Librarian's Practical Guide for Surviving Constant Change.* New York: Neal-Schuman, 1999.

Thurow, Lester C. "Regional Transformation and the Service Activities." In Lloyd Rodwin and Hidehiko Sazanami (Eds.), *Deindustrialization and Regional Economic Transformation: The Experience of the United States* (pp. 179–198). Boston: Unwin Hyman, 1989.

Tomlin, Anne C. "From Dowdy to Dandy: Spiffing Up the Journal Club." *The One-Person Library: A Newsletter for Librarians and Management* 12 (April 1996): 1–3.

Toye, Sue. "The Business of Books: Rotman Students Say Broad Approach to Reading Key to Developing Good Business Skills." *The Bulletin: University of Toronto* (November 4, 2002): 5.

United States Census Bureau. *2001 Statistical Abstract of the United States.*

Walsh, Mary Williams. "Corporations Revise Wish Lists." *New York Times* (November 7, 2002): C1, C5.

Walter, Frank Keller. "In a Quiet Corner with a Little Book." *Collection Management* 6 (3/4): 28–35. Reprinted 1984; original article 1925.

WashTech. "Amazon.com to Begin Outsourcing Customer Service Operations to India." 2000. *WashTech News.* Available at http://www.washtech.org/amazon/090700_india.php3 (accessed March 1, 2001).

White, Marilyn Domas. "Diffusion of an Innovation: Digital Reference Service in Carnegie Foundation Master's (Comprehensive) Academic Institution Libraries." *The Journal of Academic Librarianship* 27 (May 2001): 173–187.

_____. "Digital Reference Services: Framework for Analysis and Evaluation." *Library & Information Science Research* 23 (2001): 211–231.

Wildman, Sarah. "Tuning Out the World." *The New Republic* (September 9, 2002). Available at http://www.tnr.com (accessed September 7, 2002).

Wisner, William H. *Whither the Postmodern Library: Libraries, Technology, and Education in the Information Age.* Jefferson, NC: McFarland, 2000.

Wyer, James Ingersoll. *Reference Work: A Textbook for Students of Library Work and Librarians.* Chicago: American Library Association, 1930.

Index

Academic librarians: extent of reading fiction and non-fiction 73–82; extent of reading newspapers and magazines 31–42; how reading fiction and nonfiction helps with personal and professional growth 104–106, 107–110; how reading newspapers and magazines helps with personal growth and professional growth 65–68; how reading newspapers and magazines helps with understanding technological developments, outreach, programming, and bibliographic control 57–58, 62–65; importance of knowing languages 177–182, 185, 190, 193; importance of reading scholarly journals and monographs 190–199; importance of subject-specific knowledge 176–207, 216–218; improving bibliographic instruction through reading fiction and nonfiction 106–107, 171–172; improving bibliographic instruction through reading newspapers and magazines 61–62; improving collection development through reading fiction and nonfiction 102–104; improving collection development through reading newspapers and magazines 59–61; improving reference service through reading fiction and nonfiction 82–101, 110–113; improving reference service through reading newspapers and magazines 27–30, 43–57, 202–204; local newspapers 69–71; readers' advisory services 95–97, 163; types of newspapers and magazines read 35–38, 39–42
Alguire, Patrick 215
Amazon.com: call centers 15–17; relationship to digital reference models 18–19
Anderson, Jon Lee 247n1

Bain, Peter 14–15, 17, 211
Belt, Vicki 12, 13
Bibliographic control: improvements through reading 65, 101
Bibliographic instruction: improvements through reading 61–62, 106–107, 171–172
Bontis, Nick 220
Bourdieu, Pierre 209, 211–212
Bowles, Scott 254n62
Bryant-Friedland, Bruce 13
Buchanan, Leigh 250n10
Buchanan, Ruth 13, 14, 15, 16, 17–18, 19
Burke, Jim 2

Call centers: development 9–10, 15–16; ideological aspects 17–19; model for digital reference service 8–9, 10–12; negative aspects 12–17
Cary, Karen 254n48
Chowdhury, Gobinda 210
Coffman, Steve 8–9, 10–11, 12, 15, 16, 18, 19, 210, 213
Collection development: improvements through reading 59–61, 102–104
Conlon, Ginger 13, 14

Croom, Philip 254n48
Curtis, James 13, 14

Daisey, Mike 15–16
Danton, J. Periam 207, 252n6
Deprofessionalization: reference function 7–12, 19–20, 210–214, 220–221
Dervin, Brenda 20
Deskilling: call centers 9–10, 15–16; reference departments 10–12, 210–211
Digital reference services: ideology 7–12, 19–20, 210–214

Ebbert, Jon 215
Edwards, Richard 253n44
Ellis, Steven 18, 19
Equatorial Guinea 5–6
Evaluating reference service: academic libraries 174–176; ideology 212–213, 252n19, 253n23, 253n28; metrics 220–221

Ferguson, Chris 8, 12, 18, 19, 211
Fernie, Sue 13
Fiction see Reading
Finotti, John 13
Fischbacher, Colin 253n44
Foucault, Michel 12
Frenkel, Stephen 14

Gibbons, Andrew 254n49
Gramsci, Antonio 19
Gray, Jackie 253n44
Greenhouse, Steven 249n70, 249n71
Grogan, Denis Joseph 22–23
Guidelines for Behavioral Performance 213
Guyatt, Nick 249n68

Hamilton, William 251n8
Harris, Roma 9–10, 11–12, 18
Hay, Fred 207
Heckart, Ronald 7–8
Higgins, Mark 13
Hildenbrand, Susan 248n19
Horne, Andrea 254n48
Hutchins, Margaret 21
Hyman, Jeff 14–15, 17, 211

Ideology of reference service
    7–20
Intellectual capital 209–214,
    220–221
Interdisciplinarity: academic
    librarians as researchers
    199–207; need for academic
    librarians to have subject
    knowledge across disci-
    plines and fields 176–207

Janes, Joseph 6
Johnson, Haynes 143
Journal clubs: history 215–
    216; relationship to libraries
    216–219; see also Reading
    communities

Karetzky, Stephen 2
Karr, Angela 13
Kennedy, Noah 19
Kirkpatrick, Jane 210
Koch-Schulte, Sarah 13, 14,
    15, 16, 17–18, 19
Korczynski, Marek 14
Krashen, Stephen 2
Kuhlthau, Carol 20

Language skills: improvement
    in reference service in acad-
    emic libraries 177–182, 185,
    190, 193
Leibovich, Mark 15
Lengermann, Patricia Madoo
    210
Levy, Stephen 247n3, 247n5
Librarianship: evolution 11–
    12, 18–20, 21–23, 220–221
Linzer, Mark 215
Lizza, Ryan 149

Magazines see Reading
Marshall, Neill 12, 13
Marshall, Victoria 9, 11–12, 18
McFarland, Joan 13, 18
McGlamery, Susan 8–9, 12,
    18, 211

Medical Library Association
    216
Menzies, David 13
Metcalf, David 13
Mitter, Swasti 18
Montori, Victor 215
Mulvey, Gareth 14–15, 17,
    211

Newspapers see Reading
Niebrugge-Brantley, Jill
    210
Nonfiction see Reading

Onishi, Norimitsu 5, 247n1

Peterson, Lorna 221
Portugal, Frank 220–221
Public library reference staff:
    extent of reading newspa-
    pers and magazines 139–
    142; extent of watching
    television news shows and
    listening to radio news pro-
    grams 143–148; improving
    non-reference related
    library services by paying
    attention to various media
    sources 163–169; improving
    reference service by paying
    attention to various media
    sources 148–162
Putnam, Robert 37–38, 122

Radway, Janice 2
Ranganathan, Shiyali Ramam-
    rita 21, 22
Readers' advisory services
    95–97, 163
Reading: denigration by pro-
    ponents of digital reference
    models 10–12, 219–220;
    fiction and nonfiction
    books 73–84; helps in pro-
    viding better reference ser-
    vice in academic libraries
    43–57, 69–71, 173–207;
    helps in providing better
    reference service in public
    libraries 148–162; helps in
    providing non-reference
    related service in academic
    libraries 57–68; helps in
    providing non-reference
    related service in public
    libraries 163–169; historical
    component of librarianship

21–23; inhibiting factors
    115–131; newspapers and
    magazines 32–42
Reading communities 216; see
    also Journal clubs
Reference and User Services
    Association 213
Reference service: ideological
    aspects 7–20; improvement
    in academic libraries
    through development of
    subject-specific knowledge
    173–207; improvement in
    academic libraries through
    language skills 177–182, 185,
    190, 193; improvement in
    academic libraries through
    reading newspapers and
    magazines 27–113; improve-
    ment in academic libraries
    through reading scholarly
    journals and books 177,
    182–189, 190–204; improve-
    ment in public libraries
    through reading newspapers
    and magazines 148–169;
    improvement through jour-
    nal clubs and reading com-
    munities 215–219
Rich, Frank 143, 144
Richardson, John V., Jr. 7–8,
    212–213, 252n19, 253n23,
    253n28
Richardson, Ranald 12, 13
Ross, Catherine Sheldrick
    2

Saxton, Matthew 8, 10–11, 12,
    18, 19, 211, 212–213, 214,
    252n19, 253n23, 253n28
Schultz, Henry 215
Seago, Brenda 253n48
Sheehan, John 253n46
Shire, Karen 14
Shmerling, Arnold 253n47
Siegel, Lenny 18–19
Skinner, Ewart 18
Smith, Dorothy 210
Speers, Alice 253n45
Stebelman, Scott 216–218
Stelmach, Evelyn 253n45
Stereotypes: of librarians 10,
    129–130, 221
Subject-specific knowledge:
    improvements in reference
    service in academic
    libraries 173–207, 216–218;

relationship to reading
190–204, 216–218
Swarns, Rachel 247n1

Tam, Mary 14
Taylor, Phil 14–15, 17, 211
Thaler-Carter, Ruth 14
Thomsen, Elizabeth 22, 234
Thurow, Lester 12
Tomlin, Anne 254n48

Toren, Nina 9
Turman, Lynne 254n48

Wacquant, Loïc 252n1,
253n32
Walsh, Mary Williams
254n63
Walter, Frank Keller 21
White, Marilyn Domas 210
White, Martin 253n44

Wildman, Sarah 162
Wisner, William 254n75
Women: denigration of work
roles associated with
women 10–12, 219–220;
role within librarianship
7–12, 19–20, 209–214
Work roles 9–10, 12–17,
209–214, 220–221
Wyer, James Ingersoll 21